Praise for Steven

"Steven, you carry the noble art of Astr
several charts done in my lifetime, and [illegible] but yours have
escaped the astrologer mistaking so much of the chart as a sounding board for his own ego. You have restored the divine art to its noble status."
—Robert Johnson, author of *We*

"Looking back at Steve's readings, they just increase my faith in life as a 'team sport,' which is to say that skilled support can make all the difference on game day! He insists that nothing is so grave as to be beyond repair, and correspondingly that there is no rainbow that won't be evaporated by poor judgment in the now. So I guess 'benevolent realist' would best describe his approach . . . I can't recommend him highly enough."
—Robert Downey, Jr.

"No matter what you think of astrology, if you appreciate humor, insight, poetry and astute, articulate observations of human nature, you will appreciate Steven Forrest's fascinating book *The Inner Sky.*"
—Calli Khoury, screenwriter, *Thelma and Louise*

On *The Book of the Moon*: "Steven Forrest's warmth and accessibility will immediately draw you to this gem of a book. With a twinkle in his eye, he shakes up our habitual thinking about the Moon and challenges us to see Her again with new eyes. Not only does he remind us that the Moon is much more than we imagined, he brings a distillation of deep practice and creative thinking to his writing on the lunar phase. He makes complexity fun and adds his inventive, evolutionary twist."
—Lynn Bell, Centre for Psychological Astrology

On *The Inner Sky*: "Steve's book manages to disarm the skeptic, as well as debunk the charlatanism that surrounds popular astrology, with language that is as intelligent and cogent as it is poetic."
—Sting

"Steven Forrest...One of the most gifted writers on astrology to emerge in the last quarter of a century...You will be delighted with *The Changing Sky*."
—Richard Nolle, Dell Horoscope

On *The Book of the Moon*: "Steven manages to bring fresh insight to this foundational topic, breathing life into each of the lunar phases with his gift of poetic language and his skillful use of anecdote. He navigates easily between the more technical, astronomical material – the practical knowledge necessary for any astrologer to have under their belt – and the metaphoric arena of interpretation. I heartily recommend *The Book of the Moon* to students and professionals alike."
—DenaDeCastro, Sirius Astrology Podcast

On *Yesterday's Sky*: "I was very moved by the compassionate, loving motivation underlying the whole book. This is a landmark, a master book, a bodhisattva work. I bow to Steven Forrest's realization of the paramita of knowlege of the stars, and feel so lucky that he has offered us this precious result of so many years of work and experience."
—Claire Heurté Rauwel, translator

The Book of Neptune

Also by Steven Forrest

The Inner Sky

The Changing Sky

The Night Speaks

The Book of Pluto

Measuring the Night (with Jeffrey Wolf Green)

Measuring the Night Vol. 2 (with Jeffrey Wolf Green)

Stalking Anubis

Skymates (with Jodie Forrest)

Skymates II (with Jodie Forrest)

Yesterday's Sky

The Book of the Moon

The Book of Neptune

by Steven Forrest

Seven Paws Press, Inc.
Borrego Springs, CA

Published in 2016 by Seven Paws Press, Inc.
PO Box 82
Borrego Springs, CA 92004
www.sevenpaws.com

ISBN 978-1-939510-91-4

Cover art by Manu Jobst - Kunstfabrik
http://www.etsy.com/people/StaticMovement

Printed in the United States of America
LCCN 2016902043

CONTENTS

PREFACE

Writers often say that the pot boils best with the lid on. That means, "Write! Don't just talk about it." And keep what you are writing to yourself, at least until you have produced something that is fit to be read.

I really blew that one with this project. I've been talking about writing *The Book of Neptune* for five or six years. Talk is cheap. It's been heavy clouds, but no rain, for a long time.

I don't blame my delay on laziness. I'm fairly immune to that particular vice. The main thing that stopped me from writing this present book back when I first started running my mouth about it has been my Astrological Apprenticeship Program. With eight meetings a year all over the world, each one four or five days long, and probably about a thousand students, past and present, the "AP" has become the major focus of my professional life. I relish the chance it offers me to teach evolutionary astrology in depth. It is an unalloyed joy to escape the tyranny of the 75-minute song-and-dance of a lecture at an astrology conference. It's pure glory to spread my wings beyond the scope of even a full weekend workshop. The AP meetings are not only twice as long as that, but they build on themselves. The students have mostly already done the foundational work. From the first moment of each program, we are operating on a more sophisticated astrological level, with an established common language and s shared base of knowledge.

I love it—but the Apprenticeship Program is a tiger-by-the-tail. Flitting from Australia to Italy, and from China to my three American programs, does not leave me much time for writing—or anything else.

Much of *The Book of Neptune* is based loosely on transcripts of an Apprenticeship Program I gave in Calistoga, California, in March 2013. In turning those spoken words into a book, I've tried to retain some of the immediacy of a "live" class. But spoken English and written English are different beasts. What you will be reading here is a mixture of heavily edited transcripts and new writing.

I had thought originally that I would keep the two styles separate, maybe putting the "spoken word" parts in italics—but as I dived into the project, I made the decision to keep it as "talky" as possible, mostly in an attempt to convey the feeling of an actual "live" four-day session. In converting speech to the printed page, I've deleted some repetitions (live teaching often sinks in more deeply when a person hears something more than once, while in reading, such repetition quickly becomes tedious.) I've also eliminated many digressions—a disease of Neptune to which I am subject. "Gonna" has put on a necktie and become "going to." Where I actually said "you know"...well, you know, I figured that you in fact *know* that you know, so, you know, I didn't need to leave the words "you know" in the text.

In the AP we deal with quite a lot of life-and-death material. And of course humanity's classic strategy for doing that almost always involves some "gallows humor." The problem is that humor is often signaled by inflection and body language, which cannot be easily conveyed in print. One of my horrors in turning these lectures into printed text was that I would say something in humor or irony—and readers would take it as gospel, commit it to memory, and inflict it upon themselves or others.

Sometimes—I pray—the humor is self-evident. There, I just let the transcript stand as-is. Wherever I felt there might be some risk of missing the joke and thus creating a misimpression, I simply inserted: (*laughter*). It's a little distracting; my apologies. It was the best solution I could find.

In reading the transcripts of the seminar, there are many places where I realized I could have said something more clearly, or where I had left out something important, so again, the pages that follow contain much new writing.

Recently, Neptune has been transiting across my fourth house cusp in 6° Pisces. I lost a home and a family; I gained a home and a family. My inner life has gone to new levels and new places. The Neptunian spaciousness of the Anza-Borrego desert where I now live has fed my soul as has the vast holy Silence of the place. I've learned some things about Neptune that I didn't know in March 2013 when I offered this seminar. They're woven into the pages that follow, too.

There is one more major difference between this book and the actual meetings of my tribes of apprentices: in the Apprenticeship Program, I teach broadly on a chosen topic for a day or two, then we apply the principles in the context of our own charts. I reach into what has inevitably come to be called "The Sorting Hat," á la *Harry Potter*, and pull the name of a student. We then dive into his or her chart. That's followed by the person sharing his or her reactions and pertinent biographical information. This process is very intimate and can be deeply personal. As a result, we maintain an absolute seal of confidentiality over those parts of each meeting. None of that will appear in these pages, or anywhere else, ever—at least not without explicit permission. Instead, I'll take the more conventional tack of looking at the charts of a great number of well-known public figures. We astrologers seem to have come to a collective agreement that such folks are fair game.

As you dive into the pages that follow, you'll find that you are initially in a bit of an astronomy class. Read on; we will be in astrological territory soon enough. Many astrologers work with Greek mythology. That's fine, but in these pages I take a different tack. I am trying to read the actual "book of the sky" more directly. Our understanding of the outer fringes of the solar system has exploded in the past generation. I believe—and feel I can demonstrate—that we must reformulate our understanding of Neptune in the light of those astronomical revelations. Doing that entails a fresh look at Pluto and the realms beyond it. As you will quickly see, that approach provides a context for a fresh view of Neptune.

So, thank you in advance for joining me on this space odyssey out to the fringes of our solar system. We will peer beyond the rim of everything we know—both psychologically and astronomically—into the frighteningly groundless, vertiginous Void that lies beyond it.

Welcome to Neptune.

—Steven Forrest
Borrego Springs, California

ACKNOWLEDGMENTS

My special thanks to my manager and friend, Tony Howard. He has saved my most customary place to sit more times than I can count. I am too Neptunian for this world; Tony runs liaison between me and reality. For the millionth time, all I know to say is, thank you, Tony. I couldn't do half of what I do without your help.

Our wizard-of-an-assistant, Carol Czeczot, did a monumental job of both transcribing the original talks upon which much of this book is based, as well as a meticulous job of line-editing the text. Thank you, Carol.

I thank a dear soul who chooses to remain humbly nameless for helping to make the financial end of this project work. He bought me six weeks of freedom. For a writer, that is a treasure.

Deep gratitude to the people who, over the years, have stepped up to help run my various Apprenticeship Programs around the world. This book is based on one such seminar; there have been over a hundred of these events since 1998. Each one is a logistical accomplishment on par with herding cats. I have it easy. All I have to do is show up and talk. Here they are, in lights:

In southern California, Ingrid Coffin and her team at the Blue Sky Ranch Fellowship.

In China, Felicia Jiang and David Railey, along with the amazing NoDoor team.

In North Carolina, Kathy Hallen and her able assistants, Carol McLauren and Tricia Mickleberry.

In Nelson Bay, Australia, and various places in Europe, the indomitable Mercurial Connections team, Lisa Jones and Christine Murfitt.

Finally, in Calistoga, California, I especially thank Joyce Van Horn. She gets an extra gold star here because much of this book is based on a program I gave there, under her able auspices, in March 2013.

My Apprenticeship Programs have been supported by many different coordinators over time. Thanks, emeritus, to Karen Davis, Vinessa Nevala, Barbara King, and David Friedman (R.I.P. David).

Thanks to Susie Latimer Hodge who offered her cabin in Idyllwild, California, as a writing retreat.

Chapter Thirty-One is an extended version of an article I wrote for U.K. astrologer Frank Clifford. It appears in his forthcoming Flare/LSA publication, The Astrology of Music. I thank him for his gracious permission to re-use it here.

Finally my thanks to the following friends and colleagues who were actively engaged with me in various ways during the writing process: Scott Ainslie, Virginia Bell, Gail Boulton, Cui Ying, Mike Czeczot, Beth Darnall, Kate Durbin, Rona Elliot and Roger Brossy, Michael Erlewine, Maurice Fernandez, Hadley Fitzgerald, Bunny Forrest, Thomas and Jeanne Fredericks, the Fuhrmann clan: Marc, Melina, and Kalea, Rishi Giovanni Gatti, Robert and Diana Griffin, the Grossenbacher clan: John, Tracy, and Ryan, Robert and Diana Griffin, Jonathan Hall, Bunnie and Jack Hamilton, Amy Herring, Sylvia Hsiao, Baris Ilhan, Kathy Jacobson, Magdalena Janicka, Bill Janis, Robert A. Johnson, Mark Jones, Terry Jones, Peter and Ingrid Kondos, Barbara Matson, Mary Ann McGuire, Billy Murfitt, Carey Nash, Rafael Nasser, Jeff Parrett, Carol Peebles, Star Perry, the Pleym clan: Dan, Claire, and Ileana, Steven Poster and Susan Williams, Aminah Raheem and Fritz Smith, Claire Rauwel, Dusty Recor and "Indian Joe" Stewart, Ray Ristorcelli, Evelyn Roberts, Paige Ruane and Jack McDonald, Jonathan Sacks, Fran Slavich, Cristina Smith, Susan Sokol-Blosser, Pawel Suchon, Tem Tarriktar and Nan Geary, Kay Taylor, Julia Trawick, Dick and Artemisa Walker, Kris Werfel, and Brittany Wymore.

And thanks to my partner Michelle Kondos for her sanity, unfailing kindness, and for giving me a good reason for staying aboard this crazy planet at a time when I really needed one.

To my students, clients and readers—
my infinite gratitude for the life you have given me.

Part One

Neptune: The Big Picture

1

LET'S TAKE A RIDE IN A STARSHIP

Ah, Neptune! Where do we begin with something that has no beginning and no end—a subject in which time itself is a meaningless concept, space is a meaningless concept, one in which even concepts themselves are meaningless? A realm in which causality can work backwards—or not at all? Where Reason itself becomes a joke?

Where do we start with something like that?

I'm going to start by issuing us all a free ticket on a starship. We hit warp drive and we blast about fifty billion miles straight up above the North Pole of the Sun. We stand on the ship's bridge, gazing down upon the solar system from way up there, looking down on it as if we were looking down at a large pizza from the top of tall ladder.

At first, all we see is the blinding glare of the Sun. But then as we get out our binoculars, we begin to notice the ghostly disk of the solar system floating around it. Careful not to aim the binoculars directly at the Sun, we can barely see the disk; everything orbiting the Sun is so dwarfed and blinded by its mass and brilliance. But there is definitely a faint haze around our central star. And like the DNA in a cell, that faint haze is chock full of intelligence and information. Ask any astrologer.

Let's contemplate the haze very carefully. Maybe we trade our binoculars for a small telescope.

Four spherical bodies lie close to the Sun, spinning around it very rapidly. Compared to the Sun, they are just tiny pebbles, little rock worlds—Mercury, Venus, Earth, and Mars. Earth is particularly intriguing, and not just because we call it home. We quickly see that it is different from the other three. It's bigger, but intriguingly our Moon is very big compared to the diameter of the Earth, so Earth would actually appear to be a double planet.

Out beyond the realm of the four rock-worlds, there is a wispy fog—a thin haze of stone. That is the asteroid belt. Most of us have seen *Star Wars*, where we watch Han Solo trying to navigate the *Millennium Falcon* through a field of asteroids, with the Empire hot on his tail. He's zigging to the left and zagging to the right, dodging these crowds of colliding, smashing mountains in space, just like in a video game.

The asteroid belt is not like that at all. It's actually a very thin soup. There is almost nothing there.

There's a silly myth which I still hear sometimes in metaphysical circles. It is the notion that there was once an inhabited planet there, early in the solar system, and that the people of that world were really naughty, so God blew up the planet. *Voila*: the asteroid belt—all that's left of that wicked world. The tale is a lie for a lot of reasons. The main one astronomically is that if you were to take the entire mass of the asteroid belt and squeeze it together, you would still have only a tiny fraction of the mass of a planet. The true reality of the asteroid belt is that it is very close to a vacuum. It is just a thin, dust storm of stone.

So, what do we know so far? What do we see? First, there's the brilliant, blinding Sun hogging most of the attention. Then the four rocky worlds—one of them a double planet. Then the haze of the asteroid belt—and after that, things start to get pretty spectacular.

After you pass the main mass of the asteroids, you come to another cycle of four planets, but that quartet is very different from anything we have seen so far. Here we enter the realm of the *gas giants*: Jupiter, Saturn, Uranus—and our ultimate target today, Neptune. They are all big, gaudy, gassy balloons, averaging approximately *thirty* times Earth's diameter—and, remember, Earth is the biggest of those four rocky worlds.

To our eyes, looking down from the bridge of the starship, one point leaps out: these gas giants are entirely different beasts than Mercury, Venus, Earth, or Mars. They are vast. They are shrouded in thick, colorful, swirling atmospheres, and they each have an entire retinue of moons—some of which are actually the size of Mercury.

We've left the realm of the dwarves and entered the realm of giants.

What lies beyond the gas giants? As we squint, we detect another haze of stones—icy ones this time—extending out beyond Neptune toward the infinity of space, blurring eventually into the interstellar vastness. On the inner edge of this second haze of stone, we find a famous one—a tiny little world that is often taken to be named after Walt Disney's cartoon dog—*Pluto.*

We would never confuse Pluto with one of the gas giants. In fact, we might wonder—still looking down innocently from the bridge of our starship—*if Pluto were a planet at all.* Pluto is truly tiny, only about two-thirds the diameter of our Moon. And it weighs a little less than one-quarter of 1 percent of the Earth's mass.

But Pluto is not alone. It turns out there are hundreds of little "Plutos" out there. As a group, they are currently called by various names. The term we will mostly use here is the *trans-Neptunians.* Another label for this realm of worlds beyond Neptune is the *Kuiper Belt.* ("Kuiper" rhymes with "viper.") Or the *Scattered Disk.* Or the *Oort Cloud.* You will hear them all if you read astronomy. There are some distinctions among those labels; the distinctions will not concern us here. We will just call them all trans-Neptunian objects and abbreviate the term as most astronomers do as *TNO's.*

By any name we choose to call them, the discovery of these new worlds has placed astrology in a situation that could, without much exaggeration, be characterized as "grow or die." This goes far, far beyond fighting over whether to call Pluto an actual planet, or a dwarf planet. The challenge is much deeper, and it is rattling the hearts of both astronomy and astrological practice.

Everything in the sky means something; that is the core principle by which astrology has always functioned. When we flee the emerging complexity of the solar system and retreat to a pre-Copernican image of the sky, we have betrayed our tradition and our astrological ancestors.

But how can we make sense of this new solar system—so much vaster and more complex than the one my grandparents learned about in school?

Neptune, as we will see, holds a major piece of that puzzle.

THE DISCOVERY OF THE TRANS-NEPTUNIAN REALM

Pluto was discovered in 1930, way ahead of the discovery of the TNO's as

a group. We didn't know it at the time, but Pluto was just the first representative of this whole new class of worlds. The second one—1992 QB—was discovered in 1992. That's sixty-two years down the road from the discovery of Pluto. If you're reading history, and you read that something happened in 730 A.D., and then you read that something else happened in 792 A.D., of course you think the two events happened at "around the same time." We naturally have that perspective—it's all the eighth century, so what difference do a few years make? But to us sitting here in the first part of the twenty-first century, 1930 and 1992 seem far apart. In terms of the evolution of human consciousness as a whole, as reflected in these discoveries, it is not that way at all. In the great, slow shifting of the paradigms by which humanity interprets itself, the discovery of Pluto was just the salad course for the discovery of this entire trans-Neptunian field.
At least one of them, *Eris*, is only slightly smaller than Pluto, but considerably more massive. If Pluto means anything astrologically, then Eris must mean something too. Some of them are diminutive and we can probably ignore them, just as most astrologers safely ignore some of the 14,000 or so named asteroids. But Eris—and a number of others—exist on the scale of Pluto. And no competent modern astrologer can ignore Pluto.

For a while, astronomers actually began to call these new-found objects *plutinos*. That's a word that didn't seem to catch on—I don't read it in the astronomy magazines very much anymore. "Plutinos" would work fine as a term, though, because all of these worlds are roughly similar to Pluto, at least in comparison to the four rocky worlds or to the four gas giants, which are entirely distinct in a number of ways.

Wait a minute! Isn't this supposed to be a book about Neptune?

Don't worry, we will get there. But for reasons you will soon see, by understanding Neptune's *position* in the solar system, we can understand its function in human consciousness more deeply.

PLUTO BECOMES A DWARF

Back in 2006, the International Astronomical Union held the infamous meeting in which it declared that Pluto was no longer a real planet. It was declared a "dwarf planet"—and so we can now take astrological assurance from the IAU that we need not worry about our Pluto transits anymore, right? Astrologers got angry—and were generally ignorant of the astronomy I've just gone through.

Maybe the IAU was correct. Clearly, Pluto is in its own category. Should we call it a "planet?" One can make a reasonable case for giving it a different label.

Meanwhile, many astronomers got self-righteous, and tried to paper over the deeper reality—which is that "planet" is inherently a *cultural* term rather than a rigorous scientific concept.

We astrologers, by the way, have conveniently been calling the Sun and Moon "planets" for a long time, simply based on our practical concern with objects that, unlike the starry constellations, "wander" along the ecliptic. It all goes back to the Greek word *planetes*, which means "wanderer." The deeper point there is that we astrologers don't need to argue with the IAU. We have a long tradition of using the word "planet" differently than astronomers do.

Back to our starship ... Let's try counting these "plutinos." Good luck! As of mid-2014, over fifteen hundred of these trans-Neptunian objects have been discovered. The presumption is there are quite a lot more of them than that. This is somewhat conjectural, but the following statement is mainstream astronomy based on current estimates of how many of these objects are out there. If we take *the entire mass of this realm of trans-Neptunians, including Pluto, and squeeze it down into one single planet, it would still not equal the mass of the Earth.*

That's pretty significant. Now, Pluto, as we have seen, is a tiny little thing—its total mass is just a fraction of 1 percent of the Earth's mass. For perspective, Uranus is nearly fifteen times heavier than Earth's mass, while Neptune is more than seventeen times as massive. Jupiter, meanwhile, is over 300 times more massive than Earth. As for Pluto and the rest of the TNOs—Sedna, Quaoar, Eris, Orcus, and so on—while they are really interesting subjects, astrologically, and astronomically, they are *tiny*. Again, squeeze them all down into one planet, and you've still got a mass smaller than the Earth. And that squeeze includes Pluto.

Thinking of the TNOs is analogous to thinking about the asteroid belt. You squeeze all of the asteroids down into a ball and you do not have enough mass for a planet either. This hypothesis—that there is a strong analogy between the asteroids and the TNOs—will become important, I believe, as astrology goes forward into the twenty-first century.

THE EMERGING SOLAR SYSTEM

All that I'm saying here is pure astronomy. So far, I've barely mentioned astrology, and I haven't yet begun to focus specifically on Neptune. I promise, I will!

But let's start by going right back to First Principles. What is astrology? *It is basically the notion that the structure of human consciousness and the structure of the heavens mirror each other—that they are built around the same laws, organized around the same principles, and that we can understand the logic of the mind by observing the form of the solar system.* All of that is nicely encapsulated in the familiar Hermetic formula, "As above, so below."

What I have just described in some detail is the actual structure of the solar system as we understand it today. Just quickly jamming through all this again so we can take it in all at once, we have the big yellow-white blaze of the Sun in the center, dwarfing everything, practically blinding us to everything else. The Sun is the mass that holds everything together.

Then come four rocky worlds.

Then a haze of stone.

Then four giant, gaudy gas-balloons.

And then another haze of stone.

So far as we know, that's it. That's what we would see from the bridge of our starship. And if there is anything to astrology, those two quartets and those two hazes of stone constitute a map of consciousness—one that is only emerging in our lifetimes.

Neptune's place at the frontier of the gas giants as they face the trans-Neptunian vastness holds the key to everything we will be investigating in these pages.

2

DEEPENING SPACE, DEEPENING MIND

Seven hundred years ago, this "starship" perspective was not understood. None of this was known to the astrologer-astronomers of that time.

What about the astrologers of 50,000 years ago? God knows what they were thinking, but I am sure that humans have been thinking that the sky signified something since the beginning of time. The Hellenistic renaissance of two millennia ago notwithstanding, I believe astrology is ancient. As far as I'm concerned, some form of it is probably as old as human consciousness.

Who can look at the night sky and fail to think deep, transcendent thoughts about why we are here in the first place? From there, it is a very short step to the roots of what we could broadly call "astrology."

Inevitably, inescapably, astrologers have always constructed their metaphors of human consciousness based on their current understanding of the sky. Early on, that was simply about how the sky *looked.* As centuries passed, starting with telescopes, we humans discovered increasing detail about the actual structure of the solar system.

Might we, as astrologers, hypothesize that this increase in astronomical knowledge would suggest a simultaneous discovery of greater detail about the human mind?

I think we can prove that.

THE DISCOVERY OF THE UNCONSCIOUS MIND

When Sigmund Freud began to publish his theories about the existence of the unconscious mind, what was the mainstream intellectual response? It was common for naysayers to flat-out reject his theories. We can imagine pretentious pseudo-questions like, "So, Professor Freud, you're suggesting that there is a part of my own mind of which I am unaware? Well, I guess it's not going to be much of a problem for me then, is it?"

I don't mean to dismiss the intellectual history of Western civilization. My simple point is that we have come a long way. Picture two young women in a Los Angeles café: One says, "He's, like, *so* totally unconscious." The second one nods sagaciously and adds, "Too true—he's, like, never dealt with his *mother issues*."

Those young women are not geniuses like Sigmund Freud, but they have grown up in a different cultural paradigm—one in which much of what Freud first described is simply assumed to be true by almost everyone. We all stand on Freud's shoulders. *As a culture, we have discovered the unconscious mind.* Everybody just assumes its existence now. It's almost inconceivable for us to realize that this was a radical idea when it first entered public discourse.

When did this change happen? Obviously, one cannot give a specific date for social or mythic sea-changes of that magnitude. We are not talking about when Freud first published his work. (Interestingly, that would be around the time of the Neptune-Pluto conjunction in the last decade of the nineteenth century.) Rather, we are interested in when that imaginary conversation in the Los Angeles café might first have happened. That is, when did *human culture* discover the unconscious mind? I'd give any answer plenty of breathing room, but as an astrologer I would center the shift on 1930, the year Pluto was discovered. If someone wanted to take it back to the discovery of Uranus—the first "invisible" planet—in 1781, I wouldn't argue. But Pluto seems to have a particular affinity with, to use Freud's words about psychoanalysis, "making the unconscious mind conscious."

The key here is that as our knowledge of the cosmos has deepened, so has our knowledge of the human mind.

This is not a "coincidence," this is *coincide-ence*. Those two words are obviously the same, but if we say, "coincide-ence"—mispronouncing it—

we might think a little more deeply about the word. A less awkward term is *synchronicity*. That's a word we're going to be hearing a lot as we begin to focus more specifically on Neptune.

Here's the point: when we discovered Uranus and Neptune, it shook astrology. But when we discovered Pluto, we had no idea of the size of the fish we had hooked. There were at least fifteen hundred more "Plutos" waiting for us out there—or we might as easily say "in here," since they each resonate with structures in the deep mind.

CAN ASTROLOGY DEAL WITH THE 21ST CENTURY?

As we have seen, we have the Sun, four little rocky worlds, four big gaudy balloons, and two hazes of stone. Those are the basic building blocks, the basic *meta-structure*, of the solar system.

They must also represent the basic vocabulary of astrology, which in turn represents the fundamental syntax of human consciousness.

We can quibble. That astronomical model oversimplifies things a bit—those two stony hazes somewhat permeate the two groups of four "planets." But if we look freshly and objectively at the solar system, I think we would quickly realize that the four rocky worlds, of which Earth is one, are very different from the four gas giants. Gazing from the observation deck of our starship fifty billion miles above the north pole of the Sun, we might speculate that we should go further than the IAU ever dared, *and just dump the word "planet" entirely*. Maybe we need two words, one for the four rocky worlds and another one for the four gas giants, which are so clearly in a distinct category.

And that leaves Pluto in a funny position.

Historically, culturally, and astrologically, it is a planet. But in fact, as we can plainly see from our starship, it is simply one of the biggest, brightest and closest representatives of a huge group of "trans-Neptunian" objects. Astrologically, we might assume that they have an entirely different meaning than that of the gas giants or the rocky worlds—or the Sun itself, for that matter.

So what do the TNO's mean? Let's review our clues: the discovery of Pluto in 1930 coincided effectively with the collective discovery of the unconscious mind. And then, slightly further down the timeline, starting in 1992—at the conjunction of Neptune and Uranus—we learned that Pluto was not alone. We began to find swarms of these trans-Neptunian objects.

Suddenly we had an explosion in terms of our awareness of the structure of the deep solar system.

Astrologically, this explosion in astronomical knowledge suggests that we are living in a time that coincides with an explosion in our understanding of the depths of the mind.

THE COSMIC WALTZ OF NEPTUNE AND PLUTO

To go further, let's consider some interesting dimensions of the *relationship* between Neptune and Pluto.

The unique thing about Pluto's orbit—and what increasingly I have come to believe is the source of Pluto's obvious observed astrological power in our lives—is that for about twenty years of Pluto's 248-year orbit around the Sun, it lies *inside* Neptune's orbit. That is, Pluto is then closer to the Sun than is Neptune.

It's amazing how few astrologers know this, let alone people in general. To pass fifth grade science class, you have to name the planets in their order from the Sun. The litany is always, "Saturn, Uranus, Neptune, Pluto." But in fact, that's sometimes wrong. Pluto inched closer to the Sun than Neptune on February 7, 1979. Twenty years and four days later, it inched back out beyond Neptune again. That was February 11, 1999.

So with Pluto, we have a planet that weaves in and out, spending most of its time beyond Neptune, occasionally swinging inside, as if it were *carrying messages back and forth*. Like a shaman, Pluto seems to have one foot in both worlds—the "planetary" world inside of Neptune and the mysterious world outside of Neptune. What are exact natures of those "two worlds?" This is our critical question. Our understanding of Neptune pivots on the answer since Neptune marks the boundary between them.

Let's try to answer it. If we succeed we will have the key to understanding both Neptune and Pluto—and I believe the master key to astrology's inevitable future.

(Let's note here that Pluto is not the only one of these little iceworlds that crosses Neptune's orbit. It is simply the biggest one by far. Further fine-tuning lies ahead . . .)

GOD?

I was involved once in a panel discussion at one of those big astrology conferences. There were six or eight of us sitting at a long table up there in front of a large audience. We were invited to discuss the symbolism of the Divine in the chart—the symbolism of God in the chart. And I think I probably had the simplest response. I believe that the astrological symbol of God is simply the circle of space around the outside of the chart.

What is that circle of space, really? It's called the *sky*. Or, if we want to get precise about it, it is both halves of the sky—the sky overhead, and the half of the sky that we can't see, the half that's beneath the Earth, or beneath the horizon. The technical term for this space is the *celestial sphere*—that great sphere of space that appears to surround us.

That seems to me like as good a definition of God as we are going to find in an astrological chart.

Let's consider the same question from a more subjective, heart-centered, viewpoint. Lie back on a blanket on a summer evening and behold the heavens. We look at the sky and it conveys a *feeling of vastness*; it *encompasses us*. It has a quality of *infinite depth* about it. It feels *ancient and timeless and eternal.*

Aren't those all pretty good metaphors for God or for the Divine?

Place all that in the context of the idea that your nature, your personality, can be *defined via planetary positions*. That's how practical astrology works. We draw our personalities and psychological selves down from the higher realm of sky—but let's not forget that it can work both ways. We are all also capable of closing our eyes, going into the big silence, feeling that space, feeling the sky within. Feeling—dare I say it?—"the inner sky?"

Astrologers have long attributed these kinds of *mystical feelings* to the planet Neptune. That's right—but by the time we are done here we will understand Neptune's actual function more rigorously. Suffice it now to say that these "oceanic" feelings are really more about *our potential attunement to the sky as a whole*—to the Divine—than they are specifically functions of Neptune.

Neptune, as we will see, is merely an intermediary.

So, we exist in the world of personality—I could say the world of "ego," not intending that word in a negative way. In that world, we are individuals responsible for creating our own experiences and destinies, dealing with our own karma and the issues that come up in life. To be sane, all of that personality-work has to be done honestly and authentically.

And that's one half of what we are.

Then there's this vastness outside us—or is it inside us? Close your eyes for a moment. Feel your oneness, feel your silence, feel your spaciousness. There's the direct experience of what I am calling "sky symbolism." It's the place we all come from, the place to which we will all return, the place that is out there, encompassing us.

For our purposes here, the critical point is that this represents the level of consciousness that is *beyond Neptune*. This is the great space beyond the walls of the personality, beyond Neptune—beyond the outer rim of your birthchart.

AND PLUTO?

What about Pluto? Is Pluto part of the personality or not? There's an interesting question! It weaves in and out of Neptune's orbit. We can make a practical case that, yes, absolutely, Pluto is part of your personality; I can analyze Pluto's position in your chart and say intense—even intrusively personal—things about you. That's just the nature of Pluto. I'd quickly add that they're not all bad things! There are some powerful, wonderful things about your Pluto too. So of course it's part of your personality. Who could doubt that?

But Pluto also relates strongly to the unconscious mind. And that is a deep realm. It may start at its surface layers with some "standard-psychology" perspectives about your wounds, your defenses and your darker motivations—but the unconscious mind quickly gets more profound, more mysterious and ultimately clearer than that. Ask Carl Gustav Jung.

Pluto weaves in and out, crossing Neptune's orbit, moving from deep space into—what, exactly? What lies *inside* Neptune? What is defined astrologically by Sun, Moon, the classical planets, and Uranus? Let's call it the *realm of the personality*. Or we could say "ego," so long as we know we don't mean arrogance or self-importance—just our specific identity.

AND NEPTUNE?

So what, then, is Neptune? What does its actual astronomical position as the last of the four gas giants mean? What about its placement on the frontier of what we might term "the personality?"

Neptune is not quite the same as "deep inner space;" we will be careful not to make that common astrological mistake in this program. But astrological experience suggests that Neptune is not exactly "ego" either.

We can call Neptune the *outer wall of the personality*, that which separates the ego-self from psychic—or cosmic—vastness. Better than calling Neptune a "wall," I prefer to call it a window.

Neptune is the window through which consciousness peers at cosmos—and through which the light of the cosmos pours into us.

Your home has windows. Would you say that the panes of glass are inside your house or outside it? Hard question? Yes—but more seriously, it is the *wrong* question. If you try to answer that question on its own terms, any answer you give will be fatally flawed.

It is exactly the same with Neptune. The implications of this ambivalence are vast, and we will take the rest of this book exploring them.

WE ARE "VOYAGER"

Let's turn our attention back toward the vastness of space. Pluto spends most of its time out there, but it occasionally comes a little closer to the central fire. Thus, it represents *our capacity to make the unconscious conscious.* But as we have seen, Pluto is just the closest of the major TNOs to the Sun. There are many others. One of them, Orcus, shares orbital characteristics nearly identical to those of Pluto and ultimately must be woven into the cloth of this emerging theoretical construct. That's beyond where we're going here—and in all honesty, beyond where my own thoughts and observations have gone. Jeremy Neal wrote a good book about Orcus, by the way. And I love the work that Melanie Reinhart has done with it.

Let's stick with the macro-picture. Out beyond the boundaries of ego consciousness—or simple self-awareness, as defined in conventional astrological language—we find the realm of the TNOs. These bodies all represent various vortex-points in the unconscious mind—a term that we can extend to include what we might call "soul" or "spirit."

My sense of it is that all of these objects could be helpfully framed under the historical metaphor of *angels and demons*—or, to be little more modern about it, *psychological complexes.* Or, to be Jungian about it, *arche-*

typal forms and structures.

We are looking out *through the window of Neptune*, gazing out into all that—*while it gazes back in at us.*

How deep does it go? As we keep gazing out into that space beyond the ego, we eventually punch through the primal haze represented by the trans-Neptunian objects.

What do we find beyond it? Remember our starship hovering fifty billion miles above the North Pole of the Sun? Let's punch warp drive again. Let's go out another few billion miles. And now, from this vantage point, we see the hazy, vague edge of the Kuiper Belt. What's out beyond that?

No one knows, exactly.

There's some evidence from the gravitational distortion of TNO orbits that there might possibly be an Earth-sized planet or two out there, somewhere in the dark. But that's just speculation. Again, no one knows exactly what is out there. We've not yet discovered that cold, distant, Stygian part of the solar system—nor, correspondingly, that part of the human mind.

But beyond that *terra incognita*, there's a place where the radiation of the Sun encounters a limit. It collides with the subtle pressure of the near-vacuum of interstellar space, an endless wave of incoming starshine. There, the particles radiating from the Sun are basically stopped by an equal incoming pressure. That's called the *heliopause.*

Beyond the heliopause, we enter true interstellar space.

A very interesting phenomenon happened in August 2012, mostly unnoted in the astrological community. Right then, *as Neptune was settling solidly into Pisces*, one of our *Voyager* space probes, launched in 1977, finally reached the heliopause. It was the first humanly-created object to "go where no one has gone before," to quote the familiar *Star Trek* phrase.

I think that was a deeply symbolic event in human life and experience. Suddenly, humanity had "probed" out *beyond the realm of psychology*—and see how we just left astronomy and entered astrology? An event in the sky always has meaning in your head and mine. When *Voyager* crossed the heliopause, we tentatively reached beyond the structure of anything you can define as the human psyche—even in the spacious definition of the human psyche that would be characteristic of the Jungian view of things, where we include the archetypes and all those mysterious realms.

Something lies beyond that deep psychological realm. Astrology proves it. Space itself proves it. But what is it? And did *Voyager's* reaching the heliopause in 2012 represent some kind of evolutionary breakthrough, as did the discovery of Pluto?

We discovered Pluto with a telescope and a camera. We discovered the heliopause with a space probe. Is there any difference between these two instruments, from a synchronistic perspective?

This is probably a question for the next generation of astrologers.

Our questions here are centered on the last of the true planets—that mysterious gas giant marking the edge of everything we can call "human" in any simple sense of the word: pale blue Neptune, the god of the sea.

3

CLEANING WINDOWS

Here is the question upon which everything Neptunian ultimately pivots: *What is the symbolism of space itself?*

Neptune, as we saw in Chapter One, is the window between our normal self and the larger framework of consciousness. Astrologically, that larger framework is represented by the sky—or by space, or by the entire trans-Neptunian realm.

That which we normally experience as "the self" is centered on the solar ego—remembering always how the Sun's gravity holds the rest of the solar system together. The solar system, as it is defined by the Sun, the four rocky worlds, the asteroids, and the four gas giants, corresponds to what we might call "the personality." This realm is the standard domain of astrological inquiry. Neptune lies at its edge. Like a window pane, the question of whether it is positioned "inside" or "outside" is ambiguous.

But we are looking through it into—what?

That brings us directly back to our opening question: What exactly is the symbolism of space itself?

Whatever the answer might be, we are contemplating it through the haze of ego and the haze of the unconscious, and maybe even what we could call the *haze of our souls.*

What could lie beyond the "haze of the illusion of our own souls?"

Ask the sky. It never lies. Sky is just pure spaciousness—so much vaster than the ego consciousness, so much vaster, even, than the self-awareness generated by a profound system of self-inquiry, such as Jungian psychology. With the view through Neptune into the Great Beyond, we are entering the realm of pure mysticism. Neptune is the window through which we contemplate these unimaginable realms of darkness, light, and mystery.

NEPTUNE'S EXACT FUNCTION

In a conventional astrology class, working at a reasonably sophisticated level of our craft, you're going to learn that Neptune is, among other things, the planet of mysticism or the planet of *spirituality*. And I think that is correct. I've used those words myself a lot, and I'm going to use them a lot in this book. They are good words to capture the higher possibilities inherent in this planetary archetype.

But here at this early stage of our thinking, where we are still laying the foundation, I want to be as precise as I possibly can. I want to say, loudly and clearly, that Neptune is in fact *part of the ego*. Space itself proves that. As we saw earlier, physically Neptune is one of those big four gas giants. The sky doesn't lie. Neptune is part of your ego, as certainly as Jupiter, Saturn, and Uranus—but there's a catch: Neptune also represents the *interface* between the ego and the unfathomable spaciousness of the deep psyche. Again, Neptune is the window through which we're looking into deep space, and through which deep space is looking back into us. It has elements of both; Neptune is not free of ego's distortions, nor is it purely defined by our more narrow egoic drives and appetites. To understand it, we have to dance on the razor's edge of that paradox.

We all have literal windows in our homes. And, as we asked earlier, are these windows inside the house or outside the house? The question is kind of instant Zen Buddhism, isn't it? "What is the sound of one hand clapping," and all that. It seems almost like a silly question. With literal windows, we'd consider the obvious answer to be, "windows are both inside and outside the house." It's not really a trick question, there are just two different ways of looking at it. The window is part of the house, but it also lets us see beyond the house.

And that's very much the nature of Neptune.

WASHING THE WINDOWS

Maybe you decide your house could use a little spring cleaning. You decide you don't want to do the work yourself, so you're going to hire somebody to help. You see an ad in the paper—someone is willing to clean your house for twenty bucks an hour. But there is one proviso: "*I don't do windows.*"

That proviso is easy to understand. Most of us have cleaned windows, and we know that it is a difficult job. Sometimes even getting the window open is hard work. The metaphors are abundant here! You want your Neptunian window to be clean. You want it clear so that you can see what is actually outside, and so the light of day gets in. A little dirt or grease can really make a mess of it.

A window is a weird thing in that when it's working perfectly, it means you can't see it at all. You could walk right into it. That's why birds fly into them all the time.

Funny—*if you can see the window, there's something wrong with it.* And I'm not just talking about the windows in your house, of course. I am talking about the Neptunian windows in your soul.

What would we see if our Neptunian windows were completely transparent to deep space? That's a question we're going to be wrestling with for quite a while—certainly in these pages, but really also for the rest of our lives. And it's going to take us to some scary places, some out-of-control places, some places where there is no safe ground to stand on. We will sometimes not be sure which side of the famous line between sane and crazy we're on. We will wrestle with defining the line between madness and mysticism. We don't always know where that line is, but we sense that it is very real—and when you're straddling it, you've never felt so naked.

Neptune is edgy. Neptune is scary. Washing the Neptunian windows entails the cultivation of a vulnerability so total we can barely stand to contemplate it, to consider it, to integrate it.

But I'm getting ahead of myself with that.

THE ASTROLOGICAL ASPECT WE ALL SHARE

Neptune and Pluto work together, as I've described earlier. As we will soon see, this cooperation between them is particularly true now, during this present period of history. This is territory that is absolutely critical to our understanding, so I want to explore it carefully. We start with Johannes Kepler, one of the great minds of human history. He was both an astrologer and an astronomer.

Some background first. The idea that the planets orbited the Sun rather than Earth being the center of the universe is often attributed to Nicolaus Copernicus, back in the Renaissance. It's a notion that actually goes back much further, to the Greeks, even though it was mostly in eclipse until Copernicus' time. One problem was that nobody could figure out exactly how such orbits worked—until Johannes Kepler came along. It's easy enough to postulate that Earth was not the center of the universe, despite the "obvious" reality. The hard part was explaining precisely how planetary orbits actually worked, reconciling theory with observation. Until Kepler's time, arguments for the heliocentric solar system were not actually much stronger than the "crystalline spheres" of the geocentric thinkers.

Kepler made some very basic observations, and they're quite intuitive. One of them is a basic physical law. Picture a string with a weight at the end. And imagine swinging this weight around your head. The tether is, say, about six feet long. What happens? You can hear it—swoosh ... swoo sh ... swoosh. And now start shortening the string, pulling it in. Swoosh, swoosh, swoosh.

See how it goes faster and faster?

Gravity is like the tether. As Kepler figured out, the farther something was from the Sun, the more slowly it would move forward in its orbit—just like our weight at the end of the string. Something closer to the Sun would move faster, just like what happens when you shorten the string.

Earth goes about eighteen miles a second forward in its orbit; Pluto goes about three miles a second. Thus, we could say that Pluto is on "a much longer string." Johannes Kepler figured that out and described it mathematically. He also figured out that planets orbit in *ellipses*, not in circles. That too was a big breakthrough. A given planet moves faster when it is closer to the Sun, and more slowly when its orbital path is farther out.

Kepler was even more precise. A planet might advance one week forward in its orbit. If the planet is far from the Sun, it is moving more slowly so *it would not have gone as far forward* during that week as it would when it was closer to the Sun.

In that first instance, the planet would have swept out a triangle with the Sun at the apex. Ditto in the second instance, but think about it. Imagine that some time has passed and picture the planet closer to the Sun. That means it is located at a point in its orbit where it is moving faster. At that greater speed, *it goes a little farther* in a week. It again sweeps out a triangle, but a *shorter, fatter* one this time. Here's what was perhaps Kepler's greatest insight, and really one of the most elegant ideas in the science of astronomy—the area of those two triangles created by the planet's motion in a week *was the same in each case.* In any given week, planets sweep out *equal-area triangles.*

You don't need to understand this in order to understand astrology. But it leads us to understanding something absolutely basic about what's going on in the world right now.

Bear with me please. We've got just a little more "science class," and then we are going to come face to face with what I personally view as the single most significant astrological feature of our time in the world: the Neptune-Pluto aspect we all share.

A corollary of Kepler's work is that two planets that are an equal distance from the Sun would be orbiting at the same speed. Bottom line, If we know how far a planet is from the Sun, we know how fast it's going—those two factors are utterly locked together. Now, for most of the planets, we don't have to worry about that, because we have that nice fixed order: Mercury, then Venus, then Mars. They never interfere with each other.

But wait a minute—what about Pluto and Neptune? As we have seen, for twenty years of Pluto's 248-year orbit, it lies inside Neptune's orbit. The rest of the time, it is outside, farther from the Sun. More critically, for a long period of time, Neptune and Pluto are *almost the same distance* from the Sun. In other words, Pluto is kind of "closing in" on Neptune's distance for an extended period. Then it crosses the line and it's inside—but not too far inside. Then Pluto slips out a little farther, but again it takes a while to really slow down a lot.

The result is that *Pluto and Neptune are going at about the same speed* for a long period of time—way longer than the twenty years in which Pluto is actually closer to the Sun than Neptune. That is the key insight—that in every orbital cycle Neptune and Pluto march more-or-less in lockstep for sixty years or eighty years. We can't be rigorous about the duration because ...well, what do we mean by "they're pretty close together?" It's sort of a vague statement. But it's in that sixty-to-eighty year range.

This leads us to our Grand Finale . . .

THE BIG SEXTILE

Neptune's orbital period is 165 years, Pluto's orbit, 248 years. They vary slowly over vast periods of time, but they've stayed pretty constantly in that range throughout human history. Against the backdrop of a human lifetime, those are very long periods. Against the backdrop of the history of humanity, Pluto and Neptune have done this lockstep dance many, many times. But around the time of World War II, during the early 1940s, Pluto got close enough to Neptune's orbit that it was going at pretty much the same speed. It didn't really cross Neptune's orbit until the late 1970s, but by World War II, it was pretty close. And so basically around then, Pluto fell into step with Neptune. They were going forward at more or less the same speed. You could see it in the sky, and you could see it represented in your astrological ephemeris.

Again, this astronomical event has happened many times in human history—but there are some weird features this time. And, by the way, it's still happening now; they're still going at about the same speed and will be until the 2030s.

Weird feature number one is that Neptune and Pluto fell into this lockstep when they happened to be in a *sextile* aspect to each other—more or less 60°apart. So they locked in at the same speed while in a sextile. Therefore, t*he sextile aspect itself locked in.*

This is why nearly every one of us alive right now has a Neptune-Pluto sextile in his or her chart. It may be out of quality—that is, in the "wrong" signs. Or the orb may be a bit wide. But it's there, unless you were born before World War II.

Isn't that strange? A period of history in which just about everybody is sharing the same aspect their charts? We tend to think of aspects as more transitory and individual. To me, this is maybe the single most interesting feature of this historical period—that everybody's chart shares the Neptune-Pluto sextile. How often has this happened in history? I don't know. The conditions are very unique. Doesn't it seem like it should mean something? Isn't God trying to tell us something with that?

Again, it was around World War II that this phenomenon started. There are a lot of people in the world who are older than that, and I wish them a long life. But we will soon come to a time when all of them will be gone. This sextile is not going to break up until the 2030s. We will soon enter a period when, essentially, *all the people on the planet have the same aspect in their chart.*

Weird feature number two: even though Pluto and Neptune have fallen into lockstep many times in history, another critical difference this time is that Pluto was only discovered in 1930. And Neptune was only discovered in the middle of the nineteenth century—the standard date given is 1846. *So this is the first time in history that these two planets have both been* ***consciously*** *integrated into the collective and locked into synchronization this way.* And it just "happened" to coincide with a time in which they were not just marching in lockstep in terms of orbital speed, but also locked into an active aspect—that amazing sextile.

Earlier, I mentioned the obvious historical significance of Pluto being discovered in 1930, and how it coincided with the *collective discovery of the unconscious mind.* We live in a psychological age now. We didn't used to.

The discovery of Neptune is a big subject that we'll talk about in more detail later on. But its discovery coincided synchronistically with the *collective discovery of personal mysticism.* The idea that we needed "an intervening priesthood" between us and the Divine began to break down. This was the discovery of the "kingdom of God within," with individuals having direct access to it, and our not needing to put our money in the collection plate in order to be "right with God." That, in a nutshell, is what Neptune *entering collective consciousness* meant.

So a critical insight into this ongoing sextile of Pluto and Neptune is that it has coincided with these planets *becoming activated* in the collective unconscious and the collective mind. Everybody is relating to them.

THE NEPTUNE-PLUTO MYSTERY DECODED

What does this long-running Neptune-Pluto sextile mean? Every one of us is so much a part of it that no one can stand outside it and see it clearly. It is tempting to ask, what does the fish know of the sea? But we can use the fine telescope of astrological theory to peer into it more deeply.

A sextile is stimulating. I annoy some people in the astrological world by pointing out that in the word "sextile," there's one syllable that most of us like better than the other one. Will you have "sex" or would you prefer to have a "tile?" I'll bet that we would all vote for the same syllable. And of course, eggheads are quick to point out, "That doesn't mean sex, you pervert!" And yeah, I know, it means six. But who can resist?

The universe is so full of synchronicities. And this is one of them. Even though "sextile" is obviously not sexual in any narrow sense, when we think of being attracted to someone, even if nothing is going to happen and it's just kind of a social event, we have all experienced how much wittier we are, how bright our eyes are, how alert we are, how attentive we are, how alive we feel. This is Eros, the face of life. It's not just sexual energy, but sexual energy is the most obvious illustration of this "erotic" interaction—and that is the exact nature of the sextile aspect. It's not just "a watered-down trine," as is sometimes said. It has a very distinct quality. Sextiles are more exciting. In a sextile, the two planets excite and stimulate each other. Just like two people who are attracted to each other, two planets in sextile relationship experience that same kind of cross-stimulation.

Here is the whole point in a single sentence—with Pluto and Neptune in sextile, *spirituality and psychology are exciting each other.*

There are other combinations of words we could use, but that's the high end of it, the purest expression of the lockstep sextile that dominates the evolutionary intention of our present age.

We are living in an epoch that not only embraces the discovery of the unconscious, but also an equally important discovery that doesn't get talked about as much. You could almost fit it on a bumper sticker. *We are leaving an age in which people can be viewed as spiritually healthy if they have not done their psychological work.* To have a healthy Neptune, you have to have a healthy Pluto. If you haven't dealt with your mother issues, for one concrete illustration, that's going to put a big limit on your spiritual growth.

Doesn't that make sense to you? Doesn't that seem like obvious common sense? If you hate your mother, that's going to interfere with your spiritual journey. *Everybody knows that.* What we can easily miss because life goes by so fast is that this sextile-synthesis of psychology and spirituality is a relatively new development. Our ancestors didn't think that way.

This may sound like blasphemy, but many of the so-called "saints" of history showed distinct signs of mental illness. Just think of the extremes of "the mortification of the flesh" to which some of these men and women aspired.

Or ask them about sex.

Now try this—turn the sextile around. Reverse Pluto for Neptune. *We are leaving an age when anyone can be viewed as sane—as having "done their psychological work"—if they do not have a spiritual life.* This is the other side of the sextile—that Pluto depends upon Neptune, as well as the other way around.

The ancient dance that these two planets have been doing since the beginning of planetary time—this weaving in and out of their orbits—is now coming into full flower. It is coming into full consciousness. It is happening "now"—which is to say, in the lifetimes of our grandparents, parents, our children and ourselves. That seems like a long time only because our viewpoint is so small. We are mosquitoes discussing glaciers. But when we let our viewpoint become more all-embracing, we see it—what an extraordinary time to be alive!

So, what is the meaning of the long-running sextile of Pluto and Neptune? *It is the marriage of psychology and spirituality.*

PSYCHOLOGY AS A TRIBAL BELIEF-SYSTEM

Imagine a psychiatrist—academic, solid, effective. He rests solidly on that kind of existentialist viewpoint that runs through conventional psychology, where one tenet is that we "shouldn't force our beliefs or our values upon the client." That line sounds so noble. If you are a psychologist, you shouldn't try to turn your clients into Zen Buddhists or Presbyterians or Republicans or Democrats. An honorable psychologist knows that. I agree with that principle. I bet you agree with it, too.

But *everybody* comes from a belief system. The idea that we can stand here and assume that there are indeed no ultimate truths, and that everybody "creates their own truth"—which is essentially the essence of existentialism—well, I don't want to make fun of that position. But I want to call it what it is: *a belief system.* We might as well call it a *religion.* That's because it can't be proven, it can only be believed.

Nobody can look at the universe without looking at it through their values and their assumptions. We all look at it through that Neptunian window—and unless our window is utterly clean, we're surely confusing what is actually out there with some of our own fingerprints on the glass. There is an existentialist foundation in modern psychology—that much is clear. Once again, I'm attempting to say something subtle here; I don't mean to be attacking psychology. I just mean to stand outside it.

And so, among some conventional academic psychologists, a patient who believes she has psychic experiences might be viewed as delusional. Ditto for one who believes in reincarnation, or one who believes he exists in other bodies in other times besides this one. Or one who takes the dream-world to be a separate reality as authentic as this one. The very experiences that Neptunian mystics have been reporting since the beginning of time—are they delusional? In a narrow psychological framework—a narrow *Plutonian* framework—they could be viewed as forms of pathology.

We need to keep a grip here. People who think that they've been personally selected by wise aliens for a joy-ride on a UFO with Elvis Presley and Sasquatch at the helm *are* crazy. Delusion is real. It's a reality. That's dark Neptune. But some of that amazing, cool, Neptunian stuff is real.

So, the question facing all humanity now is, how do we generate a model of sanity that includes those higher possibilities? *How do we generate a model of sanity that includes human spirituality*? And by "human spirituality," I don't just mean religious practice and being nice. I am including the truly weird stuff—which, as we will soon be exploring, is part and parcel of Neptune. I am including our human capacity to encounter other dimensions and other realities.

Generating that model is the work of this tribe of souls who began incarnating in World War II and are still being born among us. The last ones will be born in the 2030s as the Neptune-Pluto sextile breaks up. And their lives and their work will run into the next century.

THE UNIVERSAL SEXTILE: NEPTUNE AND PLUTO

Have a look at the following table "The Universal Sextile." It summarizes parts of the Neptune-Pluto synthesis that is trying to happen—and casts some light on what happens when these two planets bring out the worst in each other, which is also observably part of the current process.

During the period from early in World War II until the middle of the third decade of the 21st century, everyone alive experiences (and everyone born on earth embodies) the creative synergy (or the violent collision) of...

NEPTUNE		PLUTO
Spirituality	and	Psychology
Faith	and	Questioning
Religion	and	Existentialism
Spirituality	and	Psychology
Idealism	and	Cynicism
Soul	and	Psyche
Trancendence	and	Social Justice
Trancendence	and	Sexuality
Sensitivity	and	Harshness
Belief	and	Truth
Pacifism	and	Violence

RESONANCE

Neptune's orbit is 165 years; Pluto's orbit, 248 years. Those numbers themselves don't seem very evocative. But watch. Three times 165 equals 495. Two times 248 equals 496. This means that as Neptune orbits the Sun three times, Pluto orbits twice, *within just a tiny fraction of one percent of error*. This is not chance. This is a law of physics called *resonance*.
Here's another way to say it: *Neptune's gravity steers Pluto.*

Now, Pluto's gravitational pull is very weak because Pluto's mass is very small—just a quarter of one percent of the Earth's, as we saw earlier. But Neptune's gravitational field is enormous, with Neptune being seventeen times more massive than the Earth.

On that basis, let's go a little bit further, relying again on some basic physics.

Back in sixth grade science class, many of you "passed the test" because you could define the *inverse square law.* That simply means that if one object moves twice as far away from another object, then—since two squared is four—the gravitational attraction between them is *one-fourth* as strong as it was originally. The distance doubles, so the gravity is one-fourth as powerful. If the distance quadruples, the gravity is down to one-sixteenth of its original power. That's how the inverse square law works.

So, there's Neptune—massive, plus out on the edge of our "four-and-four" solar system. Usually, just beyond it lies Pluto, representing the gateway function into this larger realm that Neptune is contemplating. *Via gravitational resonance, Neptune is controlling Pluto's orbit.* And not just Pluto's; Neptune's gravity organizes the orbits of a lot of the TNOs. Many of these distant planetary bodies lock into various resonances with Neptune's orbit—resonances that actually correspond to the musical scale and the tonal intervals between the first and the fourth, and the first and fifth, and all of that. Mostly these bodies orbit the Sun in a 1:2 or 3:2 resonance with Neptune's 165 year cycle.

The "Music of the Spheres" actually is, in other words, a reality. And, even though it is really tempting, I don't want to launch into that juicy subject right now either. But following are some of the key details.

The Music of the Spheres

- Pluto's orbit of 248.6 years is locked in an approximate 3:2 resonance with Neptune's orbit—that is, Neptune orbits three times for every two orbits of Pluto—or Pluto's orbit is about 1.5 times longer than Neptune's orbit of 163.72 years.

- Pluto's orbit is locked into an approximate 3:1 resonance with Uranus's orbit.

- Neptune's orbit is locked into an approximate 2:1 resonance with Uranus's orbit.

- Chiron's resonance with Saturn is 7:12. Chiron's resonance with Uranus is 5:3.

- 21 orbits of Jupiter equal approximately one orbit of Pluto.
- 7 orbits of Jupiter equal approximately one orbit of Uranus.
- 5 orbits of Jupiter equal approximately 2 orbits of Saturn.
- One orbit of Neptune equals almost exactly six progressed lunar cycles of 27.3 years.
- Mercury's Synodic period is 115.88 days. Venus's is 583.92 days. That equals about 5:1.
- Three time Mars orbit = four times Venus' orbit to within 0.1%. (Resonance 4:3) Thus, every 6.4 years (2338 days) Mars and Venus return to the same positions relative to earth (heliocentric).
- Venus orbits the sun 13 times while the earth orbits the sun 8 times.

An interesting area of exploration is the relationship between these planetary cycles and the musical scale:

NAME	FREQUENCY RATIO	DISTANCE IN SEMITONES
Unison	1:1	0
Minor Second	16:15	1
Major Second	9:8	2
Minor Third	6:5	3
Major Third	5:4	4
Perfect Fourth	4:3	5
Perfect Fifth	3:2	7
Major Sixth	8:5	8
Minor Sixth	5:3	9
Major Seventh	16:9	10
Minor Seventh	15:8	11
Octave	2:1	12

Suffice it to say that resonance actually makes itself felt among the rest of the more familiar planets as well—double Uranus' eighty-four orbit, we are pretty close to Neptune's 165. Three times Mars' orbit equals four times Venus' orbit to within a tenth of 1 percent. It goes on like that.

For our purposes, the critical idea is that we see Neptune organizing, through its gravitational field, much of the orbital structure of the field of the TNOs beyond it. Everything else in the solar system has a gravitational effect on their orbits too, but it is a much smaller effect. Obviously, the Sun is the hub of the wheel, and everything orbits the Sun. Being much closer to the Sun than Neptune, Uranus lies *much farther from the TNO's*. The result is that, via the inverse square law, the Uranian gravitational influence on them is much smaller than Neptune's—remember, something four times further away has only one-sixteenth the gravitational effect. Jupiter is by far the most massive planet—but it lies so much closer to the center of the solar system that Neptune's gravitational impact on the TNOs is much greater.

This is all pure astronomy. But everything in astronomy can be used to generate astrological insight.

By the way, some of you may be seeing this kind of technical astronomical material for the first time, and maybe you are starting to feel like your cup is running over. That would be understandable. This perspective is not usually discussed very much in the astrological world. As a group, we astrologers seem to prefer mining Mediterranean mythology over reading the book of the sky. I've got nothing against Mediterranean mythology! I've learned a lot from it myself. But the sky has always been the mother of astrology, and our sense of what is out there has grown exponentially since the good old naughty days on Mount Olympus. It's time we looked at it, and let our inner poets digest what the astronomers have uncovered for us.

In the early 1990s, the Uranus-Neptune conjunction occurred, signaling a vast paradigm shift—and the need for new mythology. We'll look at that in some detail later on. From the parochial point of view of pure astrological history, the main thing that was going on with that Uranus-Neptune conjunction was the discovery of the Kuiper belt—or, more broadly, the discovery that the solar system is infinitely more complex than we had ever known before. Talking to other astrologers who are interested in exploring these new discoveries—Melanie Reinhart, Philip Sedgwick, Jeremy Neal, Henry Seltzer, there are a number of them—many of them complain that it's hard to get people to show up at talks about these new worlds. Orcus and Sedna and Quaoar—it's like, "Argh! Don't tell me about them!" Astrologers stick their fingers in their ears. In my opinion, this flight from complexity is a plague in the modern astrological world. We are turning away from treasure.

CHAOS

The urge to flee chaos, to replace it with controllable order, is natural. Astrologers turning away from the newly-discovered worlds is understandable, maybe even intellectually necessary, given our human limitations. It certainly seems like total chaos out there beyond Neptune. But is it? As we have seen, Neptune, via its gravitational field, organizes some of the TNOs. It organizes this complexity—or much of it.

Now, humanly, doesn't it seem like it could use some organization? Wouldn't some organization help you resist the temptation to return to a simpler solar system? And as you face the idea of doing a reading with fifteen hundred more planets, you inevitably have that human reaction of resistance. If we could somehow put them into categories, maybe you could stay on top of it all more easily. Maybe we could think in terms of *classes* of TNOs. Wouldn't that be helpful?

Neptune does some of that, I think. Despite its reputation as a space cadet that can't remember where it put the car keys, when it comes to the deep unconscious, Neptune is actually the great organizer. I am pointing here to a great frontier of astrological study. We can begin to reap the harvest of what the astronomers are doing in terms of dividing these TNOs into these families that are organized by harmonic resonance with Neptune's orbit. My guess is that Neptune will provide that key. We will find structure out there—or structure "in there," which is to say the same thing. Rather than dealing with fifteen hundred new planets one at a time, we will be dealing with the TNOs that are in the two-to-three resonance with Neptune. For one example, take Pluto. We'll also find a lot of them in the three-to-two resonance, and so on.

I have a happy fantasy that there may be somebody reading this who takes this idea and runs with it. And we will thus have a piece of the astrology of the future; we will have the Rosetta Stone for understanding the new system.

The point is, Neptune is the gateway to all of it. Pluto may be the first stage of the outward journey, representing, among other things, *conventional depth psychology*. But there is so much beyond Pluto. And Neptune controls much of it.

IN SUMMARY . . .

In what we have seen so far, we have been focusing very heavily on astronomy. We have been attempting to understand the nature of Neptune simply through an analysis of its place and its function in the physical structure of the solar system. We have not taken the usual astrological tack, which is arbitrarily assigning meaning to Neptune based on its Greek and Roman mythological associations.

Because of synchronicity, that method usually works well—but not always. Take, for a fine example Richard Tarnas pointed out, the observed wild, rule-breaking qualities of the planet Uranus and compare them with the repressive, conservative mythic god by the same name. And what will we do with asteroids with names like "Superbus" or "Springsteen?" There really are asteroids with those names!

Instead, what we are doing here is deriving astrological theory rigorously from Neptune's actual place and function in the solar system.

Turning briefly to mythology, we have the classic synchronicity that Neptune is, of course, the Roman god of the sea, paralleling the Greek god Poseidon. Here we are looking at a planet that references the great *sea of consciousness*. So you're standing on a physical real-world shore, literally gazing out into the ocean. And you know the feeling you get there, that feeling of spaciousness and infinity, of being in the presence of something so vast and ancient that you can't comprehend it. You have no visceral idea of where the sea ends or might lead, only school-learning. These are the ancient human feelings about the sea—and they coincide quite exactly with the feelings you get if you simply close your eyes and tune in to your own inner vastness. Pay attention to what's in there, to that feeling of infinite spaciousness—that is what we have begun to map through these discoveries we've been exploring.

How do you get your window as clean as possible so you can clearly see all that magical, multidimensional inner seascape? How do you get your window so clean that *you don't know it's there*? Or, perhaps getting a little ahead of myself, how do you get your window so clean that you don't even know that *you* are there?

Those questions will plop us into some really deep water.

4

LIFE'S LITTLE TRAFFIC JAMS

Everyone has Neptune in his or her chart. It's like having the gene in your DNA for eyes or a nose. We all have them too—but in each of us they take different forms. We've begun to introduce the basic archetype we call Neptune in its intrinsic nature—the "gene itself," so to speak. We will go more deeply into that now. All we have seen so far and all we will see in the next three chapters is held in common by everyone.

Later, we will add individual complexity and context by looking at specific examples, such as what it means to have, say, Neptune in Scorpio in the ninth house.

YOUR PLACE IN THE GALAXY

Imagine one of those stylized pictures of our galaxy—the great barred spiral galaxy that we call the Milky Way. And you see an arrow pointing to a spot on one of the spiral arms, about two-thirds of the way out from the center. There's a little sign by the arrow. It says, *You Are Here.*

We've all seen that image a million times. It has become a cliché. But it does kind of give you a Neptunian perspective on things.

Now picture a couple stuck in a traffic jam. They're in a hair-on-fire rush, and yet here they are in the midst of this damned snarl. They're feeling frustrated. You notice them in the rearview mirror of your own car. They are practically apoplectic, banging on the steering wheel, mouthing maledictions you have no trouble lip-reading. You know the type—they are totally agitated because they're being delayed by ... what? Ten minutes? From your perspective, their futile rage actually looks comical.

Pan back from that little tempest-in-a-teacup. Here are five thousand other people stuck in the same traffic jam, many of them in that same stressed-out condition. Pan back a little further, and here are five thousand more traffic jams in North America. Pan back further still, and envision all the traffic jams on the planet. Zoom back even further, and the Earth becomes a dust mote. Back a little further and you take in the galaxy—*You Are Here*—and then you pan back a little further, and there's the tiny little Milky Way, just kind of a fuzzy patch in a cluster of galaxies. And you pan back a little further, and you pan back a little further, and . . . you see where it all goes.

Thinking in that Neptunian way, we gain perspective on how upset we get when stuck in life's little traffic jams. Here you are, a *really, seriously pissed-off* little microbe on a dust mote. We laugh, when it is about other people. But for you, your agony at being delayed ten minutes is currently the center of the universe. As individuals, that is basically how we interpret things. *Fundamental to the way we organize our perception of the universe is that we are the center of it.*

And that is famously called the *ego*. In conventional spiritual discourse, I would next launch into an attack upon the folly of ego and the illusions it generates. I am not going to do that . . . not exactly. Before we are done, we will see a *necessary symbiosis* between the Sun and Neptune—between ego and the spiritual path. But first: some more familiar territory.

In the context of the traffic jam, the spiritual—or Neptunian—wisdom would boil down to the familiar question, "What will this matter in five hundred years?" And the people experiencing that high level of agitation in the traffic jam might benefit enormously from a little such Neptunian reflection. Our *You Are Here* arrow in our map of the galaxy makes exactly the same point. It's just a little perspective on our perpetual upset—a little Neptunian medicine to counter the endless ego-generated drama.

We've all been through this. We've all gotten bent out of shape because of some minor exhaustion or frustration or insult or vexation. Life is like that. And then maybe you muster a moment of mindfulness. You remember to take a breath and let it out. We've all done that, too. *That's your Neptune in action.* That's what Neptune is, astrologically, at least at its best. That is its higher function in the psyche. Those moments of *mindful perspective* point directly to your Neptune, and derive from it.

Maybe you are literally caught in a traffic jam. Maybe you get upset—and then you remember to get yourself un-upset by reflecting on that larger perspective. If you were to look at your chart at that very moment, there's an excellent chance you would see some Neptunian stimulus. That's just practical astrology at work. The fact that you have that *moment of mindfulness* in the traffic jam would have a natural correlation with the planet Neptune. The event itself may be trivial, just a mindful breath amid the exhaust fumes and the bad vibes—and maybe that's correlated with a little thing astrologically, such as Mercury or Mars transiting through a trine to your natal Neptune.

Or such Neptunian evolution may be unfolding in the dramatic context of some hugely important existential passage, such as *remembering to breathe* when you are going through a divorce or a bankruptcy. Such a spiritual breakthrough would likely correspond to some more significant and long-lasting Neptunian configuration—transiting Neptune conjuncting the natal Moon, for one possible example.

Getting slightly more technical, maybe your natal Neptune lies in 7° Scorpio. And at that moment in the traffic jam, 7° Scorpio would be the Ascendant of the chart, as if a baby were born right then and there. That's a kind of astrology to which we often don't pay attention because it changes so fast. It's not that important because it is so fleeting, but the sign and degree that's currently *rising* over your present location will often trigger a planet in your chart and correlate with your moment-to-moment experience.

Again, that's not a central point, but it illustrates the broader idea that in Neptunian times—be they trivial or epochal—we are *invited to mindfulness.*

We are invited, to move to the *pole of consciousness that is opposite the ego.*

SUN AND NEPTUNE: THE CENTER AND THE EDGE

So we have one core insight: *Sun equals ego.* The center of the solar system equals the center of your personal narrative. Meanwhile, Neptune, lying at the edge of the solar system, is the *window beyond the ego*—the window through which we peer into the trans-Neptunian realm of deep space, with all its comforting "galactic" perspective.

To be human is to oscillate between these two modalities of perception.

Neptunian wisdom: What will this matter in five hundred years? *You Are Here.* Those lines sound vaguely holy. They may be clichés, but they are holy clichés, and hard won. You know what those people looked like in your rearview mirror. They were ridiculous—just angry little monkeys. If you forget Neptune, that's what you will look like too.

But here's some perspective: *the Sun also has wisdom.* There is wisdom in the ego. We need to understand it. To keep our relationship with Neptune healthy, we need to keep our relationship with the Sun healthy as well. Failing that, Neptune provides us with a classic slippery slope.

Here's a way to understand what it looks like to slide down it. Imagine you're a woman in college. A nice but rather unremarkable guy has been sitting next to you in history class. He's inoffensive. You've become sort of politely friendly with him, chatting with him. There's no attraction, there's no zing; it's just kind of a pleasant, casual acquaintance based on circumstance. You like him fine, and you happen to be sitting next to him in the class; that's all.

One night your phone rings. You pick it up and it's him. He says, "Let's have dinner." It's slightly odd. Is he asking you for date? Because going out to dinner could be kind of a date, and you're not really feeling that kind of energy. On the other hand, the relationship is friendly. Maybe he's just being friends with you. Why be mean to him and refuse? And anyway, you think—*what will it matter in five hundred years*? You agree to go out to dinner.

At dinner, he's a gentleman, even though he is obviously attracted to you. Afterwards, he walks you up to your front door. His body language indicates that he wants to plant a chaste little kiss on your lips. Well, *what will it matter in five hundred years*? We're all God's children, right? *Smack!*

He calls you again a couple nights later. "I really enjoyed dinner with you, let's go out again." *What will it matter in five hundred years*? A week later, he is kissing you a little harder. *What will it matter in five hundred years*? "Take your clothes off." *What will it matter in five hundred years*? "Will you marry me?" *What will it matter in five hundred years? (laughter)*

See, there's a definite downside to that powerful holy phrase! There's the slippery slope. There's a downside to Neptune—it can mean *living like a ghost*, living like you're nobody, living as if your ego did not matter. *Living as if you had no Sun in your chart.*

Astrologers often talk about drunkenness and escapism with Neptune. They're right; those are often Neptunian issues. But this ghostly tendency is maybe the heart of the matter. *We have egos for a reason*, just like we have legs and feet for a reason: they can all carry us to where we need to go. They can also carry us to places we should never be.

THE EGO "VERSUS" THE SPIRITUAL PATH

So should we live as though our egos mattered, or should we live as though our egos did not matter? Isn't that an essay question? This is an issue with which we'll be wrestling throughout this book: this paradox of our dual natures.

Each one of us is the embodiment of the Sun, and we have a responsibility to do that right. And by cosmic birthright, each one of us also has this Neptunian access-point to a transcendent condition in which we are not identified with the little ego self. As we will discover, these two functions are utterly interdependent.

A right relationship with Neptune is, of course, a desirable thing. In a nutshell, with a right relationship with Neptune, we do better in the face of life's little traffic jams. I also want to add that a right relationship with Neptune helps you avoid a wrong relationship with Neptune! And an illustration of a wrong relationship with Neptune can be found in the story I just told of that hypothetical woman who drifted into an empty marriage. *A wrong relationship with Neptune boils down to not taking assertive responsibility for our own journeys, not claiming the experiences that we need to have in this world.* Neptune can drift and dream and live a life that has nothing to do with the evolutionary needs of the Self.

As we go forward in our investigation, we will explore the substantial range of the Neptunian shadow in a lot of specific detail. I also want to focus on its higher, positive meaning. That's a good way to keep astrology honest: always remembering that every front has a back, and that every astrological configuration has both higher and lower expressions. So, Neptune is the pane of glass between us and the larger universe, be it clear or greasy—this window through which we gaze into outer and inner space, and through which "space" gazes into us. Like the rest of the planets, it can carry us to heights of exaltation or drag us down into the hellish depths of our own dark side.

"IT'S BRIGHT"

I heard a comedian perform at an astrology once several years ago. I forget her name, but she was completely wonderful. She was making fun of most of the astrologers. I got off the hook for some reason; she didn't take a shot at me. But here's the line she used to poke fun at a colleague of mine who has a Pisces Moon. She said, "He would be a terrible person to have with you if your house caught on fire." She illustrated what she thought he would do by staring into space for several long seconds, as if transfixed. Then, still pretending to be him, she said, wide-eyed, "*It's bright* . . . "

The crowd laughed, of course. It was funny—and the line served well as an illustration of the *useless, dazed side of Neptune*—just looking at the fire while the house burned, saying, "*it's bright*..." In other words, we can see the "ghost" again: a person just watching his or her life go by, and not engaging with the necessity of action.

There is a dark side to "*just accepting things as they are*." We become as passive as a person addicted to television—which, by the way, is another Neptunian "symptom."

"Just accepting things as they are." Doesn't that phrase sound wise and wonderful? Doesn't it sound positive and healthy? I'm not going to say the opposite; it is positive and healthy. But once again, you can also feel the darker, riskier spiritual and psychological side of it.

Neptune can be spaced-out in the simple, absent-minded, sense of the term—forgetting to pick up the milk in the grocery store, losing the car keys, and so on. But this more extended, existential "ghost" spaciness is the deeper threat by far. Life can go by like a dream.

THE BLINDING VEIL OF OPINION

We are walking a tightrope here, with the pitfalls of the Sun on one side and the pitfalls of Neptune on the other. Let's continue our high-wire stroll by taking a respectful look at the positive side of "accepting things just the way they are." This is easy to say, but hard to do. Imagine looking at the world *with no opinions at all*. No attachment, no resistance. No approval, no disapproval.

Just try that one on! It's not easy. There's one face of high, clear Neptune—no *wall of opinion* or judgement between yourself and the world;

everything simply is what it is. You just let it be.

So, without getting embroiled in politics, let's simply imagine that you intend to vote for a liberal or progressive candidate. Let's say that you meet somebody wearing a button for the opposing candidate—a political conservative. This stranger hasn't *said* anything political, but he's got that damned button on his lapel. There you are, confronted with it. And you're a liberal. Feel that gritting of the teeth? Feel that biting of the tongue? What goes on in your head when you spy that telltale button? "Here's a real dupe, enslaved by his wealthy oppressors! A lowly, stupid, insensitive, uncaring *snake* of a human being—wrong about everything. Sexist! Racist! Homophobic!"

Which may not be true about that person at all.

In that scenario, you are not seeing the person; you are looking straight into the eyes of your *opinion*. Your projection has blinded you to any possibility of seeing reality, of *seeing things as they actually are*—which may or may not resemble your projection.

Of course, we can turn that scenario around—the conservative looking at the liberal and projecting terrible things: laziness, immaturity, dependency on the nanny state, entitlement, whatever.

The pressure on us all to have opinions is very strong. *And the part of us we call the Sun loves it*; opinions and views are its specialty. If you're American, you'll be asked, "Are you a Democrat or a Republican?" Having an answer is part of being a good citizen—that's true too. But you have to decide. "Who is wrong? Which side are you on?"

Opinion goes way beyond politics.

Maybe we are hanging out with a child who is coloring with crayons. We try to make conversation. Maybe we ask the kid about her favorite color. That sounds innocent, doesn't it? Kids love to answer that one. *But why does everyone need to choose one color above all others, rejecting the rest of the rainbow?* What is the lesson we are teaching that child simply by expecting him or her to have an *opinion* on the rainbow?

Neptune is the part of you that lets the whole rainbow be what it is.

As synchronicity would have it—and synchronicity is everywhere—just before I started this session, I was sitting outside, having a conversation with two students. Somehow football came up. One of the students was pointing out that he lives in Minnesota, and how if you live there you have to be a *Vikings* fan—and may God forgive you if you support the Green Bay Packers. I heard recently that some poor guy was beaten to the point that his brain was damaged after a game because he was a *Giants* fan. Some fans of an opposing team were so passionate they beat him up for it. There's opinion!

Ask the Sun: *you've got to stand for something*. And may God help us all.

The point is, there is endless social pressure on us to be defined by our opinions about everything from sports teams to politics to the colors of the rainbow. Ego soaks it all up.

Further ego-adrenaline: opinion usually implies the idea that I'm right and you are wrong. That's generally the structure of opinion. This need to make other people wrong is quite fundamental to solar logic, which is the ego's logic of separateness and individuality.

Now, if the Sun-function is made very pure, it probably wouldn't be like that, but the ego does have those tendencies. We all live with them. One can easily see why the ego gets bad press in spiritual circles. It is, rather literally, the ultimate source of all our human problems.

Still, as underscored earlier, we *need* the Sun or we become nothing but leaves in the wind. We watch our life burning down and say, "It's bright . . ." Life *happens to us*. We drift along, living like ghosts.

So, Neptune needs the Sun, and the Sun needs Neptune. We've all got to stand our ground—and to know when to let go of it.

There is no simple answer here, only an endless, intuitive, improvisational dance. To get it right requires success at two simultaneous processes: the first is taking care of the solar ego, keeping it healthy and on track with its core values and developmental aims. And the second—cleaning our Neptunian windows—is the subject of the rest of this book.

5

I GOTTA BE ME

I am a Capricorn with Saturn in Virgo smack on my Midheaven—a hopeless case, huh? (*laughter*) As even a beginning astrology student might speculate, I tend to work hard. Some might say "too hard."

Now, many of you have studied with me a long time so you know the positive and affirmative logic of evolutionary astrology: if you're a Capricorn with Saturn and Virgo on your Midheaven, you're *supposed* to work hard, right? Isn't that why God made you? Isn't that part of why you were born? With a chart like that, you have a mission, you have a purpose in the world; that's what you're *supposed* to do.

Nobody has the wrong chart. There are no bad charts. Your chart tells you how to live. And your chart makes you a solemn promise. It describes a life that, if you live it more or less successfully, you will conclude it with a smile on your face. You will lie on your deathbed feeling, "I nailed it. I did what I came here to do."

There is no greater victory in this world than that. And that is the vow your birthchart makes to you. If you trust anything in this world, let it be that.

And yet I am surrounded by caring people who say, "Oh, Steve, we're worried about you! You shouldn't work so many hours. Learn to say no to people. You should relax more. You really should take better care of yourself."

Maybe there's truth in all that; I don't want to be rigid or defensive about any of it. Given my chart, there's indeed a danger that I might lose perspective and push too hard. But the deeper point is that we humans are not scaled to any "one-size-fits-all" standard. *There is an inherent rightness about your individuality as it is reflected in the mirror of your natal chart.* Not everybody was born to be mellow, for example.

Now, if you're a quintuple Taurus with Libra rising, and lots of Neptune, maybe mellow is right for you. And if that's your chart, and you are doing fine with it—then you're going to be surrounded by people who get on your case and say, "You should get a better job," or, "You really should try to lose fifteen pounds; I'm worried about you."

But wait a minute! "I'm a quintuple Taurus—why was I born? *To eat ice cream!*"

My ice cream line there was obviously intended playfully. But there's also seriousness in what I just said. *Why* would somebody be a quintuple Taurus? That straightforward question is what separates evolutionary astrology from the mainstream. We evolutionary astrologers wonder why we have the chart we have, knowing and believing that there is some larger purpose in it. Conventional astrology "delineates the personality;" evolutionary astrology does some of that too—but we frame the personality as a vehicle the soul is using for some deeper purpose.

So, back to our question: why would somebody incarnate as a quintuple Taurus? *Because Taurus reflects an evolutionary need to calm down, to get back into the body, to return to instinct, to recover from some earlier, past-life trauma.*

Without making too fine a point of it, maybe relaxing enough to fully and mindfully enjoy a bowl of ice cream is a spiritual step forward for that person.

But remember—just like me, just like you—that person is going to be getting constant pressure to conform to other people's opinions about good behavior—in other words, pressure *not to be a quintuple Taurus.*

You may notice how I deftly I dodged over to that quintuple Taurus, turning attention away from my own sad case—but it's the same for all of us. I get all this pressure to act like I'm not a Capricorn with Saturn and Virgo on the Midheaven. *And the point is that I could say similar things about every one of you.* The world's got a self-improvement plan for you—and the plan always involves you becoming different than what you really are.

You've got to fight off those distorting forces. *And Neptune can't do that. That holy war is the Sun's job.* As we've been saying all along, you need an ego.

One beauty of astrology is that it is founded on the core principle of respect for the uniqueness of each human being. If people are interested in a career in astrology and they don't celebrate human diversity, they're in the wrong field. Astrology *is* a celebration of human diversity. We're all different; we're all on different paths. Different experiences work for different people. Amen.

THE GOOD OLD SOLAR EGO

So what is the upshot of all this? T*he ego must defend itself.* See how that follows logically? The ego is a necessary piece of equipment for our spiritual journeys. Neptune cannot function without the help of the ego. Without the Sun, all that's left of Neptune is a biddable ghost in this world, doing what it has been told to do, following the path of least resistance to an early, meaningless grave.

The solar ego must defend itself against that poisonous intrusion on its own sovereignty.

You are who you are. You have a right to be yourself, and you probably know yourself better than anybody in the world does. You also have more access to your own soul than anybody else in the world. So, you peer through that Neptunian window into the source of all true wisdom and you listen to it. After that, acting on that wisdom is the Sun's job. And when you act on what your soul is telling you, other people will give you "corrective feedback" that is antithetical to following that good path. You have to go forward and be true to yourself anyway—and again, that's the Sun's domain.

This sense that "I am different from you" is based on certain truths about the human spiritual condition. It arises naturally. Sadly but inevitably, so does the "military buildup" that the ego requires in order that we can d*efend* our right to be who we are against the pressure of everyone else's opinions.

I don't think that issue is going to go away; I think it is absolutely fundamental to human experience. In many spiritual circles, the word "ego" has been demonized—but for us to turn taking care of it into the "work of the devil" is really misleading.

All that I have just lauded flies under the banner of the Sun. This capacity to *know ourselves* and to *take up some space* and to *stand up for our-*

selves is not Neptunian—even though Neptune's health depends upon it.

Fundamentally, this is solar symbolism in astrology: your natural right to have an ego. Without one, you'd be a cook without a kitchen.

I'm hammering an important point here, but I want to make sure I don't hammer it too hard! In words usually attributed to Albert Einstein, "everything should be made as simple as possible, but not simpler." That requires that we complicate all this a little bit. Taking care of the ego is not *strictly* a solar issue. I would add a little dollop of *Uranian individuation* to what we have said here about the Sun—that you have a right to be what you are, as distinct from what you've been trained to be. We might add a little dollop of some *Plutonian psychology* in there, as we begin to sort out some of the pathological things that have probably happened to each one of us that make us weaker or lead us to underestimate ourselves, or to carry shame that might interfere with our ability to fully honor the flowering of what we are. The Moon is part of it too—knowing what you actually feel.

In other words, we are really talking about the entire edifice of astrology—the rest of your chart. The Sun is just quick astrological shorthand for the ego, which is actually a more complicated phenomenon. *But it is the Sun that holds us together as egos, just as the literal gravity of the Sun holds the solar system together.* When it comes ego, the Sun is truly is the heart of the matter.

And it is no accident that the Sun lies "at the other end of the planetary solar system" from Neptune. They are true opposites.

TONAL AND NAGUAL

Now, for some old hippie lore. A lot of the best of it was articulated by Carlos Castaneda in the famous "don Juan" books about Yaqui shamanism. There's much to question about how truthful Castaneda was in that series of utterly Neptunian books, but even his biggest detractors mostly acknowledge that, at least, his representation of the ancient Mesoamerican shamanic worldview was based pretty solidly in the anthropological literature.

I am also happy to bring in perspectives on human life that don't have their origin in the Mediterranean basin two or three thousand years ago. We astrologers can dine at a much richer banquet if we just dig for treasure in other cultures for a change.

I find it absolutely fascinating that a shamanic tradition that evolved completely independently of European influence could cast such a helpful light on what we astrologers would call the interdependent relationship of the Sun and Neptune. I also wonder about how old these traditions are, and I imagine the answer to be "very old indeed." Might they be so ancient as to have had their origin on the other side of the Bering Strait land bridge? Might they thus share roots with Asian, and specifically, Tibetan traditions? They certainly seem to me to share philosophical DNA that suggests such a link.

My favorite of Castaneda's books was *Tales of Power*, and my favorite chapter in it is called "The Sorcerer's Explanation." Attempting to get his Ph.D. in Anthropology, Castaneda tried to get the shaman don Juan to finally make some sense—which is kind of hilarious, thinking about Neptune, a planet which opens us up to a universe far beyond sense or reason. Don Juan decided to indulge Carlos and offered "the sorcerer's explanation." He said that there are, essentially, two poles to life, or to the human personality. One is called the *tonal* and the other is called the *nagual.*

Tonal is everything you know; *nagual* is everything else. Don Juan pointed out that the *nagual* is much vaster than the *tonal.*

Carlos Castaneda said to don Juan, "So, the *nagual*, that's like God?" And don Juan laughed at Carlos and said no, you know all about God; God is a concept in your head; God is part of your *tonal. Nagual* is much bigger than God. Don Juan added that entering the *nagual*—and our translation here is "entering the trans-Neptunian territory"—is easy; anyone can do it. Don Juan said the hard part is *getting out again.*

Here's a critical clue for our purposes: don Juan added that the secret to being able to *move fluidly between these two worlds* is a healthy tonal. I believe he is essentially describing healthy personality; a healthy psyche. Again, we translate into our own astrological language: *To handle the Neptunian vastness in a way that doesn't destroy you, you need to make a strong response to your birthchart, and specifically, to the Sun.*

There's your *tonal*, translated out of the ancient Yaqui framework. It is your birthchart. We might say, "Everything in you that is not sky."

Don Juan cryptically added one comment that has always utterly delighted me. He said that the *moment of your birth* is related to the nature of your *tonal.* Here are his exact words:

> *The moment we take the first gasp of air we also breathe in power for the tonal. So it is proper to say that the tonal of a human being is intimately tied to his birth. You must remember this point. It is of great importance in understanding all this. The tonal begins at birth and ends at death.*

Doesn't that ring your astrological bells? *Tonal* and the moment of birth are intimately related—and ask any astrologer: the personality and the moment of birth are intimately related. They are the same thing, or at least they overlap significantly.

OUR BOTTOM LINE

So for me personally, given the nature of my own birthchart, to have a healthy relationship with that Neptunian vastness, it is important for me to be a worker bee. That's my birthchart, or my tonal. For our quintuple Taurus, maybe the secret to a healthy relationship with that Neptunian vastness is eating ice cream—lucky you, there's your spiritual practice. (*laughter*) And again, I'm not trying to make fun of Taurus. I am just trying to speak simply.

Bottom line, you have to be yourself. You have to know yourself and be yourself in order for the psyche to be healthy enough to live in sane relationship with these Neptunian realms. Otherwise, those realms eat you alive in ways we have already seen and in some we have not yet explored.

So your ability to open up sanely to the Neptunian vastness is in direct proportion to the health or the sanity of your ego. That's worth saying—but it's not as simple as that. There's another potential hitch: we can also open up to the vastness *prematurely*. Then we might personally illustrate the idea that the *nagual* is easier to get into than it is to get out of. This is path is often called *madness*.

Indulge an old man here, please. I am an old hippie, so let's go back to the 1960s for another moment. Castaneda's books had the reputation of being "drug literature." That was only true of the first couple of them. Don Juan basically said he used drugs—sacred plant medicines—on Carlos to whump him upside the head because he was so clueless about the larger reality. The experiences they induced actually did seem to open Castaneda up to a wider view of reality than what was then being presented in university psychology departments.

But back then in the 1960s and 1970s, there was a common social phenomenon: someone who "took too much LSD." These were often genuinely tragic stories. Some people just weren't wired for these extreme experiences, so they "screwed themselves up with drugs." They got into a place from which they could not escape, echoing don Juan's warnings about the *nagual.*

On an edgier parallel note, I would also like to recognize the phenomenon of people who took *just enough* LSD—for example, the modern guru and spiritual teacher, Ram Dass. He didn't go crazy; he maybe got near the edges of it. He entered the *nagual* and he came back out again—wiser and still with an intact, functional *tonal.*

There are definitely, however, people who took psychedelics prematurely, before they had prepared their landing strip. They entered the *nagual* and they couldn't leave, so they were trapped within it. Some of them are still there. Some of them died in that condition, which must be truly terrifying.

One point that I'm really trying to underscore here is that working with Neptune is *dangerous.* It can threaten your mental health. Sacred plant medicines are not the point; to me at least, psychedelic drugs are merely a footnote in the book of Neptune. What I am saying is that there is a tendency to equate Neptune with the word "spirituality." That's fair enough; that's accurate. But we have to be very careful not to let Neptune become too safe a word, the way "spirituality" has—not to let it be absorbed entirely into the *tonal.* It is stranger and wilder than that by far.

When we have a "safe God" who holds no surprises, we are seriously off target.

And we are in for a serious surprise.

6

NEPTUNE AND PSYCHIC PHENOMENA

Among all the loftier things we might say about it, Neptune is really, really weird. In talking about Neptune, I want to be careful not to be *too* weird—but I want to make sure I'm weird enough.

For example, your telephone rings. You pick it up. Imagine this one in slow motion: the telephone is moving toward your ear. Before it arrives, the image of a friend's face forms in your mind. The telephone hits your ear and that's who it is: the same friend, calling you. You had his face in your mind before you heard his voice in your ear.

I doubt there's anyone in this room who hasn't had that kind of experience. That's Neptune in action.

When you stop to think about it, how could that subtle communication have happened? More pressingly, what are the larger implications of that kind of experience? Some people might be tempted to call it "chance." But we all know that kind of thing happens far too often for "chance" to hold water as an explanation.

Or try this one. Maybe you're out with a bunch of women friends. You're in a Mexican restaurant drinking margaritas, relaxing, joking around, bantering. Maybe one of the women needs to leave—it's time to go home and relieve the babysitter. She's a single mom. As she's turning away from the table bidding everybody goodbye, she says over her shoulder, "Pray for me. I've got a date with some guy this weekend."

It's the first time she's mentioned the date; it appears that it is not something hugely important for her—just "some guy" has asked her to go out, and she's agreed. Some of the gals make bawdy suggestions about safe sex. But as you hear her words, it hits you: *she's going to marry him.* How did you know that? Two years later, sure enough, it's wedding bells.

Once again, I doubt there's anyone in this room who hasn't had that sort of experience. It's the same story as the telephone, just playing for higher stakes.

Let's raise the stakes even higher. Picture a mother living in Los Angeles whose grown son is serving in Afghanistan in the military. Tragically, he steps on a landmine and his legs are blown off. That happens at 2:13 in the morning, Los Angeles time. And his mother awakens, bolt upright in her bed—at precisely 2:13 AM—from a terrible nightmare she cannot quite remember.

How many times have you heard that kind of story?

What makes these three experiences I've just described so subversive is that they are so common. *But how does that work?* Somebody on the other side of the planet has transmitted pain. Through what medium? Ditto about the phone call or the intuition that your friend in the Mexican restaurant would marry the guy.

How weird the world is when you look at it honestly—or, dare I say, when you are brave enough to look at it *realistically*? None of this makes any sense within the context of our conventional descriptions of reality. This is all pure Neptune, and it runs very much counter to the dominant, "official" beliefs of our society.

The more deeply you get into thinking objectively about Neptune, the more you realize that "common sense" is mostly incorrect. Common sense is, at best, a gross oversimplification of reality. It represents a fundamental distortion of the nature of our actual experience in this world. *Under the tyranny of "common sense," we have almost everything wrong.* Reality simply does not work that way.

Let's get weirder yet. Let's go deeper into Neptune—which, somewhat counterintuitively, I have come to think of as the true *planet of reality*. In this age of Relativity and Quantum Mechanics, I think it's time to take that title away from Saturn.

So, if I knock on my chair—tap, tap, tap. It hurts my knuckles a little bit. It's solid. It's made of atoms. But what is an atom? I got this imagery, by the way, from Gary Zukav's book *The Dancing Wu Li Masters*. Picture a few grains of salt on the sidewalk. Picture a fourteen-story building. Picture some dust motes on the roof of that building. Now *take away the building.* That's an atom. Salt, followed by fourteen stories of emptiness, followed by dust. The rest of the atom is empty space. Isn't that amazing? The chair I knocked on with my knuckles is "solid." It's what we have agreed to call "solid."

Think of all that in relationship to your physical body. You are made of atoms too. *You're barely here*! Any physicist would be nodding his or her head. There's nothing conjectural about any of this. You are mostly empty space.

Recall the traditional metaphysical language about the "spirit world" for a moment—a realm where we might find ghosts or angels, or a place we go when we die. As we imagine such a world, we think of people in this kind of insubstantial, nonmaterial form. *But that's where and what we actually are.*

Neptune is the part of you that knows all that.

WHAT THE SUN THINKS ABOUT ALL THIS

I'm saying things that are objective and real. But I have an ulterior purpose: I am asking you to direct your attention to how you *feel* about what I'm saying, how you experience it. I suspect that there is a part of you that really *likes* what I'm saying. But there's another part of you that's thinking, "Steve, get a grip. If you stub your toe, it's going to hurt. Reality is—*real.*"

In practical terms, we do think of ourselves as solid objects in a substantial world. But there's also a Neptunian part of us that grasps all that I have been saying, that knows all this—that we are actually, in reality, something more like spirits. I can hear Sting and the Police singing in the back of my head: "*We are spirits in the material world.*" But he's wrong about the material world; this world is barely material. We are spirits in it, but *is there a material world out there at all?*

What a question. Welcome to Neptune.

Our experience of ourselves and each other, on one hand—and the actual reality of ourselves and each other on the other hand—are at sharp variance with each other. What am I actually looking at when I look out at your faces? I think I'm seeing bodies; I think I am this body, and you're those bodies. But is that really true? What I am seeing has nothing to do with what's actually out there; what I'm seeing *is my own mind.* It's all in my head—whatever "in" means. Or "head" means. That's all you're seeing, too.

"Hi, I'm Steve—a figment of your imagination." Which of course isn't exactly true, but it's closer to the Neptunian truth than "common sense" can ever carry us.

Again, feel that solar voice in your head saying, "get a grip." Feel the *tyranny of the Sun's gravity*, always trying to pull us back to the predictable, safe world of "common sense." We want that "solid ground," which ultimately boils down to the illusion that we understand what's going on here. Let's have common sense and reason: we are physical objects in a physical universe, making sound investments—that comforting fiction.

And yet, reality is so much weirder than that. And Neptune is the perceptual window into that deep weirdness.

Still, we need to remember the other half of the fundamental paradox we explored in that last chapter: to survive Neptunian states with our sanity intact, *we have to take good care of the Sun*, or everything mists out into a big, dull "whatever," where nothing matters—not our integrity, our ability to love, our creativity, our courage. Everything fades into triviality—and *what will that matter in five hundred years*?

And yet, here is the active element: if I'm good at holding the solar side of the equation together, I can also go into Neptunian space—and still pay my electric bill on time.

FIRST THERE IS A MOUNTAIN . . .

In Zen Buddhism there's a *koan*. "*First there is a mountain, then there is no mountain. Then there is.*" The singer Donovan made a song of it; many of you older folks have heard it.

Back and forth we go, swinging between these two incompatible interpretations of reality—the Neptunian one and the solar one. Am I looking at a mountain? Yes. Of course. There it is. But am I really only seeing my mind? In other words, is the mountain really in my mind, and the thing in my mind has little to do with the actual reality of the mountain—if there is any reality there at all? Yes again. But, on the other hand, if you run into that mountain in an airplane, you're dead. Then there definitely is a mountain.

Notice the tug of the gravitational center of your ego-mind here. You may have the feeling that you have to choose between these two interpretations, to take a position, *to have an opinion*. Is there a mountain there or not? The instinct arises in us: "OK, bottom line, there is a mountain, damn it. Get a grip. Keep a grip. Or you'll go crazy."

And that's the Sun talking.

Neptune is the part of you that can just sit there with the idea that, "there is no mountain." And that gives you a sense of how vast your mind is—and how small a segment of its actual scope exists in the conventional understanding of the mind.

The psychologist's version of the mind operates within your skull. It's a function of the brain. And, in that belief-system, we can make this very neat distinction between that which happens inside your skull—biochemical and electromagnetic phenomena in your cranium—versus what happens in the outer world. They are different from each other.

But are they really? Ask Neptune and, no surprise, you get a very weird answer.

SYNCHRONICITY

Absolutely fundamental to astrological understanding is the idea of *synchronicity*—that what happens in the outer world and what happens in the inner world are intimately entangled. As Carl Jung put it, things happen in this universe for two reasons. One is that something makes them happen; that's *causality*. The second is that it would be *meaningful* for them to happen—that's synchronicity.

You have a vivid dream about having been an architect helping to build one of the pyramids of Gaza. Maybe you sense that it might be a past-life dream. Two days later, you're in the doctor's waiting room. The doctor is running late. You've got to kill forty-five minutes. You pick up an old *National Geographic*, and you open it up at random. There's an article about the pyramids. Interesting coincidence? Three days later, you are having lunch with a friend. She says, "Guess what I'm doing next summer? I'm going to Egypt!"

You're startled by the synchronistic pattern, even if you don't know the word "synchronicity." You excitedly tell her about the dream and the *National Geographic* article. She senses your emotional engagement, and she says, "Why don't you come with me?"

What's your response? You know the answer already. "*I guess I'm supposed to.*" Right? Wouldn't that be your line? You had the dream, and you saw the article—by sheer chance? Those words, "by sheer chance," embody the "common sense" Western model of *existential randomness.* "What a coincidence!" What a coinCIDEnce, more accurately.

Now, the root of this little Neptunian anecdote about your trip to Egypt lies with a dream. Maybe, for reasons you cannot fathom, it's very important in your larger evolutionary journey for you to go back there and visit those pyramids. Maybe it would be *meaningful* for you to do that—and thus, *your evolutionary need triggers the synchronistic mechanisms of the universe*—that is, you "happen to" see that article in National Geographic and to have lunch with your friend.

But how does the deep psyche initially set the stage for your visit to the pyramids? The answer is through that most Neptunian of direct, otherworldly experiences, a *dream.*

All this is standard Jungian thinking—that dreams can alert you to directions that you might follow. But let's look at the question more broadly: How does the universe tell you you're supposed to go to Egypt? It wasn't just via that dream, which we can understand as a purely mental manifestation. The universe also directs you to Egypt in two other ways. First, as you sit in that doctor's office and open a *National Geographic* that just "happens to be" sitting there, there's that article. Second, your friend with whom you "happen" to be having lunch "happens" to be going to Egypt this summer.

It is tempting to say that, unlike the dream, these two "random" events have nothing to do with the psyche—but that's not quite true. *Meaning* is the common denominator, linking the dream and magazine, not to mention your friend's plan to go to Egypt and the fact that you are having lunch with her that week.

The implications of synchronicity will make you dizzy if you really reflect on them. They suggest that the psyche and the outer universe are not as unrelated as conventional psychology would have us believe. They mirror each other and are ultimately inseparable.

The more you think about this, the more it subverts everything you learned in eleventh grade science class.

There's an ancient formula in the Upanishads, the Hindu sacred text, "Atman and Brahman are one." *Atman* basically means "soul"; for *Brahman,* you can say God—but it does not refer to the old guy with the long white beard, ruling Heaven. Brahman is more like the cosmos, the universe. The idea is that if you go deeply enough into yourself, you realize you've gone out into the universe. In a nutshell, the experience of synchronicity teaches us that *the skull is a fictional wall.* The inner and outer worlds are not just linked; they are a unity.

And this reflects a pivotal Neptunian truth: no boundaries, no divisions.

Here is the critical point for our purposes: *we've all experienced such meaningful coincidences and inexplicable patterns.* They are not rare. People who want to hold on to the kind of standard Western "common sense" model of things will hear these kinds of stories and call them "interesting coincidences." But as Carl Jung observed, *there are just too many of them* for that to be a reasonable position. We cannot explain "chance" by chance. And there are *patterns* in "randomness"—which of course means that randomness is not random, but rather governed by principles that are simply not recognized by the First Church of Materialistic Science.

ENTER ASTROLOGY

If we look at your chart during times characterized by a density of such *signs* and *omens*, we see Neptunian stimulus. Maybe it's transiting Neptune hitting a sensitive point. Maybe it's your natal Neptune receiving a significant transit, progression, or solar arc. We will explore all that in detail later on. But the Neptunian signature will be there. *During these times, the veil between the worlds parts.* We might call it the veil between the spiritual world and the material one. But that's a somewhat fictional distinction. Let's call it what we, as astrologers, should call it—the veil between the conventional planets and the trans-Neptunian realm. The exact nature of these experiences will be in accord with the nature of your natal Neptune, flavored by whatever planet is the passing trigger.

Now, those are two big ideas—transits, progressions, and arcs connected with Neptune, on one hand, and the nature of your natal Neptune on the other. We're going to be unpacking those elements of interpretation later. So far, we are just exploring general Neptunian principles. And they boil down to this: *the fundamental description of reality that you have inherited from our culture is wrong and is breaking down.*

Hallelujah! You can take off those tight shoes.

INTUITION

Lord Kelvin, the head of the Royal Society in England who lived from 1824 to 1907, once famously pronounced that, "There is nothing new to be discovered in physics now. All that remains is more and more precise measurement." Born William Thomson on June 26, 1824, in Belfast, Ireland, Lord Kelvin had the Sun opposite Neptune in his birthchart.

These lines are a fine illustration of "famous last words."

Along came Albert Einstein, who said, "What if space and time are not constants?" That's Einstein, the Pisces; Einstein, the Neptunian (Einstein was born March 14, 1879 in Ulm, Germany, with a Pisces Sun, Pisces on the MC and Neptune sextile the Ascendant). Here's the origin of the special theory of relativity: as a kid, Einstein was riding his bicycle as fast as he could down a hill. And he noticed that the world was looking a little different as he sped through it faster and faster on his bicycle. He started to wonder, "What would the world look like if I were going as fast as anything can possibly go?" That's 186,282.3 miles per second in a vacuum—the speed of light, the speed limit in the material universe. Einstein was just wondering, what would it look like if I could ride my bike at the speed of light?

And suddenly he knew.

How? Who knows? But he just *knew* the answer. His Neptunian intuition spoke to him. Then, by the way, he had to prove it all mathematically. The result is called the Special Theory of Relativity, one of the greatest intellectual triumphs of the human species. But he "got it" intuitively. And he later said, "I didn't arrive at my understanding of the fundamental laws of the universe through my rational mind." In other words, he came to them through Neptunian means.

How much do you "just know" in your bones, without any reason for knowing it? You meet somebody; you've literally known them for one minute. And yet you know that you're going to be friends. Love at first sight happens. People meet each other, and sometimes they just know. Given the complexities and pitfalls of mate-selection, what an incredible illustration of Neptunian intuition that is! This remarkable transmission happens through trans-logical methods; *we do not come to our understanding of who our soul mates are through logical means*—or through any other kind of rational analysis.

If we sat in a circle and just shared stories about encounters with people we might call our soul mates, how many astonishing "coincidences" would we hear about? How many tales of amazing omens would we encounter? There are often truly freaky "coincidences" that allow such people to come together and recognize each other.

These stories are amazing and inspiring—but they are also fairly commonplace.

Under the banner of quantum mechanics, science has just begun to figure some of this out over the past century and a quarter or so. Mystics have been saying it since the beginning of recorded time. Life is short. I don't have time to figure all this out logically—but maybe I have time to tune into my Neptune and surrender all control, surrender my illusion of understanding, and surrender to the great mystery of what's actually out there.

Maybe then my window will be clean and clear.

BURNING DOWN THE HOUSE

I recounted a joke in Chapter 4 about a Piscean person watching a house burn down and just standing there uselessly saying, "*It's bright.*" We all laughed. But let's consider the qualities of women and men who are making a strong, healthy response to Neptune, and doing so systematically over the years of their lives. Their house catches fire. It is out of control, and the fire department hasn't gotten there yet. It is clear that the house is going to be a total loss. *And they accept it.*

Wisely—and much to their comfort considering the situation—they're experiencing a moment of pure Neptunian transcendence: "I am not this house. These are merely things I have had; I no longer have them. I am still here. *The house is burning down; it's bright.*"

There is a neutrality. A clarity. A transcendence. These inspiring souls take refuge in the ultimate truth of reality, which is that we are all Neptunian beings; we are insubstantial. We are indeed luminous spirits in the material world.

So, *faith*—there's another word we might roll out. Somebody is watching the house burn down, but retaining equanimity and spiritual perspective—we might call that "faith."

Personally, I don't like that word too much here. "Faith," to me, implies belief in things that we don't know for sure, as if we've just chosen to believe in something, maybe without evidence. *But with Neptune, we can have direct evidence.* I can go into direct relationship with my Neptune and just feel this spaciousness, or this groundlessness. I can become it. You can too.

That's another word I like to keep coming back to: *groundlessness.* Because if I have a house, I'm identified with that house; part of me is thinking, "I am this house, I am the person who owns this house." And now my house is burning down. So who am I? What will I become? I'm tempted to break down in the face of the burning house and say, "I am this house! I am the stuff in this house! I am Steven Forrest of 381 Ocotillo Circle! I am burning up! Soon I will no longer exist!"

Feel the solar ego getting its knickers in a serious knot as the ground falls out from underneath it? This "groundless" condition is so human, so poignant, we can only have compassion for the suffering that can arise at such times.

And yet, what an inspiration to know that, out at the edges of the inner sky, there is a place inside us all that is capable of enduring any material loss with absolute equanimity. Given the realities of life, how wise it is to cultivate a relationship with that ultimate place of refuge.

LOVE, SURRENDER, AND VULNERABILITY

Like most astrologers, I didn't like it when Pluto was demoted. And as I've sat with the change for over a decade, I've come to realize that calling Pluto a "dwarf" doesn't diminish Pluto at all. Instead, it refines our understanding of the actual structure of the solar system and thus prepares us to place Pluto in a larger and truer context.

Closer to our purposes here, this development also enormously clarifies Neptune's role as the frontier between the world of personality and the transpersonal realms. Inside Neptune lies the realm of the ego, like a kind of bubble within the measureless universe. But the bubble has windows; it is transparent. The universe shines in through it; our attention to the universe goes out through it. And the glass that separates them is the planet Neptune.

Each chart—and we'll look at this carefully and specifically—suggests certain optimal methods for cleaning that glass. Now that we have laid the foundation, we will be able to be specific about, say, Neptune in Scorpio in the third house and square Saturn. Those details can really emerge. But right now we're still just putting down the roots that can feed the various branches of this wide-open, nonresistant, accepting, transparent state—this permeable Neptunian membrane surrounding what we experience as the ego.

THE DARK SIDE OF THE FORCE

Let's look at the other side of the coin. What happens when the Neptune function is weak? Here, we're not yet concerned with flat-out negative responses to Neptune—just what happens when the higher functions of Neptune are failing to balance the Sun's natural self-orientation.

Think of all that fury that underlies the headlines. Behind the rage, there is ultimately all that fear, all that bleak despair, desolation, and hopelessness. We are talking about all the children with AK-47s in their hands; all of the abused humans, all of the animals being slaughtered, all the trees being mowed down.

I could throw us all into miserable despair here, just by going on and on about this endless pain. So I won't. Let me just point to it, and add that all of those beings are *radiating* those dreadful feelings, spilling them into the psychic atmosphere—and you're swimming in that energy. You're feeling it all through your Neptunian antennae.

So, in the light of that, *how do you really feel about opening up psychically*? Good idea? If I asked that question for openers, out of context. most of us would welcome such an opening in principle. But this deeper consideration of its implications should give us pause.

Positively, opening up psychically can really add fairy-dust to everyday life. Sometimes you can just "tune in" and get answers. Maybe you've got a big question in your life, and you ask yourself, "What should I do?" And it's as if you've asked the God within. And immediately an answer pops up "out of nowhere."

Where did that answer come from? Our astrological answer is "Neptune." That's a precious function. We would naturally like to magnify it.

Would you really like to be more open to that? Well, as we just saw a moment ago, there is a parallel question: *How would you like to be more open to the agglomerate pain and suffering of all embodied life-forms?*

These two forms of perception are a single package. With Neptune, *you have no control over what comes in through the window.*

Remember that what we are cultivating here, right at this frontier of our psychic development, is to try to make the windowpane more transparent. We want to clean the window. No opinions. No judgments. Total vulnerability. Nothing but radical acceptance of what is out there. We are wide open, so we stand back, and we let it be what it is: there's Neptune. We're not controlling it, we're not interpreting it, we're just letting it be itself, according to its nature, as it arises and as it falls. That's the challenge here.

When we look honestly at the bleeding edge of this challenge, we realize that we are opening up to a lot of pain as well.

NEW HOPE FOR THE GALAXY

How can we live with that pain? Here's the right answer—but like a lot of right answers, it's in the realm of cliché. We have to be careful to hear it freshly. The right answer is some kind of *spiritual practice*. That's how we can live with this edgy challenge.

When I speak of "spiritual practice," I promise that I'm not going to hand you Hare Krishna literature or Jehovah's Witnesses tracts. Everybody has their own spiritual practice, and we'll be looking at how our birthcharts convey the most efficient and effective practices for ourselves in our particular evolutionary predicaments.

In terms of spiritual practice, there is one Neptunian common denominator for everybody, and that is that we remember to log some minutes every day in that Neptunian state of spaciousness—to be mindfully, gently and consciously swimming in that Neptunian state of wide-open undefendedness.

We could call that practice "meditation;" we could call it "prayer." Some people might call it dancing. Some might call it sitting in the garden. I always picture a simple man fishing. He's got his line in the water, not really caring if the fish bite or not; he's in a trance. He is surrendering to that spaciousness. He is logging hours there. And he may not be able to spell "meditation."

Remember the galaxy and the arrow saying, "You are here?" Or the person in the traffic jam, so angry and upset? There's the solar experience, the ego experience. "The sheer injustice of my terrible misery is the current center of the universe."

And then there's Neptune: What will this traffic jam matter in five hundred years?

Notice that with Neptune, we're still seeing the pain; we're not denying it. It's not escapism. The pain just looms a lot smaller against the backdrop of the galaxy, of five hundred years—or against the backdrop of the rest of the collective suffering in that moment in the world.

Keeping that larger perspective is the trick. But it is not a concept. It's not a philosophy. It is the result of a kind of deep *mind-training*. Spiritual habits, instincts and reflexes are formed, and they serve us well when the extremities of life hit us.

If, on the other hand, we are not doing some kind of spiritual practice, and we come to a time of Neptunian stimulus, we might make a startling discovery: there is a kind of "ready or not, I am coming" feeling connected with these events. To some extent, the psychic opening occurs anyway, only now we can't handle it. We haven't built the basis for it. We are in a real jam. We hurt and we don't know what to do.

Synchronistically, beyond the psychic opening itself hurting us, we often have other more obvious, outward hurts. Earlier we spoke of the pattern of collapse in the structures that support our perceived identity during Neptune periods. Unprepared spiritually, we begin to try rather desperately to *control everything*, to try to cling to old crashing structures.

It can get worse—we may go down a path of trying to numb our feelings, numbing the psychic centers. There are lots of ways to do that—too much alcohol, too much shopping, too many video games, pornography, compulsive exercise, bad love. We might find ourselves frantically trying to hold onto dying structures and interpretations of ourselves—endless therapy for a dead marriage, trying madly to keep your tape-cassette business afloat in the age of MP3 files. Holding onto our dramas, we attempt—with some success, sadly—to shut out this Neptunian opening.

So there are ways to get Neptune right. And there are ways to get it wrong. We aren't going to pull punches about the dark side of any of this. But we're also going to make sure we concentrate on the higher ground and how to get there.

Soon, as promised, I want to dive right into how we begin to work with Neptune in the individual birthchart. What does it mean in aspect to various planets? What about its house position? What sign is it in? We will see that Neptune is like a chameleon, taking on the coloration of its surroundings. As we move deeper into this material, I'm going to be focusing on how we can work with the moving kind of Neptune events, Neptunian developments in your life—transits, progressions, and solar arcs involving Neptune. So, we'll build the foundation by first embracing Neptune's unique and specific message in the natal chart. Then we will explore predictive theory.

But first, we have a strange tale to tell, one fraught with manifestations of synchronicity, one that will make you laugh and I think make you marvel.

It is the tale of how humanity discovered Neptune.

7

NEPTUNE, DELUSION & ECSTASY

During Neptune events, there are two schools of thought in standard astrological counsel. One is that you're "going to make a terrible blunder." And the second school of thought is, "Be careful, or you *will* make a terrible blunder." The second sounds pretty close to the first, but there's a difference. At least the second one affirms your freedom to possibly *not* make the blunder. But, sure enough, people blunder, often spectacularly, in Neptune times. They become deluded; delusion arises.

Here's the heart of it. What does Neptune mean, in its deepest essence? What is the simplest message that Neptune has for all of us? One answer is truly glorious: *You are far, far better than you think you are.* You are an ancient, evolving consciousness in a mysterious universe. You just *look* like a monkey! But don't worry, it's a temporary condition. Deep inside the monkey is this luminous emptiness that has existed since the beginning of time. And by the end of time—whatever that means—you will be *one with all that exists.*

This is your true nature; you're far, far more than you think you are. Be proud of that. Trust that. Gradually clean the window so you can see that.

Isn't that a beautiful thing to say? And it's all true—it's the most fundamental truth of the universe.

So, when we experience a Neptunian stimulus, the possibility arises that we can begin to move in that direction, we can start to see all that—but maybe "through the glass darkly."

This is exactly where delusion sets in. Picture a guy who has a job with the post office. He's carrying letters. He's doing all right. He's got a couple of kids and is married to his sweetie from college. They love each other, they've got a home. He begins a Neptune period by transit or progression and starts thinking, "I'm more than I think I am. *I'm not just a letter carrier for the United States Postal Service. I'm far more than that. I'm – I'm – I'm – a guitar god!*"

Now, the "guitar god" is a cultural metaphor for grandness, at least in my generation. We think of Jimmy Page or Eric Clapton, or Jimi Hendrix—and they are really just human beings, of course, but they were elevated in the mythology of our culture to Mount Olympus. They became transformed into exalted *metaphors* for achieving something greater than "working for the post office."

This false exaltation is the basis of Neptunian delusion. But remember the compassionate perspective on it: We truly *are* greater than we think. We get that much right—but then, following that lofty instinct in a deluded way, we sell our souls for some cheap, tawdry *metaphor of greatness.* And, even in the rare scenario where we attain the thing for which we reached, it feels empty when we achieve it. Delusions are always empty; they are always mirages. Ask Jimi Hendrix.

"Guitar god" was just a way to focus that idea. There are countless others. "I am an undiscovered movie star." Or, "I have the potential to manifest fabulous wealth! I could be one of those gods—like ... like ... Donald Trump." That was fun to say. Donald Trump is a ridiculous character to me, and probably to most of you too. And yet, for people who worship money, Donald Trump can become a cheap metaphor for the Divine. He is one of the gods of money. Just as easily, we can become enamored with the delusional gods of beauty, or the delusional gods of sports—any of them can become *delusional metaphors for the transcendent.*

So, instead of aiming for our highest Neptunian potential—the complete identification of mind with the spirit-body—we settle for cotton candy.

Now, what happens to the guy working for the post office who decides he's an undiscovered guitar god? Maybe he looks at his post office job and thinks, "Why am I wasting my life here?" Maybe he looks at his wife—his sweetheart from college—and he thinks, "A guitar god's not going to be seen with some pear-shaped woman like this."

You can start to see how sad this kind of scenario can be. Maybe he leaves his wife, quits his job, and moves to Los Angeles to be discovered. Before long, he's down and out on the streets of L.A., screwed up on cocaine. Isn't that a familiar story? I mean, in its bones, in its basic form, you've heard it a million times.

So an astrologer who predicts that "you will blunder" can often be correct. Sure enough, you can see *why* that prediction has traction. Look at the postman story; it worked. It's basically a true story. But if we understand the deeper logic of it, we realize the letter-carrier settled for a *metaphor*, a Neptunian *mirage of greatness*, rather than aiming for the actual essence of what Neptune means.

This is the basis of Neptunian delusion.

Let's add the next step. An astrologer might predict that during a Neptune time you will experience *disillusionment*. Fair enough, but every disillusionment needs to be preceded by an "illusionment," so to speak. That's not an official word, but it ought to be! So, we succumb to an illusion—and we've just understood the mechanism whereby we can do that—and then the illusion collapses, leading to bitterness, which eventually leads to disillusionment.

So what about ecstasy?

Let's start by talking about two words that are closely related and often mistaken for each other. One is "happiness" and the other is "pleasure." We like both of them, of course. But pleasure and happiness don't really mean the same thing. High Neptune is linked to happiness—which may ultimately be a better word than ecstasy. In a state of happiness, we realize that life has pain in it. And if we have right relationship with Neptune, we keep perspective on our pain. We don't collapse into it. We remember to wonder *what that pain will mean in five hundred years*. We remember that others are suffering too. We have, in other words, a deep, transcendent place inside ourselves where we can retreat to during life's storms. It doesn't make the storms go away; it doesn't numb us to them. But it eases the suffering. And so, with a strong spiritual life, we're not knocked off center quite so much by pain when it inevitably arrives.

That, at least, is the ideal; most of us are going to be knocked off center for a little while. But at least we have a way for finding our path back to some kind of equilibrium. This becomes a *foundation for happiness*.

There is a feeling of contentment that arises in us when we accept things the way they are. That's a simple phrase, but let's just sit with it for a moment—a feeling of contentment that arises when we accept things the way that they actually are. It's almost self-evident. When we're looking at things and saying: "That needs to change! I don't like this, I don't like that, this isn't working for me," we are not happy. We are too engaged in trying to change things, often things we can't actually change, over which we have no power or control. I can't help but think of the famous Serenity Prayer here—*God grant me the serenity to accept the things I cannot change, the courage to change the things I can, and the wisdom to know the difference.*

So, the deeper the spiritual life, the calmer we are, the happier we are: there's one cornerstone of lasting ecstasy, or at least something like it. And of course the weaker the spiritual life, the more likely it is that the opposite happens. Remember how, when you were a kid, the world was going to end because you didn't get a lollipop? That pain was real.

Now, the idea of *pleasure*—people so confuse pleasure and happiness. So, if you win a contest and you've suddenly got an extra $138 million in your pocket, would that make you happy? Of course few of us would turn down the money. We naturally think that would make us happy. But would it? Here's what I can guarantee—that money would buy you a lot of pleasure.

People get that kind of money all of a sudden and what are they going to do? They buy themselves a new car, a new house, maybe they go on a world cruise—they nip over to Paris for croissants. Extravagant new things like that are fun. They give us pleasure. I am not going to shame that word; pleasure is not a bad thing. But it's so easy to imagine a person expecting *happiness* from all that money. They start off doing things that give them pleasure, and pleasure makes them happy for a few months, but probably not much longer than that. And then they start trying to hold on to that "happiness" by feeding themselves more pleasure. "I bought a Lamborghini; maybe what I need is a Rolls-Royce . . . and a Lexus sedan, and a Land Rover in case it snows, and . . ."

You see where it all goes. After a while, you can't even remember all the cars you've bought. They're not making you happy anymore. Pleasure and happiness—they are so different. So different; but not unrelated. It is easy to confuse them. With Neptune, we can fall into the delusion that pleasure is happiness; we can be obsessed with pleasure. And this can spin us down into delusion, and even addiction, and block us utterly from authentic happiness.

So, turn all that around. If we really clean our Neptunian window, we find a refuge inside ourselves during life's storms—even the ultimate storm, which is the time of death. Even then, we have a place to go. *Our fundamental happiness becomes much more stable as it becomes less dependent on how the circumstances of life are presenting themselves to us.* This core of happiness does not make the pain of life go away, but it does point to our map of the galaxy and reminds us, *You Are Here.* That Neptunian perspective puts a floor under us beneath which we are not likely to sink.

What about ecstasy itself? Truly blissful states?

The central point we need to grasp here is one that has been underlying many of my comments—that *ecstasy is an internal condition of consciousness*, not a necessary by-product of certain attractive outward circumstances. Observably, people can be miserable in situations that seem as if they should support happiness. Famously, not all rich people are happy. And unfortunate people in situations of real privation are often seemingly content. Picture happy Andean villagers dancing in the village plaza, or the poor in Bhutan, where "Gross National Happiness is more important than Gross National Product."

With Neptune, we are looking at the actual *foundation of ecstasy*—at its actual source, which lies in consciousness itself. In terms of ecstasy, all the other planets are secondary.

We gaze through Neptune's window into deep space—in astrological language, into the realm of the trans-Neptunians. Out there—or in there—we encounter angels of ecstasy: truly blissful states. We also encounter some demons. My sense is that the further out—or in—we go, the more blissful it becomes, and the fewer the demons. Eventually we pass the "heliopause"—or whatever that means in our inner realms. And beyond it, we are one with the mystery.

8

THE WEIRD TALE OF HOW WE DISCOVERED NEPTUNE

When was Neptune discovered? The standard answer is 1846, but the truth is a lot more complicated. The discovery of Neptune was quite a "Neptunian" process, as you will soon see. I encourage you, as you hear the tale, to think of the story in terms of the inherent qualities of confusion and vagueness that are often associated with Neptune—the planet of illusion and uncertainty, mirages and hallucinations.

In light of that, we start with Galileo Galilei, straddling the turn of the sixteenth and seventeenth centuries. Galileo didn't invent the telescope, but he was one of the first people to aim one at the night sky. He discovered the four major moons of Jupiter—the so-called "Galilean moons." He discovered that the Milky Way was in fact not a cloud, but composed of what he called "congeries of stars," lots and lots of faint stars.

Here's the key point for our purposes. Galileo's drawings show that he first observed Neptune on December 28, 1612. Remember—that's 234 years before the official discovery date you learned in high school. Basically, Galileo got very lucky—as he was making his observations of Jupiter's moons, Jupiter and then-unknown Neptune had formed a tight conjunction in Virgo. He drew a picture of Jupiter, mapping its moons' positions—and there's Neptune, right there on the paper. And he did it again, on Jan. 27, 1613.

So Galileo was actually the first human being to see Neptune. But on both occasions, he mistook it for a star. Hence, he is not credited with Neptune's discovery. During the period of his first observation, in December of 1612, Neptune was making a station. It had just turned retrograde that very day. So, it was basically not moving. Of course, a month later when he made the second drawing, Neptune was in motion again—the "fixed star" that he had drawn in fact had shifted its position. But he didn't notice that.

The plot thickens a bit. Fast forward to the summer of 2009 when an Australian physicist named David Jamison announced new evidence suggesting that Galileo was at least aware that the "star" he had observed had moved. So...hmmm. Feel that Neptunian signature of uncertainty? Galileo was looking at a new planet, but he doesn't notice it. He sees it move, but *he didn't know what he was looking at.*

It's critical here to remember that early in the seventeenth century, *no planets had ever been discovered.* That was an experience that humanity had not yet had—even the discovery of Uranus was, at this point, over a century and half in the future. So, the *paradigm of planetary discovery* did not exist in Galileo's mind. His *description of reality*—there's a deep Neptunian concept—did not include the idea of discovering planets.

We might say he did not observe the sky; instead he observed his *opinion* of the sky.

A BRIEF DIGRESSION

This of course is the core Neptunian question: to what extent do we live in an agreed-upon description of the world? Not in "reality," but instead in a socially-engineered mythology that we project mentally onto the fabric of reality? The idea can sound exotic until you reflect on it a bit. Think for a moment about a scantily clad, pretty white woman. How does she look to a pornographer? Now think of how she looks to her loving and protective father. Now imagine her to a repressed Cistercian monk from a millennium ago. Now try Kalahari Bushmen who have never before seen a white woman. The woman is "out there," but what forms in the mind of the perceiver is largely an interpretation.

Is anything at all really "out there," or is it in fact nothing but our own mind that we see? I get the feeling that any clear answer will inevitably be a lie—we might say that there is one true answer from the Sun's point of view and another, different "true answer" from Neptune's.

There's deep water here. I think we would need to be enlightened to understand it. There's also some shallow water that is plenty deep enough and unsettling enough for me. I go back to the disconnect between the "common sense" view of how the universe works through cause-and-effect and so on, versus the reality that psychic experiences happen, that there are many examples of living people communicating with "dead" people, that miracles seem to be an occasional reality. What "everybody knows" is fundamentally wrong—and in each historical age, we can count on two things:

* *First, that reality will be described and understood differently.*
* *And second, that the belief will be that our ancestors were obviously wrong about almost everything, but nowadays we're on top of it.*

In Galileo's reality, there were no planets to be discovered. So, objectively, this brilliant man mapped a "star" moving—an impossibility—and that reality was so far outside his description of things that he didn't register it at all.

AND BACK TO FINDING NEPTUNE

Fast forward to 1821—which, by the way, coincides very closely with the previous historical Uranus-Neptune conjunction, before the one in the 1990s that I discussed earlier—the one that coincided with the discovery of the trans-Neptunians, in our present time. Back in 1821, in a similarly fertile time of paradigm-shift, a French astronomer named Alexis Bouvard published predictions for the orbit of Uranus, which had been discovered just forty years earlier. Telescopic observations revealed that Uranus was not behaving as predicted, which led Bouvard to guess that another undiscovered planet's gravity was to blame. He was right, but he couldn't prove it.

Note the Neptunian fingerprint again: *something invisible is interacting with us. Some people believe in it, but no one can prove it. Some people who don't believe in it think that the people who do believe in it are crazy.*

A generation later, in 1843, John Couch Adams, a professor at Cambridge, used the "errors" in Uranus's orbit to hypothesize the orbit and mass of the undiscovered world. Adams sent his work to the Astronomer Royal, Sir George Airy. Airy was open, but he asked Adams some specific questions before he attempted a tedious observational search—remember, Adams is the mathematician and Airy is the astronomer.

Now, get ready for Neptune's invisible hand to make itself felt again: Adams began to compose a letter replying to Airy, *but he never sent it.* Why? In the language of the modern world, it is tempting to say that John Couch Adams simply *spaced out.*

What?! He has personally discovered sound mathematical proof that there is a new planet out there. He even thinks he knows about where it is. With a little luck, Neptune might have been *named* Adams! The Astronomer Royal himself has expressed interest in his work, and he starts a letter, and . . . what happens? "*Oops! I thought I mailed that letter . . . Didn't I mail that letter? Geez, I would've sworn I'd mailed it!*"

Can you feel the Neptunian signature in this? This presents another fine illustration that there is a fundamental flaw in our common sense understanding of how reality works. We hear this story, and our culturally-induced reaction is to shrug our shoulders and say, "This kind of thing just happens." Well, it does—synchronicity is everywhere. We can see it here with John Couch Adams—you start to interact with these gods in space that we call "planets" and the synchronistic principle kicks in like crazy. Adams didn't just "happen" to forget to send that letter that could have made him one of the luminous figures in the history of astronomy. He was messing with Neptune.

Two or three years down the road, we meet another player in the tale: a Frenchman, Urbain Le Verrier. I've been told that his name, "Verrier," sounds like "glassmaker." Glass. Windows. Feel the synchronicity? Again, it's everywhere, once you start noticing it.

In 1845 and 1846, Urbain Le Verrier, independently of Adams, did basically what Adams had done: he looked at distortions in Uranus's orbit and calculated a likely position for the new, undiscovered planet. He couldn't, however, seem to trigger any interest among his French colleagues in looking for the new planet. The British Astronomer Royal—you may remember Sir George Airy, still waiting for John Couch Adams' errant letter—was on the ball. He saw Le Verrier's estimate of the missing planet's position and noticed a similarity to Adams' estimate. Interest piqued, Airy persuaded Cambridge Observatory director James Challis to have a look through the telescope. Challis searched the heavens for a couple of months that summer. Meanwhile, Le Verrier wrote a letter urging a Berlin Observatory astronomer—Johann Gottfried Galle—to search simultaneously with that observatory's world-class telescope.

A student at the Berlin observatory, Heinrich d'Arrest, suggested to Galle that they could compare an existing recent chart of that area of the sky with current observations. The aim was to see if anything had moved—the clue that Galileo had missed over two centuries earlier.

Le Verrier's letter to Berlin arrived on September 23, 1846. That same evening, Neptune was finally officially discovered within one degree of where Le Verrier had predicted it to be—and about twelve degrees away from Adams' prediction.

Neptune's fingerprints again: A bit later, James Challis later realized he had seen it two times during the previous month. He'd just not been paying much attention to what he was looking at. *So, once again, somebody's looking right at Neptune, and they don't see it.* As you can tell from this story, we've got a nice long tradition of exactly that.

The tales goes further. After Neptune was officially discovered, there arose the pressing question of who exactly deserved the glory. The French and British each had some basis for the claim. And naturally, the Froggies versus the Limeys has provided one of history's great rivalries. Eventually, history declared it a draw—a consensus emerged that Adams and Le Verrier each deserved equal credit.

Settled? Not exactly. Even now, a century and a half down the road, Neptune's foggy fingerprints are still mucking up the looking glass. The year 1998 marked the discovery of "The Neptune papers"—historical documents apparently stolen from the Royal Observatory in Greenwich by a respected astronomer named Olin Jeuck Eggen. They had been missing for decades; Eggen went to his grave denying that he had taken them. But there they were among his personal papers when he passed away in the fall of 1998.

These are important documents, at least in the history of astronomy. They imply that John Couch Adams does not deserve equal credit with Urbain Le Verrier—that the French were robbed by the English, which naturally is a story that plays better in Paris than it does in London. The essential message of these lost or stolen papers is that, while Adams had done some calculations, they were fuzzier than subsequent *culturally agreed upon* versions of the story suggest.

So, who the heck discovered Neptune? When was it discovered?

Doesn't all this sound just like Neptune?

That the discovery of new planets is a synchronistic event is a commonplace astrological idea. In earlier chapters, we spoke of Pluto's 1930 discovery coinciding with the collective discovery of the unconscious. Famously, Uranus's discovery in 1781 lined up with the very Uranian American and French Revolutions. Neptune's story here is not as spectacular as world revolution, but if anything, it is even more vivid. There are thieves, there's deception and confusion, there are people spacing out. There are forgotten letters, people not following up—the whole Neptunian nine yards.

More deeply, down in the veins and arteries of the tale, we see people looking at Neptune but not seeing it—instead, *seeing their beliefs*. In parallel fashion, many of us, if we saw a ghost, would rub our eyes—and then decide that *our eyes had been playing tricks on us*. We live in a mental construction that we call the universe. And that mental construction is, at best, only a small subset of the actual nature of reality.

Reflecting that notion, we see that Neptune was the first planet to be discovered *indirectly*, by inference. Up until the discovery of Uranus, the planets were just "there" in the sky; anyone could see them if they weren't blind. Even Uranus is faintly visible to the naked eye, if you know where to look. More importantly, Uranus was discovered visually and more-or-less by chance when William Herschel was searching for comets. It was there to be seen; not so with Neptune. *Exactly like what Neptune symbolizes, we knew it was there only because of its indirect influence upon visible reality.*

If you have ever walked across an old battlefield and gotten the shivers, you know exactly what I mean.

PART TWO

NEPTUNE'S ASPECTS TO THE PLANETS

9

HOW ASPECTS WORK

Our focus up to this point has been on exploring Neptune broadly, as an archetype. All the principles at which we've been looking really apply to everyone across the board. If you have Neptune in your chart—which is an excellent bet—then you were born with this window in your psyche. You can gaze through it into the eyes of angels or into the eyes of devils. Or you can spray-paint it black with delusion and addiction. But that Neptunian window will always be there inside you, hardwired into your mind, body, and spirit.

We all have Neptune in our charts—but for each one of us it is ultimately a different Neptune with its own unique fingerprints. In each of us, Neptune is conditioned by a specific network of sign, house and aspectual symbolism. That's the basic paradox in the heart of astrology: we are all built out of the same few elements, but there is an effectively infinite range of variation in their arrangement. We are as different—and as alike—as snowflakes.

How do we understand these distinctions among the various possible faces of Neptune? Here in Part Two, we dive deeply into the technical craft of astrology. How does Neptune fit into the specific realities of your own birthchart? What house and sign does it occupy? What aspects does it make? *What does it tell about you as an individual?* How is its message to you different from what it is telling the person sitting next to you?

And then there is the imponderable question: how well are you responding to your Neptune? That is not something we can determine through any technical analysis of your chart—but we can almost surely see its imprint on your life.

Here, we'll be looking at specific examples of all these themes. I want to start out by looking at Neptune in aspect to other planets. Have a look at the following table.

NEPTUNE IN ASPECT TABLE

With planets in aspect to your natal Neptune, meditation is enhanced by concentration on:

Sun	Selfless non-duality
Moon	Compassion; kindness
Mercury	Mindfulness
Venus	Loving empathy
Mars	Warrior-mind
Jupiter	Generosity toward all beings
Saturn	One-pointedness
Uranus	Sudden Enlightenment
Pluto	Shamanic intensity

INTEGRATION: THE HOLY GRAAL

All aspects are about integration. That's the most fundamental thing you need to know about aspects.

A virulent plague in conventional astrological practice has its origins in the sadly pervasive idea that there are "good" aspects and "bad" aspects. Astrologers are often obsessed with that notion.

Good and bad aspects are not useless concepts, but I would never use those exact words—better to say "easy aspects" and "hard aspects." Those equally simple terms work a lot more effectively. The distinction may seem like hair-splitting, but it is not. "Hard" and "bad" only mean the same thing to lazy people. We have all done hard things that were good for us. We have all even done hard things that we enjoyed doing. Why would anyone explore the arctic? Why would anyone read James Joyce's *Ulysses*? Why would anyone learn to play the piano?

The pivotal concept here is not some pop psychological shibboleth about avoiding "judgmental words" like good and bad. It is that when two planets are in aspect, the reality is always simply that they are *trying to work together*. They are trying to *integrate their energies*. If it's a so-called "bad aspect" that joins them—typically a square or an opposition—that integration is more difficult. If it's a trine or a sextile—"easy" aspects—it is indeed easier, but there is also a danger of a certain laziness in them. Easy aspects don't hurt us—and hurt can get us going. Easy aspects can therefore be unmotivated.

One of the soul-dangers particular to Neptune, as we have seen, is a kind of spacey "drifting along through life." I am getting ahead of myself here, but immediately we can recognize that one of the potentially "bad" things about "good" Neptunian aspects in general is that they can represent a real risk for staring transfixed at the "house-fires" in our lives while saying, "It's bright . . ." There can, in other words, be a risky synergy between Neptune's potentially lackadaisical qualities and the *mañana* attitude of trines and sextiles.

Meanwhile, a potentially good thing about all the so-called "bad" aspects is that they are dynamic. They're not easy, but you want to fix the issues they represent. They hurt. Your foot is in the fire. You are motivated to do the integrative work.

My suggestion as you are confronted with any astrological aspect—whether or not it involves Neptune—is to organize your thinking as follows:

1. Start by simply thinking of the energies the planetary archetypes represent. Realize that if they are linked by any aspect at all, they are trying to work together. Imagine what that integration might look like if it were healthy. Pay some attention to what it would look like if it were unhealthy, because that is always a possibility too.

Notice that what I've said so far is totally independent of what aspect we are talking about—it could be a trine, a square, or a sesquiquadrate; it doesn't matter.

2. Think of the *nature of the aspect* itself. Are we talking about *friction* between the archetypes (squares) or about the *reconciliation of opposites* (oppositions)? Those kinds of issues pervade any of the other more difficult aspects, too—for example, sesquiquadrates. Or are we in the realm of the easy aspects? Are we thus talking about *mutual enhancement and support*—and the possibility of laziness, a lack of motivation, and dark collusions? Those are good words for trines. Or cross-stimulus and excitation—good ways of thinking of sextiles? Or just simply *fusion*, which is the heart of all conjunctions?

3. In a nutshell, *put the planetary integration first and the nature of the aspect last.*

KEEPING PERSPECTIVE

One final note here, and this notion is critically important. What follows in the next few chapters is an analysis of possible integrative paths, for good or for ill, of Neptune and each of the other planetary archetypes. *Your mileage may vary!* What I mean is that maybe you have a Mars-Neptune square in your chart. Read that chapter and hopefully you will learn something relevant to your experience. But what if that Mars is conjunct your ascendant and thus very emphasized? What if, on the other hand, it is your Neptune that is on the ascendant? In which direction are those two energies balanced? Which is more dominant? Those are different situations.

What if it is an *uber-hot* Mars-in-Aries squaring your Capricorn Neptune—versus a *softer* Mars-in-Pisces squaring a Sagittarian Neptune? These too are very different situations.

Add the rest of your chart to the mix, as we always must. Maybe your Sun is in the twelfth house, and thus you are particularly responsive to Neptune. Or maybe your Sun is in Aries and you feel every nuance of your Mars—but perhaps Neptune is a more alien energy.

Astrological reality is always complicated that way. *That's why it works so well.* It can describe literally billions of realities in separate, individual detail.

So, keep perspective. These next few chapters are only starting points for the analysis of the Neptunian pieces in a far more complex puzzle.

WHAT ABOUT ORBS?

The question of what orbs to use is tricky. There are many, many variables that go into determining the most appropriate orb. Some of the variables are technical. Some are actually personal, even arbitrary, depending a lot on your own nature and your astrological style. I just shake my head when I read or hear specific dictates like, "Trines are seven degrees, sextiles are five."

With slower planets, everything else being equal, you may generally use smaller orbs than with the faster-moving planets. That's a good rule of thumb. But "everything else being equal" is, of course, the corker, because nothing usually is. For example, there is another rule of thumb in astrology: the more powerfully-placed a planet is, the wider the orbs you can employ. Some of that "power" is *intrinsic* to the planet—for example, astrologers almost universally use wider orbs with the Sun or the Moon than they do with anything else. That's good practice. But planets can become more or less powerful because of their position in the chart. Are they Angular? Do they rule the ascendant? Are they in the sign they rule?

A good starting point with Neptune's aspects is to set your orbs somewhere between five and seven degrees. Don't read that as religion though—what I am trying to express here is the deeper, and ultimately more accurate, perspective.

Maybe you were taught to use, say, a three-degree orb with the outer planets. But then you are confronted with a chart that shows Neptune rising and Uranus on the nadir, and they are in an eight-degree square. You could accurately build an entire interpretation around that aspect! Being angular like that gives those planets tremendous torque.

Neptune is currently in Pisces, the sign it rules. That's an example of a placement that makes it stronger. For every child being born now with Neptune in Pisces, we need to use a wider orb for any Neptunian aspect because of its inherent strength in Pisces. It's more central, so our orb grows.

We have to consider many such variables when deciding what orbs to use—rulership, aspects to Angles or to the Sun or Moon, and so on.

MAKE IT PERSONAL

There is another dimension to all this, and it's one that doesn't get enough attention. Everybody's mind operates differently. We have to customize astrology to the nature of our own consciousness. The core of the reasoning here is fairly simple: *the wider the orbs you use, the more aspects you have.* So, for you personally, *how many aspects can you handle at once?*

There are questions of simple intelligence here; some of us are smarter than others—not to shame anyone, but of course that is a reality. If you can juggle a lot of information at once—and maybe we should add, you are more experienced—you can naturally handle looking at more aspects. That's straightforward enough.

More importantly, *there are people whose minds are oriented to dealing with a whole lot of data at one time, and other people whose minds are better at going deeply into a few core points.* That's not to be confused with intelligence in the sense of raw IQ, but rather with a *style* of intelligence. For example, if you're in the Capricorn and Scorpio kind of family, you are probably more one-pointed; if you're in the Gemini or Sagittarius family, you are probably more capable of dealing with large fields of data. You are good at *pattern-recognition.*

Each astrologer, as he or she advances, has to tailor astrology to his or her own nature. If you have a mind that can deal with a whole lot of complexity all at once, then use wider orbs. If you're better at focusing on a few concepts really deeply, then you want to make sure you're focusing on the most important concepts and not being distracted by things that are less central. So in that case, you tighten the orbs—because the tighter orbs will correlate with the more powerful and vigorous aspects in the chart.

What I've just said is kind of Neptunian, if you think about it. First, it is about *attention to your own consciousness.* We might also say that it is about *astrological mind-training* rather than astrological academics—and our field needs more inner work and fewer talking heads, in my opinion.

Not to be too *schmaltzy* about it, but this approach to aspects is also Neptunian in that it is about loving yourself and being gentle to yourself. Don't beat yourself up if, for example, you don't work with septiles and noviles, or you haven't become proficient in distinguishing the seventeenth harmonic series from the twenty-third. Those harmonics are real factors. I'm not making fun of them or astrologers who use them. But in the real world of astrological counseling, you'll surely spend a lot more time going deeply into the major aspects—the so-called Ptolemaic aspects, conjunctions, sextiles, squares, trines, and oppositions. That's where the most pressing information resides.

10

NEPTUNE AND THE SUN

The catchy phrase I use for Neptune-Sun aspects in the Neptune Aspects table from the previous chapter is *selfless non-duality*. Like most of the rest of those short phrases, I fear it is one that you might read and understand—and yet not wind up any wiser than when you got out of bed this morning. As I mentioned earlier, these phrases are intended as mnemonic devices designed to trigger a mental reference to the much more complete and complex perspectives we'll soon be exploring at length.

Earlier, I wrestled with the creative tension between the Sun and Neptune—that is to say, between the naturally self-oriented *ego state* and the *selfless non-ego state*. We emphasized how both functions must be healthy for either of them to be healthy. *Tonal* and *nagual* are interdependent. As Neptune attempts to integrate with the Sun—and this could be through any aspect at all—we are trying to sit in the middle of that paradox. To be both of these things—a personality and a wide-open, transparent soul—simultaneously.

That's a lot easier to say than to do.

With healthy Sun-Neptune connections, there's the Sun—the ego, essentially—*getting its own joke* and simultaneously trying to do a good job of being itself. It is laughing at itself, but still continuing to *be* itself, to follow its own course and to defend its righteous boundaries. All the while, the Sun maintains that sense of humor, which keeps the creative tension on the situation. The ego doesn't *like* to have a sense of humor about itself. So always, with Sun-Neptune aspects, there is that sense of letting a little more space into the ego.

For perspective, we need to remember that with the astrological Sun, we are talking about one of the biggies. Anything in aspect to the Sun is absolutely central to the identity. If you have a Sun-Neptune aspect of any sort, you are on a seriously Neptunian path. You're Neptunian to the bone, across the board. Through the ever-reliable laws of synchronicity, you will attract into your life an awful lot of *psychic experience*. You will attract *teachers*, probably a lot of them. You will visit *holy places*, sometimes without intending it. *Metaphysical books* will fall off of bookshelves and land on your feet. Ghostly fingers will stroke the back of your neck. Someone will call your name when you are all alone in the house. Constantly, you will be invited to let a wider reality touch you.

You can ride that wild horse into the heavens of evolution—or it can spook you into numbing yourself, leaving you drifting along as a ghost, wondering what all this will matter in five hundred years.

On the dark side, temptations and pressures to *erase yourself* will press at you. With Sun-Neptune aspects, conventional astrological literature warns of excesses relative to *alcohol* or *drugs*. That's worth mentioning, but let's not be so limited in our imagination about the ways people can escape from themselves. Some of the most subtle escapist traps here come disguised as virtues: extremes of *work*, extremes of *exercise*, for two examples—where deep down what is going on is that the Sun-Neptune person is trying to exhaust himself or herself into a state of oblivion.

We can also find escapes into seemingly "saintly" behavior—that is another Trojan Horse that dark Neptune can employ in order to sneak through the natural walls of the ego and erode the Sun. For two edgy examples, try caring for a child with Down's syndrome or a senile parent. Either one can illustrate this face of the Neptunian soul-cage. Obviously, such behavior can be genuinely virtuous and morally necessary—but in the dark version of it, certain *exaggerations of the responsibilities* arise and are the telltale sign of Neptunian dysfunction. Is it really true that "no one else can take care of Mom?"

One point is certain. If you have a Sun-Neptune aspect in your chart, you are "majoring in Neptune." Thus, the course are likely to be harder!

MY STORY

The best way I know to go a little deeper and to be a little more specific here is to be personal. I've got a nearly exact Neptune-Sun square in my own chart. I'm a solar Capricorn with Neptune in Libra. I don't like using myself as an example too often—that always feels kind of wanky—but maybe that's actually my Neptune talking, come to think of it.

And of course the heart of our apprenticeship program family lies in sharing our own charts and own experiences. So here I go—please throw tomatoes if I go on too long.

So being a Capricorn, there is a clockwork-loving part of me that would really prefer a nice, orderly nineteenth-century universe—one that actually makes comprehensible sense. I think sympathetically here of a fellow Capricorn. Johannes Kepler, whom I mentioned earlier. Kepler was born with Neptune rising on his Gemini ascendant. He lived at a time when astrology was falling out of favor. Challenged on it, he made the most wonderful comment. That "the unfailing correspondence" between what happens in the sky and what happens on the earth "*has compelled my unwilling belief*."

In other words, Kepler didn't want astrology to work. But he saw that it did. And he had to believe it. You almost get the sense of astrology annoying Kepler. I can relate to that! Astrology has rarely actually annoyed me, but illogic always does. Disorder does. I have this goaty affinity for things making more sense than they actually do.

I can laugh at myself now at all of this, but when I was a kid in the 1950s, I was definitely on a "science track." With my Sun-Neptune square, the laws of synchronicity would not allow me to stay on that path—at least not as it was defined in those days.

All through my life I have attracted amazing Neptunian experiences. As a little eleven-year-old proto-scientist, I innocently got into amateur astronomy—looking through telescopes at the sky, reading books about astrophysics, thinking of it as "science." But I started to have these *feelings* looking at planets ... In my book *The Night Speaks*, I draw a parallel between two experiences I once had: one was looking through telescopes at galaxies. The other was looking into the eyes of a dolphin that surfaced very close to me when I was at the helm of a sailboat in Pamlico Sound in North Carolina. I recount the experience of looking into the infinite eye of that dolphin, and just feeling the intelligence and life in the creature—and then looking through the eyepiece of the telescope at galaxies and *feeling the same intelligence and the life in them.*

This was not a logical experience. Nothing like it occurred in any of the science books I was reading. But it was my subjective, Neptunian reality. It was like the universe saying, "Steve, put that in your pipe and smoke it. *The universe is a living being*."

So, synchronistically, I drew those Neptunian experiences to myself. They did not marry easily with my solar Capricornian need for reason and order, nor with my social training. There's the square, representing the *creative friction* between my mystical Neptune and my "rational" Capricorn ego.

Again, I feel a little self-conscious yacking about my own chart. On the other hand, for all of us, some of these Neptunian realities are so deeply, subjectively *personal* that it is hard to get to the heart of them in the usual astrological way—which is basically to illustrate our ideas in reference to big outward events in the lives of famous people. That approach works way better with, say, Saturn than it does with Neptune.

In any case, if you will indulge me, let me continue to use my own experience as a vehicle for talking about the larger principles behind any Sun-Neptune aspect.

"By chance," on a family vacation in upstate New York, I encountered a girl from Germany. She was about sixteen, I was thirteen. She taught me the rudiments of palmistry. On your hand, you have a "Mount of Venus," a "Mount of Jupiter," a "Mount of Moon," and so on. This was the beginning of my encounter with the *language* of astrology, even though at that age, I barely knew anything beyond the fact that I was "a Capricorn."

Why did I encounter that German girl? Synchronicity strikes again—and my Capricorn Sun had to deal with more Neptunian input. I found myself—while trying to be a little science-egghead of a kid—doing palm readings for my friends and schoolmates—and actually getting good results. Again, the universe was *creatively bothering* me, telling me to put that in my pipe and smoke it: *palmistry works.* Neptune was integrating with my Capricorn Sun. Awkwardly.

Note how in these stories there is always something "happening to me." The Neptunian experience is *coming at me from outside*, from a point outside my ego—from the trans-Neptunian realm, which manifests so often through these synchronistic patterns that give order to the "chance" elements of experience.

This is true for everybody—but if Neptune aspects your Sun, the universe is bombarding you with Neptunian opportunities and "reasons to believe" in the larger mysteries.

The pattern continued.

When I got to college at the University of North Carolina, Chapel Hill, in 1967, I signed up for a non-credit evening class in psychic phenomena. It was an intimate group. I ended up reading the palm of the fellow who ran the program. It turned out he was one of the researchers at the then-world-famous Rhine ESP labs at Duke University, just a few miles away. If you've read much about parapsychology, you've probably heard of the J.B. Rhine laboratories. In the 1930s, '40s and '50s, something like 10 percent of Duke University's budget was based on the study of psychic phenomena.

So there I am, wet behind the ears, eighteen years old—and shaking hands with J.B. Rhine himself—probably the most famous man in the world of serious parapsychology at the time. Talk about being invited into the Neptunian realm! There's synchronicity in action—like everybody else, I was magnetizing into my life the experiences that I needed to have.

If you reflect for a moment, you can see how being in contact with the Rhine labs mirrored the perfect integration of my Sun and my Neptune—the *rational, objective study of psychic powers.*

With the universe's help, I was making progress.

During "business hours," the Rhine people were consummate scientists. After hours, there was much activity around mediumship, Ouija boards, and that kind of thing. I had some occult experiences in that context I will go to my grave not mentioning, but one I will mention—my roommate, a physics major, saw a compass needle deflect 45° *at the instant* a partner and I "made contact with a spirit via the Ouija board."

That compelled *the pants off* my unwilling belief!

Why was I drawn to look through telescopes? Why did I meet that girl who taught me palmistry—which is to say, why did she *arise in my life* as an answer to my question about the *meaning* of the planets that arose in my consciousness while looking through telescopes? How, as a result of learning palmistry, did I, a clueless eighteen-year-old, wind up a subject at the world-famous Rhine Parapsychology labs? It's all about synchronicity.

The pattern continued—and continues rather obviously in my life today via the work I do. Through synchronicity, my solar Capricorn self was constantly confronted with Neptunian realities. The integration of the Sun and Neptune foretold by that aspect was supported by experience—and, as usual, Neptune made a mockery of the delusional distinction between the so-called inner world and the so-called outer one. This is part of what I mean when I speak of "selfless non-duality"—not getting so caught up in our ego-self that we need to create a duality between "what we are" and everything else. Rather, we allow it all to merge into one thing. There is a continuum between individuality and the larger universe.

Notice here how I am really hammering the theme of synchronicity. It pervades astrology—it pervades life, for that matter! But is particularly obvious when planets aspect the Sun, partly because the Sun is very biographical and thus quite obvious outwardly in life. And partly just because the Sun is so important that anything connected with it is always in the existential spotlight. So, when you see a Sun-Neptune aspect, you need to hammer synchronicity too! Astrology needs to be psychological—but not too narrowly so. Life doesn't just happen between your ears.

I believe that future historians will look at our current pan-cultural ignorance of synchronicity in about the same way as we look presently think about people who believed the earth was flat.

ENOUGH ABOUT ME . . .

I've been going on about myself, but the point is that all these ideas are generalizable. Let's talk, for example, about a *Sagittarian* with Neptune in aspect to the Sun. That's a whole different beast than a Capricorn Sun. With Sagittarius, there's an underlying drive to have a big sense of the *meaning* of things—to make sense of life. This is why Sagittarius was, in times past, seen as the sign of *religion*. Among other things, it represents the urge to have a philosophy that "explains life."

And yet, with Neptune in aspect to the Sagittarian Sun, one faces *philosophical shock*. The *trans-rational* realm constantly makes its presence felt. Experiences arise that challenge one's current belief systems. The ego is relentlessly pressured to integrate Neptunian input—without denying its own personal reality. So understanding arises—followed by realizing the error of the understanding, followed by another understanding, followed by another realization of error, and so on. If the person with that particular Sun-Neptune aspect succeeds at the integration, her mantra becomes, "*Whatever I see, it's more than that.*"

If you are the person with this particular Sun-Neptune aspect, you have got to continue to be "Sagittarian." That's Sun-work, which is to say that is how you hold your *tonal* together well enough that you can handle the inrushing flood of Neptunian information. The latter, for our purposes, correlates with don Juan's *nagual.* These two sides of your being have to be in balance—interdependent, as we explored in earlier chapters.

As always, the secret of being able to stand the Neptunian influx is to have a healthy relationship with the ego. With all the Sun-Neptune contacts, that is the bottom line. For a Sagittarian, doing that entails a *philosophical quest*—and probably some *traveling*, some *learning*, some *adventures.* For a Capricorn, it requires some focused *great work.* In either case, the point is to keep your ego strong, and surf that Neptunian wave.

As I mentioned earlier, you can ride that wild wave into the heavens of evolution—or it can spook you into numbing yourself, leaving you drifting along as a ghost, wondering what all this will matter in five hundred years.

Those are familiar Neptunian admonitions. The trick, with a Sun-Neptune aspect, is to remember that you are "majoring" in Neptune. It will press on you.

Get it right, or you will just have to repeat the course.

11

NEPTUNE AND THE MOON

Here is the higher nature of the Moon in two simple words: *compassion and kindness.* We cannot understand the Moon's marriage to Neptune without them. The roots of this symbiotic connection are truly primeval. As we attempt to integrate Neptunian consciousness with the nature of the Moon-function, we run headlong into the ancient notion that the Moon represents the *Great Mother.*

"Mother" of course sounds very female, but be careful not to "genderize" it too much. Men have Moons too!

To grasp the link between the Moon and the Great Mother, just think of the attitude that any sane mother has towards her baby—that infinitely protective, infinitely forgiving, infinitely *caring* kind of energy. Such language expresses the highest energy of the Moon. It is *sweet.*

To mix Neptune and the Moon is to mix the sweetness of the Great Mother with the Neptunian qualities of mysticism or spirituality. As you can probably sense already, the natures of these two symbols are similar; they tend to get along well. Together, the Moon and Neptune represent an evolutionary path animated by *love.* It is very much a path of *devotion*, a path of the heart.

Initially, in order to spotlight the Neptunian dimensions of the process in particular, my intention is to pay a lot of attention to Moon-Neptune aspects as they pertain directly to effective spiritual practices. Remember, our main aim is to explore how we can "clean our windows."

In the modern world of "alternative spiritualities," it is common and natural for people with strong Moon-Neptune interactions to find themselves literally *devotees of the Great Mother*. It doesn't mean that you must "worship the Mother Goddess" if you have a Moon-Neptune link—but rather that contemplating the maternal or feminine face of God is simply a very natural way to embody the Moon-Neptune energy. You resonate with "Her" spontaneously. We can certainly experience lunar devotion, however, without feminizing the object of the devotion. It doesn't necessarily have to take the form of Mother Mary, Kwan Yin, Green Tara, or any of the pagan Mother Goddesses—or any other variation on those "God-is-a-Woman" themes. The point is simply that for people with a Moon-Neptune aspect, there is great benefit connected with emulating the loving, tender face of the Divine by whatever name we call it. "Mother" is just a metaphor.

Close to the core of all this is the classic lunar behavior of *nurturing, loving and healing actions* towards others. We might, for example, imagine somebody with a Moon-Neptune aspect who volunteers in a *Meals On Wheels* program, helping to deliver food to people who are not able to leave home. And you can just sense that primal, warm—and utterly lunar—feeling that comes from giving food to someone who is hungry.

Remember that in physical astrology, the Moon rules the stomach—it rules the sign Cancer, and so it is connected with food specifically. But naturally it links to nurturing behavior when it is defined more broadly and generally. *All healing behavior is Moon behavior.*

Link the Moon to Neptune and we add pure compassion to the mix—along with those weirdly Neptunian elements of *psychic or paranormal* powers of perception. Just think of a person who is a gifted practitioner of some kind of *touch therapy* or who is a *medical intuitive*, and you have the feeling of this particular expression of the broad Healer archetype behind such Moon-Neptune aspects.

From a logical point of view, The Moon-Neptune knot quickly becomes more tangled—it always does with the Moon, which is so inherently transrational. For examplе, think of a person who goes to Mass every Sunday. And maybe one day she tells you that she doesn't relate to half of what she hears in church. But she attends anyway. You ask her, "Why do you go if you don't believe it?" And she says, "*It feels good. It gives me a good feeling.*" I've heard exactly this from a lot of my Roman Catholic clients.

Now, many intellectual people would have a big problem with that disconnect between reason and religious practice. You don't believe half of what they're saying, and yet you espouse this religion? You say you're Catholic, but you don't really believe that the bread turns into the body of Jesus (or whatever the belief happens to be)? You practice birth control? You are Pro-Choice? Yet, here is the key we need to turn in the lock of our understanding: *that Moon-Neptune person doesn't have a problem with the illogic*. And that is OK. Their path is a path of devotion, not a path of philosophical reason. It's not about intellectual rigor, it's about the heart. They want the *vibe*. They want *soul*. They want the *energy*. Here. for another related example, is the Roman Catholic who prefers the old Latin mass. Maybe she doesn't even understand Latin. But there's something about the "vibration" of it that works.

Go to a traditional African-American worship service, with that gospel music ringing out and the preacher taking off his suit jacket and wiping the sweat from his brow. He shouts out, "Can I get an amen, children? Let me hear you say amen!" And, before you know it, you are shouting, "Amen!" Forget the theology; what we are experiencing is a massive outflow of vibrational juju.

Who's to say which is more feeble in the face of the Divine mystery—the human intellect or the human capacity to feel?

So, with Moon-Neptune aspects, how do we clean our windows? It's *heart work*. It is about *feeling*. It's the polar opposite of some dried-out prune of a seminary professor discussing theology in the abstract—although we have to remember that God made that professor too. That intellectual form of spirituality is an authentic path as well—it's just not a Moon path.

Let me give you another piece of the Moon's puzzle. And let me warn you right away—this is nothing you're going to hear in a mainstream astrology class.

If you have a Moon-Neptune aspect, a really powerful spiritual experience for you—and a very efficacious one in terms of the evolutionary trigger it provides—is literally *to expose yourself to moonlight*. Literally. Spend time in the moonlight. Let it wash over you. Take your clothes off, if you are brave and in a place where you won't be arrested for it.

This sounds kind of romantic and fun and vaguely silly, but there is some truly deep lunar water here. You know how you feel if you step outside on a moonlit night and just kind of breathe it in for a moment. There's no electric light around—just that beautiful, weird, magical moonlight. *You feel a mystical luminosity that seems to pervade the whole world.* Right away, notice how you are instantly catapulted into an altered state of consciousness? Moonlight does something to your head. Everyone knows that. We just don't know what to *do* with it. As a culture, we have lost that thread.

Now let's take a very short step from literal moonlight. Let's go beyond what I would call the "meditation practice" of bathing in it. This carries us into a whole class of "legal lunar psychedelics." Say that a friend of yours is responding positively and consciously to his natal Moon-Neptune conjunction. You pay him a visit and you notice that all around his home you see candles. They show evidence of having been used. Immediately you flash on the image of him sitting alone in his house while it is illuminated only by candlelight.

Think about it—candlelight is not quite the same as moonlight, but it is similar. *You know the feeling you get when you walk into a candlelit room.* It's a sweet mystical feeling, much like what moonlight does to us. You can just feel your psychic centers opening.

Why did they make the old churches and temples so dark? And why do these brightly-lit mega-churches not, er, "hold a candle to" a Gothic cathedral? *There's something about that darkness that seems to open the inner eye.* People with Moon-Neptune aspects generally love that. They understand it. So if you have such an aspect in your natal chart, *spend time in candlelight.* Spend time in moonlight. Don't think about it too much. Just let that energy wash over you. And if you well up in tears and you don't know why, just let that happen. Those are real Moon-Neptune spiritual practices. They feel good to say—and even better to experience.

Let me make one more suggestion. This one is quite mundane, but still effective. If you have a Moon-Neptune conjunction, think about replacing the light switches in your home with rheostats. That way, with those "dimmers," you can turn down the lights without turning them off. What does it feel like when you walk into a room with the lights dimmed? You know the answer. It's not as satisfying as talking about moonlight or candlelight, but the effect on the brainwaves is rather similar. It's just the Moon and Neptune dancing together.

There's a fundamental concept in practical Buddhism—the idea of *skillful means.* The Buddhists say that good intentions are commendable, but because life is very short, you need to take those good intentions and ally them with methods that are well-suited to your actual karmic predicament. That creates an efficient marriage between those good intentions and the techniques that you are using. Exploring that notion is really the heart of this whole book. In this particular chapter, we are applying that idea to Neptune and the Moon. Acts of kindness, the development and expression of healing skills, heart-centered devotion, and remembering to do a little Moon-gazing—for you, those are skillful means. They will propel you forward on your path.

THE DARK SIDE

Earlier I pointed out that the Moon and Neptune share a lot of common ground. That is not automatically a good thing. Agreement can be dangerous; planets can agree on errors and lies. Active Facebook-addicts don't generally benefit much from asking other active Facebook-addicts if they perceive any evidence of a Facebook-addiction problem. Similarly, planets that are alike can lack perspective; they can exaggerate each other's dark sides. That's the risk with these two bodies.

First and foremost, the Moon's and Neptune's shared affinity for emotion can make them positively *sappy.* If it's just about sweet, treacly expressions of affection designed to embarrass an Englishman or a Capricorn, that's maybe not so bad. But remember: Neptune is attuned psychically to the suffering of the world—and that can be authentically painful. Meanwhile, the Moon is the Great Mother, always attuned to the suffering of her children.

Put them together and you see a classic train wreck: *infinite sensitivity meets infinite pain.* These two can really cry in their beer. Put on a doleful Country & Western tune about a dead dog, and it's all over for them. Get out the handkerchiefs. Feeling deeply is of course not an inherently negative thing. Down the dark road, taken to an extreme, life can become a long meditation on *whining.*

We can have compassion for a soul caught in that particular Moon-Neptune condition—but let's call the condition what it is: a form of egocentricity and self-absorption. The soul-window stays dirty and distorted by all that self-referential emotionalism and drama. Sheer emotion can flood the psyche as sure as a levee breaking can flood the bayou. This overwhelming condition can lead quickly to those various patterns of escapism we explored in earlier chapters: escape into alcohol, drugs, television, and so forth.

Let's add another one. Remember how the Moon is connected with food? We looked at the act of *offering food* positively a few minutes ago. Now we face another obvious dark side of Moon-Neptune contacts: *escape into eating*. Here we often encounter food addictions, compulsive dietary obsessions, eating disorders, obesity.

The Moon is about devotion, so what about devotion to unsound spiritual practices or unsound teachers? That is another potential face of the dark side of Neptune-Moon interactions. Going to Mass "for the vibe" is a legitimate expression of this planetary integration, as we saw. Following a Jim Jones or a Charles Manson—or any of the other Rasputins of the age—is not.

Finally, the self-sacrificial "ghost" qualities of Neptune can collude with the all-giving Great Mother, and together they may produce situations where a person chooses to hang on the cross, endlessly serving the needs of ungrateful, unworthy parasites. With the Moon's natural connection with *family*, the domestic dangers in that regard are acute: to be swallowed alive by needy family members, to become a shadow in one's own home. These are terrible risks for the Moon-Neptune person. Her kindness hangs her as sure as a noose.

MOVING ON

So far, I've just been working with Neptune in connection with the "Luminaries:" the Moon and the Sun. Such aspects are always particularly significant, of course—anything involving the Sun or the Moon is absolutely central to the psyche. That's why I've spent a lot of time on them. I want to investigate the rest of the planets in terms of their aspects to Neptune in similar detail. They're important, too—just not quite so central. Someone with a Neptunian aspect to the Sun or Moon immediately qualifies as a "Neptunian person." They are majoring in Neptune, so to speak. People with, say, Neptune-Mercury sextiles might not qualify for that title—but they are still souls on a journey that has Neptunian dimensions. We can help them on that path by understanding how Mercury can help them "clean their windows" too.

Before we're done, we will look at Neptune in each of the twelve houses as well. We'll explore how Neptune's expression is modified in the various signs too, concentrating more on those of the living—with its 165 year orbit, it's tough to find anyone with Neptune in Aries or Taurus!

There are a lot of Neptunian variables, in other words. Every chart mixes and matches them in an ultimately unique way. And, as you unravel the symbolism, you come up with a very specific set of instructions that will work efficiently for you as you develop spiritually. And this is not the kind of magisterial, cookie-cutter spirituality that leaves you feeling bad about yourself because you're not meditating the way some authority says you should meditate. Once we have understood Neptune's placement in your chart, we'll see you "meditating the way you should"—which might be walking, or playing a drum. Or even not meditating at all—and instead feeding the poor. And, in all cases—as is true with all higher Neptunian pathways—loving yourself as comfortably, deeply, and easily as you possibly can.

12

NEPTUNE AND MERCURY

We come to Neptune's dance with Mercury. Unlike what we saw with the Moon, here we have two functions that are very distinct from each other. Mercury deals in mental constructs—perception, cognition—and the ability to communicate them. Its energy is crisp and precise; it concerns distinctions, boundaries, and definitions. As you can see, in a great many ways, Mercury is opposite Neptune in meaning. So do they do battle or do they complement and correct each other? Those are the core questions.

I want to refer again—in the light of our basic Neptunian paradox—to the fact that not only are we human beings Neptunian, but we are also Solar. We have to be ourselves. Your *ideas* about yourself and the world—your Mercury, in other words—are close cousins to your Sun. And of course, Mercury is enslaved to the Sun astronomically because it orbits the Sun so closely—from the Earth's point of view it can never be more than 28° away from the conjunction.

That sky observation really says it all. Mercury and the Sun—your ideas about the world and your ego—are famously in bed together.

You have to be who you are. You have a path through this world, and it is not the same as everybody else's path. The Sun may be the heart of all that—but Mercury plays a critical role in it too, defining your perceptions and your understanding.

Of course, the rest of the planets come together to constitute the natural, healthy form of your ego. It's not just about the Sun, although the Sun is the essence of ego-formation.

Just to get in the spirit of specifically how Mercury plays into this process of ego-formation, imagine that when we *think*—and I am using that word "think" very narrowly here—when we think about Neptunian spiritual practice, the mind might immediately go to the word *meditation*. Say a friend of yours is going through a Neptunian period, so you suggest meditation as a tool to help her. It seems like good advice—and it probably is. You have great respect and love for her. She is caring, loving, and self-aware. But after you bring up the idea, she says, "*I just can't meditate*. I'm not wired for it. I sit there and I get all fidgety and nervous, and my mind goes all over the place."

How many times have you heard that? Maybe it even applies to you personally.

What is meditation? Well, you can get pretty rigorous about it, if you want. You might ask a very traditional Buddhist and he would tell you, very specifically, that you need to be in the sitting position with your butt the height of four fingers off the ground. So you need a cushion that compresses down to four fingers. And you must sit cross-legged, and your hands have to be at the same height—ideally, they should be resting on your lap. Palms up or palms down? Your call—although there are certain schools of thought about that too. And you sit there and your chin is in a certain position, and your eyes are slightly open, and there you sit, following your breath. That's how you meditate—if you are a very traditional Buddhist.

Feel the fingerprint of Mercury in all that? It is something you can *learn* and *memorize*. It's a *technique*. Google "the seven postures of Vairocana" and read all about it, if you want. And that kind of meditation can work well for some people.

But remember your friend? She's tried all that. She says, "I sit there for a few minutes, and I get the fidgets."

That specific kind of formal meditation just doesn't work for her. A "fundamentalist" would pressure her anyway, try to get her to fight against her own Mercurial nature—and, directly or indirectly, probably only succeed in shaming her.

Enter astrology.

Let's say your friend has natal Neptune conjunct Mercury. We start off by stating the core principle that *there is nothing wrong with that*. Neptune conjunct Mercury is an evolutionary path as legitimate as any other. The culture has given her a definition of meditation—and implicit in where I'm going with all of this is that this definition of meditation is not going to work for her. She tries it, but her experience is that whenever she sits and tries to meditate, a voice in her head starts chattering.

Analyze her language here. There's a "chattering voice" in her head. If she thinks of it that way, she has made the voice in her head the enemy. But what is the very essence of Neptune? No enemies! No veil between Self and Other. No resistance. No opinion—in this case, the *opinion* that the chattering voice in her head is a problem is the problem! With that attitude, she will make no progress at all; she has violated the fundamental spirit of Neptune, which is *loving, nonresistant acceptance*. Always remember to include self-love in the Neptunian formula; that is absolutely critical. Neptune is love; that includes a *unified field* of loving the self and loving everything else, which equates with *not resisting* everything else—and that includes not resisting the nature of the self.

What if she were to make the voice in her head into a friend? What if she embraces the chattering voice in her head as part of her meditation?

Now, what might that look like? In practical terms, what could that mean? We could go down a few roads with that question, but here's one of them. Let's make the inner voice her friend by giving it something to talk about. Let's embrace it. So, let me give our friend some advice about what the voice in her might occupy itself by saying (or in this case, chanting): "*Om Mani Padme Hum, Om Mani Padme Hum . . .*"

Perhaps your friend has Christian roots and feelings. Then she might try: "*Our Father, who art in heaven, hallowed be thy name . . .*" If she grew up in churches, that prayer is really familiar. She can recite it without thinking about it very much. There's a Neptunian power in that "chant" too. The Lord's Prayer, memorized, recited ritually, to the point that it has no intellectual content for her anymore—that gives the part of her mind that wants to talk *something to say*. We are not making the voice in her head the enemy anymore. Instead, we're working with it. To that Mercury, we say, "You want to talk, then talk! Here's what you need to say." And a kind of harmonious compromise is reached—a loving compromise is reached with the part of the mind that wants to chatter.

Neptune in aspect to Mercury: the *union of meditation and speech*. If you have such an aspect, try mantra or prayer.

See the elegance of this? In pure Neptunian fashion, we've evaded the dead-end folly of making part of the self "wrong." Instead, we have let the chart suggest a method of unification. We have surrendered to the actual nature and path of this particular individual.

Let me go a little further with the same example. It is not just about speech. Mercury has a strong affinity for *sensory experience.*

A slight digression here into astrological nuts and bolts: Mercury is the natural ruler of the third house, and that house is often viewed as the house of *short journeys.* At a most primal level, we could speak of the third house in connection with *walking*. Equally, you could relate it to driving a car or riding a horse or anything else that makes you mobile through the environment. But at the most primal level, it's about just walking. I want to focus on Mercury-Neptune aspects here; later we will dive specifically into Neptune in the third house. It suffices to say for our purposes here that Mercury is about walking too.

Here's a hypothetical conversation with someone who has a Neptune-Mercury aspect: Question: Why do you go for a walk every night? Answer: I don't know; it just kind of calms my mind, clears my head, makes me feel peaceful."

Now we go to an unpretentious monk and ask, "Why do you sit in meditation?" And the monk says, "It calms my mind, clears my head, makes me feel peaceful."

The point is that there are some Mercury-Neptune people for whom *walking can be a spiritual discipline*. Such practice again reflects the complementary union of Neptune and Mercury. In fact, there are traditions in which walking is raised very consciously and literally to a spiritual practice. In the deeper Christian traditions, we might point to walking a *labyrinth*. That's an old technique that seems to be undergoing a renaissance lately. Or we could think of an Australian Aboriginal going *walkabout* in *dreamtime* in the Outback, just walking. Zen Buddhism has a tradition of walking meditation. Walking can be a very powerful spiritual practice.

The underlying point is that if you have a Mercury-Neptune aspect, your Neptune is stimulated. It's busy—that's the nature of Mercury. It wants to be busy. Don't make that urge the enemy. Instead, find a way to cooperate with that need; find a way to be in harmony with it. That way, a method opens up for your own Neptunian unfoldment that is in harmony with your true nature.

Mercury loves books; it loves to learn and study. And we humans are blessed with a vast library of spiritual literature. Famously, much of Neptunian reality "cannot be put into words." That doesn't mean that wise words can't help! They can. In modern popular spirituality, there is a great emphasis on the heart. That's fine; we live in such a mental culture that we probably need that balance. But with a Mercury-Neptune aspect, *spiritual scholarship* is a productive path. The mind can be trained, thereby speeding one's evolution. If you have such an aspect in your chart, that high-speed evolutionary freeway is wide open before you.

THE DARK SIDE

As always, every front has a back. There are ways to get a Mercury-Neptune aspect wrong, to have it become a soul-trap instead of a soul-path forward. They all boil down to two problems. One centers more on Mercury's liabilities, the other on Neptune's. If we balance too far toward Mercury, we wind up *thinking too much*. If we balance too far toward Neptune, we can become *hypnotized by own description of reality*. Let's look at each of these traps in a bit more detail.

If we think too much, something inside us becomes desiccated. We may be saying brilliant, truthful things, but we are basically a "talking head." We have mistaken the universe for an idea in our mind—and, while that notion is very close to the truth, it's not quite there. "An idea in your mind" quickly becomes impervious to wonder. Nothing new can get in. And, touching briefly on very deep waters, Neptune does not teach that the universe exists only in your mind—not exactly. It teaches that the part of you that would make a distinction between "your" mind and "the universe" is the problem.

If we fall into the second Mercury-Neptune pit and become hypnotized by our own description of reality, some similar traps open up—but we go down a somewhat different road here. One trap is that we might fall into the *pit of preaching*; there is a charisma in this kind of spiritual certainty, so followers often appear. And "being right" can become addictive—and deadeningly repetitive.

Another trap is pure *delusion*; a wrong idea, held faithfully, can trap a soul for lifetimes. For one vivid illustration, consider the spiritual folly of believing that "God wants us to slay infidels." From the outside, such a belief is transparent error. There is evidence on the nightly news that from the inside, for certain deluded souls, it is endlessly compelling.

Famously, the most dangerous kind of liar is the one who believes his or her own lies. When Mercury and Neptune interact, that sad phenomenon can easily arise. There are, for example, people who actually, truly, *believe* that God wants them to slay infidels.

When we truly believe a lie, we have entered into a *delusional state*—and that is another dark expression of Mercury-Neptune energy. A classic cartoon-cliché about "a crazy person" is that "he thinks he is Napoleon." In such a case, a Neptunian incursion from the inner psychic realms has erased the person's ability to function socially in the collectively agreed-upon matrix of "reality." I phrase this carefully because one core message here is that Neptune *wants* us to question reality. But of course not everything comforting or cool is actually true, and Neptune-Mercury people are susceptible to such delusions. In its mild form, this can express itself as a harmless addiction to weird and groundless thoughts and theories—someone hooked on endless conspiracy theories, for example. In severe form, these aspects can correlate with truly *psychotic ideation*.

Plain liars are not in short supply in this world, and some of them are very skillful. That can be a dark expression of Mercury-Neptune aspects too. Here the person knows what he or she is doing, so we are not dealing with a delusional state. Instead, we see more of the *master actor* dimension of Neptune entering the equation.

How to avoid the dark side of Mercury-Neptune contacts? Keep it fresh. Value good questions more than comforting answers. Value learning over being right. And make friends with the itchy, antsy part of yourself. It will lead you to some fascinating places.

13

NEPTUNE AND VENUS

Sometimes astrologers say that Neptune is the "higher octave" of Venus. I like that idea; I think the notion of planetary octaves makes a lot of sense—that Uranian genius is the higher octave of Mercury's simple intelligence and perceptiveness; that Mars, the warrior, has a higher octave expression in the best of Pluto, which can crusade for things that are bigger than itself. So what about Neptune and Venus? Venus is famously "the goddess of love." And Neptune is connected with love as well—but of a very different sort.

Love is a very popular word with scoundrels. That's partly because it has so many different, legitimate meanings. Love is a necessarily slippery term. Compared to Venus, Neptune's love is less person-specific, less connected with meeting our own needs. There's a link between Venusian love and Neptunian love, but they represent very different levels of energy.

I had an experience when I was a young astrologer, just starting out. I was probably in my mid-twenties, so this was back in the early 1970s, when the so-called "sexual revolution" had stampeded. I was doing a reading for a very pretty woman about my own age. She had a strong Neptune, right on her Libran Sun. I remember sitting alone with this beautiful woman in an office in a house in Charlotte, North Carolina. She expressed her view that if anyone wanted to use her body, who was she to say no? She was "on the spiritual path" and loved everyone.

As a normal, twenty-five-year-old guy, I had to think about that for a moment!

So what was wrong with her viewpoint? Hey, if you really love everybody in a divine way, why have any boundaries at all? Would *God* shut anyone out? And your body is just the physical expression of your spirit, right? Just channel the God within, and open your zippers! Right?

This played better in 1974 than it would today.

I passed the test, by the way. I've often fantasized that angels were watching, and that if I had flunked that test and made a pass at the woman, my path through life would have been very different.

That's my Neptune talking. I can't prove what I just said, but I don't need to. *I feel like I know it.*

Can you recognize a kind of satanic logic in that woman's position? I bet you can. "Satanic" is a funny word to use, I guess. I don't mean to demonize her; I actually suspect that within a few months, she had figured out that she wasn't doing herself any favors. To say it simply, that kind of sexual free-for-all can be a psychologically dangerous way to live for all concerned. And of course it is physically dangerous too. That all seems obvious today, but the 1970s were ... let's say, "giddy with experimentation."

Underlying this little tale is the key principle for our purposes: *Venusian love and Neptunian love ain't the same creature*. But as with the Moon and Neptune, we are faced with two energies that have many similarities.

That synergy produces certain advantages, but also certain risks.

I startled the students in one of my Apprenticeship Programs while teaching a synastry seminar. I said, "The main function of Venus is to reject people." And that statement naturally raised some eyebrows. That's not how we usually think about Venus. But let's say that I am your best friend—I'll just leave it that way, without even getting into sexuality. I am your best friend—and, as we all know, that doesn't just mean that I am "friendly" towards you. It's more special than that. We share, we email, we talk—we stay caught up with each other. I know what's going on in your life, and you know what's going on in my life. That's what being "best friends" means.

And you can't do that with everybody. There's not enough time in the day.

Further, we just don't have that kind of *deep affinity* with everyone we meet. For us to become best friends, in essence, I've had to say no to lots of other people. Any process of *selection* implies a process of *rejection*.

This principle is even more vividly obvious when we talk about committed sexual relationships. For most of us, there are a fair number of people—potentially or theoretically—who could have been worthy, loving partners for us. Using a very Venusian word, let's say these are attractive people in the grown-up sense of the word: a multidimensional, body-mind-spirit sense.

But how many of them will fit in your bed?

So with Venus we have to say, "Not you, not you, not you, not you, not you . . ." Thus, strange as it sounds, most of what Venus does is rejection. And that's why it is connected with discrimination. That's why love between two people, in deep friendship or sexual intimacy, is such a unique and special thing.

Now, with Neptune, we are looking at an entirely different face of love. We could call it "universal love." It is wide open. On one of his solo albums, Pete Townshend of the rock band *The Who* wrote a song called *The Sea Refuses No River*. The tune is about what we might call "God's love." The lyrics explore the idea that no matter how polluted a river becomes, the sea accepts it without hesitation or resistance. What a lovely metaphor! Pure Neptune is like that; *it loves everybody.*

But that doesn't mean it sleeps with everybody. With that idea, we see something closer to the shadow-side of Venus-Neptune aspects.

I owe my public astrological career, literally, to this next insight. It involves another astrologer whom I respect, so I will leave out his name. He was also writing for the same publisher when I was negotiating to get the contract for my first book, *The Inner Sky*. There was a crossroads in the negotiations. The publisher—one of the big, mainline house—was already doing pretty well with his book, and their question was, how will your book be different from his? In essence, they were asking a very fair question in the context of that industry—why should we publish your book when we're already publishing his?

My agent, bless her, had prepared me for this juncture. I had a copy of his book, and I had literally opened it at random—thank you, synchronistic universe—to a place where he had said, "*Neptune conjunct Venus suggests promiscuity.*" Now, as we have seen, promiscuity is one of the possibilities with Venus-Neptune contacts. He wasn't wrong, but his understanding of the aspect was too narrow, depressing, and rigid.

Here is the gist of what I said to the executives there in New York that day, back in 1981: his words are not just an erroneously narrow statement; but also potentially a damaging one. Imagine you are the reader. You have a Neptune-Venus conjunction and you read this statement. *What if you already have a certain vulnerability to making bad judgments in the sexual arena?* And now along comes an astrologer, with the authority of the planets behind him, saying, "Of course you're like that; you're *doomed* to be like that. You have Neptune conjunct Venus."

You can see how the lazy side of the human soul might say, "Whew! Thank you! That's not a problem after all, then, is it?" And the person hurts herself or himself, and probably hurts a lot of other people. That's destructive astrology—dangerous, negative astrology. The publisher understood and published *The Inner Sky*.

Positively, Neptune conjunct Venus means that the only kind of relationship that is going to be stable for you is one with a *spiritual basis*. If you don't have that kind of connection, then the relationship will feel empty. Exactly what do we mean by a "spiritual basis?" Let's start by being clear that we do not mean that you are both Presbyterians, Jews—or Rastafarians, for that matter. It is not about *theological* agreement. In relationships with a spiritual basis, the *spirits connect consciously*. It's as simple as that. But those words can sound vague. They don't need to be. We can be quite specific, testable, and grounded here.

Here's how: Let's say that you are single. You've gone to Italy on vacation. You find yourself attracted to someone in the tour group. Wednesday morning is free; you pair off and decide to go visit a certain cathedral together. On the way there, you are yacking and yacking; it feels good; you're connecting well. Together, you step into the cathedral. It is empty. No worship service is in progress. *But you are both knocked out by the energy of the place*. People have prayed there for a thousand years. Immediately, you are both quiet. You separate as you explore the Caravaggios hanging in the alcoves.

After a while, you sit down alone on one of the pews and close your eyes. A few minutes later, you feel your friend's eyes on you. *How?* He or she is standing fifteen feet away, waiting patiently. A wordless conversation happens: "Ready to go?" Arm in arm, you walk out to the street—and begin yacking again as soon as you leave the building.

Think about this story. It says everything we need to know about the higher dimensions of Venus-Neptune contacts. The vibrations of that cathedral sunk right into the perceptual center we call your natal Neptune. *And your friend felt it too*. There was a wordless connection between you.

Your *spirits were relating*.

It is such a simple idea, such a common little miracle in this world. We meet people with whom words are not necessary—or to say it more precisely, we meet people with whom it is sometimes necessary that there are no words. This is how spirits relate. This is the deepest meaning of Venus-Neptune aspects.

Tweak our little story about the cathedral. You walk into that holy building—and *your friend keeps talking*. He or she is a nice person; you get along fine at the level of personalities. But if you bond with that person, something will be missing for the rest of your life. Remember, one of the main functions of Venus is to reject people. That sounds mean—but timely, wise rejection is ultimately a tremendous act of kindness.

Let's go further. Wherever Venus lies in your chart, you *need some help*. That's the nature of Venus. It is about *trust* and *love* and *sharing*. Venus reminds us that no one is an island, so to speak—that to continue efficiently on our evolutionary journeys, we sometimes need the catalytic impact of other souls.

Say you have a Neptune-Venus aspect. You are walking alone by river in a forest. Suddenly, cold fear grips you. Scared, you look around. You see nothing unusual; you hurry forward along the path. A hundred yards later, you begin to calm down. What was that all about? Was it a panic attack? Who knows? Welcome to Neptune. Let's say that two centuries ago there was a massacre on that very spot. And when you passed by, you felt the lingering psychic energies connected with that violence. *But you don't know that*; you don't know about the massacre. So far as you know, maybe you are "just crazy." Maybe you're having an issue with your blood sugar.

Now, let's tell the same story, but with one pivotal change—you are walking along that river with a soul-friend. That same edgy feeling hits you. You say to your friend, "Do you feel anything weird?" She looks at you and says, "I'm so glad you said that . . ."

Note how this is an utterly different experience. The presence of the friend transforms it entirely. She feels it too! Thoughts of "being crazy" vanish. *Someone else has corroborated your psychic impressions*. And that is the heart of the matter with these Venus-Neptune aspects. Your "faith" grows with the spiritual support of souls who are on your wavelength.

By the way, we will see all this again when we look at Neptune in the seventh house. But that's another story.

In just a few paragraphs, we've come a long way from "*Neptune conjunct Venus suggests promiscuity*." We have entered the realms of *sacred love* and *sacred sexuality*, which is where we belong when these two planets interact.

Venus is not just about loving relationships. It is also connected with our *aesthetic responses* to life. As most of us know, Venus was the Roman goddess of the arts. This perspective leads us down a new road—and to a new method for "cleaning the Neptunian windows."

There is a long tradition of *religious and spiritual art*. Could you, for example, imagine the Italian Renaissance without Christian iconography? Buddhism without mandalas? Islam without its lovely mosques? We can talk here about the *contemplation of uplifting art* as a Venus-Neptune evolutionary path.

Just lie down, close your eyes and turn up the volume on the last movement of Beethoven's Ninth symphony and you will know exactly what I mean.

But Venus is not just about the art that humans create; it's about our *response to beauty* in general. A friend of yours tells you that she is going to the mountains for a week of meditation. That makes sense; mountains are beautiful. And for centuries, mystics have been drawn to meditate in beautiful places. If instead your friend announced that she is going to sit in the New York Port Authority Bus Terminal for a week of meditation, you might question her about that... although if you can meditate there, you've really accomplished something!

But with both Venus and Neptune, we *cultivate gentleness* toward ourselves—so why torture yourself with meditating in the bus station? Off we go to the mountains, or to the concert hall or to the museum. Or we join the drumming circle, or we lose ourselves in the trance-work of painting or poetry. These are all efficient expressions of Venus-Neptune aspects as avenues of conscious evolution. Why? The answer is simple: when we are caught up in aesthetic rapture, we are in a wide-open, loving, nonresistant state. Venusian beauty has seduced us into a higher Neptunian state.

THE DARK SIDE

With Neptune, we are always dealing with a power that must be kept carefully on track, lest we slip into delusion. We are *getting over ourselves—but not too fast.* We need to guard that delicate balance between *tonal* and *nagual*, between the solar ego and our sense of those soaring spaces out beyond the Neptunian window. When we get it wrong, we blur. We become ghosts in our own lives. We hang on crosses.

To hang on the cross of an empty marriage—that is not a rare tale in this world. No marriage is perfect; it is that most nakedly human of institutions. But if you have a Venus-Neptune aspect in your natal chart, you need spiritual relationships, at least with friends. A committed life-partnership operating on that basis is a powerful soul-stimulant, for reasons we explored earlier. But a dark response to a Venus-Neptune aspect can leave you *trapped in the belief-system that you must remain in an empty relationship.* What will it matter in five hundred years, right?

There's another, very different, intimate "cross" available to Venus-Neptune people: *romantic addiction.* This disorder can take several forms. The simplest expression is an endless, desperate search for that great myth: perfect love with the "twin soul." When you read the fine print, this usually boils down to a search for a relationship that requires no work and no evolution.

People with such a belief actually do find each other from time to time, experience a few weeks of blissful psychiatric projection—then, as reality sets in, they punch reset and start over again with someone new.

Other forms of this same addiction are "carrying a torch" for someone who is unavailable and always will be—or just plain endless, longing, aching loneliness.

When the phenomenon of *promiscuity* is seen here, as it is sometimes, it is not so much simple "monkey business" sexual compulsivity as another expression of this urge for Venusian soul-connection—but with a kind of "shotgun" approach. What I mean brings me back to that woman I mentioned at the beginning here. She was open to "connecting with the Divine in everyone," which sounds like a fine idea in principle. But we do run into difficulties when we attempt that connection via our genitals. Remembering this is helpful when counseling someone who expresses Venus-Neptune aspectual energy in this misguided way. As you speak with them, underscore that in the framework of their own consciousness, they are not about using, objectifying, or exploiting anyone. Motivationally, they are all about genuine soul-connection. By saying it that way, you will go a long way toward maintaining that precious bridge of rapport.

One of the saddest things that can happen in this world is to encounter a soulmate who has gone down a dark path. With a Venus-Neptune aspect, you surely have some Neptunian soulmates. But when Neptunian people go down dark roads, they become overwhelmed by their own sensitivities because they have not done the soul-work they came here to do. Therefore, they might become addicts or escapists, as we have been seeing all along. They sit in front of televisions in dark bars at 2:00 in the afternoon—bars often full of strangers who have made the same mistakes. If you have bonded with someone like that, you are holding a ticket for a First Class cabin on the *Titanic*. Tear it up and walk away. That is easier to say than to do, but it is the right advice.

Remember, with a Venus-Neptune aspect in your chart, you can't do what you came here to do all by yourself. You need help from those who are your *spiritual equals*. Don't hang on the cross. Don't settle for anything less.

14

NEPTUNE AND MARS

Neptune and Mars—at first glance, it doesn't seem like a marriage made in heaven. Mars the Warrior and Neptune the Mystic. Warriors practice violence; Mystics turn the other cheek. Warriors force the issue; Mystics let it all be. The two seem irreconcilable. Their synthesis does present an integrative problem. But all along we have been seeing that these kinds of "problems" in aspects—a core of incompatibility between the two planetary archetypes—can actually be an advantage. In a nutshell, they can *potentially balance and correct each other.*

One primal theme we explored back in the foundation material lies in s the *complementary interdependency* of Neptune and the Sun. The other side of that coin was revealed when we looked at Neptune's interaction with the more comfortable energies of the Moon and Venus—and the challenges that can potentially be created by their penchant for *dark collusions.* So let's not be too quick to assume that Mars-Neptune contacts are inherently troublesome.

But let's also not ignore the elephant in the living room: warriors hurt people, while mystics practice kindness, forgiveness, and surrender. There's a gulf of difference between these two planets, for sure. At worst, it's a chaotic combination.

At best, we are talking about the archetype of *the spiritual warrior.*

Let's add a familiar warrior cliché to the stew—*There are no atheists in foxholes.* I don't want to glorify war—and a true understanding of Mars takes us light-years beyond war—but when we are faced with any kind of edgy, scary situation, the experience can often reduce us to our spiritual bones. I am sure that men in combat, men who may have professed atheism or agnosticism, have found themselves literally praying—in "foxholes" or elsewhere. But let's go beyond war in the narrow sense. What if your child was in a life-threatening accident and his or her life were hanging by a thread? What if you were in an airplane that experienced engine failure?

If such events don't call you to prayer, probably nothing will.

Maybe your kid recovers just fine, maybe that airplane pilot gets the engines working again—but those moments of tense uncertainty tend to turn us all to our Higher Power. Such moments viscerally integrate Mars and Neptune. We don't even have to think about it. And that is one unique feature of the evolutionary potentials that these Mars-Neptune aspects indicate: *their integration can unfold very quickly, triggered by the kinds of instincts that arise when we are under fire.* Much of our evolutionary work in general comes from committed effort over time. Mars-Neptune integrations can happen in seconds, while the results can last a lifetime.

"We've tried everything; there's nothing left to do now but pray." Arguably, that is the most deeply human statement that has ever been uttered. When every option and strategy under our control has been exercised, we face that moment of powerless waiting. The dice have been rolled.

There is "nothing left to do now but pray." If Neptune could speak, it might raise the question of why prayer is the last thing on our list. That's a really good question, but it is very difficult to fight human nature. When we're scared, we're wired to do everything we can to take care of ourselves. And maybe that's not such a bad reflex. It reflects the healthy basic solar quality of simple self-preservation. As we will see, this reflex also often has a big Mars signature too—we *fight back*, we trust our own power, we "shoot first and ask questions later." Sometimes those kinds of reflexes and attitudes keep us alive, and most of the time staying alive is a pretty good choice.

But at some point, in some dire situations, we realize that we have to surrender to 'the fates."There is no choice because there are no choices left. Sometimes life says "checkmate." We all face such a crossroads at some point. When we are there, our only hope—quite literally—lies in our relationship with what we are calling Neptune. You might call it God.

I think here of the Buddhist teaching about "entering the *bardo* of dying." Buddhists define that life-passage very precisely. When you enter it, you are actually still alive. It occurs at the moment when we *see the cause of our death coming*. It could be a doctor telling us that we have six months to live. It could be an oncoming car seen through our windshield. The bardo of dying can be long or short. But it sure gets our full attention. And in it, we see a synthesis of Mars and Neptune. Can there be a greater spiritual teacher?

More Mars imagery: I think of a warrior literally going into battle—and I mean this in a genuinely human sense, not in the context of some bloody Hollywood hero-myth. Picture a man going into battle. With real bullets. He knows he might die today; he might be dead an hour from now. One possibility is that such a thought *truly composes his mind*. Perhaps in that moment he becomes the spiritual warrior.

From here, let's take what might seem like a long leap, to another Mars-Neptune concept: *shamanism*. Shamans—or Mages, or Wizards, or Medicine people—represent a synthesis of Neptunian mysticism and Martial warrior-courage. Meditating on them is an aid to attuning to the meaning of this whole family of astrological aspects.

Now, here in California, every third neurotic claims to be a "shaman." But I am talking about the real deal here, not the endless, ego-posturing in the spiritual fashion show.

Go to a museum of anthropology and look at the masks that traditional shamans wore. They are terrifying. They're *intended* to be terrifying. And if you can feel that frightening energy in a museum, under fluorescent lights, can you imagine what it would be like to be stoned on something in a little clearing in the forest and some guy dressed in that mask leaps through the fire and yells "boo" in your face?!

So, the *shaman invokes fear*. The shaman lives in a world of fear. Not panic—there's an important difference between fear and panic. Panic means we are "losing it" in the face of overwhelming fear. We've stopped thinking. That's not what shamans do. Instead they *harness fear* to develop one-pointed, highly-focused attention. They are the consummate spiritual warriors.

One of my favorite quotes here goes back to my old sailing days: "There is no pump in this world like a frightened man with a bucket." There's something about fear that, if it doesn't paralyze us, brings out levels of strength and intelligence in us that we didn't even know we had. When we are in survival mode—again, not in panic, but fighting intelligently for our very lives—we have powers of which we'd never dreamed.

Here's how these Neptune-Mars aspects plug into the web of synchronicity: if you have such a contact in your chart, *your life will attract emergent situations that call for that same kind of super-human focus.* It's a bit like that famous sequence in *Star Wars* where Luke Skywalker tells Yoda that he is not afraid of the Dark Side of the Force, and Yoda answers, "You will be."

Think of somebody with a Neptune-Mars aspect who is about to bungee jump for the first time. In fact, let's think about the spiritual aspect of bungee jumping. I know how crazy that sounds. But in all honesty, if I were about to jump off a bridge and fall two hundred feet, and then, hopefully, ten feet above the rocks "boing" back up again, I'd pray first!

We can laugh at this last image. Me too—and fear not, I'm not even slightly attracted to the idea of bungee jumping. But for someone with a Mars-Neptune aspect, it could actually be a significantly spiritual experience. They might bounce back up, giggling wildly, and say, "Whoa—a near-death experience! Who's next?"

Think about how often you hear of people who, when coming to birthdays with zeroes in them, elect to celebrate with a parachute jump or a ride in a hot air balloon. It's all the same thing. With a Mars-Neptune aspect in your chart, you need these kinds of "kicks in the soul" from time to time. You are wired to benefit from them. They compose your mind. They help you remember who you are and what is truly important in your life.

So, with Mars-Neptune aspects, we need adventure, we need some edginess, we need risk. We intentionally need to strip ourselves down to what is really true. Bottom line, with a Mars-Neptune aspect in your chart, you are attempting in this lifetime to *constellate the archetype of the spiritual warrior in yourself*—and that is pie that's baked in an oven of scary events.

You will seek them, or they will seek you.

WHAT ABOUT SEX?

Passion is a classic key word for Mars—and for anybody older than twelve, it's a short step from that word to sex. Mars energy is sexy, for sure. People who are not "beautiful" but who still take your breath away often show strong Mars features in their charts. Add some Neptune to the Mars-mix via an aspect and the combination becomes *erotically beguiling*. Right away, we see synchronicity—human beings with Mars-Neptune aspects tend to attract sexual interest and attention over long periods of their lives. And they need it, not just physically or psychologically, but for evolutionary reasons.

In really hot sex, there is a kind of surrender to our instincts. We trust the body and let it do what it does. And in truly hot sex—which is actually almost the polar opposite of pornography—the surrender between the lovers is not just physical. There is a kind of undefended soul-surrender that happens too—that, or we are back to mere pornography.

Great sex is physical, of course. But it must also be spiritual, in other words. See the Mars-Neptune integration? Too much Mars and we are back to starring in our own dirty movies. What about too much Neptune? That's a little bit more subtle, but we need to understand it. If someone has a compulsion always "to make sex a sacred experience," they might sound pretty holy. But might they also just be afraid of their own bodies? Or the instinctual body of their lover? What we are talking about here is surrender—but a surrender to the inner animal that occurs simultaneously with a surrender of souls.

THE DARK SIDE

What if we aim this Neptune-Mars energy in the wrong way? Let's talk about the dark side of these aspects. Always with Mars, one reliable sign of the energy having gotten off its tracks is *exaggerated* or *inappropriate anger*. That is a classic dysfunction connected with any weak response to Mars.

Imagine somebody is going on and on about how much they hate the President. Now, of course, people might legitimately have a different political philosophy. They have rational reasons to disagree. I want to respect that; as astrologers, we have to respect diversity. And argument fuels democracy, and so on. But this person I am invoking is practically foaming at the mouth. You get the feeling that something other than politics is going on. Spittle is forming on the person's lips—this sounds just like your alcoholic Uncle Joe talking about Washington DC over Thanksgiving dinner, right? Characters like this seem to come straight out of Central Casting. What are they really angry at? If we ask them that question, they just get even more furious.

On the simple level, with a Neptune-Mars aspect, there is a danger of a *delusional dimension to one's anger*. There is a risk of misdirecting it, aiming it at *symbolic targets*. We are often talking about *displaced anger*—what you are seeing in your alcoholic Uncle Joe is actually an angry little five-year-old boy who wants to kill his father for not taking him to the baseball game in 1958. But say that to Joe and he'll just get angrier.

Let's add another, very different, layer. A weak response to a Mars-Neptune contact can simply manifest as *apathy*—a state devoid of any passion at all. What will anything matter in five hundred years? That's a whole different beast than what I was just talking about with your Uncle Joe, which has that violent edge. Mars is our enthusiasm, our passion in the larger sense. What if we give up on it? What if we, in the fashion of dark Neptune, just hang on the cross? At that point, something vital inside us dies. *We just don't care anymore.* We lack the spark plug that makes us *want* things, and to *do* things—and, basically, to get out of bed in the morning. But when Neptune-Mars goes dysfunctional, we move into numbness and escapism. We don't give a damn. Apathy rules.

Always, a core insight into Neptune's shadow is that patterns of active escapism can arise. A further insight is that those patterns of escapism are a response to unintegrated, ultimately clueless, Neptunian psychic sensitivity. We escape to numb ourselves to ourselves. There are a lot of ways to do that. With Mars flavoring the picture, let's think about a person who is compelled by some inner demon to take truly stupid physical risks. There are judgment calls to be made here—not every bungee jumper is crazy. But if you catch me bungee-jumping, call the mental health unit and tell them to bring the bazooka! I'm being playful here, but I am serious too—for me, bungee jumping would be a Mars-Neptune "cry for help."

The key here is the realization that when people are faced with such extreme stress, for a while they *don't have to be themselves.* If being ourselves—taking conscious responsibility for our own creations—becomes agonizing enough, we will do anything to turn it off, even for just a little while. There's the root of the escapist pattern. Call it *compulsive risk-taking.*

And of course, let's not forget about sex! Talking about Neptune-Venus contacts earlier, we looked at a kind of romantic escapism. With the dark Mars, there is less emphasis on the needs of the soul, even delusionally, for intimacy. There is, more frankly, a desire for purely physical sexual contact. Sex is an intense experience, of course. In sex there is such a profound attention to the sensations of the moment that we can forget ourselves. There are high expressions and uses of this energy, as we saw earlier. But it can also serve escapist needs.

One more step: As we all know, sex with a new partner is a particularly intense experience—and there is no shortage of potential new partners in the world. Mars-Neptune contacts, gone down a dark road, can be genuinely promiscuous, even more so than Venus.

I don't mean to sound prudish here. The problem is not the number of partners; the problem arises if one's partners are all *objectified* and ultimately *dehumanized.* The root problem is that if you're thirsty, all the popcorn in the world isn't going to quench it. You can never get your fill of the thing for which you are not really looking.

Lastly, another sexual expression of Mars-Neptune gone bad is simple *sexual apathy*. Libido disappears. We have no interest in passion at all. We have given up.

15

NEPTUNE AND JUPITER

When Neptune contacts Jupiter, the critical evolutionary synthesis is *generosity towards all beings.* That phrase says it pretty well. One dimension of Neptune is nonresistant, compassionate engagement with everything and everyone "out there." Jupiter, at least in its positive manifestations, lives up to his famous title, the King of the Gods—and, like a good king, Jupiter's spirit is *expansive* and *big-hearted.* When you dine at his table, he feeds you well. And your job is to eat, drink, and be merry.

Put Jupiter and Neptune together and they radiate a big Yes into the universe.

Say you're at a party. You've been trapped in conversation with a boring person who's cornered you. He is rambling on and on about something that does not interest you at all. We've all been in that kind of situation. What is the high Neptune-Jupiter response? *Listening to that boring person with apparent interest and patience.*

We are not doing that because we are really engaged with what he is saying—as already indicated, we're struggling to be patient. We are paying attention for two reasons. First, because it is *Jupiter-generous* and *Neptune-compassionate* to offer this person a few minutes of our time. And second, because it would be really *cheap* for us to reject this person with expressions of disinterest or the body-language of dismissal.

There, in that simple moment, we see the evolutionary magic of this combination of energies. From an egocentric point of view, a few minutes of your time are wasted. But from a Neptunian perspective, you have turned that moment into a real evolutionary opportunity. You have used it to become more loving, less opinionated, more open, and less resistant to accepting what is.

Infinite, loving generosity to all beings—that's the Jupiter-Neptune ideal. By "generosity," we mean radiating an attitude of palpable kindness. We mean interpreting other people's actions in a positive way, giving them the benefit of the doubt, looking at their various lapses of conduct in a forgiving way.

Yikes! Some people don't exactly inspire that emotion in us. The ones whom it is easy to treat that way—the people we love—don't present us with much of a lesson. There's not much evolutionary potential there. Loving them is still a virtuous action, but we don't learn so much. Therefore, probably the highest expression of Neptune-Jupiter aspects would be wishing *success and happiness to our enemies.*

Obviously, I'm setting a gold standard here. Who can possibly live up to it? You would have to be a saint. You would, in fact, actually be a saint.

It is so tempting to add, by reflex, that expecting ourselves to be saints is unrealistic. But let's bring the energy of Jupiter up a little louder in the chorus. Always, with this planet, the question is *how have I underestimated myself?* How have I sold myself short? Jupiter invites us to think *idealistically* about ourselves and our potentials. Humility is a virtue—but it is not the virtue that Jupiter seeks to cultivate. Jupiter represents *healthy pride.* That's not to be confused with arrogance or ego-inflation. In plain English, it boils down to faith in yourself—to being your own best friend.

If you have a Jupiter-Neptune aspect in your chart, keep your eye on the grand prize: a loving, compassionate, nonresistant relationship with all of God's creatures—yourself included. You may not get there quickly, but *never forget that you can get there.*

Bottom line: don't be so quick to dismiss the possibility of your finding sainthood in yourself! Realizing that you could get there is part of a healthy response to a natal aspect of Neptune and Jupiter. Delusion and inflation are not the points; the point is to be wary of holding yourself back with limiting attitudes. All those saints were once just like you.

What if you're living a middle-class kind of life, doing all right, but counting your pennies at the end of the month? A friend of yours buys the right lottery ticket and suddenly has $238,000,000. *Can you feel unambivalent joy at your friend's joy?* Or are you thinking squirrelly thoughts, such as, "I wonder if she'll give me just one stinking million? She has hundreds of them ..."

Do you feel that *grab, grab, grab* kind of acquisitiveness? That's the opposite of Jupiter; Jupiter is generous—we celebrate our friend's joy as if it were our own.

Funny how people, even friends, can become competitive with each other. I picture a group of women who are single and in midlife. And part of their bond with each other is talking trash about what total dogs men are. And it's partly humorous, but there's also a certain truth in it for them, because these are women who have all had their hearts hurt by men. And so part of their bond is a shared rejection of males. Who would want those sour grapes anyway? They comfort themselves by devaluing males.

We'll carry this story further—but let's stop and have a mindful moment; let's walk our talk. In good Jupiter-Neptune fashion, let's be generous towards these women as we contemplate their negativity. Calling a spade and spade, they are condemning and dehumanizing half of humanity—but we know two things that help us to forgive them. First, their attitude is a response to their pain. And second, it is part of the basis of their loving friendship with each other.

Now, the plot thickens. One of these women falls in love with a wonderful guy who treasures her. Let's make it even worse: He's rich, faithful, and cute as a button. How do the other women in the circle feel? Do they experience unambivalent celebration of their friend's happiness? I doubt it! They are a bunch of monkeys, just like you and me. You can almost hear them, "He's *maybe* a nice guy, but ..."

In calling all humanity "a bunch of monkeys," I am not trying to turn any of us into cartoons. And God knows I'm not trying to beat up women with that story; I could tell the same story about a group of male buddies—just reverse the genders—because men who have been hurt by women will often band together in similar ways. And there are parallel structures in the LGBT community too, of course. The Jupiter-Neptune question here is, *can we celebrate our friend's joy at having found love without comparing it to our own poverty*? Can we do it without feeling some ambivalent taint of resentment towards the victory or the success of the other person?

This discipline of *warm-hearted supportiveness* toward others is the core of the spiritual path indicated by a Neptune-Jupiter aspect. It is powerful, and it can carry you a long way toward sainthood.

So far we have only looked at how the Jupiter-Neptune family of aspects can express itself helpfully relative to other people: unconditional generosity of spirit toward them. We can extend the principle much further. Let's talk about *an attitude of unconditional trust toward the universe as a whole.*

Here we are ultimately looking at the idea of faith. By that word, I don't mean a belief system. It is more like an assumption that you are guided, protected, and cherished by some basic benevolent quality that is inherent to the fabric of reality. Call it God or your guardian angels. Whatever you call it, *it wants to support you whenever you are willing to take an emotional or material risk for the sake of your own evolution.*

Illustration: you feel the inner call to visit a sacred site—say, the Camino de Santiago, the famous "pilgrim road" in northern Spain. Trouble is, you don't have enough money. You decide to go anyway, on faith. And a week later, grandma dies and leaves you $10,000. Synchronistically, your inward faith in the universe has triggered an outward expression of welcome and support. That kind of "lucky" life-event is correlated with this family of aspects. When Jupiter gets together with Neptune, the water of life flows—if you remember to prime the pump with faith.

THE DARK SIDE

Never be fooled by the idea that Jupiter is inherently "benefic." Jupiter can get you into worlds of trouble as easily as Saturn, Mars, or Pluto. In thinking about Jupiter's dark side, I always go back to that delightful quote from Oscar Wilde, "I can resist anything but temptation."

As we mix Jupiter's inherent vulnerability to ego-inflation with Neptune's spirituality, one pitfall that quickly arises is *spiritual pride*. Ego, unfettered, wants to be the king of the cosmos—there's the dark Jupiter. Ego wants to be the center of everybody's attention, the most important thing that has ever happened or ever existed. There's the ego's basic drive, at least when it runs amok.

Add Neptune, and this compulsion morphs in the mystical direction—the desire to be seen as a *glamorous figure of wisdom*. The Vedic word for Jupiter is *Guru*—link it to Neptune and you can see the danger that arises. When others think of you as "the guru," it's a terrible trap. It's ego-candy.

We have both a baby and some bathwater here, for sure! Spiritual pride—in the sense of an inflated assessment of our own level of inward accomplishment—is an awful trap. Ego obviously gets pumped up in delusional ways—plus, we create the mucky karma of merrily misleading other souls on their own paths. It's a full-blown Jupiter-Neptune catastrophe.

On the other hand, *faith in ourselves at a spiritual level is an important soul-vitamin.* That is essentially the positive Jupiter-Neptune point we have been hammering from the beginning. Imagine you started every meditation with the following affirmation: *It probably won't work this time. I will never achieve enlightenment. I just don't have what it takes.* How effective would that be? A basic tenet of most mystical traditions is that, deep down, you are already there. The Buddha-nature is inherent in your consciousness. The Kingdom of God is within you. Remembering all that—and having absolute faith it—is in the very DNA of all the Jupiter-Neptune aspects. You have got to believe in yourself!

Sorting all that out from simple spiritual pride can be subtle business. Bottom line, you need to *remain real.* And the reality is that you are an ancient luminous being who sometimes worries too much about money, sleeps with the wrong people for the wrong reasons, and gets really annoyed in traffic jams.

Keep your eye on both sides of that equation, and you will keep your Jupiter-Neptune aspect on an even keel.

Not everybody who falls into the traps of a Neptune-Jupiter aspect starts thinking of themselves as saints, gurus, or spiritual masters. For one thing, those are cultural words, and not everyone is of that culture. To be fully alert to the shadow here, we need to think more broadly.

Consider the delectable temptation of *being right all the time.* And then drop that down a notch from "spiritual ambition"—that is, being right all the time about God, the universe, the purpose and meaning of life. Think instead about being seen as "important" or "cool." Think of the *glamour of this world.* Think about "the lifestyles of the rich and famous." These are all soul-cages from Neptune's perspective—and, to Jupiter, they can be as tempting as spilled ice cream to a colony of ants.

Jupiter imparts "star quality" to whatever it touches. It can be magnetically attractive, persuasive, and convincing. It can therefore often *get what it wants* as surely as a Hollywood star, a rock star, or some phony, expensive media-generated "guru." Earlier, we spoke of how Jupiter-Neptune aspects support you whenever you are willing to take an emotional or material risk for the sake of your own evolution. But what if, instead of your own evolution, you want to take risks simply to satisfy your various ego-appetites? These aspects can "help" you there too—and sometimes "getting what you want" is exceedingly perilous to the soul's well-being.

Addictions in all their forms are commonplace with this class of aspects. In Greek and Roman mythology, the "King of the Gods" famously likes to eat and drink and fornicate. Not to sound prudish here, but when is enough enough? Don't ask these two planets when they are in cahoots with each other!

Technically, it is helpful to remember that Neptune and Jupiter traditionally share rulership of Pisces—one classic, one modern. They can cooperate in wonderfully creative ways in pursuit of the higher meaning of Pisces: *spiritual opening*. But don't ask them if they've "had enough yet" in any category of appetite. And don't limit your attention to the standard spectrum of appetite-driven escapist behaviors, although they are quite relevant. Remember to add the terrible risk of an addiction to other people's *attention* and *adulation*. Power and glamour are famously heady drugs. Once they get into your bloodstream, life is very drab without them.

16

NEPTUNE AND SATURN

When Neptune and Saturn form an aspect, again we see a familiar scenario: two very dissimilar energies are trying to integrate. As we have been underscoring all along, that tense type of planetary combination offers potential advantages of *mutual correction* and *perspective*—but it also presents the possibility of planets working at crossed purposes.

So what does Saturn bring to the Neptunian mixture? How can it help balance Neptune? Saturn's gifts are: *One-pointedness. Focus. An absolute commitment to realism.* Saturn is *discipline*; Saturn is *effort, method, and structure.*

In the last chapter on Jupiter and Neptune, I used the words, "Hey, you're there already. You already have the Buddha-nature." From Jupiter's point of view, that's helpful to remember. That attitude deepens your self-confidence and your faith: Jupiter virtues. Enlightenment is not such an exotic condition. One day you will surely get there.

But now along comes Saturn to rain on Jupiter's party. "You think you're *there* already? Give me a break! Just take a look at yourself . . ."

Saturn invites you to *get a grip*, to be realistic about your actual evolutionary condition. Saturn goes on, sort of depressingly: "Oh, the road is long! How many more lifetimes will you have to struggle just to get over your basic selfishness? How long before 90 percent of your waking thoughts are no longer about satisfying your multitudinous monkey-hungers? *Enlightenment?!* Who are you kidding? You're lucky just to stay out of the psych ward."

The Buddha's followers asked him once, "So how long does this take? I've been meditating for, like, hours." OK, maybe that's the modern Los

Angeles version. Here's ancient India: "I've been meditating with you for thirty years, so how long does this take?" And the Buddha, who could be a real Saturn guy sometimes, replied, "Imagine there's a stork, and he's got a silk scarf in his mouth. Every century he flies over a mountain peak and drags his silk scarf over it. *How long does it take him to wear down the mountain*?"

So what do we do in the face of that kind of obstacle? Saturn says, "*All right, let's get on with it then.*"

Which is a good attitude. If you've got Neptune and Saturn interacting, you've reached a point in your evolution where there is no rocket fuel so effective as simply *sticking with it*. We are talking about *spiritual discipline. Sustained effort*—Saturn's domain—is trying to integrate effectively with *mystical, spiritual aspiration*. That's how you are going to clean your windows in this lifetime—via hard, day-to-day work. There is no magic bullet. Saturn is the face of the Divine that asks you, "*So how badly do you want it?*"

I am going to represent Saturn, the taskmaster, the lord of discipline. In other words, I'm going to afflict you. I'm going to be a serious boil on your butt. You sit down in formal meditation and I am watching. After fifteen minutes, you get up. I say, "I see you've stopped meditating."

You: "Yes, I have."

Me: "Why?"

You: "Well, I've finished."

Me: "How did you *know* you were finished meditating?"

You: "Well, I think I got what I came for. I sat and meditated for a while, and now I feel calmer and attuned . . . and I'm just done. I just know it."

Me: "So, let me ask a related question—what are you going to do next?"

You: "Well, it's about noon; I think I'll have some lunch."

Me: "Are you hungry?"

You: "Well, not particularly but it's noon, so I think I'll eat."

Me: "Do you mind me asking what you're going to have for lunch?"

You: "I have some leftover pizza in the refrigerator and I think I'll just eat a piece of it, cold."

Me: "Let me get this straight. Two minutes ago you were sitting in meditation. You were sitting in the presence of God. And now you feel like getting up to eat a piece of cold pizza even though you're not really hungry? *How much power do you want to give the part of yourself that prefers cold pizza to the presence of God?*"

You: "Well, I wouldn't phrase it that way . . ."

Me: "How else *would* you phrase it? Isn't that exactly what you are doing?"

You: "Give me a break . . ."

Me: "Sit your sorry ass back down and meditate!"

Of course this is a caricature that I hope you found amusing, and I wouldn't talk like that to anybody! But if you have Neptune-Saturn aspects, that's how you need to talk to yourself at times.

I would draw an analogy here with long-distance runners. Sometimes they are running right at their limits of endurance. They feel like they can't take another step. They feel like there is a knife in their chest—*and they keep going anyway*. On sheer courage. On guts and determination. And those runners have a saying for what happens next: they *go through the wall*. That's a metaphor they often use. And once they go through the wall, they can run for many more miles.

Where did they get that second wind?

So forget about the slice of cold pizza and sit your sorry butt back down in meditation! If you have Saturn—the lord of discipline—working with Neptune, there are treasures awaiting you. Spiritual breakthroughs literally beyond your imagining are available to you in this lifetime. But your ability to find them hinges on one critical question: Can you go through the wall? Or its second cousin: How bad do you want it?

Saturn loves *structure* and *method*. With a Saturn-Neptune contact, your inner practice might benefit, for example, from committing to a particular spiritual tradition, especially a practical one that really tells you "exactly where to put your foot next." Vague, lofty metaphysical theologies are of less value here than concrete practices. Examples might be formal Buddhist meditation, walking a labyrinth, Iyengar yoga practice, fasting for Ramadan, or saying the Rosary. Again, structure and method, not abstraction—those are Saturn's signatures.

Further, you've got to do those practices even when you *don't want to.* That is critical. That's what discipline means. Ultimately, with Saturn-Neptune aspects, you are *making your will dominant over your desires and ego needs.* Therefore, you'll benefit enormously from practicing certain *austerities* if you have a Saturn-Neptune aspect. Going without food—the ancient practice of *fasting*—is a good illustration. Such an aspect doesn't mean "Thou shalt fast." That's just an example. But think about it: going without food is kind of psychedelic. It opens up consciousness in weird and interesting ways. Fasting is a *method.* It has been used by mystics in every culture for countless millennia.

As I say these words, I'm quite aware of how unstylish and un-modern they sound. Today one might hear, "You should always listen to your body." And indeed, the phenomenon of hunger is a clear example of your body trying to tell you something.

But what if your body feels like staying in bed all day? What if it feels like pigging out on junk food? Is that a spiritual practice for you? Well—and I love this answer—for some people without Saturn-Neptune contacts, the answer is, "*Yes indeed! Stay in bed, if you want.*" How can that be? Maybe you are learning to practice absolute kindness to yourself. Maybe it's the *Moon* in aspect to your Neptune, not Saturn, and you need to bring some of that Great Mother energy into your relationship with yourself. We are astrologers, so we celebrate diversity here.

But that kind of self-indulgent attitude will not work with a Saturn-Neptune interaction. There, it is more like saying, "So, you're a little tired of meditating? *Let's see what happens on the other side of that tiredness.*"

This is fierce Saturn talk. It is disciplined talk. In this Age of Instant Gratification, Saturn is out of style. But this kind of *total commitment* is the soul-victory that unfolds when Saturn's true aim integrates effectively with Neptune's mystical aspirations.

Austerities—let's go a little further down that road with that idea. If you have a Saturn-Neptune aspect, I would like to recommend periods of *celibacy*—say, up to thirty-six hours in length.

Of course those words make us all laugh. But I am serious. And don't be alarmed—we're not going to play that old, toxic game of shaming human sexuality. But when you make love with someone, your energy bodies interact—they should! Your lover's energy body is impressed upon yours, just as you have impressed yours upon him or her. And that can be a delicious, beautiful, wonderful thing. But in meditation, we want to *quiet the mind.* And it might benefit us a lot not to have interacted sexually with someone for a while as we sit down in meditation, just for the calm and the clarity that comes with such a quieter energetic condition.

Note the Saturn signature here: we are being utterly real, utterly objective, and utterly practical. We are not within a million miles of making sex dirty or shameful, or any of that crap that we get fed in some of the older, more patriarchal spiritual traditions. What we are doing, bare bones, is simply being mindful of the energetic, psychic reality of what sexuality does for us—or to us.

When we hear the word "celibacy," most of us probably think of a monk's or nun's lifetime vow to restrain one's self from sexual expression. But here, with Saturn-Neptune contacts, we may literally just be speaking of thirty-six hours of celibacy. Often the desire for "thirty-six hours of celibacy" really boils down to a need for some solitude—and there's another venerable Saturn word: *solitude.* With a Saturn-Neptune aspect, *periods of solitude* can really benefit your spiritual practice. Mystics in all traditions have practiced this sacrament of solitude.

All of this reflects the higher expression of Saturn's interaction with Neptune—a very specific, practical, concrete path composed of *solitude, fasting, and disciplined meditation practice.*

As with everything positive about Saturn across the astrological board, it really boils down to relentless effort. *You will get what you earn* spiritually, not a penny more, not a penny less.

THE DARK SIDE

Saturn loves logic and reason. There's nothing wrong with that. True spirituality goes beyond logic and reason, but it is not opposed to them. The trouble is that often under the banner of logic and reason, what Saturn is really after is *control.* It would like to "control the universe" by being able to understand it and predict it. That is of course an illusion at many levels. But, hey, we're talking about the dark side.

A lot of astrologers in particular seem to succumb to this Saturn-Neptune trap—the urge to control the universe through *prediction.*

There's a very poignant story—and this is connected with a fine, prominent astrologer whom I will not name because it is a very intimate story. But his wife was dying of cancer. And he was visiting her regularly in the hospital. She was an astrologer too. Lying on her bed in the ward, she was busily predicting the day she would die, based on her transits. He became exasperated with her as he realized what was going on. He said, "You would rather be right about the day you die than to get well!" Isn't that disturbing? She would rather be *right* in the prediction than to *survive* the prediction of her own death!

As I recall the story, she died on the day she had foreseen. Which came first, the chicken or the egg? Was it a self-fulfilling prophecy? I cannot help but wonder what might have happened if, instead of visualizing herself dead, she had visualized herself in remission. I don't want to be Pollyanna about cancer, but I do wonder . . .

So, with Saturn in aspect to Neptune, there can be a sort of "*Father Knows Best*" need to be "right about everything," spiritually. The need to be "the expert" in such matters is a real danger here. You get a lot of rigid fundamentalism with this aspect—and when I use the word "fundamentalism," I do not just mean Christian fundamentalists. There are plenty of New Age fundamentalists. And Science fundamentalists. You name the belief system and we're going to find fundamentalists within it. These people are always offended when reality turns out to be more complicated than their beliefs. And they will try to stomp on anything that doesn't fit their existing beliefs. They have a desire to control the universe—and if you step outside the circles they have drawn for you, they will want to control you, too.

Neptune, as we have seen over and over again, can be connected with escapism and addiction. Adding Saturn to the mix gets tricky, since this planet is generally good at keeping an even keel in this world, showing up for work, keeping its promises—attractive moral qualities which we don't naturally associate with addicts and drunkards.

But addicts and drunkards don't all look alike. One dark expression of Saturn-Neptune contacts is the *high-functioning alcoholic*—a person who "keeps his act together" despite such a dependency. It is quite possible that only people very close to him or her would recognize the existence of the issue. That recognition would come through the eternal signature of a person on an escapist path: simply said, they have escaped. They are not "there," really. You sense that quality of absence whenever you attempt to make any kind of intimate, authentic emotional contact with them.

With Saturn-Neptune contacts, we can also see addiction relative to a whole range of Saturnian activities. *Work* would probably be at the top of the list—thus, the aptly-named disorder we call *workaholism*. We can also observe addiction to *exercise*, to *rigid dietary restrictions*, to *schedules*, to formal *social manners*, to *traditions* ... the list is long.

And underlying every excess here is our addiction to that classic Saturn fingerprint: *the empty promise that we might control everything*.

17

NEPTUNE AND URANUS

We now cross the boundary of the solar system as it was conceived before 1781 and come to the interactions of the planets Neptune and Uranus. They both move slowly, so their aspects last a long time. Therefore, they affect "all the kids in your graduating class."

That's a good way to say it. Obviously, a "generation" would be too big a term—these two planets don't move *that* slowly! But it is typical to see a Uranus-Neptune aspect lasting for a year or two, perhaps a little more—so, again, if you have such an aspect in your chart, it's a good bet that "so did all the other kids in your class."

While these two outer planets can act very powerfully, their natures are totally different. Neptune's meaning can be telegraphed just by referencing the familiar metaphysical cliché *transcending one's ego*. With Uranus, the basic logic is almost the polar opposite: *the perfection of one's individuality*. There is therefore a creative tension between them. They aren't enemies—and, even if they were, all aspects are still about integration anyway.

Here are the core questions:

- *Can radical individuality serve our spirituality?*
- *And can spirituality offer not only balance, but also direction to the free expression of the ego-self?*

The essential Uranian idea is that each one of us is in an absolutely unique karmic predicament. And each of us has a treasure inside ourselves—a set of instincts about *exactly what we need to do in order to address that karmic predicament*. We can potentially be true to ourselves and follow a very efficient Uranian path forward in our evolutionary journeys. Doing that would be easy and natural—except for one issue: *we humans are like ants in an anthill.* We are herd creatures. We believe what we have been told to believe.

That all sounds terribly negative. I don't intend it so darkly. I am actually glad in a lot of ways that we are herd creatures. When the traffic light turns red, most people are going to stop. Thank you! There's a social agreement that red means stop and green means go. And we all live a lot longer because of that agreement.

And that's just about traffic lights. More broadly, as a society we have come to agree upon various norms and assumptions about moral behavior, decency, practicality—just simply how to get along with each other in a crowded, interdependent world. And we have arranged that those who break the rules create all kinds of trouble for themselves.

Civilization is a joint effort; being part of one involves *surrendering to the social contract.* Yet, adhering to such agreements can blur our instinctual attunement to our actual natures. In other words, there are people who, in the quest to feed their souls, require certain experiences that *they are discouraged from having*. And that, in a nutshell, is why God made Uranus.

Let's start with an obvious example. Consider a man born under the sign of Cancer in 1935. Cancer indicates an evolutionary path that has to do with attuning to one's inner life—attuning to the heart, feeling deeply. But a male born in 1935 was taught that "*girls cry and boys don't.*" He was taught that a prime virtue in a man is a stoic endurance of everything.

In this example, we see social training that runs absolutely counter to the person's actual evolutionary needs. All the principles that we need to understand about the planet Uranus are built into that sad little story.

Can that man recover his ability to feel, and to express what he is feeling? Yes—but whenever he takes good care of himself, doing what he came into this world to do, he is going to be viewed by people around him as *wrong* or *crazy* or *defective*. Or weak. Or "unmanly."

Now, we humans love approval. We love respect. We love to be taken seriously. We love it when everyone else thinks we're cool. To get the planet Uranus right, we need to be very mindful of those traps and not fall into them. Uranus is about being true to yourself—which always boils down to *overcoming our pitiful human hunger for approval* and being accepted.

Neptune, of course, relates to mystical, spiritual matters. It is the windowpane we need to clean if the light is going to enter our heads. And when Uranus and Neptune are in aspectual contact, cleaning that windowpane is inseparable from the Uranian processes of *individuation* and *self-liberation*.

Let's imagine that you go back to your hometown after some time away at a spiritual retreat. You discover, to your shock, that everyone there has decided that you are the Messiah. You are just the coolest thing that ever lived because everyone knows you're so spiritually evolved. You walk down the streets of your community and people fall to their knees before you. "Hallelujah! I can die now, I've seen the Messiah." They are touching the hem of the garment, and running away shouting ecstatically, "I've been healed, I've been healed!"

Now, what does that actually say about your spirituality?

And here's the answer: *absolutely nothing*. Nothing good, nothing bad. That's just people talking. Nothing more than that. It has absolutely no relevance one way or the other. If you can fully internalize that truth—not just understand it, but rather *be* it—then you have made an "A" in your Uranus-Neptune lessons.

But that kind of glory, that kind of respect—it can become addictive. If you were to be greeted that way, you would understand how dangerous it is. And if you started to believe it, you would be in serious trouble. Still, there is something inside all of us that likes to read positive reviews of ourselves, something that wants to believe them. Of course, the other side of that coin is that we all get negative reviews too sometimes. We have an inclination to believe those as well. And that represents another kind of danger.

The underlying point is that we humans are *social creatures*. One effect of that is our vulnerability to internalizing other people's views of ourselves. This creates a terrible risk of distortion in the human psyche. So the universe—the solar system—contains the planet Uranus, which is the natural antidote for this primal human vulnerability.

Here's a story I like to tell when I see this Uranian-Neptunian archetype activated in a person. You're sitting in a meditation group with ten other people. Let's say the leader of this meditation group is a good-looking, charismatic guy. And he's the real deal—there's nothing phony about him. But he has a kind of star-power about him. One day as the group forms its circle, he says: "There's something I want to share with you today before we start. I'm just too blown-away by it to lead today unless I get it off my chest. I was hiking in the desert last weekend by myself. And as I was walking up a canyon way out in the boonies, I saw there was an old man sitting there on a stone ahead of me. As I approached, I saw that he looked like a Native American. *And as I got closer, he called me by name.*"

So we are already in Neptune city here, right? Everyone gets goosebumps at that last line.

The leader goes on: "The old man said he had been waiting for me for three days. The Great Spirit had told him that I would come. He had a healing quartz crystal that was given to him by the grandson of Sitting Bull. And the Great Spirit said that I was to receive this sacred object. It was time for the sacred stone to be shared with his white brothers."

With that, the leader of the meditation group reaches into his vest and pulls out an old buffalo skin package. And he opens it up dramatically and there it is before you—the sacred crystal of Sitting Bull!

Everybody is wide-eyed. You are sitting right next to the leader, on his left. He reverently passes the crystal to the person on his right. She holds it—and tears start streaming down her cheeks. Onward to the next person—a beatific look spreads across his face. As the stone goes around the circle, everybody is blown away by its power.

Finally it comes to you. And up above, your guardian angels are praying that you get this right. The crystal is passed to you. You accept it with wide-open expectation. You honor all these people. They're having a real experience, it seems. You expect to have one too.

You hold the sacred crystal. *Nothing.* To you, it's just a sweaty rock. And you look around the room nervously. Everybody's looking at you. They like you. That's good—but that's *important* to you too. Their expectation that you will have an amazing experience is so strong you can feel it pulling at you. You wonder what's going to happen to you if you say, "I don't feel anything. It just seems like a sweaty rock."

Well, your spiritual Dow Jones average is going to plummet—that's for sure.

Feel the social pressure on you to fake a spiritual experience? This is why your guardian angels, knowing you have a Neptune-Uranus aspect, are up there with their hands in prayer hoping you have the courage to say, "I don't feel anything."

You are developing a certain kind of courage which helps you to *individuate spiritually*—and that is what Uranus-Neptune aspects are all about. *What the rest of the monkeys think of your spiritual evolution does not matter.* It is simply irrelevant. Nothing matters except the truth as you experience it. That realization is the heart of this aspect. It is a very difficult attainment—again, because we are social creatures. Our survival, literally, has always depended on our maintaining membership in a tribe. You are trying to liberate your psychic experience from the thralldom of collective beliefs and socialization.

Synchronicity supports this dimension of the soul's journey, of course—synchronicity is ever-present once we start noticing it.

So what kind of experience and circumstances do you draw to yourself in order to facilitate this unfoldment? The answer is, ones that get you into a lot of interesting trouble!

Maybe you were raised in a very religious Roman Catholic family, and you meet a Buddhist lama who blows you away. Maybe you are like "the sleeping prophet," Edgar Cayce—kind of a backwoods, rustic Protestant who starts remembering people's past lives. Maybe you are a mainstream scientist who has a mind-boggling, accurate astrological reading—or who sees a ghost or a UFO.

In all these cases, *shocking spiritual experience* offers you a choice: you can deny your own reality and thus maintain your social identity—or you can claim the evidence your own mind and senses present, and thereby trigger an avalanche of judgment, criticism, and social attempts at "correcting" you.

It's your call.

In talking about all this, I want to be careful to keep a balance between Neptune and Uranus. Uranus is fiercely devoted to truth, and it can be harsh about it. You probably have some friends who are so truthful that sometimes they seem mean. And, even if unintentional, that's often the spirit of Uranus. It has that kind of edge.

But Neptune is all about love. It's about loving others, and it's about loving yourself. It's about surrender. It's compassionate. It's sweet. Neptune knows that whatever the truth may be, we always have to be gentle in presenting it to that insecure inner monkey. We never want to condemn the monkey for its need for other people's approval and support. *This tension—*

essentially between the spiritual usefulness of truth and the spiritual usefulness of love—pervades every aspect made by Uranus and Neptune.

So, with a client who has this kind of aspect, I often tell the story of the meditation group and the sacred crystal. But I could also imagine a person who has a Neptune-Uranus aspect who is a member of a Pentecostal Holiness congregation in rural Georgia. And there's a healing service in the church—people throwing away their crutches and all that. And our Pentecostal friend is offered a healing in front of the congregation. And after all the hoorah, imagine this person saying, "I honestly don't feel anything. I don't feel any different. My rheumatism is still bothering me."

The person is honest, in other words, rather than succumbing to the social pressure and exclaiming, "Thank you Jesus, I've been healed!"

I don't want to be cynical about it, I just want to be real about it. Let's recognize that it is very difficult to go against the grain of everyone's expectations. In going against their expectations, we lose status in their eyes. There's the trap. How hungry are we for that status? What price will we pay for it?

So *keeping truth more important than approval*—there is the higher meaning of Neptune-Uranus aspects.

THE DARK SIDE

How long can we talk about true spirituality without bumping into the word "surrender?" One inescapable Neptunian reality is that the ego must drop its shields. In this book, that's just a translation of our central metaphor of "cleaning the windows." The highest Neptunian state entails nonresistance to everything that is. It is wide-open. It accepts everything. It has surrendered.

But "surrender" is not in the Uranian vocabulary. The point of Uranus is *not surrendering*—to social pressure, to conformity, to tradition, to expectations. Its mantra is, "I am what I am. Deal with it." And given human cultural reality, that mantra quickly turns into a familiar self-versus-society battle. Adding a dollop of Neptunian compassion to our understanding here, we realize that this Uranian process is hard. It is a struggle. Part of us wants to be loved and accepted and will pay any price for it.

Because of all that, in practical terms *Uranian energy usually must become at least somewhat defensive*—if it doesn't defend itself, it gets steamrollered. Abstractly, a *perfect* Uranian response could simply be to "be itself" without any need at all for self-defense—but that's up there with Enlightenment: a good goal, but tough to reach.

This leaves us with the basic dilemma facing everyone with a Uranus-Neptune contact: How can we "surrender"—without surrendering our individuality and integrity? It is easy to see how we can get this wrong. And error opens us to the expression of the dark side of such a configuration.

Always, across the board with Neptune, we need to be alert to addiction and escapism. Here, with Uranus in the mix, we can see an *addiction to freedom*. That doesn't sound too bad, but it can manifest as contrariness and stubbornness, and boil down to a commitment to never learning anything from anyone.

Spiritual quirkiness can become a kind of fetish. Attacks on other people's religions can become compulsive. If I have inward doubts about whether I am right, then I probably need to defend against them by making everyone else wrong—there's a soul-cage for anyone with a Uranus-Neptune contact.

Surrendering to the Divine is fundamental to any positive response to Neptune; that is inescapable. Surrendering to spiritual teachings is very close to the same thing. Surrendering to spiritual teachers is close as well, although perhaps not quite as close. So we have two rings around a bull's-eye here—surrendering to teachings and surrendering to teachers. And these both lead us into delicate territory. If you have a Uranus-Neptune aspect in your chart, should you follow any spiritual teachings? On one hand, it would be a shame to ignore the treasure offered to us by those wise ones who have gone before us. On the other hand, there is something positively Uranian to be said for an innocent, fresh approach to your own consciousness.

How do we sort this out? Check yourself for *attitude*. If you have a lot of "attitude" about teachings, you've probably slipped over into the dark side, and you need to consider your own resistance.

We can say essentially the same thing about our outer ring—*surrendering to spiritual teachers*. Not everyone needs a guru or a priest or a mullah, or an analyst. Sometimes you just need to go sit on the mountaintop by yourself. That is an honorable path, and if you have a Uranus-Neptune contact in your chart, exploring that kind of spiritual independence may be an important evolutionary step for you.

But again, check yourself for attitude—if, for example, you feel a compulsion to make fun of other people's dependency upon their gurus or a need to project dark assumptions onto all such teachers, then you are likely slipping into shadowland here.

Let's say you've fallen into that pit. Ask Neptune what to do, and Neptune will say, "Simple. Forgive yourself and try to stop doing that as best you can."

AP STUDENT QUESTION: First a comment, then a question. Not really related, but I was inspired to remember a Carl Jung quote. He said, "One does not become enlightened by imagining figures of light, but by making the darkness conscious." The latter, he added, is more difficult, and therefore unpopular. The question I have is about the Uranus-Neptune conjunction of the early 1990s. Could one speculate that the generation born with it has the ability to merge science and spirituality?

STEVEN: A great quote there from Jung, and a very good point about that group of young people. The Uranus-Neptune conjunction, of course, embraced a few years of time, given the eighty-four-year orbit of Uranus and the 165-year orbit of Neptune. The conjunction actually repeats on a cycle of 171 years. We should maybe start paying some attention to it as early as 1988 or so, when Uranus first joined Neptune in Capricorn. It peaked in 1992-93 at the actual conjunction, and faded into the middle '90s when Uranus crossed into Aquarius.

Every time these two planets come together, there is an absolutely extraordinary—and very obvious—shifting of the cultural paradigms. This could turn into a long digression, and I'm not going to do that, so let me just go back to the last time it happened, before this one that we've all experienced. We will look into the rearview mirror of history and see what we learn. This takes us back to about 1822—make that about the center of it, and give it a couple or three years on both sides. In that time-frame, we have the harnessing of steam, the first trans-Atlantic steamship, railroads beginning to really take off; you get the whole kind of *fossil-fuel-driven* version of civilization—the beginnings and roots of the *industrial age*. And if you think of what that symbolized in terms of the next 171 years of history, you start to get the picture.

But if you were living back there in 1822, you'd have no idea of the mythic implications of humans harnessing the power of fossil fuel in metal compression structures. You would have no idea what that development would turn into. The world changed at a fundamental level, and yet no one living then could really understand it.

Here's another one of my favorite illustrations from that time: There's an English gentleman by the name of Michael Faraday. We visit his home for a spot of sherry one evening. And Michael takes us down into his laboratory in his basement and demonstrates that he has arranged a coil of copper wire, and a magnet in the center of it, and a handle so he can spin the magnet. And when he does that, something amusing happens: sparks shoot out of the end of the copper wire.

And here we are, sipping our sherry, English aristocrats. What do we say? "Ah, Michael, how fascinating! Truly droll! Who would have imagined that you could ever create sparks that way? Bravo, my man! ...By the way, what are we having for dessert?"

Faraday's "trick" would have seemed completely insignificant to us, in other words. Yet he had figured out *how to generate electricity*. This was under the Uranus-Neptune conjunction! Humanity figuring out how to generate electricity—doesn't that seem like a pivotal moment? A paradigm shift? But it is also obvious that we would have no idea of its meaning at the time.

This is how the Uranus-Neptune conjunction works. There is a *Uranian revolution in our Neptunian dream of the world.*

Let me add one more, rather different, example, right back in that same period. This one puts the cherry on top of the mythic sundae. I want to make a reference to one of humanity's great holy books—a book of prophecy. You will not think of it as a holy book. Mary Wollstonecraft Shelley published *Frankenstein* anonymously in 1818, then under her own name in 1823.

Now think about *Frankenstein* in the light of all we have just seen—in that book, *science creates a monster whose effects it cannot foresee or control.* There's the story of Dr. Frankenstein, reflected in the generation of fossil-fuel-driven culture and the generation of electricity.

Doesn't all that kind of cohere into one unified field of symbolism? Haven't we played that seed-moment out for the 171 years that came after it? Under that Uranus-Neptune conjunction, the basic paradigm upon which we found our myth of the world changed in a fundamental way, essentially ushering in the modern era. And may God help us all.

This brings our attention to the early 1990s, where once again, a paradigm shift occurred. I would link it to the epicenter—not really technically the beginning—but the *cultural epicenter* of the digital revolution. I remember looking at letters to the editor in *Time* magazine in the 1980s. Somebody wrote a letter to the editor, and signed with a name and "@aol.com." And I wondered, "What's that?" I actually remember that—wondering what "@aol.com" meant. I didn't know what email was! I still went to libraries to look things up at the time. I didn't know about the internet. I had no cell phone. I had zero Facebook friends—and neither did you!

We can barely imagine that world anymore, and yet it existed within the lifetimes of many folks still alive on the planet. That was part of the paradigm shift, then—the digital revolution. And here we are still at the beginning of it, with no real idea what its ultimate implications will be. What does the fish know of the sea?

With all that said, let me add that I am not sure that the digital revolution is the most important part of the Uranus-Neptune revolution of the early 1990s. Earlier, I pointed to the discovery of the first of the Kuiper belt objects other than Pluto, right at that same time, right on schedule—a major paradigm shift for astrology. The implications of the discovery of the Kuiper belt extend far beyond the hallowed halls of technical astrological practice. When we think about what the discovery of those objects means in terms of the revolution in consciousness, centered in the 1990s, we begin to recognize the far vaster implications of that shift.

Here's the most important part—all the kids born under this Uranus-Neptune conjunction carry within themselves the hologram of this new world. There was a phrase that was popular back then, one that seems to be fading from general usage lately—that these kids were the "*indigo children*." People sensed something different about them—that they carry within themselves the seeds of a new way of being human.

What about the synthesis of science and spirituality? Sure—Uranus has that "science" feeling to it, and Neptune is surely spiritual. I think this new wave of humans will not feel the need to put the Grand Canyon between mysticism and science any longer.

The one thing I feel absolutely confident in saying is that they will surprise the pants off us all.

We always get change of this magnitude under Uranus-Neptune conjunctions. I've already put a lot of time into it here, so I'll stop. If you are interested in a more in-depth historical overview of the whole thing, let me recommend a recorded lecture I gave on the subject back when it was actually happening. It's available on my website, and it's called *Again The World Ends: Uranus Meets Neptune*. Not to be a shill, but it would make an interesting gift for anyone you know who was born in the early 1990s. They are carrying this hologram inside themselves, and they are getting old enough to wrestle with it.

18

NEPTUNE AND PLUTO, AND BEYOND

We've looked at Neptune in aspect individually to the Sun and to each of the planets from Mercury all the way out through Uranus. Neptune can't aspect itself, at least not in the context of a natal chart—sorry kids, nobody gets more than one Neptune.

That leaves us with Neptune-Pluto aspects.

I will be relatively brief here, because we covered this topic earlier in fairly exhaustive fashion when we talked about the ongoing Neptune-Pluto sextile—an aspect that almost everyone alive today has. In quick summary, we are looking at *an emerging global paradigm that involves the synthesis of Plutonian psychology and Neptunian spirituality*. I suspect we may come to a time when the two words become synonymous—or disappear entirely, to be replaced by some new word that refers to them both at once.

Because of the strange universality of this Pluto-Neptune sextile, essentially everyone on the planet is part of this process now. That covers a wide range of humans, of course—and a wide range of human responses to the possibilities this sextile represents, from the lowest to the highest.

In a sense, evolutionary astrology is a good representation of the higher potential inherent in this combination. One way I like to define evolutionary astrology is *the synthesis of astrology with ancient metaphysics and modern psychology*. Evolutionary astrology is all about consciousness, past lives, psychic phenomena, energy healing, contacts with the spirit world—the whole nine yards of subject matter that would get you thrown out of a modern university psychology department. It is pure Neptune, in other words—pure human mysticism.

But evolutionary astrology is also very hard-hitting psychologically. Nobody gets away with a "flight into Light," so to speak. Let's say you have transiting Pluto squaring your fourth house Saturn, and maybe it's time to deal with your anger at your father. Forgive him? Not so fast—before you can forgive him, you've got to get in touch with the part of you that wants to murder him. I hope you're laughing. That line makes me laugh too. My point is that *evolutionary astrology embodies the Pluto-Neptune sextile*. We really are on the cutting edge here, synthesizing spirituality and psychology.

At what moment in time did the term "evolutionary astrology" emerge and start take hold in the culture? I chronicled that story, as I understand it, briefly in my book *Yesterday's Sky*. Basically, my view is that the movement arose organically as the result of the combined work of several people—many of whom would not call themselves evolutionary astrologers. Could we have done it without Dane Rudhyar? I don't think so. Could we have done it without the English Theosophical astrologers of the nineteenth and early twentieth centuries? I don't think so. And of course we have many modern astrologers to acknowledge for their unique contributions: Jeffrey Wolf Green, Martin Schulman, Stephen Arroyo, Patricia Walsh, Jan Spiller—basically, anyone and everyone who brought reincarnation into the fold with psychological astrology.

My point here is that the term "evolutionary astrology" emerged right on synchronistic schedule with the ongoing sextile of Pluto and Neptune. It has flowered under that stimulus, a reflection of a vast impulse that arose like a tide in the collective awareness. Its roots are older—ancient, really. But the practice itself is part of the present cultural wave.

And of course the Pluto-Neptune sextile is not just about evolutionary astrology. Under this transit we have also seen the emergence of *transpersonal and archetypal psychology, energy-healing, body-mind-spirit integration, and parapsychology* as legitimate fields of study.

All of you have this sextile in your chart. Some of you have it placed very prominently—that naturally ties you more closely to the unfolding process. Some of you were born between late 1983 and early 1995, with Pluto in its own sign, Scorpio. With that signature you are carrying more of the juju of the *psychological* side of this revolution, helping to establish a new human relationship with the unconscious—and, really, with many things we humans have been so scared of for so long that we have demonized them. You're sitting down to dinner with those demons, brave souls—and thank you for that. You are an essential part of this evolutionary process.

There are some young ones now, born after Neptune entered Pisces in 2011 and 2012, who will be Earth's new mystics. I suspect they will be defining spirituality in a post-religious age—whatever that will mean. I don't claim to know what it means, but I believe that, in their bones, they do. And that remarkable generation of souls has of course just begun to show up for earthly roll call—most of them are still hanging around in the bardo, not yet born. And some of them are lying in hospices, waiting to catch the next bus out.

But they'll be back.

This Neptune-Pluto process is ongoing. What an exciting time to be alive!

THE DARK SIDE

Yikes, just read the newspapers. Pluto deals with all the manifestations of the unconscious mind, including the most nightmarish ones. Neptune, as we have been exploring, correlates with madness and delusion. *Just think of what happens when the dark side of religion gets in bed with unresolved human rage, human fear, and human projection.* These two devils have been stimulating and exciting each other since World War II—in fact, just look at World War II and you'll see some excellent illustrations of all this. The nightmare of Nazism, the nightmare of Hiroshima ... take it forward through the sheer madness of the Cold War—what an example of simple psychological projection that was! We feared the old Soviet Union and they feared us, so we each projected our own shadow onto the other. And of course, subsequent history suggests there never was a serious intent on either side to actually *start* a nuclear war; it was all in our heads. Oops, a near approach to accidental Armageddon, gazillions of dollars and rubles down the toilet—and how many schools not built?

Take it right up to the present with the religiously-inspired terrorists on all sides—it's all Pluto and Neptune "exciting" each other in ways that illustrate the dark side. And how many souls are addicted to all that madness?

Part Three

Neptune in the Twelve Houses

19

HOW NEPTUNE INTERACTS WITH HOUSE SYMBOLISM

Back to our basic *mappa mundi* for a moment: where are we in our investigations? We now have a broad sense of the role that Neptune plays in the human psyche. We have explored some one-size-fits-all suggestions about how humans might care for their own souls and spiritual well-being:

- Universally, we all benefit from quiet, reflective time
- Practicing compassion is good for all of us.
- Being wary of how opinions create unnatural walls of separation between the self and the cosmos helps us keep our hearts open.
- We all need that inner "map of the galaxy" with that arrow indicating "*You Are Here*" to help us keep perspective on our little dramas.

All of that applies to everybody. All of that is intrinsic to Neptune's fundamental nature, at least at its higher levels of expression. All of that flies under the banner of our ruling metaphor—that taking care of our souls boils down to window-washing. We've got to keep that Neptunian glass as transparent and free from distortion as we possibly can.

But for each one of us, beyond those broad statements, there are *specific evolutionary techniques indicated in our birthcharts*—spiritual techniques of dazzling efficacy, custom-designed to impact our blind spots and open our inner eyes, propelling us as rapidly as possible toward illumination and enlightenment.

In the previous section of this seminar, we began to let Neptune reveal its specific, individual messages via a consideration of how it is flavored by aspects to various planets—for instance, my Neptune-Sun square suggests a different path than your Neptune-Mercury trine, and so on. In this section, we take the chart's message further by thinking about the differing meanings of Neptune in each of the twelve houses of the chart.

THE HOUSES

So what are the astrological houses? Concretely, they are very simple. They answer the question: *at your birth, where would we have to point in the sky in order to be aiming at Mars or Mercury or any of the others?* Overhead? To the western horizon? Down below the earth?

Houses are at the core of astrological theory—but they are often misunderstood in practice. Specifically, there is a pervasive tendency to blur the meaning of signs and houses. In the literature of astrology, we often encounter a phrase such as, "If your Neptune is in the ninth house or Sagittarius . . ." And since in either case we read the same words of interpretation, logic dictates that the astrologer is telling us that there is no difference between the ninth house and the sign Sagittarius. And that is not true! The distinction is not difficult to make, either. When we succeed, our astrological lens becomes—rather literally—twice as clear.

My favorite line is that *we are our signs and we do our houses.* Houses are *behavioral*; signs are *energetic* and *motivational.* Houses are about actions, while signs are about the underlying values and priorities that are reflected in those actions. Is he an introvert or an extrovert? That's a sign question. Does she work long hours? Is her life a constant relationship drama? Those are behavioral questions—house questions, in other words. Signs are *being* and houses are *doing*. Naturally, "being" and "doing" are in a feedback loop with each other; consciousness and action are mutually reflective. Making too sharp a distinction between signs and houses is overly rigid. But keeping a sense of their differences focuses our work more sharply.

In what follows, as we investigate the specific meaning of Neptune in each of the twelve houses, you will see a particular concentration on certain *actions* and certain kinds of *decisions* made at life's *existential crossroads.*

That's house-theory in action.

SOME GUIDELINES FOR THE FOLLOWING CHAPTERS ABOUT NEPTUNE'S HOUSE POSITIONS

At the start of each chapter on the house placements, you'll see a few keywords and keyword phrases about each placement. We will repeat that pattern over each of the twelve chapters.

Always, when I offer these kinds of keywords for a chapter in a book or in a class handout, they are not intended as a full analysis of a configuration. That deeper perspective is what I want to offer here in the pages that follow. The keywords are intended merely as aids to memory. My hope is that these short "tweets" will make a lot more sense after we have been through the deeper perspectives—and that later, as you refer back to them, they will help you recall the heart of the matter.

With each of these thumbnail descriptions of Neptune's various house placements, I have tried to amplify the hints by adding a familiar cliché or a saying that captures some of the spirit of the configuration—for example, in the First House Chapter you'll see: *You can't make an omelet without breaking a few eggs.* There is an *attitude* implicit in that cliché—one that conveys the mood of Neptune in the first house.

In addition, I suggest a few key phrases for *Leaking Energy.* The phrases apply to the ways we can leak energy with that particular placement. They are meant to telegraph the notion that if we get that Neptune placement wrong, we dissipate our life-force. We have already explored these leakages in broad terms. You'll see house-specific expressions of them here. In each case, we can slip into a deer-in-the-headlights state of paralysis or psychic shock. We can become a ghost in our own life. That will be true, as we will be seeing over the next several chapters, of each and every house placement of Neptune—those symptoms arise, in house-specific fashion, whenever we miss the higher potentials of the configuration.

The bottom line, still thinking of "leaking energy," is that if we fail to rise to Neptune's higher range of potentials, we will surely have a staring contest with the lower ones. We will forget about our *You Are Here* arrow on the galactic map; we will have no concept of *what this will mean in five hundred years.* So, what happens? We worry. We squander our energy in trivial dramas.

Those are just some key ideas. Most of them will apply across the board to all of the Neptune house placements—but we will also see how the first house can tilt all that in a different direction than the fourth house does. Let's get on with the show and look specifically at our first house placement: Neptune in the first house.

20

NEPTUNE IN THE FIRST HOUSE

Seemingly selfish or egocentric actions facilitate the evolution of consciousness. Leadership. Defense of boundaries. Growth-triggering experience claimed assertively.

You can't make an omelet without breaking a few eggs.

Leaking Energy: *A deer-in-the-headlights state of paralysis or psychic shock. Feeling trapped in a "role." Watching one's life in a daze, as if it were a movie.*

Roll the drums and blow the trumpets: anything in the first house is pivotal in our understanding of a birthchart. Such a planet is "in the Ascendant"—not necessarily *on* the Ascendant, but *in* it. That statement helps us remember that the ascending degree is really just the cusp of the entire first house, and cusps are always simply more concentrated versions of the entire house that follows.

I think of any planet there, in the Ascendant, as simply being *in the spotlight*. The person will be deeply identified with its energy, both subjectively and also socially and visibly—he or she will be tagged as the embodiment of that planetary archetype by everyone around him or her, even if they don't know astrological jargon.

So, as soon as we see Neptune in the first house, we immediately know that the person is a certifiable, card-carrying *Neptunian.* We don't need to know anything more about the chart to recognize that much. If you have Neptune in the first house, then this book is for you, period.

We can be more precise about it than that. The first house has a very specific meaning, and this will quickly get us into much more personal territory than the idea that you have "a big Neptune."

The Ascendant—the sign that was literally dawning when you were born—represents *how you dawn on people.* At the Ascendant, we attempt a difficult task: to *translate the multidimensional, paradoxical realities of our inner lives into the relatively two-dimensional world of actions and choices.* Of all the lives you might live, which one will you actually live? Of all the different people you could be, whom do you choose to be? We have to edit ourselves so much, and sometimes the choices feel brutally black and white, when our feelings are actually shades of gray. Will you have the baby or not? Will you marry X or Y—even though you love them both? Those are first house dilemmas. It is the house of hard choices.

We might make a characterological statement about a person, such as, "She is shy." Now, how exactly do we know that somebody is shy? Well, she walks into a room full of strangers with her eyes downcast and seeks out a familiar face at a table in the corner. "Shyness" is a word that refers to a certain quality of psychological energy. *But shyness becomes visible through action.* The quintessential, internal qualities of the personality make behavioral choices in the world. And thus our energetic potential is crystallized in the world of concrete action. That is the core of our understanding of the Ascendant—it is how we *translate our psychic essence into specific worldly expression.* Thus, anything connected with the Ascendant or the first house has a certain quality of the *obvious* about it. Anyone can see it. No one can hide it.

More broadly, the signature of any planet in the first house is vividly present in the biographical narrative of a person's life. This is one of the reasons that astrologers tend to put so much emphasis on any planet in the first house—it is simply because everyone can recognize it so clearly. It is absolutely evident in a person's repertoire of behaviors.

Note that I haven't described Neptune specifically yet, I am building a foundation for our specific understanding of having Neptune there, in the Ascendant.

The first house is *expressed*; we can call it our *style.* People with a lot of planets in the first house "have a lot of style." That doesn't mean they're always stylish in the sense that they're necessarily fashionistas or anything like that. *But you remember them.* They have presence. They are the embodiment of an archetype. Because of that, you often find them in positions of influence or leadership. It will get a little trickier with Neptune, of course—Neptune can fade into the background—but, as we will see, these ideas are the basic DNA of understanding the healthy functioning of *any* first house planet, including Neptune. Sometimes a person with Neptune here finds himself or herself in a position of overt leadership, but other times it's more subtle, manifesting as a kind of subliminal influence upon others—and that latter observation carries a bit more of the Neptunian fingerprint.

There are people who *set styles*—whose vibrations make a strong impact upon a social environment. With some planets placed here, the effect is quite evident. These are people who kind of "take over," some of them naturally and gracefully, others more brashly. That's typical of the first house across the board. With Neptune in the first, we see the same effect, although it operates less in the manifest realm of ego and more in the subtle realm of psychic influence.

I am still going back and forth between the general meaning of planets in the first house and the specific meaning of Neptune here. You probably already sense which way the wind is blowing in terms of Neptune's presence in this part of the chart: *there is an absolutely fundamental tension between the meaning of Neptune and the nature of the first house.* It's ego versus transcendence once again. But let's complete our foundation before we dive into unraveling that paradox. We need to look at the dark side of the first house to complete the picture.

If you are interacting with someone with a strong first house, you might find that the person seems to "take up too much space." He or she seems to be claiming too much influence over other people—or over you. You might experience that person as *bossy* or *pushy*. This is kind of a delicate moment. I'm not saying that a crowded first house makes a person bossy or pushy. That is not fair. It can be the case, but such misbehavior is fully over into shadow territory. What I am saying here is a little different—that a person with a strong first house may very well be *perceived* as bossy, self-centered, or pushy.

The key lies in understanding that such risk is implicit in the realities of leadership. A leader has to make hard decisions in an imperfect world. Even a good leader will sometimes have to make a choice that involves treating someone unfairly—in order to avoid treating ten other people unfairly. And when that happens, the leader will probably be criticized as unfair, insensitive, or dictatorial by the person who got the short end of the stick.

So, in being a good leader, sometimes you have to hurt people. *You can't make an omelet without breaking a few eggs.* There's never been a good leader who has been free of the accusation of insensitivity and selfishness. Sometimes the accusation is fair, sometimes it's not.

What I'm getting at here is right in the heart of the evolutionary path represented by the first house in general. And I am still speaking of it across the board, no matter what specific planets lie there—Neptune included. *The soul lesson here involves recognizing that whether you are influencing others or simply leading your own life, you have a right to take up some space.* You have a right not to be manipulated by shame or guilt-rays aimed at you. You are the boss, at least in your own life.

These are healthy, positive first house energies. But every front has a back. The first house, when emphasized, can indeed simply be selfish. With that said, we must also recognize that "selfishness" is always at least somewhat in the eye of the beholder. It may be real, or it may be perceived as real.

Now we can wrestle directly with the meaning of Neptune in the first house. We already know that a person with this configuration is simply very Neptunian. But we can take it further—we are finally ready to face what a truly weird combination of energies this structure represents.

Neptune—transcendent, without opinion, transparent, letting things be as they are, not resisting, turning the other cheek, surrendering. Those are Neptunian words. *And none of them fit the first house at all!* There's our dilemma. Where it gets slippery is the attempt to reconcile *Neptunian selflessness with first house selfishness.* How can you turn left and right at the same time? The obvious answer—you can't. How can selfishness serve your spirituality?

There is an answer, as we will see, but it is not so obvious. There are ways to get it right, but let's be clear: it can be pretty confusing to have Neptune in the first house!

Here's how the two archetypes come together. *There are times when we need to be aggressive or even selfish in pursuit of our spiritual goals.* There are times when choosing your right—and righteous—soul-path is going to frustrate or frighten or threaten other people.

Too bad for them! Whose life is it anyway? There's the spirit of Neptune in the first house.

A woman in her fifties came to me for a reading. She had Neptune in Libra in the first house, with no other planets there to confuse things, and Libra itself on the Ascendant. She had been a Roman Catholic nun most of her life, but had recently left the Order. She told me that when she was nineteen, she informed her parents of her intention to enter the convent. They didn't like it. They wanted her to marry and have children so they could have grandchildren. And she had to say to them, "Sorry, Mom and Dad. Your sweet dream of holding your grandchildren on your knee—*kiss it goodbye.*"

She didn't put it like that, but that was the essence of it—"Dad and Mom, I am off to the convent, deal with it."

Remember that at the simplest level, a planet in the first house has a lot to do with your style, your "energy," your vibrations. Accordingly, this ex-nun had a Neptunian and Libran style. Personally, as is often the case with nuns, she was self-effacing, gentle, and sensitive—Neptunian, in other words.

But the bottom line was that she had to *claim her right to be a nun*—even though it was going to break the hearts of her parents. Her "selfishness" was a tool that her spirituality needed to use. Synchronistically, she attracted that particular evolutionary challenge into her life. She got it right, I think. She made the hard choice to take care of herself even though it created pain for her parents.

What I have told you here is the story she actually related to me. The story she didn't tell me—but that she was actually living—was that she had recently left the Order. And I am sure there were other nuns who didn't appreciate the choice she made to leave—nuns who were threatened by the fact that she chose to say, "This cloistered style of life is not feeding me spiritually any longer." Of course, that action of hers would be threatening to at least some of the other Sisters who had made that sacrifice and committed to that path. And she had to say to them, "Sorry. Adios, I'm out of here."

Let's take a different tack. Remember, anything in the first house is connected with "the mask we wear in the world." But Neptune's nature is the polar opposite of any mask at all—it is about the trans-Neptunian spaciousness, the clear windowpane, the luminous empty sky. This presents a serious dilemma because when the phone rings, you can't pick it up and say, "Om."

Here I sit before you doing *absolutely fantastic Steven Forrest impressions.* Am I really Steven Forrest? Are you your name? You're not that really, not in any ultimate sense. Are you your appearance, your present station in life, your age? They change constantly. You aren't those things—not ultimately. You are something ancient that has incarnated in the body of an intelligent, social primate living on the third stone from the Sun. This imagery is a way to get very quickly and directly to Neptune. I am *doing Steven Forrest impressions*—and you are doing "impressions" of whoever you are. But, really, you are *the thing that is looking through your eyes.* You are the clear blue sky behind it all.

There's wisdom in all that. Ask any mystic from any tradition. But it also contains, as we meditate upon those words, a certain *distancing from the solar personality.* We see that edgy Neptunian fingerprint—what will my personality matter in five hundred years? So what does it matter what I do? What does it matter what stand I take? Let me simply flow with everything. All of that can sound pretty good, but it sort of depends on what you're flowing with. We can flow right down the sewage pipes.

So let's say you have Neptune in the first house. As a little thought-experiment, we maroon you on an island in the South Pacific—you and 1,122 neo-Nazi skinheads—for a year. *And, with that Neptune in the first, you can probably find a way to get along with neo-Nazi skinheads.* You will find something decent and human in many of them. That's Neptune—compassion for all beings, nonresistance. You will find a way to get over yourself enough to build a bridge to a bunch of neo-Nazi skinheads.

Is that good for you? Did I just praise you or did I criticize you? Talk about essay questions, right? And who would you be after a year on that desert island? Remember, as a Neptunian, you are very sensitive to environmental influences. Maybe, after a year, you've found the inner neo-Nazi skinhead.

Bottom line, with Neptune in the first house, there is a potentially *chameleon-like* quality to your outward persona. You wear the *mask of the master actor*—and in fact you would literally be good on stage, able to play many different kinds of roles. But with Neptune in the first, you have to watch which "island" you're marooned on, which role you play. And the key to getting that right lies in a certain quality of consciously-directed selfishness.

Here's an image straight out of Central Casting: a woman with this Neptune configuration finds herself sitting at the country club bar even though she's not at heart a country club kind of person. Let's add that she's not a racist. Somebody at the bar makes a racist quip, and everyone chuckles. *She chuckles too.* She fits in there at the bar because that's the society she was born into. *She learned the role.*

But how does she feel, as she goes through the motions of being somebody she isn't? The answer is very simple: *she feels like an actor on stage.* Because that is what she is. And that is one face of the dark Neptune in the first house. We can be so flowingly adaptable that we "adapt away" our own lives, squandering them. In work, in society, in relationship, we can play roles that don't reflect who we actually are—just like a skilled actor.

How do we address that risk? What we need in order to heal it—or avoid it entirely—is some *healthy first house Neptunian ego.* Remember our basics here: when we do that, people who don't like it will label it selfishness. Let them! It's your life.

Positively, with Neptune in the first, who are you actually? What do you truly want? What does your life look like when you are not acting? What do we mean exactly by "some healthy first house Neptunian ego?"

Answering those questions well and clearly is how to avoid the dark traps we have described—and when you are sane and real and authentic, your honest, self-aware answer is: *I am a mystic. I am here in this world exploring consciousness.* What you are here in this world to claim is *Neptunian experience.* That's what you actually want. That is who you really are.

"Neptunian experience" is a big subject; it can take a lot of forms. But as a broad generalization, you want to be *on some kind of the spiritual path.* But let's be wary: that term—spiritual path—can be a little too pat. There are many different spiritual paths. In a way, exploring their variety is what this whole book is about. But which path is yours? To focus your wise first house Neptunian selfishness helpfully, you need an answer. Astrologically, that question leads quickly to others. What sign does your Neptune occupy? What aspects does it make? What does the rest of your chart look like?

There's your spiritual path—at least insofar as we can determine it astrologically. The answer would be very individual, but we can count on certain elements being present. With Neptune in the first house, you are here on Earth *exploring the nature of consciousness.* To do that, you need to *assertively claim certain kinds of experience* as catalysts for that exploration. Neptune in Sagittarius? Travel might be a part of it. Neptune conjunct Mercury? Teachers and teachings trigger your evolution.

In every case, you need to lead your spiritual life, not follow it. You'll need your ego working in alliance with your soul in order to claim those catalytic experiences. If you succeed, you will have a significant impact on the soul-lives of other people—you will take on the persona of a *spiritual leader* in some sense of the word.

Claim those experiences forcefully and decisively or you will become a ghost in the world, an actor on the stage of your life. The choice is yours. Those are the terms of the soul-contract you signed. And you can't make that particular omelet without breaking a few eggs. *Even though it is hard for you to accept this, get used to the fact that in following your natural path you will surely hurt some people's feelings.* You will frustrate some people. A few acts of selfishness on your part will be the salad course for spiritual breakthroughs. That pattern will show up again and again in your life. Your soul has manifested these evolutionary conditions, and you can reap the fruits of those actions. *Don't turn the other cheek.* Take a stand. Claim what you need for yourself. Others will benefit from your actions in the sweet by and by.

In this lifetime, *enlightened selfishness* serves your soul.

21

NEPTUNE IN THE SECOND HOUSE

Honoring your attainments on the Path—and avoiding the underestimation of your actual evolutionary state. Choosing appropriate and effective levels of inner practice. Being "willing to pay for it." Benefits deriving from relationship with sacred objects: statues, stones, relics. Proving one's self spiritually.

Bet the house.

Leaking Energy: *Wasting time on practices that are no longer useful given your actual evolutionary condition. Dithering self-doubt. Complications stemming from financial confusion.*

Classically, the second house is called the house of money. We will soon see that its actual meaning carries us far beyond the financial realm, and not just because we are talking about lofty Neptunian concerns—in fact, when we consider its lower expressions, we will see that money ranks near the top of the list of people's favorite Neptunian addictions.

In the second house, we often encounter issues of *self-confidence*, along with actual financial ones. The key is that the former can masquerade as the latter. In the second house, we wrestle with our willingness to take care of ourselves, or reward ourselves, or to be kind to ourselves. We wonder *if we have what it takes.* These are the psychological dimensions of the second house. In thinking about Neptune in this position, we will need to deal with them—as well as with the more purely practical financial and material dimensions of the symbolism.

But let's start with money, plain and simple.

Neptune and money? Hey, isn't Neptune supposed to be *spiritual*? Money is an extremely symbolic subject as well as a practical one. It invokes strong emotional reactions. In our culture, we often idolize rich people—and then resent them for their wealth. We simultaneously wish that we *were* them and delight in their misfortunes. And how do we feel when we hear about some "expensive Hollywood guru" taking home several million dollars a year? Smell a rat? Obviously, in thinking about Neptune in the second house, we have some labyrinths of prejudice to thread.

Say you have Neptune in the second. Here's a question for you: *How much are you willing to invest financially in your own spiritual journey?* This is a totally concrete, dollars-and-cents question. If you're not willing to invest financially in your spiritual journey, what does that say about you? What does that say about how much you value the spiritual journey—or how much you value yourself? We bounce right back to questions of self-worth, in other words.

Sometimes, given the realities of modern life, it costs money to take care of your soul. That feels uncomfortable to say, and I suspect it sounds a little uncomfortable to hear. We can always sit in meditation—that's free and always will be. But there are certain experiences we might need in order to support that inner journey. And a lack of money—perceived or real—can potentially place an obstacle between us and having those experiences. If you have Neptune in the second house, there's a good chance that issue is going to get stirred up. And we need to be alert to the possibility that the real issue is self-worth, with money only acting as a kind of paper tiger.

Somewhere out there in the world is a person who would love to be part of my astrologer apprenticeship program, but resists attending because he says he "can't afford it." I'm using the words "can't afford it," but I have the phrase in quotation marks. Why? A lack of money is simply reality sometimes.

I want to be really careful here not to pontificate. I am not one of those wealthy, privileged New Age types who believes that people are only poor because "they've chosen to manifest poverty." A lot of what is popularly called "prosperity consciousness" teaching is, in my opinion, nothing but tarted-up materialism and nose-in-the-air, class-based condescension. There are people who are genuinely disadvantaged. Poverty is a disease. It's a social disorder and a terrible, grinding thing. I want to express that loudly and clearly before continuing.

But I also want to recognize that in this particular story of the person who claims he "can't afford" to attend an astrology workshop he really wants to experience that maybe—just maybe—there's more to the story than a lack of funds. Possibly, there are other issues that are not entirely financial, but rather have to do with his lack of confidence, or perhaps a weak sense of self-worth. A lack of cash might be a literal reality. But what if he were also afraid that he didn't know enough astrology? What if he were afraid that no one would like him? Or that he would make a fool of himself? *What if his father used to call him stupid so often that he began to believe it?* Taking refuge in a "lack of money" gets him off the hook. It's a bulletproof argument for not taking any risks.

Let me add something to the story: that it might be really good for his spiritually to attend the workshop. If he talks himself out of making the effort to attend—even if it's financially a stretch—he might miss out on an experience that would have fed his soul just because he didn't feel worthy of claiming it.

Let's not avoid the concrete financial reality either: attending a workshop, especially one he has to travel to, might cost a thousand bucks. For most of us, that is a substantial sum. But consider it this way: *Is the care of his soul worth a thousand bucks?*

Still sticking with money, but widening our horizons a little—why is money so popular? We laugh because the answer is rather obvious—money buys food and shelter. And of course, money buys more than that. Money buys fun, money buys status, money buys comfort and relative safety. But at the most primal level, we look at the second house as *the material basis of physical survival.* Food is a good example of that. Nobody lasts long without food. And most of us would be dead in less than three days if we had no water. These are totally concrete, second house realities. In the days before money, these are what the second house meant.

Calling the second house "the material basis of survival" aims our attention at its raw heart. It also directs us right back to its psychological dimension—*if outwardly you have no food, then inwardly you are definitely going to feel insecure.*

With Neptune there, maybe it does you good to affirm the fact that you can go a day without food—to remind yourself that your spirit can be strong enough to push through that wall of hunger, and to embrace, Neptune-fashion, your ultimate physical insecurity in this universe. In other words, literally *fasting* is a second house Neptune practice.

More broadly, throughout human history we see traditions of *austerity* among mystics. Not only mystics fasting, but the monk sleeping under one thin blanket in the Irish winter, yogis facing long periods of solitude—all the spiritual variations on the theme of *doing without.* This kind of thinking—austerity-as-a-spiritual-path—is almost totally out of style in the modern world, and yet it reflects a long tradition. Maybe our spiritual ancestors were not completely wrong about that process. Maybe that method still works. So, with Neptune in the second, you might benefit enormously from fasting or from intentionally putting yourself through other deprivations for spiritual ends.

This is shaky ground, as excesses of "doing-without" can arise here, and they represent one extreme expression of the dark side of this configuration. The aim is not to hurt yourself, but rather to *let the inner animal know who's boss.* That is an ancient spiritual tradition. Monks, mendicants, and native Medicine people have been doing it for millennia. And again, such practices affirm that edgy Neptunian wisdom: we are not ultimately these bodies; there is no safety in them and no safe ground to stand upon except the clear, luminous core of our eternal windowpane.

A classic form of monastic austerity is poverty itself. Spiritual figures throughout history have often lived very simply, intentionally. Monks and nuns have taken *vows of holy poverty.* Of course there is nothing intrinsically holy about poverty! Poverty is just an outward condition, that's all. But the human attachment to money and its symbolism is very strong. We live in a culture that makes a god out of money. There is powerful medicine in turning away from that madness, in affirming that our natures are ultimately spiritual rather than material. With Neptune in the second house, you might benefit from such simplicity. Periods in which you lack money—provided that they are used consciously—can be good for you. Accordingly, depending on your karma, you might draw such times into your life. They can be a helpful school for learning where your treasure really lies.

By the same synchronistic token, with Neptune in the second house, you might equally draw periods of wealth into your life. There is no better school for wrestling with the fierce and beguiling *glamour* of money.

"So, Steve, does my Neptune in the second house mean I'll be rich or poor? Just give me a straight answer, please." And here's my straight answer: "Yes." I say that because one of the real meanings of this configuration is that you're dealing with the question of *how much power you are going to give to money in your life*. Wealth can be an even greater challenge here than poverty.

On the dark side, let's take a short step to another obvious second house Neptune pitfall: simply *becoming addicted to money*. Down that road, we see the fundamentally insecure man who needs everyone in the room to know that he drives a Porsche, keeps apartments in the French Quarter and Montreux, only drinks the finest wine, has beautiful buxom babes on both arms, and so forth. You know the type. Such a person is trying to compensate for self-doubt by shoring up the ego with physical objects—and of course, even those "babes" are objects to him. He has no idea who they are.

The irony is, his gambit doesn't work. He is giving too much power to money—power it does not actually possess.

Equally, though, we might look to a person obsessed with *financial fears*, thinking of himself or herself in terms of poverty, chronically terrified of "what might happen." Such a person is just as addicted to money as the show-off we just described. That's a second house Neptune trap too: *endless money-worries*, driven by the illusion that there is some bank account level at which one has attained safety in this world. Often such worries have the additional Neptunian signature of being groundless neurotic fantasies.

One very practical road to go down with Neptune in the second house is to speak of *material possessions that might be relevant to our spiritual lives*. Let's say a woman born with this configuration, after long years of negotiations with herself, finally coughs up sixty dollars for a meditation cushion. She finds it helps her meditation practice a lot, that it's easier to hold the right posture, and it gives her the physical stability that allows her meditation to occur in an undistracted fashion. For years, she dithered, trying to make do with pillows. Buying a cushion seems like such a trivial thing, and yet it isn't. The meditation cushion is a synchronistic expression of her Neptunian evolutionary issues. Does she love herself enough to invest sixty dollars in her own spirituality? Again, she is wrestling spiritually with the question of the power of money in her life.

We might point out that, assuming that she is even in the lower reaches of the middle class, it has probably been many years since she didn't actually have sixty bucks. That's not the issue—that's a smokescreen.

Maybe a person comes to a place in his or her journey where there would be benefit in having some kind of *religious or spiritual icon* as a focus for meditation or prayer—a crucifix, or a statue of the Goddess or the Buddha, or something like that. Maybe she needs an incense burner. Maybe he needs to spend some money on helpful, inspiring books. These are all physical objects, and yet they can be relevant to Neptunian work.

What might stop you from taking the simple action of giving yourself such tools? What might stop you from supporting yourself in using every precious minute of this incarnation as efficiently as possible? It's usually not actually a lack of money. More likely, it is self-doubt or an underlying penchant for self-punishment.

Now let's get right to the heart of the matter. The spiritual path, broadly and inclusively defined, embraces so many different levels and practices. They range from mundane things, such as attending church on Easter, up to nine-day fasts in the desert. *Earth is kindergarten through the twelfth grade.* There are many primitive souls here. Let's respect them and have compassion for the suffering they inevitably create for themselves. They give evidence of their condition through their abject materialism, by a denial of spirituality, by believing that violence will solve things. We're not making fun of them, we're not busy feeling superior to them—we're just looking at them with clear Neptunian eyes.

And then, at the other end of the spectrum, we have, for one example, the Dalai Lama. To me, he illustrates a very lofty state of Neptunian evolution.

Now imagine that I have dinner with the Dalai Lama—a happy thought. Halfway through the meal, I put down my fork and I say, "Dalai, I hope this doesn't seem pretentious of me, but I've been meditating now for several months, and I'd like to share a few tips with you."

I hope you're laughing! I am laughing too. What's wrong with this picture? Obviously, I am in no position to share meditation tips with His Holiness the Dalai Lama. He is in a higher grade than me.

There is a certain grace in not overestimating ourselves spiritually—in not falling into *spiritual pride*. Earlier we talked about that as a possible Neptune-Jupiter trap. But with Neptune in the second house, the danger lies in precisely the opposite direction: *too much self-doubt in mystical matters*. The aim with this configuration is not to avoid spiritual inflation—that is generally not an issue here—but rather to *attain clarity about exactly where we are on the spiritual map*. If we have clarity about where we are in the journey, we will avoid inflation and egoism. But we will also avoid the equal and opposite error of deflation—which is a soul-cage very much available to you if you were born with this configuration.

In the Himalayas, there are yogis in caves fasting and meditating on generosity toward all beings. In rural Mississippi, there are Evangelical preachers fulminating against "the heathens and their sinful ways." *Let's honor both lineages as forms of spiritual practice*. There's our Neptunian compassion; there's our Neptunian clarity—our freedom from putting a veil of opinion between us and reality. But here's the point: if we took a nice old grandmother out of that congregation in Mississippi and sat her down in a Himalayan cave, *we would only frighten the poor thing*. She would not benefit. Such practice is too fierce for her; she is not yet sufficiently evolved. She probably *needs* to be sitting in that church, singing hymns. It's good for her. And if we took that yogi out of the cave and sat him down in that rural church, he would be respectful of these simple souls doing their simple practice, but *he would not benefit from being there*. He is already too advanced to be helped by that kind of church.

So, why are you sitting in church on Sunday when you should be fasting in a Himalayan cave? There's the Neptune-in-the-second question! I hope it is obvious to everyone that I am speaking figuratively. *The point is that if you underestimate yourself spiritually, you will be drawn to practices that are no longer effective for you*. That's the core trap for people with Neptune in the second house. That is the heart of the matter.

There are Neptunian practices that are appropriate for each evolutionary level. With Neptune in the second house, the aim is to know objectively and in clear-eyed fashion where you are in the journey and to behave accordingly. The main distorting risk is self-doubt, which leads to practices and beliefs that do not trigger any real progress. That innocent mistake quickly blossoms into a feeling of being lost, of treading water, of being spiritually jaded or stale.

Why? Ultimately, it is because we have not trusted ourselves enough. We haven't given ourselves the tools we need, we have not challenged ourselves enough, and we haven't given ourselves a practice that actually moves us forward.

With Neptune in the second house, it all boils down to self-love—with a clear eye.

22

NEPTUNE IN THE THIRD HOUSE

The five senses are attuning to the Otherworld. Visions. Free-associative conversation with the Divine; "Channeling." Learning. Reading omens, symbols, and synchronicities. Clairvoyance.

I didn't know I knew that.

Leaking Energy: *Worry. Scattered speech and thoughts. Wool-gathering. Dithering. Not believing your own eyes.*

A weird opening line here: "The five senses are attuning to the Otherworld." Sounds eerie, doesn't it? It actually can be. By "Otherworld," I mean the dimensions beyond our three-dimensional world—the ones the mystics have been talking about since we were chipping stones in the Olduvai Gorge, and the ones the physicists have been exploring for the past century or more. We could of course also use our own astrological jargon here and simply call the Otherworld the trans-Neptunian realm.

Conventionally, astrologers think of the third house in connection with *communication*. That's valid; let's begin there.

So, maybe you have Neptune in the third house, and you encounter someone who has gotten wind of the fact that you're interested in metaphysics. She bumps into you in a shopping mall, starts a conversation, and quickly progresses to asking you, "Do you believe that if you visualize yourself being in love with the perfect person that you'll attract that kind of love into your life?" Out of the blue you are confronted with that question. And it's in the framework of a conversation—feel that third house context? You open your mouth and words come tumbling out. And they are exactly the right words. You have the experience of saying something that you *didn't know you knew.*

There's a classic expression of Neptune in the third house. With this configuration, you will have many occasions to say, "I didn't know I knew that."

Neale Donald Walsch wrote a book that was popular a few years ago called *Conversations with God.* The basic premise was that this fellow could just ask God questions and God would answer, taking the form of "a voice in his head." It went like this: "So God, is reincarnation for real?" And he hears an answering voice saying, "Duh . . . yes." At first he was startled by the voice. "What? Who said that? Is that really you, Lord?"

My point is that this is not actually such an unusual experience when you strip it down to its bones. We all sometimes just *know things.* It may not come in words and we may not take it as the literal voice of the Divine—but with Neptune in the third, words are a likely channel.

So, what exactly is the nature of that voice inside us? Is it actually God's voice? Calling it "God" is as good a metaphor as any, isn't it? A psychologist might say, "Ah, the unconscious mind!" But as you've seen, we have already drawn at least a fuzzy equal sign between the unconscious mind and the soul. And of course it's not too hard to draw a fuzzy equal sign between the soul and God. "Atman and Brahman are one," in the Hindu version of that Neptunian perspective.

Conversation is a standard third house key word. The term of course generally implies verbal communication. But if a friend told you that she stood before the great marble colossus of *The David* in Florence, Italy, and felt like she was having "a conversation with Michelangelo," you wouldn't bat an eye at her syntax. Communication is indeed the heart of the third house, but not all communication is verbal. All of it, however, is *sensory*, as sight, sound, touch, taste, and odor communicate information about the world to us.

To complete our profile of the third house, along with the familiar five senses, we just have to add the famous "sixth sense" of psychic, extrasensory, or intuitive phenomena—and that "sixth sense" is particularly central to any specific understanding of Neptune's presence in this house.

What happens when we attune our six senses and our mind to the Otherworld? Insights enter the picture. The third house is mental—not as in "crazy," but as in *conceptual* and *cognitive*. With Neptune there, we experience an attraction to metaphysical *ideas, thoughts, and understandings*—spiritually useful mental constructions that can be put into words, more or less.

Let's put our hands together and thank God for all those fantastic one-liners about the spiritual path—every pithy inspirational quote that you could put on a bumper sticker. I say that and it sounds like I'm making fun of them. But these one-liners are often actually complex ideas that are encoded as clichés or familiar sayings. Some of them have their origin in folklore and popular culture. *Be careful what you pray for—you might get it.* Others are scriptural, even though often people don't recognize that. *Do unto others as you would have them do unto you.* Isn't that wonderful advice, actually? Just make yourself innocent, as if you've never heard that saying before—terrific, eh? The words of Jesus. The first time you hear the line and reflect on it, it is utterly profound. The hundredth time you hear it, the reaction is muted: "Yeah, I know." The thousandth time you hear it, it might as well be a parrot or a cuckoo clock. And yet, encoded in all these phrases is real wisdom about how to live. There's an endless list of such phrases we can recall. *Think positively. There are no atheists in foxholes. Be kind to animals. That which does not destroy us makes us stronger. Let go and let God.* And so on.

If you have Neptune in the third house, even these little sayings are useful. Remember them; they will steady you on the path. More broadly, you have reached a place in your evolution where some manner of *spiritual education* is crucial—and it's not just about one-liners. As we go deeper, we'll find that there will be some parallel structures between Neptune in the third house and Neptune in the ninth house. I don't want to confuse things by launching into the ninth house now, but I want to make you aware that I'm going to say some similar things about the two. They both relate to the role that intellect plays in the soul's journey.

We're also going to see some pretty significant differences between them. For starters, the third house is very much about *questions*, as opposed to the ninth house which deals more in answers. Historically, in medieval astrology, the third house was the house of *heresy*. That was because it was opposite the ninth, which was the "House of Religion." And "religion" meant the One True Faith—"answers" again. So what *opposes* the one true faith? The answer, again, was heresy.

And there is nothing more heretical than questions.

With a third house Neptune, you are *cultivating questions* in this lifetime. I always love to quote a wonderful line from the brilliant musician Peter Gabriel, in his song *That Voice Again*, "It's only in uncertainty that we're naked and alive." There's a classic line for anyone with Neptune in the third house—praising that fertile uncertainty that makes us far more "naked and alive" than memorizing someone else's catechism of answers. Peter Gabriel, by the way, actually has Neptune in his third house.

Once again, as I often do in trying to understand the wiring of the deep mind, I revert to acute observations from the Buddhist tradition. They speak of the five senses as we would—eyes and ears, taste and touch, smell. But they often add a sixth one, and it's not so much a psychic sense, but more broadly *the mind itself*. In the Dharma-teachings, the mind is a sixth modality by which we engage the world, and mind itself colors the perceptions of the rest of the senses. I like this approach as we attempt to understand the third house. It represents the senses, but includes the mind's *interpretation* of the sensory data. So the five—or six—senses feed the mind, and the mind turns the perceptions into ideas, interpretations, thoughts—and, of course, opinions.

Let's try to unravel this third house knot, starting with the senses themselves as they interact with Neptunian levels of perception and cognition. Here again is an experience that I imagine every one of us has had. It's kind of a weird one. You're watching somebody teaching. You suddenly flash on this glow around her head. Then it's gone.

Hmm ... that's what you saw, but was it really there? And what do we actually mean by the word "really?" Did you see the teacher's energy body? Did you just actually see her aura? Mystics have always assured us that the human aura is real. They have also assured us that it is possible to see it under certain conditions. They say that, as you evolve, you become more attuned to that Neptunian wavelength of visual perception.

But did you really see it? Sometimes you stare fixedly at anything and it leaves a kind of afterimage on your retina. Could that explain it? You can almost hear Mister Science talking—Get a grip! Stay in reality! Don't be crazy.

On the other hand, maybe you really did see the speaker's aura. *It is only in uncertainty that we are naked and alive.* Let go of your need to know. With Neptune in the third, your senses might play tricks on you. You are human, and that happens. But the symbolism of Neptune in the third house assures us that you have reached a stage in the evolutionary journey where your *bandwidth of perception is beginning to open up, beginning to expand.* You have within you the potential of actually beginning to see the aura, as well as many other phenomena. You also have the potential of entering into a delusional state in which you convince yourself that you saw the aura, when what you just saw was only an afterimage.

Which is it? Remember: in the third house, we learn to live with unanswered questions. *We are heretics; we have no religion to defend.* You do not need to answer the question; you only need to live with it.

You have Neptune in the third house and you're alone in your home one night. *And you swear you hear somebody call your name.* Now, was that voice something in your head? Or were there actually sound waves in the air? Or no sound waves—but rather some more ethereal version of the same thing as your guardian spirit called out to you? The next obvious question: *are you going nuts?* Go to a psychiatrist and report these symptoms and they'll have an easy answer for that question. Yes, definitely nuts! And they have some pills for you . . .

At some point in the soul's upward journey, the senses expand beyond conventional reality. We begin to see that "reality" is, to a great extent, a cultural agreement, and a very limited one. *How much do we miss simply because we have all agreed it is not really there?*

These realizations correlate with a high, conscious response to Neptune in the third house. We are claiming our actual heritage as energy bodies, as ancient *perceivers* in this multidimensional universe. And as you go down this path, you'll find a lot of people who think you're going crazy—probably at times including yourself.

So you may "hear things." You may "see things." You may "smell flowers" when there are no flowers there. I put quotations around those lines because I am quoting the "normal" people—which is yet another word that demands quotations marks.

We sometimes talk about someone who "looks at the world through rose-colored glasses." But we all look at the world through some kind of glasses. No one can see it as it actually is; we consider everything from the perspective of our values, interests, and tastes. One really powerful way of thinking of a planet in the third house is to think of it as your *colored glasses.* It tints the world. With Mars there, you might tend to see the world dialectically—ideas facing off with each other. With Venus there, maybe you see the world through the eyes of an artist. And so on.

What about with Neptune there? *You are seeing the world through the eyes of a mystic—or a dreamer.*

This third house quality of perception tints your thoughts. And your speech rests upon your thoughts. So there is the classic trinity of interacting processes that defines the third house—*perception supporting thought, thought supporting speech.* The third house is tied inextricably to language, but language is the flowering of the other two processes.

Let's take a harder look at that connection. I began this section with a story about a conversation. You respond to a stranger's question about visualizing true love by saying things that you didn't know you knew. Where did those things come from? *Really, where do any of your thoughts or ideas originate?* We open our mouths and just chat with people. What could be more commonplace? But it is really extraordinary when you think about it. Something happens automatically here; speech and thought simply arise out of the psychic depths. You'll get dizzy—or mute—if you think about it too much.

With Neptune in the third, these thoughts and this speech can have the feeling of "channeling." There is a sense of "another being" somehow speaking through us.

That's a complex area, fraught with potentials of genuine delusion. But it's also a real phenomenon. In fact, when you told that stranger something "you didn't know you knew," were you channeling? If not, then where did those words come from? Or if you are just having a chat with someone, and you really start to think about the process ... well, again, you can get vertigo pretty quickly.

Maybe we are all "channeling" all the time—which of course would mean that another word for channeling is simply talking.

All this is a universal third house reality, but it is more vivid with Neptune there. Why? Because Neptune links us so directly to the trans-Neptunian realm. We are directly connected to that transcendent, mysterious source inside us all. Psychic powers are common here—or to put it in more down-to-earth terms, we have a lot of sensory experiences that can't be explained logically. Once more, insights and interests of a metaphysical nature—that is, a Neptunian nature—arise naturally. Poetry—and poetic, or metaphorical language—flow naturally with this configuration. One high flowering of Neptune in the third house is the *brilliant poet or novelist*. Another is the true *spiritual teacher*.

Getting Neptune in the third house wrong typically creates confusion in the mind. There is, in this lower response, a verbal signature of mental chaos that is very typically evident in a person's speech, writing, or thought. Often their ideation is simply disordered. We've all had the experience of listening to a person go on in great passion or irritation about something—and when he is finished, we realize *we have no idea what he was talking about*. He was "all over the map." This particular disorder of mind, manifesting as confusing speech, often correlates with Neptune in the third house. It is typically what happens when the person is choking on the Neptunian flood in his or her own mind. Too many thoughts arise too fast.

To get Neptune in the third house right is, as usual, the cure for getting it wrong. To get it right is to sit in contemplative states. To allow the universe to be complicated and paradoxical. To adjust the mind to a state of some comfort with its innate uncertainty.

Strange how, if we get comfortable enough with that confusion and we're not fighting it, we seem to be able to speak more clearly. We've relaxed enough to let the *whole self speak*. If we're fighting it, there is turbulence in the mind and it comes out as turbulent speech. So we need the *medicine of silent observation*. We need contemplation. And we need to get comfortable with not knowing anything for certain.

If someone came to me experiencing dysfunction with Neptune in the third house and was receptive to the deeper kinds of insights, I would encourage them to sit quietly, in formal meditation, with their eyes open. And to just simply observe what they observe in a state of detachment. Just watch the mind. If they find sitting still to be difficult—and some people do—then I would suggest that they *walk* in a meditative state. The third house, ruled by Mercury, is innately curious, and thus it gets bored easily if it finds itself in a very static environment. We do not need to fight that impulse or make it into an enemy. We cooperate with that need. We stay engaged, we stay active, but we observe the mind. Walking meditation can do that.

Let me add one more idea, and it is a very old one. With our eyes open, we can come to realize that, in a sense, the whole world is mind, the whole world is the content of our meditations. One practical effect of that notion is that the universe is *continuously communicating with us in the form of signs and omens.* You are walking down the street, puzzled by some existential dilemma in your life. Suddenly, out of the psychic depths, a solution arises. You see a workable path ahead. *And in that very instant, the clouds part overhead and you are bathed in rays of sunshine.* In the old days, they would call that a sign or an omen. Another, more modern, word for this phenomenon is *synchronicity.*

You don't need Neptune in the third house for synchronicity to work. It's there for everyone all the time. But with Neptune in the third, one of your soul-contracts in this lifetime is to learn to pay attention to these signs and omens. It is a question of mindfulness—and that is one of those "officially spiritual" terms that quickly free-associates to "the inner life" and the idea that "the kingdom of God is within." But the "kingdom of God" is *without* too! It is everywhere, not just "in" your mind, and it is always feeding back information to you.

With this configuration, if you keep your eyes open, you will find that precious guidance is everywhere.

23

NEPTUNE IN THE FOURTH HOUSE

The need for withdrawal from worldly stimulus. Attention to dreams. Literal darkness; candlelight; moonlight. Literal silence. Acute psychic attunement to the land-energy and local daemons. The search for one's spiritual home.

Into the Great Silence

Leaking Energy: *Navel-gazing. Myopic psychology. Sacrificing one's self to one's family. Losing the sense of the miraculous nature of the outer world. Lack of roots. "Homelessness."*

With Neptune in the fourth house, we again find ourselves in an angular house, where any planet is going to wield a lot more torque in the psyche. A planet in the fourth house is absolutely fundamental to the *roots and the core* of what we are. You might say it correlates with our *myth of our self.* Strip away the layers of somebody's onion and get right down to the person's essence, as if you had slept with him or her in a spirit of love for ten years—there's the heart of the fourth house. With Neptune there, if we strip away the onion layers, we find the *mystic*—or, of course, the drunken escapist.

Either way, this Neptunian energy is operating in a very *emotional* framework—emotion is quite fundamental to the fourth house. We might define it as the house "where psychology happens." Psychology, of course, cannot be reduced to emotion, but it cannot be separated from emotion either. Here, in the fourth house, we encounter the basic engines that drive the psychic states of love, fear, attachment and joy—the whole spectrum of human feelings. In the fourth house we experience them in a very raw and direct fashion. Fourth house people in general tend to be inward, psychological, and subjective. Add the powerful Neptunian sensitivities and you sense how easily such a person can be *overwhelmed by feeling*. In related fashion, we should add that the fourth house, buried under the earth, is *an excellent place to hide*.

Imagine that you are really upset. Something terrible has happened, and you're so shaken that you feel you need to make a real effort to collect yourself. You try to meditate. Good luck, right? So there you are, attempting to sit in meditation, trying to follow your breath, trying to calm the mind. But you're just too upset to meditate. We've all been there. Whatever shock has been delivered to you, you can't get it out of your mind. Emotion is so powerful. It can overwhelm the steadiness, serenity and transparency that are characteristic of all high responses to Neptune.

Thus we see an *emotional* expression of Neptune—there is one face of Neptune in the fourth house. Furthermore, in Neptunian fashion, you are *psychically sensitized* to emotion. To be "psychically sensitive to emotion" is to experience it with almost brutal vividness. With Neptune here, that is your dilemma. Your mind, if you blow this, becomes too upset to focus—too psychologically charged to do its Neptunian work.

So that's the challenge. How do we address it? What does Neptune in the fourth house look like when we are nurturing it skillfully and successfully?

We start off with a very practical strategy. *Whenever we need to, we shield ourselves from all emotional stimulus.* In fact, we shield ourselves from stimulus altogether. We simply *cultivate the quiet of the mind*. I think of a classic meditation metaphor—that we have a glass of water, but the water is dirty, turbid with silt. And if we sit it down and just don't bother it for a while, the dirt settles to the bottom of the glass. Gravity pulls the silt down and the water becomes clear. Meditation implies the same notion—that if you just keep the mind steady for a while, clarity, silence and serenity will naturally arise in it.

This is the spiritual discipline that allows a fourth house Neptune to shine.

Remember that, in practical astrology, the fourth house is the *house of the home*. Thus, there is a powerful *domestic* connection with Neptune in the fourth. Home plays a pivotal role in your spiritual health, positively or negatively. Say you've had a busy, crazy, upsetting day. You come home, walk into your house, and *you close the door to the world behind you*. This is a primal, archetypal fourth house moment. You've closed that door. And maybe you lock it. It's as if you are saying, "So, world—you're out there. Self, you're in here." And the next line: "Ahhh, it feels so good to be home."

It is thus helpful, if you have this configuration, to have *literal walls* between yourself and the world and to log a lot of hours inside them. Those walls are a primal need. With Neptune in the fourth house, you periodically need shielding barriers between yourself and all that worldly stimulus, just so the dirt can fall out of suspension in the water of your consciousness. You need quiet time.

Maybe you've had the kind of day I just described. You close the door behind you, and things start to quiet down a little bit. And the damned telephone rings! Maybe the world has entered your house through the telephone. Maybe what you hear on the telephone upsets you again. This is why the Lord God Almighty created voice mail. Or you can just silence your phone.

With Neptune in the fourth house, in other words, you're going to need more than the physical walls of the house; given the realities of modern life, you're going to need *electronic walls* as well. Consider the dreaded Get Messages button on your computer screen or your cell phone. Maybe you don't need to hit that button when it's been "one of those days." Maybe you need to recognize that it's time to take care of your fourth house Neptune.

One further illustration of a strong response to this domestic dimension of Neptune in the fourth house is to create a *sacred space* in your home—and to use it. It could be an altar, for example—and it might not even be recognizable as such to other people. You don't have to be spiritually pretentious or fancy about it. But you might benefit from having a place in your home that you have made sacred. And, with your deep sensitivity to the *energy of place*, after a while you will notice that good *juju* seems to have accumulated around your altar because you have used it with spiritual intention over an extended period. Just the sight of it creates a stimulus-response, reminding you of your higher Neptunian functions, bringing you back into that spiritual space.

As we dissolve into a fourth house Neptune, a process occurs that is quite analogous to going to sleep. In fact, we might define a particular fourth house meditation as the attempt to *go to sleep without losing consciousness*. How do you do that? It is not such an easy thing to accomplish, but the words focus the intuition on an effective strategy.

More specifically, I would invoke the notion of *lucid dreaming* with Neptune in the fourth house. Which means that in the midst of a dream, you *realize* that you're dreaming. With Neptune in the fourth house, you may have some natural inclination in that direction.

Let's keep perspective here by putting lucid dreaming on our list of a thousand other effective spiritual practices. Charitable giving is a spiritual practice. Doing yoga, going to Temple, practicing *boddhicitta*, saying the rosary—there's a long list of spiritual practices available to you, and lucid dreaming is on it, with an extra asterisk if you have Neptune in the fourth house.

I'm going to sneak up on lucid dreaming by speaking a bit more generally about dreams in the broader, more conventional sense. *With Neptune in the fourth house, your spiritual life is supported and conditioned by dreaming.* Now, almost everybody dreams. Some of us don't remember our dreams. Others do. If you get interested in dreams, you might want to study Jungian dream work or something of that nature. In that world, there is a weird phenomenon which is reported over and over again. Somebody says, "I have difficulty remembering my dreams." And the psychoanalyst says: "Get yourself a notebook and put it beside your bed. Put a flashlight there, and a pencil or a pen. And when you have a dream and it wakes you up, immediately write it down."

What happens? *You find that you are dreaming more frequently*, and you're remembering the dreams in greater detail. Why, exactly? Having the notebook beside your bed has *set an intention in your mind.*

Now here we come to the very Neptunian heart of the matter—what or who, exactly, is having these dreams? The answer, obviously, is you. Or we could say "your mind." But "mind" is a big, slippery word. Dreams do not come from the part of your mind that balances your checkbook. They are more autonomous than that by far. They originate in the deep self—in the trans-Neptunian realm. So, you've told your deep mind what to do and it displays some degree of obedience to your little mind—or some *agreeability*, at least. Thus, by using this dreamwork technique, you are creating a *cooperative alliance between your conscious mind and these deeper, Neptunian layers of your being*. You are bringing them closer together. This is one face of the sacred "psychological" work particularly available to anyone with Neptune in the fourth house.

In much of what I teach, I depend on the Jungian path. I want to underscore that I honor it and acknowledge that my work could not exist without it. God bless Uncle Carl! Where would we be without him? But he famously said, "Thank God I am Jung, and not a Jungian." So I am going to go down a heretical road here.

Imagine a woman who is conditioned by the Jungian view of the world. She's read a lot of his work; she's been in analysis for some years. She is on that good path. Now, she wakes up one morning and realizes that she just had this amazing dream. *But she can't remember it.* "Dammit"—right? That is a familiar experience, of course. Her dream has slipped through her fingers. "I know it was important ... it had something to with ... with ... an *artichoke*." And I'm picturing her as a kind of "cartoon Jungian," just having a fit. She's whining to herself, "Damn, damn, damn! Why couldn't I remember that dream? Now I've failed. It's lost. I can't bring it to my analyst. My shrink will hate me."

All that is a familiar, and rather reflexive, lament among people doing psychological dreamwork. The dream is forgotten, and so it is lost treasure, squandered, wasted and of no use.

Let's question the basic assumptions underlying that attitude. Just because this little cork floating in the ocean of your consciousness—this little cork that we call the conscious mind—couldn't do some kind of intellectual exercise based on that dream, is *everything truly lost and wasted?* Does that mean the dream did your larger self no good at all?

As soon as I say that, we *shift the center of our perception from a psychological level to a Neptunian one*. We understand that a dream might have served a purpose for the larger self—one to which the ego's obsession with understanding or analysis was quite irrelevant. Your spirit is not to be confused with that little cork floating in the ocean. The dreams you have and don't remember at all are part of your spiritual journey too.

To dream is a powerful spiritual path. And with Neptune in the fourth house, dreaming plays a critical part in how you "clean your windows."

One irony is that sometimes your conscious mind will be left entirely out of the loop. A strong response to Neptune in the fourth house implies a particular emphasis on the benefit of paying attention to dreams across the board—including some benefit from trying to remember them, and doing that whole psychoanalytic two-step. But, Neptune-fashion, I would also encourage you to be kind to yourself, to love yourself. Don't beat yourself up because you "stupidly" forgot the dream. Just reframe the experience—that was not a dream you were *supposed* to remember. That was a dream that served a purpose in the larger psyche that did not necessarily have the potential to benefit you intellectually. Perhaps "angels guided you" to forget the dream. Even if you remembered it and tried to interpret it, you would probably misinterpret it and tie yourself into a knot.

All of this talk of the role of dreams in our spiritual lives leads us to a real piece of "chicken soup" advice for anyone with Neptune in the fourth house. *You need a lot of sleep.* Sleep creates the necessary preconditions for dreams to arise. Your mind-body-spirit system knows that and will likely get you yawning a little sooner than others might.

To say that people with Neptune in the fourth house sleep longer than others—I don't know, but I'll bet it's true, especially in the more evolved segments of the population. The length of sleep isn't really the point; the point is the states of consciousness that we access "behind sleep." The majority of them are beyond the grasp of our understanding. *But the fourth house is not about understanding*; it is about a direct experience of layers of the mind that are deeper than everyday consciousness.

I worry a lot about people who stifle their dream-lives with sleeping pills, especially those with this configuration. Sleep is not just about the physical body's need for rest.

Accepting the idea that there is a basic goodness and rightness in the natural processes that arise in the mind is pretty fundamental to Neptune in general. Remember—no opinions and no resistance, not to others and not to yourself. There's the very essence of Neptune. We're just looking at a specific instance of it here.

The fourth house became "psychological" in the astrological literature only in the last century or so, as psychology itself came into awareness. Historically, the fourth house represented our *roots* in the broadest sense. If I ask you, *where do you come from*, how do you answer? If I live in your town, you maybe give me a street name. If I am from Iowa, maybe you say, "California." If I am from Hangzhou, China, and we meet in Paris, then you probably say "America." It's all relative. But it always comes down to the question, where is *home* for you? And that is a classic fourth house question.

Now, as we all know, a house is not a home. A house is just architecture until there is love in it. And that brings us directly to another classic fourth house word, *family*.

Most of us, in the course of our lives, will have at least two families—we are born into one and later we often create one. The fourth house is very much the *house of family*. But that word "family" is very elastic. We are not talking narrowly about heterosexual, child-bearing couples, although God bless them too—they are an excellent source of fresh birthcharts to interpret! "Family" has become increasingly voluntary and flexible in the past several decades. Your dearest friends are "family." Your partner, if you have one, is "family." So is your cat or your dog. That's because the key concept in family is the presumption of *loyalty for a lifetime*. Your cat and your dog deserve that loyalty, right? How do you feel about people who "get rid of" their cat or their dog?

We are talking about your search for your *spiritual family*. What does that mean? How do you know when you've found them? You won't necessarily want to sleep with them, although we aren't necessarily saying the opposite of that either. These bonds will be characterized by *unquestioning loyalty* and the assumption of some kind of *lifelong commitment* to loving engagement. Those are, I believe, the core, modern views of "family" in the true fourth house sense.

What happens when we add the Neptunian element to "family?" What does that add to what we've just seen? We already have the basic vocabulary for answering. There may very well be a long-term, *shared* spiritual practice of some sort. A shared religion is not necessary, but it can potentially help cement the bond. *The family that prays together stays together*, as the billboard says. And those words are worth saying here—even if "prayer" translates as a couple doing Ashtanga yoga together.

When you're in your high Neptunian space, you are absolutely nonresistant to reality as it is. That includes being absolutely nonresistant to other humans as they actually are. And it means being completely undefended in your presentation of yourself. If I am in my Neptunian space with you, and we are "family," then *I am what I am* and we both accept it. If I do something silly and you laugh at me, I laugh at myself too—and I feel closer to you for it. Part of me is indeed silly, and you just saw it and got a laugh out of it. Your laughter makes me feel good. I have no pretenses. I'm not trying to pretend to be anything that I'm not. I don't need you to be amazed by me. I just need us both to relax and to be emotionally naked and human and real. I feel secure enough, standing on the bedrock of our bond, to know that you can see me as I am and you will not leave me. Your loyalty does not depend upon my manipulations or pretenses.

Many of us have some relationships in our lives that have that precious texture. They provide an illustration of "spiritual family." With Neptune in your fourth house, cultivating these relationships is a profoundly pivotal part of your journey. You need them.

Family and home are intertwined words. We've just looked at family. We might add that, with Neptune in the fourth house, a core quest in this lifetime is your *search for your spiritual home*. And that term embraces a *sense of place* as well as a sense of human connectedness. Someone might say, "My spiritual home is Northern California." Another might say, "Going to the south of France always feels like going home to me." A third might make a reference to the "holy coast of Maine in summertime." All those statements invoke the flavor and values of a fourth house Neptune.

Let me also mention that the condition of a person's fourth house—the planets there, aspects they make, signs involved, particularly the sign on the fourth cusp—all will cast light on the *kind of place where such a person would feel at home*. That would be a fascinating subject for further study, but our purpose here is an exploration of Neptune, so we'll limit our attention to natural homes for people with that planet in the fourth house.

Wouldn't it be nice to live in your spiritual home? Who would refuse that, in principle? But for many people, where they physically live is not really of any ultimate spiritual importance. Their evolutionary work and their natural developmental focus lie elsewhere—with a career, or a particular relationship, or creativity, for a few examples. But if you have Neptune in the fourth house, *you are particularly sensitive to the vibrations of the immediate environment and you therefore need to be in the right place.* Failing that, your windows get dirty.

Now, where is that right place? That is a very complex question. There are various techniques we can use to address it, as we mentioned a moment ago. The most fundamental is simply to follow your heart, to follow your intuition—and to follow your dreams. Let Neptune tell you where it is, in other words. Of course—and again going beyond the scope of this book—we can also use the various techniques of Astro-mapping, such as Astro*Carto*Graphy, Local Space, and relocated charts. If you are interested in exploring those techniques in the context of this style of astrology, look for my "Astromapping - Into to Relocational Astrology" workshop on my website.

With Neptune in the fourth house, in looking for clues about our spiritual home, there is a too-simple, too-literal interpretation that often proves correct anyway. So let me put it out there with some caution. Neptune is the god of the sea. *So maybe you're supposed to live by the sea.*

Without too much imagination, we can generalize that you might benefit from living by large bodies of water. We will soon go way beyond that idea, but let's just dwell there for a moment. Think for a moment about how you feel when you find yourself walking beside the ocean or when you're sitting by a big, beautiful lake. We all know that large bodies of water have a certain kind of vibration. They calm you. They open you up.

You might feel these effects especially vividly if you actually get in the water. How do you feel when you've been swimming in the ocean? Personally, I always get the feeling that a kind of electrical charge has been pulled out of my body. I just feel calmer.

Let's go beyond the literal idea that "Neptune means water." That's true, but it is also way too narrow. So we are searching for our spiritual home. Neptune is the mystic. Where do mystics like to go? There's our magical question. *What kinds of landscapes attract mystics?* There are a variety of answers. For sure, mystics have always been drawn to oceanic metaphors—water metaphors. Mystics like to meditate by the high lakes or by the ocean. They want to be that famous raindrop landing in the sea. *But mystics love mountaintops too.* Mystics are famous for lurking in Tibetan caves, which are typically high in the mountains. Want to find a mystic? Climb a mountain. Maybe there'll be one up there. How often have you seen that motif in a cartoon—the seeker climbs the mountain, comes to a ledge in front of a cave, and sitting there is the guru in robes?

Mystics like the desert too. There's a long tradition of desert mysticism—just think of the Holy Lands and all the traditions that have emerged from that piece of arid real estate, starting in the days of Pharaohs. You could hardly get more opposite to the ocean than the desert. And yet, mystics are drawn to both.

All these different landscapes we've listed—what do they have in common? *You can see a long distance.* That is their common DNA. If you want to see a long distance *into yourself*, being able to see a long distance in the physical world seems to support that endeavor. You sit by the ocean and you're more likely to have a deep meditation. You climb a mountain—sooner or later you're probably going to want to just sit there and collect yourself for a while. You hang out in the vastness of a desert. You'll feel that same thing. It's a natural instinct. *The outer spaciousness is in resonance with the inner spaciousness.*

Of course mystics are sometimes cloistered, hidden away from the world. Or hidden in the forest. We don't need these spacious places in order to be supported in our spirituality. And we have already emphasized how, if you have Neptune in the fourth house, your home must be your temple too. You need those walls between you and the world. But as we wrestle with the question of your search for your spiritual home, a simple way of organizing our initial thinking is to consider that you might benefit from living in a place with a view. You need spaciousness around you, and if you can arrange that, it will support you.

Let's take a peek at the darker potentials connected with having Neptune in the fourth house. First, very generally, mystics are forever giving things up. They give up sex, food, money, having a home. They hang on crosses. Intentionally giving up things to which we would normally experience attachment is a recognized spiritual discipline. But it has a dark side. We can make a virtue out of hanging on crosses. And when such self-sabotage is not linked to any kind of spiritual discipline or inward practice, it is simply the ignorant and erroneous notion that suffering will lead automatically to spiritual evolution.

In the case of Neptune in the fourth house, we have seen that you need your spiritual family and you need your spiritual home. You need some degree of domestic peace and quiet to be able to deal with the intensity of the inner work that you're doing.

What if you gave those things up? What if, for example, you are just going through the motions of being in a family that has no meaning to you? What if you're living in a place that alienates you? What if you are endlessly surrounded by noise and distraction, and you don't lift a finger to create that kind of sanctuary in which the fourth house Neptune blossoms? There's the fingerprint of the dark Neptune, *tricking you into surrendering what you actually need for your journey.*

Down that empty highway, all we see are the Neptunian demons of apathy, delusion, and escapism. If you do not feed your soul, your soul will starve. Better to lock the door, hide behind Voice Mail, and gaze into the twin mirrors of inner and outer space.

24

NEPTUNE IN THE FIFTH HOUSE

The "creative trance." Cooperating with the Muses. Performance. Reclaiming stolen parts of your soul from past-life associates. Lovers and love affairs. Children. Ecstasy as an evolutionary path.

You must become like a little child to enter the Kingdom of Heaven.

Leaking Energy*: Dissipation through trivial pleasures. Draining one's energy with interpersonal dramas. Escapism. Turning away from the positive need for joy.*

Let's turn our attention to Neptune in the fifth house. This will cover a lot of bases, many of them a joy to discuss, some of them pretty heavy and intense.

Here's a happy one for starters: *creative trance* as a meditative technique. Here's another: *play as a spiritual path*. And of course this is famously the *house of love affairs*—they can be fun too, but perhaps with those words and some grown-up memories of romance-gone-sour, you might begin to sense deeper waters opening up, with a few dorsal fins cutting the waves.

We will spend a long time unraveling the mystery of "love affairs," and it will bring us head-to-head with the fact that none of us come into this world without unresolved karmic business with other souls with whom our paths have already become entangled. That means that you are invited to reclaim stolen parts of yourself from past-life associates who are holding them captive.

That's a big subject. We will pursue it soon—and, by the way, these same people may manifest in our lives as *children*, as well as lovers, friends, or rivals. There, we will get some deeper insight into what is probably the most common name for this house, the *house of children*.

Art and beauty, as we simply receive them and enjoy them, or even more powerfully, as we *create* them—are activities that reflect pure expressions of fifth house energy.

I want to set a backdrop and then a foreground. The backdrop: I'm thinking of one of those painfully earnest people who is "on the spiritual path" and rather ego-invested in your knowing it. You know the type. I would compare that kind of narrow spiritual pretention with the absolute childlike innocence and surrender of creative people in the midst of making a painting or a song or a poem. They have suddenly become completely transparent to the source of all inspiration—transparent to the universe, transparent to their own soul, transparent to God, transparent to the trans-Neptunian realm.

Such artists, "caught in the act," are not likely to be thinking, "I am doing spiritual practice." *But they are.* They've gotten out of their own way enough to let the inner world come rushing in. And ain't that "getting out of our own way" really what the spiritual path is all about? If it isn't, I need someone to tell me what the word means.

So inspiration for the painting or musical phrase or next line of the poem just enters the mind from—*where*? The old Greeks would have spoken of our being inspired by the Muses. Today we might call it the unconscious mind surfacing. Whatever you call it, *the origin of creativity lies outside the scope of our normal waking consciousness*. Nobody who's ever had a creative moment has done it without engaging in that mysterious process of surrender. I call this receptive state the *creative trance*. It is the very essence of Neptune in the fifth house.

Bottom line, *creativity is a spiritual path*; art is a spiritual path. In terms of the basic evolutionary goals implicit in Neptune, this is a particularly effective path because of its unselfconscious quality—the ego simply can't be too involved without gumming up the process. And this line of development is the epitome of effective spiritual practice for anyone born with Neptune here.

I say "ego can't be too involved." That truth is limited to the moments of the creative trance itself, which is where the magic happens. Ego can jump in later, of course—just think of an insufferably self-important rock star *whose work is actually brilliant*. But even that clichéd creature had to get out of his own way for at least a little while for those lyrics and that chord progression to slip past his monumental ego.

Going further, the fifth house has an *ecstatic* quality to it. It is the house of *sheer joy*. As we abandon ourselves to joy, we are also surrendering to that larger space. Think of an improvisational dancer having thrown herself totally into the dance. Perhaps she has an experience of physical exhaustion—and she breaks right through that wall and continues dancing anyway. There's a fifth house Neptune in action!

Cut from the image of a ballerina pirouetting on the stage to an image of basketball's great Michael Jordan going up for one of those turnaround jump shots he was so good at. Look at Michael Jordan taking that shot in slow motion; *he's a ballerina too*. What possessed him? To what does he surrender in that moment? And we could ask the same questions about the dancer.

I'm not an athlete; I don't have any particular interest in sports. But a lot of people do. And thinking of *sports* as a spiritual path—there's Neptune in the fifth house again. Even in the simplest and most literal of astrology books, you see that connection: sports are a fifth house correlate.

If it's fun, it's the fifth house. For some of us, sports would not be our idea of fun, but for others, they are. Ditto for dancing. Ditto for any of the creative arts or acts. In all of them, there's a sense of surrendering to something bigger. There is always a wild ecstasy in it. *And that loss of ego-centered awareness, that ecstatic surrendering to the energies of the moment, that willingness to be ridden by a force greater than ourselves which we cannot understand or fully control is the lifeblood of Neptune in the fifth.*

Once, many years ago, I got a profound insight from the great Buddhist teacher, Khenpo Karthar Rinpoche. During a question and answer period, a man said, "I just had a son. I want to know if I should teach him to meditate, and if so, how and when?" This all was translated into Tibetan and back out again into English, and here's Khenpo Karthar's answer: "Never force him to meditate, but when he is about five, go and buy a bell. Hold the bell before him and strike it. And while it's ringing, say to your son, '*Tell me when you can't hear it anymore.*'"

End of teaching.

Isn't that powerful? Just picture a five-year-old boy listening with absolute concentration to the sound of a bell *not ringing anymore*: instant meditation. That image has a powerful Neptune-in-the-fifth-house quality. To be absolutely here and now, absolutely absorbed in this moment—that's the essential spirit of it.

When you are in synch with the archetypal field of the fifth house, *you want to smile*. It's happy. That's why creative people are often happy, at least while they are engaged in the act of creation. There's joy in it. It's not so much that joy is the goal—it's that being absolutely, transparently open to the here-and-now is the goal. And with that transparency comes joy, as a side effect.

Now we come to a giant subject with the fifth house in general, and with Neptune there in particular: *love affairs*. As I opened this section I mentioned how, with any planet in this house, you're invited to reclaim stolen parts of yourself—parts held captive by others whom you knew in prior lifetimes. This idea is fundamental to the fifth house across the board. We will look at it broadly, then we'll focus specifically on Neptune.

All of us, in this lifetime, have had relationships that did not end well. Similarly, we might reasonably assume that you have had relationships in prior lifetimes that did not end well either. But ultimately in this universe, there is no such thing as unfinished business. Those with whom you had unpleasant or unresolved experiences in prior lives will encounter you again, and vice versa. You need to meet them; it's potentially to your benefit and to theirs as well. You're both stuck—something was left unresolved, and it has to be released if you are to go forward on your separate journeys without that burden.

The narrow term "love affairs" is actually misleading here. These relationships are not always sexual; they can take a lot of other forms too. To use one gross example, to murder somebody—or to be murdered—naturally creates a lot of unresolved karma. Such a pair will surely meet again. To abuse someone, to cheat, to lie to someone—almost any action that has a negative quality—creates karma. Less negative energies can do it too—for example, *unresolved sexual longing* for someone. Or feeling as if you *owe* something to someone—she bailed you out somehow in a prior life, and you never had a chance to pay her back. You'll meet again—and when she shows up at your door asking for a loan of $500, you'll write her a check for $2,000. It's such a relief to unburden yourself from the debt.

In all such fifth house scenarios, there are certain "signs and omens" that accompany them. Essentially, there are three criteria to be recognized here:

- First, we experience an uncanny, inexplicable sense of *familiarity* with the person even though we are just meeting "for the first time."

- Secondly, we have a strong or disproportionate *emotional response* to him or her—our previous example serves well here: why do we feel so right about writing that $2,000 check? What is the actual origin of such compulsive generosity?

- The third is *compulsion and urgency*. If we stand back from the situation and think clearly, we recognize that powerful unconscious forces are engaged. Something is exaggerating and distorting our emotional response to the individual.

- The nature of the planet in the fifth house gives us insight into the nature of the business that needs to be finished, our part in it, and the nature of the other person. As I've mentioned, the energies here are not always sexual, but often our most vivid experiences of this face of the fifth house do indeed take the form of literal love affairs.

With Neptune in the fifth house, we see a particularly sticky kind of interpersonal karma. Let me dive into this in a way that is a bit like a cartoon. That way, we can turn up the volume on the basic principles, and then we can recognize how they might manifest in more subtle ways.

Let's imagine a forty-three-year-old woman who has been married for twenty years. She's got Neptune in the fifth house. She decides to leave her husband because she's "found her true love"—who happens to be a twenty-six-year-old punk rock guitar player, recently out on probation. And of course, she's frustrated that all her friends are so pigheaded with resistance about it—nobody understands! She assures you that she and the punk rocker have *a very spiritual relationship*. She intimates that, "We were cruelly separated by our evil families in Luxor, Egypt, in the third millennium BC, and now we have found each other, and we're destined to be together."

I promised a sort of cartoonish image. But we're all familiar with such sexual situations—insanely impossible relationships that people enter into, often apparently with a sincerity matched only by their foolishness.

Look into the astrological crystal ball and you will often see that there are fifth house correlates to these kinds of romantic situation comedies.

Our friend affirms the "deeply spiritual connection" between her and this young guitarist who's so recently out on parole. *And she may be right about that*—and there's the key to understanding Neptune in the fifth house. We have to honor the fact that the two people, however improbable the relationship seems on the surface today, might indeed have a deeply spiritual connection. The story about having been cruelly separated back in Luxor might even be correct as well, at least impressionistically. They may look into each other's eyes in a spirit of total surrender. They may have a psychic bond. *They surely and truly knew each other instantly.*

But with all that said, let's keep some lead in our shoes. What odds do you give this relationship of succeeding? We're kind of right back to square one, aren't we?

The fact that they have "a deeply spiritual connection" is not going to erase the fact that there's a gross age difference and social difference between them. It's not going to erase the fact that she's left her long-term marriage precipitously, and will need to deal with the consequences of that. That whole range of mundane issues is still in place. Common sense is far from irrelevant here—and the cynic's predictions for the relationship are likely to prove accurate within a month or two.

With Neptune in the fifth house, we meet people with whom in prior lifetimes, we had a genuine spiritual bond—but probably not a solid, real-world, grounded relationship. Maybe, for example, we met while one or both of us were in Holy Orders—and we kept our vows, despite the temptation to break them. Maybe there was a Romeo-and-Juliet story—a kind of longing, but unconsummated, relationship: pure *romantic projection*, with all its inaccurate idealization. Another Neptunian image: maybe we were drunkards sloshed together, feeling closer than we actually were.

The possibilities are endless. There is a *karma of fantasy* here, for sure.

The fundamental, raw nature of karma is *repetition*; karma is mostly just habit. There are other things we can say, there are subtleties with karma, but habit is the heart of it: the *repetition compulsion*, doing the same thing over and over again, and expecting a different result. In a case of Neptunian attachment, an irresolution exists between your soul and the soul of this other person. You meet again in this lifetime. The aim of this present edition of the relationship is to pick it up where it left off and carry it to where it needed to be—to carry it forward into healthy resolution. Often that simply means goodbye, and may God bless you—elsewhere. When the balloon of projection pops, when reality raises it head, many times what happens is the energy of attraction dissipates instantly.

Here is the suggested mantra—and you'll see the signature of the higher energies of Neptune written all over it—*I release you; I offer you nothing but goodwill and good wishes. Let us both be finished here. Let us recognize that this relationship doesn't work in the form we have imagined it; let us each go forward on our own journeys in a spirit of warmth and love towards each other, non-attached and free.*

That's not easy to accomplish. Maybe it shouldn't be easy. These attachments—be they in the form of desire or in the form of aversion—are very powerful. The habitual responses are very deeply ingrained. Still, *in a nutshell, the aim of fifth house Neptunian relationships is to end them.* That doesn't mean that as soon as we meet the person we need to run away. That ends nothing. That is just a way of putting the unresolved karma on the back burner again. *We must interact.* There must be some degree of *shared vulnerability.*

Maybe you have Neptune in the fifth house and you find yourself attracted to somebody. When you look into each other's eyes, there's that classic Neptunian omen: comfort with shared spiritual nakedness. That's not always a bad sign, God knows—it can be a wonderful thing. But if you have Neptune in the fifth house and you feel that link with somebody . . . *have lunch with the person.* Seriously! Have lunch—which of course is a metaphor for interacting casually, getting to know each other, and being mindful of any projections or assumptions you are making.

Don't be afraid, but be cautious.

As you're having lunch, try on the following idea: even though there is honestly a strong spiritual rapport here, there are practical differences that could make this connection not work well as a worldly partnership. *Just try that idea on.* There's an excellent chance that if you do that, sitting across the table having lunch, you'll realize the grounded accuracy of the observation. As you realize the truth of it, you find that you rather automatically release your attraction to the person—when you sense where the relationship would likely go, *you don't want to go there.*

Here's the magic. *We can, in other words, resolve Neptunian fifth house karma literally in minutes.* It is *consciousness* that does it; there's not some kind of penance we have to suffer. It is simply consciousness moving to a different level—a level that kills the *illusion* of the desire. The more quickly that awareness arises, the more quickly the karma is resolved.

When we call the fifth house "the house of love affairs," we may seem to be trivializing it. The term sounds shallow, as if we were talking about meaningless coupling based solely on lust— unimportant, immature, and ultimately of little consequence. And yet, in the fifth house, we see some of the most poignant human experiences available. These bonds can have elements of real depth to them.

But once again, the aim is always to end them; the aim is release for both people.

Underlying all of these observations is the critical insight in terms of the soul's evolutionary strategy: you need to realize that *part of your soul-energy is captured by these projections.* You are still entangled with another being in a way that is not good for either of you. Both of you are caught in habitual patterns relative to each other—patterns that always loop into the same developmental cul-de-sacs. This simply wastes time and energy; the patterns must be broken. Forgiveness and release are the goals.

What about children? As we mentioned at the beginning of this section, the fifth house is the classic *house of children.*

Let me start with a line that will sound wrong to you, at least at first, although it will ultimately connect our insights into children with our insights into love affairs. *The aim of our relationships with our children is to end them.*

Of course that isn't exactly right—one would naturally hope for friendship and a lasting bond with one's kids, not an "ending." But the point is that the natural developmental trajectory of the parent-child relationship is that the child grows up, is successfully launched into the adult community, and ceases to relate to the parent as a child. The *parent-child relationship ends*; the child is blessed and released, and the underlying logic of the relationship changes. That's the connection between love affairs and kids in terms of fifth house theory.

To be a parent is a great joy, but it is also a terrible sacrifice. You used to have a life; now you have a kid. Why would anyone pay that price? I think it is safe to say that there are always karmic connections between parents and a newborn. One of the oldest spirit-stories in the world is, "OK, I was your mommy last time. You owe me one. You have to be my mommy this time." It sounds funny—but doesn't it sound right too? Ask anyone doing hypnotic past-life regression work: that pattern is very common. Having the Moon or Saturn in the fifth house is, by the way, a good indicator of that kind of unresolved karma. There are plenty of other possible interpretations there too, of course.

With Neptune in the fifth, if you have children, there is a good chance that at least one of them will be very Neptunian. She might literally be a little Pisces; he might have a twelfth house Moon; either could simply have a strongly-placed Neptune. There are a variety of possible astrological signatures. Another piece: the connection between the two of you is likely to be very psychic—your child is having a tough day at school, and you feel that dark cloud before he walks in the door.

You may have known each other in a monastery or a convent. You may have been devoted to the same guru. Or you may have frequented the same pub!

Going further, with Neptune in *your* fifth house, your child has brought a lot of sensitivity into this world—a level of sensitivity that he or she needs your help in handling. This is a big subject, but let me just telegraph it to you with some words that will sound familiar. "Never force him to meditate, but when he is about five, go and buy a bell. Hold the bell before him and strike it. And while it's ringing, say to your son, '*Tell me when you can't hear it anymore.*'"

What about the dark side of Neptune in the fifth house?

Always when Neptune goes negative, one of the features we see is withdrawal from life through some pattern of escapism. One thing about most forms of escapism is that they are *fun*. What is easier to acquire than a bad habit? What is harder to lose? And the fifth house is the *house of pleasure*—all of life's joys and comforts are here: sex, food, alcohol, parties, shopping, games, sports. It's a hedonist's shopping list. So we can readily see the potential for a vicious synergy between Neptunian escapism and fifth house hell-raising. True to form, the fifth house is fraught with opportunities for numbing oneself. Just think of any pleasurable, repeatable experience—anything that fits those two criteria: it's fun, and you can do it more than once. Anything that fits those two criteria can be used in escapist ways.

Escapism is always an issue with Neptune, but it reaches a crescendo of risk in the fifth house context.

Pleasure is a necessary vitamin in life, for sure—without pleasure, all we are left with is pain. And if all we have is pain, something inside us hardens and begins to die. The key here is to make sure that we have some positive, healthy Neptunian pleasures in our lives. We've seen most of them already, earlier. High on the list is the *pleasure of creativity*. Meditation can be a pleasure—and, as we saw, for someone with this configuration, dancing can be a meditation, writing poetry can be a meditation, and so on. The timely ending of relationships that only drain and frustrate us may not be a pleasure in and of itself—but it can clear the path for relationships we genuinely treasure and that feed our souls.

If we get all that right, our joy is greater and our pain is lessened. And if our pain is lessened, the self-destructive escapist drive has less of a hold on us. With Neptune in the fifth house—really just as in the rest of astrology—you've been presented with a dilemma and you've been offered a path of resolution for it. Following that path to the higher ground is your choice. You can do it—and if you choose not to do it, you will embody the dilemma. It is always that way.

So, with Neptune in the fifth, is it the easel or the bottle? Is it a love affair with your own soul—or a love affair with someone bad for you? Is it a path of genuine joy—or futile devotion to joy's false advertising? As ever, the choice is yours.

25

NEPTUNE IN THE SIXTH HOUSE

The positive dissolution of ego-self in service and devotion. Participation in lineage; seeking masters. Working methodically with precise, well-defined spiritual techniques. Commitment to spiritual routines.

Where do I put my foot next?

Leaking Energy: *"Volunteered slavery." Becoming a drone. Dithering. Guilt and humiliation. Troubles magnified by irresponsibility or forgetfulness. Devotion to false teachers or teachings.*

The sixth house is all about brushing your teeth in the morning. That has to fit into your chart somewhere, right? Are any of you failing in that? Anyone want to confess?

I am obviously being silly—but real. Brushing your teeth may not be exciting, but it is an important part of your life. And since brushing your teeth is part of life, it must be part of astrology too. But *what* part of astrology? The answer is the sixth house—the house of, among other things, all the *basic routines of life.*

Take it a little further. Let's say that you had never brushed your teeth before in your life, and you decided to "get religion" and take up the policy of brushing, starting tonight. We hand you a toothbrush and toothpaste.

You've never seen either of them before in your life—and by a miracle, you still have teeth in your head. And you try brushing, after we explain the concept a little bit.

Now, how bloody would your mouth be? You'd hurt yourself, brushing your teeth for the first time. It would take you a long while too, and you probably wouldn't do a very good job of it.

But for most of you when it comes to brushing your teeth, you're kind of semi-professional, wouldn't you say? You don't really have to think about it very much. You've practiced, and practice makes perfect. *Routines allow something to become very strongly embedded in us, to become an established pattern in our lives, something at which we achieve excellence.*

And that is sixth house logic.

So, in the sixth house we find the duties, responsibilities, and patterns of habit in life—everything that contributes to the daily maintenance of physical, concrete, well-being in this world of flesh, electric bills, and teeth to brush. There are other things we'll say about the sixth house, but those elements are critical to our understanding of it.

What if we put Neptune's natural concerns in this context? We begin to speak of the *spiritual routines and habits* of life. Someone might, for one illustration, meditate every morning at dawn. That's not for everybody. And that's OK too. You just have to know yourself, be gentle with yourself. But some kind of spiritual routine is good for you—and that's true really, not only for yourself, but whether they know it or not, for everyone else in the world.

If you have Neptune in the sixth house, what spiritual routines do you choose to establish? It's a pressing question. This configuration signifies *an evolutionary intention to harness the incredible power of habit in service of our soul's growth*. Just like brushing your teeth, practice makes perfect. When you got out of bed this morning, you probably went straight to the bathroom and squeezed that famous tube, right? You didn't have to think about it. You didn't need to "try to remember." Brushing your teeth is in the marrow of your bones at this point. The habit manifested as an automatic reflex.

Imagine if you supported your soul's unfoldment with that same mechanism. How powerful would that be?

Notice how I started out making the sixth house sound pretty boring—the house of your tired old toothbrush. Now notice how exciting it can become, especially linked here to Neptune's highest expressions.

Spiritual practice is a broad subject. I'm going to focus here initially on the word "meditation," although we must always remember to let that word breathe. There are many forms of meditation, not all of which are "officially spiritual." For example, in the last chapter, we explored how people with Neptune in the fifth house can "meditate" by dancing or writing poetry.

With Neptune in the sixth house, which form of meditation do you choose? And how do you turn it into something as fundamental to you as that habitual, automatic pattern of brushing your teeth? Maybe you meditate every night when you lie down in your bed. Some teachers say that's not the optimal meditation position—that you should be sitting up instead. We will have more to say about that kind of advice shortly. Here, suffice it to say that *any kind of sustained practice* is good for you—and "sustained" is the critical word. Repetition creates the sixth house Holy Grail, which is *converting a good behavior into a habit.*

Let's turn God into the guy with the long white beard sitting on the heavenly throne for a minute. You have Neptune in the sixth. God appears before you in a flash of light, saying, "To what kind of spiritual routines do you solemnly commit yourself in this lifetime?" God adds: "It's your call. Anything you say is OK. The one thing that I would not find acceptable is for you to promise me some practice and then not do it. So just tell me what I can count on, what I can expect. It's up to you, 100 percent."

And maybe we answer, "Uh ... how about I fast for Ramadan and just forget about you the rest of the time?" And God says, "Peachy—see you later." God writes it down. "Here's your contract. You'd better not eat until the sun is down!" And God promises you that there will be great benefit to you from sticking to that promise, building that routine of fasting for Ramadan, once a year.

Obviously, I've set the bar fairly low with that little tale. But the point is about spiritual *promises kept.* Maybe instead of promising to fast for Ramadan, we say to God, "I will meditate every morning at dawn." So, there's God again, at the foot of your bed in the flash of light, saying: "Every morning? Do you mean that? If you're saying that, you'd better mean that." Along about Day Five, we decide to skip meditation that morning and sleep in. That seems forgivable and understandable, right? But in the context of Neptune in the sixth house, we are failing to live up to the contract.

And as we have seen countless times, a reliable astrological principle is that if you don't get it right, you will get it wrong. Failing to keep the promise here is an engraved invitation to the dark face of Neptune in the sixth.

We'll talk about that specifically very soon.

Famously, there's nothing in this world easier to lose than a good habit, and nothing easier to acquire than a bad habit. Those two principles work together here. *In the sixth house, we're dealing with the part of human consciousness defined by habitual logic.* With Neptune in the sixth house, you're attempting to establish healthy *spiritual hygiene*. You need to figure out what's going to work for you, commit to it—and then the main thing is to stick with it.

My little tale about that flash of light and making a deal with God—I want to be careful with that. I don't want to feed the "hellfire" imagery of that judging, damning patriarchal God. Fail here, and it's not like the mystery we are calling "God" will hate you for it and terrible punishments will be visited upon you. I'm not going to play that kind of dirty game with you. The core idea is simply to be realistic about yourself and to establish a pattern of spiritual effort that will work for you and that you can commit to strongly enough that it has a chance of becoming habitually ingrained in you—just like brushing your teeth.

And of course the critical corollary is that it is the *height of folly to establish the pattern of breaking your spiritual promises to yourself.* With this configuration in your chart, you have reached a stage in the evolutionary journey in which you are ripe for taking on new habits. That receptive structure is in place in you already. You *will* be taking on those new habits. The question is, which habits?

I'm going to go right back to brushing your teeth for a moment. I am intentionally using that utterly mundane image in order to convey the utterly grounded, utterly real-world nature of the sixth house. Now, there are good ways to brush your teeth and not-so-effective ways to do it. There is a certain *technique* to doing it right—and "technique" is another good sixth house word.

Similarly, there are ways to meditate constructively and some ways that are less likely to produce good results. To revisit an image from a few minutes ago, most of the Buddhist teachers would, for example, discourage you from meditating while lying down. Earlier, in a different context,

I mentioned the Tibetan tradition where they talk about how your butt needs to be four fingers above the ground and your hands both at the same level, ideally in your lap. They make a fuss about that very specific point—that the asymmetry of one hand being higher than the other will foul up your meditation. See how specific that is? Welcome to the sixth house—it's like, do this, do that, do this, do that. It is—literally—the house of instruction manuals.

How do you feel about being ordered around that way? Feel some resistance to being told what to do? I know I often do! And yet people who are more evolved than you or me, people who have gone down this road long before us, have been kind enough to leave detailed instructions about exactly what worked efficiently for them. They offer their experience as a gift for our consideration. They are suggesting that you try putting your hands this way; try keeping your butt four fingers up off the floor. They invite you to see if it speeds you up on your path or deepens your experience, as it did for them. They are offering spiritual *techniques* and *skills*—sixth house Neptunian gifts.

With your Neptune in the sixth house, you have reached a stage in the evolutionary journey where, basically, you just need to *read the directions, follow the directions, and apply the directions in a disciplined and routine way.* The universe, manifesting as your birthchart, has promised that this approach will work wonders for you.

There's more to the sixth house than skills, habits, and techniques. Classically, this is also the *house of servants*—or, now that servants have become scarce, the house of *service*. This brings us to hallowed, well-trodden ground: *service to others as a spiritual path.*

Here's why that is such an effective Neptunian evolutionary technique: when we are serving others, what is going on internally for us is that, in that moment, we are *making the other person's problems more important to us than our own problems.* It is hard to imagine a more powerful yoga for getting over ourselves. Thus, pretty much every religion that has achieved any kind of maturity has included some kind of *sacrament of service,* of doing for others, of doing good in the world.

If you have Neptune in the sixth house, as you learn to give of your time and energy to help other people, you are burning evolutionary rocket fuel. Service is a spiritual path. Is service a form of meditation? I suppose one could defend that idea, but it's a stretch. It's sufficient to say that service lays down an excellent foundation for meditation. It reduces the centrality of ego in our motivational profile. That certainly helps us clean our windows.

We move on from "servants" and head for what may possibly be the true, esoteric heart of the sixth house Neptune. A servant serves a master; those are interdependent concepts. In the sixth house in general, we encounter the notion of *unequal relationships*. Those can be dreadful, such as when a master rules unfairly over a slave or a psychopathic boss blames you for his own mistakes. But unequal relationships can be sweet too, such as the bond between an aunt and her niece, or a master pianist and her *protégée*.

Adding a dollop of mystical Neptune to the mix, we find the idea of *lineage*—of *spiritual masters and their disciples*.

A little while ago, we were expressing appreciation for those evolved souls who left us some record of what they had learned. With Neptune in the sixth house, you were born with the right *receptor cells* to receive enormous gifts from these lofty beings. Perhaps you will do that through the teachings they left behind, or perhaps through contact with them in a more mystical and direct way. *And, via synchronicity, you are likely to encounter such teachers here and now in the flesh as well.* Whatever form the interaction takes, you have business with them, and they have business with you. The laws of synchronicity will bring you together.

Here's another way of saying it—in the higher potentials of the sixth house, we start with the recognition that there are people in this world who, from a spiritual point of view, are simply *better than us.* I intentionally phrase it in that punchy way because it brings us to one of the most critical pieces in our understanding of a sixth house Neptune. That is *humility*. It takes a lot of humility to recognize that here is somebody who is simply more conscious than we are; here is someone who is more evolved than we are.

Say that you have a sixth house Neptune, and maybe you share with a new friend the fact that you meditate. The friend, suddenly beady-eyed, asks you exactly how high off the ground your butt is when you meditate. And you reveal that you sit in a comfy chair. Your friend announces that you *should*—oh, fearful word!—try meditating with your butt on a meditation cushion exactly the width of four fingers off the floor. You are meditating "wrong."

Now, just imagine your reaction. How close do you come to thinking, "Who the hell does she think she is to be telling me my butt should be four fingers off the floor?!"

See how the solar ego takes over? It doesn't want to be told *anything.* But with a sixth house Neptune, the right response might very well be, "Thank you." We need to cultivate enough humility to recognize that there are beings in this world who know things that can benefit us. That friend probably isn't your true spiritual master, but she may have been sent by angels to offer you some precious correction.

A moment ago, I mentioned how, with this configuration, the laws of synchronicity would attract spiritual teachers into your life. The term "spiritual teachers," of course, invokes the notion of lofty, ethereal creatures—imagine having dinner with the Dalai Lama, Ram Dass, Marianne Williamson, Eckhart Tolle, Pope Francis, and so forth. And there may actually be some of that in store for you if you have Neptune in the sixth. But the story I just told is closer to the practical heart of the matter. That friend giving you advice might not even be more evolved than you—but she *knows something you need to know*, and you have attracted her into your life.

You have also, perhaps more significantly, attracted a situation that can teach you humility.

Now, there's a certain innate *seed* of humility in the sixth house Neptune; as we cultivate it, we attract more of these teachers to ourselves. How do we cultivate the seed? By *losing our self-importance* and by *committing ourselves to some kind of diligent spiritual effort.* Service to others can really help there.

I don't want to be too mechanical in my interpretation here, but my impression is that the quality of the teachers you attract is a rather direct barometer of your success at cultivating those three virtues: humility, effective spiritual habits, and service. And, if you have Neptune in the sixth, you are just *so ready* for this. The catalytic effect of such teachers on you is extraordinary, once you have prepared the ground.

I'll walk out on some thin ice for a moment. I hope I can express this clearly. If what I am about to say comes across as arrogant, I've blown it entirely.

My astrology Apprentice Program draws in new students every year. In most cases, I'm guessing that what inspires students to attend is that they read my books or listen to a downloaded lecture online and decide they would like to come and study with me directly. Here's the edgy piece: *I want to point out that students who sit with me in person are learning things from me that they would never learn from a book.* And it's not simply that there is deeper content in this kind of teaching than I can put in a book, but rather that something else is happening—something that's operating on a different level than written words. Something is *radiating from me into them* about this style of astrology. It is not simply an academic or intellectual transmission that students are receiving; they are also receiving a transmission at a more fundamental human level.

Now, I prefaced this remark by saying that I was going to walk out on thin ice. The "thin ice" is that what I just said could so easily be interpreted as ridiculously arrogant on my part, as if I were just blowing my own horn: "I have this superpower, and I'm zapping you in your very chromosomes with astrological knowledge! Lucky you!"

But I'm not really saying that at all. What I'm talking about is a quality that is inherent in every human being—a quality we must understand if we are going to grasp the ancient core meaning in astrology's sixth house. *We all radiate what we are into the world.* And every one of us has *radiated in transmission* to other people.

Every one of us has encountered people who knew less than us in some category. They benefitted from meeting us.

Here, in attempting to grasp Neptune's specific relationship with the sixth house, we are speaking of people who are more or less *spiritually evolved* than yourself—that's Neptune's focus in particular. But if you're a golfer, and you take lessons from a golf pro, something is radiating from that golf pro to you. That golf pro might have an IQ lower than yours and might very well be less evolved spiritually than you—but he or she plays a better game of golf. And as that person expresses understanding of the game of golf to you, there's information transmitted, but also a "carrier wave" of the radiance of that person's essence.

I emphasize that this is a universal human quality. With Neptune in the sixth house, you are wired to be able to *receive such transmissions* clearly and efficiently—especially the ones coming at you on psychic, metaphysical, and spiritual wavelengths.

Every one of you is skillful at something. Every one of you has something you could teach me, where I am ignorant compared to you. So, there's no claim of any inflated nature here—just a reference to a fundamental piece of human experience that is weirdly eclipsed in our present culture.

That's a real treasure in astrological practice—how, if we really listen to the planets, they can open our eyes to things regarding which our society is blind. As a culture, we don't talk much about *mentoring* in general—and we certainly don't talk much about this function of transmission that exists between people. It is ancient and human, and has been recognized in almost every culture that has ever existed—ours being the glaring exception.

And it is symbolized by the sixth house.

As we have seen, with Neptune in the sixth house, you are wired to receive particularly Neptunian transmission. You're wired to receive directly from people who are, in fact, more conscious than you. They'll teach you useful, practical things that can be put into words or books or classes. But they also shoot you this kind of zap or charge directly into the very cells of your body, a jolt that helps you bypass an awful lot of difficulty in life, simply by consciousness being transmitted through resonance directly into your being.

To have that receptor cell—well, I can hardly think of a greater gift in this world. In evolutionary terms, it is like hitting warp drive.

Let's add that with Neptune here, you can also *transmit to others*. It is a two-way street. You are part of a *lineage*. All through your life, and probably especially so in the second half of your life, you will be *attracting disciples*.

Yikes, what a line! Attracting disciples?! You can see why humility plays such a critical role in all this. *If you are too arrogant and self-important to be a disciple yourself, you will surely never become a guru.*

This kind of guru-disciple language is dangerous because of its tendency to inflate the ego, but I use it anyway. I am actually trying to make it *less* exotic. With these kinds of sixth house Neptunian receptor cells, everything is actually very down-to-earth.

With such receptor cells comes humility. And through the beautiful doorway of humility, we enter the Shadow—we enter the dark side of Neptune in the sixth house. The point is that there is a very thin line between humility and humiliation. The two words even sound an awful lot alike. But they are very different in their meaning.

What happens if we don't attune ourselves to the higher potentials of Neptune in the sixth house? Naturally, we will start to experience more of the lower ones.

Let's start with the idea of being *erased* or *eclipsed* in life by duties or responsibilities imposed on you by another person, by a *petty tyrant.* There is no shortage of them in the world—bossy, demanding, shaming people. Remember, though, it takes two to tango! No one is so bossy or shaming that they can take away your dignity unless you let them. But there can be some real challenges here. Once again, the humility of the sixth house—the very quality that allows you to receive teaching from those who are truly more advanced than you—can also allow you to become second fiddle to a buzz saw. Someone takes over your life and you become erased by your duties—hanging on the cross, dark Neptune-fashion.

The situation can be very pressing in a practical, even moral kind of way. Synchronicity—commonly called "fate" or "luck" or "randomness"—kicks in. Your mother has Alzheimer's disease and needs to live with you, for example. Legitimate, morally-inescapable duties do arise in life, and that's a real sixth house pattern.

Maybe that's your karma; maybe you can learn humility through service to your poor mother—and do remember that selfless service is a high Neptune-in-the-sixth evolutionary pathway. But beware of "mission creep," to use a phrase out of the modern newspapers; your mission in life seems to creep and expand to the point that your work is never done, so that you are simply defined by a function. You are soon "hanging on the cross" of ever-inflating, ever-metastasizing duties and responsibilities. You have entered the soul-cage of the sixth house Neptune: a utilitarian model of yourself; you exist to serve the others—children, partner, aging parents.

There are many forms this can take in practical terms. Maybe your boss was Attila the Hun in a prior lifetime. Maybe your mother was a starving child. Whatever the form, the demands are endless, the shaming—inner or outer—is endless. These are sixth house dangers; these are the soul-traps connected with it.

Let me add one more piece with the sixth house. It has always been related to *health and illness.* The astrology of the physical body is not my strong suit; I tend to not go too deeply into medical astrology, mostly because my ignorance is nearly complete there.

Here is what I have observed: Neptune in the sixth house does often suggest physical conditions that are notoriously difficult to trace or to diagnose. They are often connected with *environmental sensitivities.* When I say "environmental sensitivities," I want to include all that we might obviously imagine—mold spores, electromagnetic fields, outgassing from synthetic carpets, and so on. But I also want to include psychic vibrations and collective mental energies and all of that—they are part of the environment too. And, with Neptune in the sixth house, the body tends to be very sensitive to that entire range of influences, registering these dysfunctions or imbalances in the energetic environment or the chemical environment outside us.

I have a feeling—I'm not sure of this, but I bet it's true a lot of the time—that the more positively we are responding to Neptune in the sixth house in all the ways that we've been exploring, the stronger our physical resistance becomes. And conversely, the weaker a response we're making to Neptune, the more we tend to experience these kinds of weird and hard-to-trace physical complaints.

I never want to enter into an overly one-dimensional view of disease; physical health is very complex, and there are a lot of factors that interact with it. I would never want to be so simpleminded as to say, "If you just meditate a lot, you'll never catch a cold." That is not how reality works. Even worse, such an attitude generates a lack of compassion towards people who do catch colds. So I want to be cautious here. But attitude and health are interactive—that's an inescapable element of the larger truth. And Neptune is very strongly associated with our attitudes.

As we think about the physical body and its vulnerabilities in the context of Neptune in the sixth house, we must always remember that Neptune ultimately references the astonishing power of consciousness itself. Body, mind and spirit interact. We live in a materialistic culture, which tends to put the body first—that's why, if you tell them you are sad, doctors will give you a pill before they ask you about your life. They assume that the condition of the *physical* brain is the origin of the sadness.

In Neptunian matters, we usually see more clearly if we put spirit first instead of the material questions. How much can the mind influence the condition of the body? Certainly almost any physician will tell you that a patient's attitude has an impact on his or her recuperative powers. There is some evidence that prayer has a healing quality. Medical literature is full of stories of "spontaneous remissions." That's all in the realm of Neptune.

Maybe you have Neptune in the sixth house. Maybe you get sick—I don't want to predict that, but let's just say it happens to you, as it could to anyone. Just possibly, that illness can be understood as a gift. Just possibly it offers you an opportunity—not to mention a serious motivation—to practice the sustained spiritual discipline of meditation on your own healing.

26

NEPTUNE IN THE SEVENTH HOUSE

The catalytic impact of spiritual friends. Truths so vast that no one person can hold them. Committed love as a spiritual path. Passing through doors that others have opened. Corroboration and confirmation of one's spiritual vision.

My God! You are a soul inside a body!

Leaking Energy: *Codependency. Wasting time on escapists and dreamers who always fail you. Quixotic romanticism. Turning away from support and affection.*

With the seventh house we enter the intricate, complex realm of human intimacy. Strike up a chorus of the old song, "Fools rush in where angels fear to tread." The song is about the naïve illusions and unconscious projections of "romantic love," and that is our pitfall here. If you fall into it, you will miss half of the meaning of this house.

Before we go an inch further, let's affirm that the seventh house is about *all* our relationships, not just the romantic or sexual ones, healthy or otherwise. Those are the ones that get us into the most "interesting trouble" and so we naturally prioritize them in our thinking. But never forget the bigger picture: whenever we feel that *we are in the same boat* with another person, when our fortunes are intertwined, we are in the realm of the seventh house.

Here is a standard, shorthand interpretation of Neptune in the seventh house: "You will be attracted to Neptunian people." And that is accurate. Often the next word would be, "uh-oh." Neptunian people—that means drunkards, junkies, seducers, sex addicts, leeches, bankrupt spendthrifts, deceivers, porno freaks, compulsive masturbators, couch potatoes, hallucinating psychos, and worthless dreamers, right?!

And we do see that sometimes. Those types represent the dark face of Neptune, for sure. You can see shades of escapism in each of them. But there's higher ground too—and here we encounter the happier notion that your natural partners and friends in life are *mystics* and *visionaries*, people with rich inner lives—sensitive souls. They are the kinds of people who will, in our culture, probably feel the need to use the word "God" sometimes—that is, without immediately following it with the word "damn." And that's because God—or some reference to the Mysteries, whatever word they might use—is a necessary part of their vocabulary, simply because it is so much a part of their experience. They cannot share the realities of their own experience without using such language.

If you have Neptune in the seventh house, you have critical soul-business with such people. *You can't do what you are here to do in the world without their triggering an impact upon your consciousness.* They hold the mirror of your own spirituality before you; they remind you of who you really are. They are catalysts for your evolution.

Here's a practical pattern I have seen over and over again in my private astrological practice: I do a reading for a Neptunian person, *and then that person sends his or her partner to me for a reading.* Often it emerges that the first person actually had to twist the partner's arm a bit about making an appointment. The partner finally comes—and that *second person has Neptune in the seventh house.* The point is, he or she wouldn't be sitting with me unless the Neptunian partner had chosen to have the experience first—and then gotten the second person to come for a reading too. And hopefully, the second person—the one with Neptune in the seventh—walks away having benefited spiritually from the reading. And—hopefully again—he or she goes home and thanks the partner for opening that door.

This does not mean that such a person, left alone, would never have a spiritual life. Saying that would go way too far. Rather, the classic pattern that often manifests with Neptune in the seventh house is that *critical spiritual experiences arise as a side-effect of the relationship.*

Picture two people on vacation in France, walking across what used to be a World War II battlefield. One of them—a person with Neptune in the seventh house—turns nervously to the other and says, "This place gives me the creeps." And the second person responds, "Yeah, me too ... I'm glad you said that."

It's a simple little anecdote. And it is utterly Neptunian. Materially, these two people are just strolling across a pretty meadow in June. But they both feel the energy of the unquiet dead—ghosts of Allied or Nazi soldiers, the residual psychic imprint of violence and fear. Phrase it however you want; it is a purely Neptunian perception. The perception is *shared*—and that sharing is the seventh house component.

Now let's tweak the story. Imagine instead that you are walking *alone* across that battlefield. You start to get that same creepy feeling. It crosses your mind that you are picking up on the spirits of the unquiet dead, that you are actually sensing them. And then the doubts creep in. "*Or maybe I just knew this place was a battlefield and I'm making it all of this up. Maybe it's my overactive imagination. Maybe it's just free-association. Maybe it's my ego playing tricks on me, telling me I am more psychic and sensitive than I really am, trying to capture me in spiritual pride.*"

There's that old solar-ego reaction to any contact with weird Neptunian reality: *Just get a grip.*

A sane person is naturally going to have those kinds of doubts arise. That's not a totally bad thing—when you think you see something that goes against all logic, reason, and probability, it's healthy to question yourself. But then your friend says that *she feels it too*—just that simple affirmation of your own perception by another person. Feel how much more valid your own initial perception seems to you then? Someone you love and respect independently had the same "improbable" experience. Soon you are both babbling about it, making it feel even more real to you.

This is one major key to understanding the meaning of Neptune in the seventh house—that shared perceptions of the spiritual, of the transcendent, of the Otherworld, of the paranormal, of the supernatural ... use whatever words you want to use, but *such shared perceptions have more authority than perceptions we have alone.* If you have Neptune in the seventh house, connecting with such people is a spiritual necessity. They help you deepen your visceral faith in your own psychic functions. They don't *give* you your spirituality; they help *give you faith* in your spirituality.

Now let's tweak our story about that stroll across the battlefield one more time. Imagine you turn nervously to the other person and say, "This place gives me the creeps." And Mr. or Ms. Wrong responds, "Yeah, what happened here was really gruesome."

In this last example, your comrade on the trip is not Neptunian at all—and if this is a romantic or sexual relationship, let's pray it will soon end. Why? Because you are with the wrong person; he or she may be a decent individual, but not the one for you. Why is that the case? Simple: love is about feeling connected to another person, in a state of rapport and mutual understanding. Feel the disconnect here when your friend misses your point about that battlefield? Your friend's response is not crazy. It is intelligent, even compassionate. Mr. or Ms. Wrong feels that he or she understood your words and made a reasonable, agreeable, connecting kind of response.

But your point was missed entirely! "What *happened* here *was* really gruesome?" Happened? Past tense? Seventy years ago? No, what you were saying was that this horror is still happening now. It's happening right before your psychic eyes, right there in the trans-Neptunian realm. *"Can't you feel it?"* But in fact Mr. or Ms. Wrong cannot feel it; they are just not receiving on that wavelength. To be angry with them would be like being angry at a person for singing off-key. Some people are tone-deaf; they don't know they are singing off-key. This doesn't make anyone "bad." This doesn't make anyone wrong—just wrong *for you*, if you have Neptune in the seventh house.

Maybe you are seeing someone in a "dating" kind of way—let's say you're female, heterosexual, and his name is Joe. Joseph P. "Wrong," by the way. One night Joe makes a little speech to you. He says: "Look, I know you're into a lot of weird stuff... I don't mean 'weird' in a *bad* way, OK? But you know what I mean: astrology, life after death, reincarnation—things like that. I mean, I don't know... maybe that stuff is for real. I respect you. We've all got a right to our own opinions. I've got no *problem* with you being into that stuff. It's just not my path. We can live and let live there, OK?"

So there's Joe's speech. I have heard worse ones. You have too. He is not actually attacking you for your beliefs. And of course he is right about people being on different paths in this world. But if you marry him, you will be lonely for the rest of your life. Why? *Because he has just rejected half of what you are.* Furthermore, he has reneged on any possibility that he might ever meet the evolutionary needs implicit in your seventh house Neptune. He is not going to be your partner in that way.

Kiss Joe goodbye, is my advice. Go to a mediation class, a yoga class, an evolutionary astrology class—go to any such place and you will meet people who are naturally attracted to the Neptunian path. They are your pool of possible mates and lifelong soul-friends. That's where you will find them.

One of the most devastating and heartbreaking things that can happen to a person on this Earth is to meet a soul mate—a genuine soul mate—who is completely fouling up their journey. As we explore astrology in this evolutionary context, our perpetual discipline is always to recognize the higher and lower possibilities in any configuration. Those lowers ones can be very tempting. At first, they almost always seem to be the easier path—although the opposite is almost always true. Everyone has free will, including our soul mates. And "free will" includes the freedom to make a mess out of things, to make nothing but lazy, self-destructive decisions. Some people take full advantage of that. We've all got scars to prove it, too, just from watching people we've loved go down such roads. It is very painful to witness.

One thing is clear: If you have Neptune in the seventh house, many of your deepest soul mates are Neptunian. Technically, they may simply have a strongly-placed Neptune—conjunct the Sun or the Moon, for example. Or they may be very Piscean, or show a charged twelfth house, or have the Moon in Balsamic phase. There are many astrological ways this signature of "Neptunian" psychic sensitivity could manifest. It is not just Neptune, but rather that whole family of astrological symbols.

All such "Neptunian" people bring tremendous sensitivity into this world. Deep down, they are learning how to handle it—that's really what such configurations ultimately mean. But let's say they *don't* learn how to handle their psychic sensitivity very well. And you already know the rest; we've already explored many of the lower expressions of Neptune. Maybe they start to fall into patterns of escapism. Maybe they become ghosts in their own lives.

When these kinds of people show up on our doorsteps, they are human wreckage. And yet, something in our hearts knows that there is supposed to be a spiritual exchange here; there's supposed to be some magical, mutual, catalytic effect. One way to express this instinctual, reflexive response is the feeling that "we signed a contract before God with each other. We agreed that each of us is to be the yeast in the bread of the other one's soul."

But the person shows up crippled and incapable of triggering anything in us except pity—and frustrated anger. It is completely heartbreaking to see such a person before you, knowing what they were potentially capable of being—and then seeing what they have done with that potential.

There's a hard bottom line here: faced with such a fallen Neptunian soul mate, you are holding a ticket for a First Class cabin on the *Titanic.* You're standing there on the dock at Ireland, with that ticket in your hand. What are you going to do?

Tear it up; throw it away. That's what you need to do.

That is very hard. This may be someone your soul loves—and whose soul probably loves yours—but through the fog. You have got to let that person go anyway. That's "advice"—good advice. But because it is so difficult—because love is arguably the most powerful force in the universe, and love binds you together—there's a fair chance that you won't pull it off at first, that you won't be able to let that person go. And then you find yourself on board as the *Titanic* sets out to sea. If things go that far without you becoming conscious of it and doing something about it, you are, by the way, fulfilling the baleful prophecies of the more one-dimensional astrologers about the "dreadful fate" that awaits you with your Neptune in the seventh house. You find yourself in love with a drunk, in love with an escapist, in love with a crazy person, a pill-head, an incompetent—you are in love with somebody who will do anything to escape his or her pain.

Sooner or later, that ship is going to sink. It is far better to get off the *Titanic* in Ireland, so to speak. Failing in that exit strategy is one way to make a mess out of a seventh house Neptune—entering into these dramatic, often parasitic relationships with people who do nothing but suck energy out of you. And then your life becomes a drama with a familiar script, and the drama boils down to one core pattern: *your partner failing you.* He or she is just not strong enough to do the hard work of loving. And your mistake was that you expected this person to be able to come through for you. That was your own Neptunian delusion.

I'm probably going to be a little too formulaic here in this last bit. I am still talking about what happens when a Neptunian soul mate has gone down a dark road. Because it is truly a soul bond, there is a compelling sense of responsibility in you toward these people—you feel that responsibility acutely, which is one reason why walking away is so hard. No matter what such a person has done, you have to live with your own behavior. And here's where I might get a little too formulaic: I think *you have the responsibility to hold the mirror of truth before them three times.* "Here's what you're doing to yourself. Here is what you are capable of being. Wake up. Please wake up."

Maybe you *can* help. If such people are addicts in the literal sense, try to get them to a twelve-step program. If they are compulsively unfaithful, call them to truth. Ask them to look you right in the eye and tell you about it. If they are addictively plugged into a video game, pull the plug from the wall and engage them about what you see.

Will it work? Maybe. At the risk of cynicism, let's say "probably not." But you will have tried. You can go to your grave knowing that you, at least, held up your end of the contract. There is no joy in that, but there is a certain dignity.

Not to despair, either. There are lots of scenarios where people actually do help each other. Somebody's going down a bad road—and somebody who cares steps in and makes a difference. I don't want to erase that beautiful truth with some formulaic idiocy such as, "People never help each other; people have to help themselves." We hear that a lot, but it is not true. We have all been genuinely helped from time to time. All that stoic attitude does is to insulate us against love. Soul mates naturally try to help each other, and sometimes they succeed.

But you have no responsibility to go to sea in the *Titanic.* That's really the bottom line. The alternative is to tolerate this terrible energy-leak in your life. The leak derives directly from being bound to people who can't pull their own weight and indirectly from your being robbed of a positive, active need for your own journey: a partner who can be a spiritual mirror for you.

27

NEPTUNE IN THE EIGHTH HOUSE

Psychic breakthrough via sacred sexuality. Exchange of strong energies. Conscious, lifelong preparation for death. Encounters with Powers, both within and without. Occult practices and experiences.

Storming heaven

Leaking Energy: *Romantic and sexual obsession. Drama. Moody dissipation. Temptations of the Dark Side. Giving up on magic.*

First, just for purposes of efficiency here, I want to emphasize that the eighth house, like the seventh, reflects the realities of our intimate relationships. It deals with very different territories as well, as we will see. But for the sake of continuity, we will start off by revisiting the world of soul-intimacy—realizing that while the seventh and eighth houses share common ground, they are miles away from being interchangeable. With the eighth house, we deal more explicitly and concretely with sexual energy. With the seventh house, sex can be part of it, but we are also looking at *friendship* and a broader, more inclusive sense of the term *soul mates*. The seventh house is not always erotic, not always romantic. With the eighth house, there is much more of a tendency to be confronted with the compelling, often confusing, mysteries of *chemistry* between people—the *mysterium tremendum* of our old friend and ancient nemesis: *purple passion.*

We meet perfectly nice people who are card-carrying representatives of whichever gender most beguiles us. By community standards, they are physically attractive enough. They are totally pleasant. We like them very much. We vote for the same rascals, love the same Thai restaurant, listen to the same music—and yet, *sleeping with any of them would feel like going to bed with a sibling.* Sex doesn't even enter our minds. There are people with whom we are just not on that romantic, partnering wavelength at all.

On the other hand, there are people we meet and—kaboom!—the hormones are flooding our bloodstreams. This seems to happen quite independently of their moral fiber or personality. We vote for different rascals, and so on. But if we are male, we need to take a seat rather quickly, and if we're female, it's as if we ovulate at first glance.

You all know exactly what I'm talking about—that unfathomable erotic fascination that we encounter from time to time in life. You feel that energy with somebody and—what? Maybe it's the beginning of a really beautiful chapter of your life—perhaps a very long chapter of your life. Or, maybe it's the salad course for a blissful six weeks, followed by a year of psychotherapy.

How do we sort all that out? Two realities—true love and romantic catastrophe—and it's hard to tell them apart when those hormones hit. Either way, it feels about the same—at first. Welcome to the eighth house, especially with dreamy Neptune there.

We'll look at the dark side of all this soon, but let's start with the higher ground. There, in the eighth house, we are looking at the secret of *lasting or sustainable sexual chemistry* between people. We are looking at the deep mystery of the successful *couple*—and let's recognize that while two such people would surely be *friends* in the seventh house sense, there is more than simple friendship binding them. When a lover says, "let's be friends," we all understand that it is a demotion, so to speak—that the quality of the intimacy is becoming less profound.

That difference—between sleeping together and just being friends—is essentially the definition of this dimension of the eighth house. Meanwhile, subtract friendship from the equation, and if there is anything left, bottle it up and call it the elixir of the eighth house. It's not the opposite of friendship—thinking that would be a big error. But it is something outside the normal scope of simple affinity between people.

Any planet in the eighth house will give us insight into what constitutes the heart of this kind of attraction. Add Neptune to the mix and we are looking at a *spiritual basis* for the sexual bond. This is not about shared religion or philosophy, although those might be helpful. This is not about cognitive agreement. It is about something felt far more viscerally. It generally is accompanied by a pattern of shared *psychic communication* peppered through the daily life. One says, "How's about trying that new Thai place over on Magazine Street?" And the partner answers, smiling—"I was about to ask you the same thing!"

Multiply that phenomenon over countless repetitions and you have a classic expression of Neptune in the eighth house. If you have that configuration in your own chart, *you need that kind of relationship.* You will, via synchronicity, draw to yourself opportunities to bond with such people. You have soul-business with them. By that sign you will know them.

Going right to the heart of the matter sexually—we are looking at the possibility of *eye contact sustained through the point of orgasm.* That moment of utter human soul-nakedness, shared. This does not have to happen, or even be intended, every time the couple has sex. But it will happen sometimes. There is hardly a deeper nakedness than that, and what is forged between lovers, if they can resist that impulse to close their eyes in that intimate moment and instead remain engaged, is the fusion of Neptunian mystical experience with eighth house sexual energy.

We are talking about *sacred sexuality.* In our broader understanding of the eighth house, this is one of the holy sacraments. There's more to the eighth house than that, though. While we are not done talking about sexuality here, I immediately want to point out that you might have Neptune in the eighth house and could potentially "die a virgin" and still do a pretty good job with it. We will get to that.

A critical point: the eighth house also refers to certain kinds of relationships that are not sexual—but let me stick to sexuality for a moment to build our launching pad into the broader framework. If two people become lovers—and I'm not talking about a casual situation where they go to bed together, I'm talking about where they are lovers for, say, six or eight consecutive weekends. It's a phrase that makes everybody laugh, but if lovers last even that long, things start to *get real* between them. The relationship becomes more raw and more human—and that's where we enter the eighth house. There is no house that is more *human*—and when I say "human," I mean warts and all.

If you're "in bed with somebody," in the larger sense of that phrase, over a long period of time, you're going to get know them better than you will know anybody else in the world. You see their rough places, difficult places, anger, control issues, fears and edgy places; you see their difficulties, wounds, and probably their tears. Lovers, in the deep eighth house sense of the word, share and commune at that level.

Now, here is where we go beyond sexuality. You have a friendship with someone. It is not sexual, but it is the kind of relationship in which *you can talk about anything.* Maybe you've cried together. Maybe you've raged. It's the kind of relationship in which you sometimes risk the relationship's entire existence in order to keep it honest. You tell each other things you don't want to hear; you say things you're afraid to say. You're not sure your words will be taken right—but the commitment in the relationship is to be that real. We are talking about *really* best friends.

Let's bridge a little deeper into understanding this kind of soul-friendship via a little detour. Classically, the eighth house is the *house of death*—and we will indeed have a few things to say about mortality as well before we are done. Let me start by imagining that you have just received a terminal medical diagnosis. *Who is the first person you're going to tell?* Who's the first person you're going to sit down with and talk to about this?

As you answer that question for yourself, you are listing your eighth house friends—or friend. Often one of them is enough.

The eighth house is not always miserable and horrible like that, but life contains plenty of "miserable" and "horrible." People are often embarrassed to share these things. "Embarrassed" seems like a strange word to use, but think about it. If you had that kind of diagnosis, do you notice how there's that inner resistance regarding telling anyone? It makes you so vulnerable to say those words—and you know it's going to make everyone uncomfortable to hear them. It's just so heavy—and there is a big cultural taboo about bringing up "heavy" topics. Therefore, we all get trained socially to keep bad medical news quiet—*except where?* And the answer lies in our eighth house relationships. With Neptune in that house, there's a great need to be able connect with someone in a spiritual way in the face of life's sheer enormity and horror. So, when the chips are down, to whom do you turn? Who can see you in your raw, real state?

Notice how we have extended our definition of the eighth house beyond the sexual framework? As we've seen, the eighth house is indeed often sexual in the grown-up sense of the word—but it actually refers to all relationships in which we can *exchange strong energies.*

We add just a little reality-check here. If you are mated with someone and you've gotten that kind of dire medical diagnosis, who is the first person you are going to tell? We understand that in almost any healthy marriage of souls, the first person to hear the news will be your partner. Sex isn't the touchstone here; raw human intimacy is. But they often go together.

To help someone with their passage out of this world—*to help someone die*—there's an eighth house Neptunian phenomenon. And I am not narrowly referring to giving someone an overdose of medicines out of mercy or something like that. That *could* be on our list; sometimes people have to make choices like that. We might instead be talking about simply *being with another person who is exiting this world*—to hold his or her hand and be present in that sacred, mysterious moment.

The phrase that almost formed in my mind was "to counsel someone who's dying," but somehow that makes it sound too heady, too intellectual and wordy. A lot of the "counseling" of people who are passing from this world boils down to sitting there with them, just being with them in that space. If you have Neptune in the eighth house, you may very well magnetize into your life exactly that experience—somebody close to you needs your help passing from this world. In some mysterious way, your souls signed that contract.

And if you hold the hand of someone as she passes from this world—she is medically alive and then medically dead, while you're holding her hand—that is an experience that is going to live inside of you forever. Socially, we might say words like, "Oh, what a terrible thing, what a horrible experience." And that's what people are going to say about it—"That must have been so awful for you. I'm so sorry." That's what you're going to hear.

That's just social talk.

But here is what you know in your heart: being there with your friend in her last moments *was a sacred experience.* Your soul-friend let you into the sacred space of his or her passage out of this world, and you were privileged to be there. You're not "happy," but you know in your bones that she gave you a gift. The memory is sacred to you for the rest of your days on this Earth. And when your turn to die comes, *you draw strength from the courage and grace of your friend's passage.*

Some people wind up doing *hospice work* with this kind of configuration. That is a high expression of the potentialities of Neptune in the eighth house, for sure. But here I'm talking about it coming up more naturally or spontaneously in your life. Such experience reflects a small percentage of your elapsed time on this Earth, but in terms of what you bring out of this Earth and what you learn from your journey through it, it's going to be high on the list.

Poignant stuff.

Going further with Neptune and mortality, we can observe that, with Neptune in the eighth house, part of your spiritual path lies in *cultivating constant mindfulness of your own death*—letting death be your teacher, death be your counselor. Because of the laws of synchronicity, you'll find you will probably get some help with this. The help may take the form of little reminders that you could die. One example is a near-accident in the automobile, or maybe a disease that could threaten your life, but then you recover from it. Maybe it's just the *imagination* that you have a disease. Maybe you just ate too much pizza and you've got some tummy pain from all the acids and you think, "Oh, Jesus, pancreatic cancer!"

And we may laugh at that image, but the idea is that for two or three days you actually have the subjective experience that something is really wrong down there and that you're going to die. Angels are laughing at you a little bit, but trying to keep straight-faced in front of you; they don't want to tell you it's just pizza. This little taste of the realness of your own death is way too useful! They don't want to waste it. Angels know that sooner or later, the pain is going to be real, and it's going to be a sign that you're getting near the exit, because of course we all die. We all get there.

Keeping death close helps you really understand what's important and what isn't. And keeping death close that way is part of how you clean your windows with Neptune in the eighth house.

It's a fierce path, this one! Sex and death—of course they are a famous pairing in all the literature on the subject. And there's the eighth house: it embraces the two most intense subjects in the world. I want to weave them together a bit more, and that will eventually launch us into a classic merging of eighth house intensity and pure Neptunian mysticism: the *occult.* Just a few steps more before we get there.

Going back to sex for a moment, I used that very vivid image of maintaining eye contact with a beloved through the point of orgasm. As you simply sit, humanly, with that image, you feel a thrill of energy run through you. Feel how your batteries are given a big jolt of cosmological amperage, even just by imagining that experience? Two people come together in that sacred alchemy and they both leave the situation stronger.

Run another step through your reality-checker: two people who have just had that sacred sexual experience are less likely to catch a cold during the next three days. I know how crazy that sounds—and of course it wouldn't be true if one of them already had the sniffles. But doesn't that basic assertion feel real, if you stop and intuit about it for a moment? Sexual love charges us with life-force. The logic is that their life-batteries were charged, and one effect is that their recuperative powers, the defensive powers of the body, are stronger.

That imagery provides a deep perspective on an eighth house Neptune—the mystical process of building that energetic charge in ourselves. Call it *prana*, call it *chi*. It goes by many names. We are nearing the realm of the occult, as promised. In many such occult traditions, this energetic load accumulates in the solar plexus. I think that's probably the right way to think about it; I think of a little Sun starting to shine in there because you have accumulated experiences that charge it.

Sacred sexuality is only one of those experiences.

Let's tie it back into death. You walk away from the hospice where, an hour ago, you were holding your friend's hand. She's gone from the body now. You have a vivid sense of your friend's spirit triumphantly leaving the flesh. You can feel that reality—even if it was never mentioned in science class. You can't explain it to anybody, and probably you have sense enough to keep your mouth shut about it unless you're with somebody you really trust. Why argue? Why squander the good energy that way arguing with a materialist?

But you sensed her spirit leaving her body. You sensed the sacred triumph of that. Go back to the moment of that experience. Feel how that solar plexus battery gets a little charge? *Conscious contact with the process of death and dying feeds the ancient soul-battery.* And, with Neptune in the eighth house, that's a big part of what you are actually here doing: feeding that battery.

Personally, I am horrified by the idea of "sacrificing" any kind of living being as a religious ritual. You won't see me doing any voodoo. But this recognition of the moment of death as a portal into realms of enormous energy is really the key to understanding even those kinds of barbaric practices.

Go further. There is a lightning storm, and instead of running for shelter, something inside you compels you to step out into it. There you are, standing before the storm with your arms spread wide, feeling the rollicking energies of earth and sky roaring through you, into you. Wow! Feel that *juju!* Here is the universe, thundering, and you open your heart to it. Can't you feel that? Of course you can—you are human and this is your inheritance. Now imagine a shaman, ten thousand years ago, doing exactly that same thing, following that same instinct. Easy, huh?

Thus, we go from sex to death to lightning storms. Notice the common denominators: Something is filling you with juice; something is filling you with energy. Why don't we, as a culture, talk about this kind of thing anymore? Why have we astrologers—purportedly holders of ancient wisdom—forgotten all this? With Neptune in the eighth house, these potentials are within your grasp. Exploring them is part of your soul's intention for this lifetime.

Now, again, I appeal to your ancient, primeval self—not to your social, cultural, or academic training, because all of those are completely irrelevant here. I appeal to something far more primal than that. *When your time comes to die, when you are leaving this world, wouldn't it be a really good thing to have that battery charged?* To have it really alive and ready? Doesn't that make sense? Doesn't it feel intuitively right that such a charge would help you as you enter the mystery of the *bardo* of dying? And don't confuse this with physical vitality—obviously, physical vitality is rare on deathbeds.

We are not talking about "standing in the Hall of Judgment," not the Sunday School stuff about dying. We are talking about the actual mystery of the death process. I am leaning in a very Tibetan direction here. We are talking about soul-navigation in the *bardo*, in the mysteries—with all of the risks and incredible opportunities connected with the moment of death. And if you have Neptune in the eighth house, I am talking about you.

We could say that, with Neptune in this position, you are spending your life preparing for the moment of death. To be ready, you need *dear friends* with whom you *exchange strong energies*. You benefit enormously from *sacred sexual experiences*. You will likely have *contact with death* during your life and can draw energy from such experiences. You need to *walk in lightning storms*—or the equivalent realities of walking by the shore as storm waves are crashing in, or standing by a volcano, or just feeling the power raining down on you from a dark desert sky full of more stars than you can count.

Spending your life preparing for death—run that idea through the cultural filters and we quickly see how easily it could be misinterpreted. We are conditioned to think it is a depressing statement. It is as if we are suggesting that you always dwell morbidly on death. That's not what Neptune in the eighth house means at all. You're *accumulating the energy that allows that astral body to remain conscious and intact through the mystery and the trauma of leaving the body.*

This gets into very deep territory. But if you have Neptune in the eighth house, you are already in that deep territory. Even if no one has ever said a word like this to you before, I believe you are wired to understand what I am saying.

Let's go further with the "occult" meaning of Neptune in the eighth house. For the majority of humans on the planet who have this configuration—which totals about six or seven hundred million people—what I am about to say would have little meaning. We are definitely at the higher end of the evolutionary spectrum here. I suspect that if you are encountering this material, you are ready to hear it.

We have seen that certain kinds of relationships play a pivotal role in the eighth house process. We have focused on human relationships. Entering some exotic territory, in various occult traditions there are beliefs and disciplines which involve *establishing relationships with invisible beings*—deities, spirits, daemons, and so on. This too is part of the eighth house Neptunian realm of possibilities.

The underlying idea is that "the couple" is stronger than either of its parts alone. That sentence would fit earlier in this presentation as a simple reference to a human couple. Here, in this occult context, it takes on a different coloring—but it still retains many identical features.

Occult traditions, for example, often reference relationships established with *power animals*—and again, there are parallels with previous eighth house patterns. With Neptune in the eighth house, you might find yourself drawn in these "animistic" directions—maybe a very weird cat meows at your door. Or maybe the relationship is not with an animal. Maybe an angel knocks on the door of your soul.

If that is your path, the universe will let you know. Synchronicities arise; you will be guided by omens. You will find teachers. And you will become more charged, more powerful, as a result.

Some occult traditions put less emphasis on the idea of "other beings" with whom we might establish energetic symbiosis. Instead, they posit "powers" of a more neutral, less personal nature. I'm not convinced that the distinction is anything more than one of personal perception, but for what it is worth, this second, "inorganic" language is closer to my own experience. Either way, we enter into rapport with "something" other than ourselves and, together, we become empowered in ways unavailable except in this kind of working partnership.

If you keep your battery charged, you will have energies of insight and creativity and inspiration you'd otherwise lack. That's something you can take to the proverbial bank.

Now let's take a look at the dark side of this placement.

The garbage-can dimension of the eighth house, across the board, is *moody, heavy, and brooding*. Just imagine a person who is morbidly obsessed with death and all the heaviness and moodiness that might be associated with that preoccupation. This condition can arise quite independently of whether death is actually consciously on the person's mind. It can be operating from the unconscious, leeching the life out of a person.

Sexually, there is a danger of dissipating our energy in endless intimate dramas. Life becomes a passion play—tragically-doomed romance after tragically-doomed romance. That's a terrible danger here.

We could talk about "sexual dissatisfaction." I don't mean some reference to a quota of orgasms that we have failed to meet—nothing nearly so mechanical. When I use the word "sexual" among grown-ups, I'm not talking simply about genital needs, but rather the need for a certain quality of connection between two people. Bad relationships speak for themselves; they are no good for anyone. But if you have Neptune in the eighth house, there is a true soul-need for energizing partnership. If it is missing, that opens up a bleak emotional pit from which it is hard to escape.

We can imagine people with Neptune in the eighth house who are afraid of going into that deep shared nakedness that I've been describing—but they don't admit that fear to themselves. Instead, they account for their feeling of dissatisfaction or disconnection in sexuality by blaming their lovers: "If only I could find the right person who was capable of handling real passion, then I would be happy." And yet, they are carrying in themselves a fear or a blockage. Perversely, they often become attracted to people who are as incapable of bonding as they are. Or, if by chance they find themselves attracted to people who could potentially "go there," they don't let them. They sabotage the situation. And so, they constantly renew and preserve their own sexual frustration. "I'm just looking for somebody with whom I could have a truly spiritual relationship"—that's what they say. "But time after time, I have been failed, or fooled."

It's a delusion; the problem is something they're creating for themselves. We could label it "sexual addiction," and that's correct. But even if we observe sexual compulsivity, the real hunger is not for genital release. Instead, it is more akin to a *morbid romanticism*. Just think of all the trouble people can potentially get into with a slight mis-definition of the term "soul mate," followed by an endless search for someone who doesn't actually exist.

The cure? We go back to square one. With Neptune, it's all about cleaning your windows. It's about clear-seeing. And that always starts with some kind of personal spiritual practice.

28

NEPTUNE IN THE NINTH HOUSE

Cross-cultural spiritual stimulation. Sacred journeys and pilgrimage. Rectifying one's views, beliefs and philosophy through disciplined metaphysical education. Mind training. Critical spiritual thinking.

I'm not dumb. I am just ignorant!

Leaking Energy: *Religion as an obstacle to true spirituality. Beliefs that block or distort your actual experience. Provincial or limited views. Cultural determinism eclipses direct experience.*

We come to Neptune in the ninth house—a more spacious, less claustrophobic environment than the eighth house, for sure. Reading the descriptive lines above, already you can feel the call of a wider world. In the ninth house, our attention turns to learning, to immersion in experience, and to the expansive world before our eyes.

Regarding the quotation, "I'm not dumb; I am just ignorant." I love that line. It's from a film about the young Loretta Lynn, *Coal Miner's Daughter*. Sissy Spacek played Loretta. In the film, someone accuses Loretta of being stupid, and she puts her hands on her hips and delivers that glorious line. A wonderfully petulant moment—and a very deep truth. There is a difference. "Dumb" is a really unfortunate condition in that it is completely incurable. But ignorance is 100 percent curable.

Ignorance is cured by *education.*

Now, the ninth house, of course, is classically related to education—to universities, literally. And that connection is real and valid, but I want to give the word "education" more breathing room. It's not just the idea of getting your doctorate or your master's degree, but rather of *learning*—just learning itself, no matter how you do it, and apart from any diploma you might earn.

Adding in Neptune, you might enroll in a school to learn electrical engineering or accounting; that's fine—but that's not so Neptunian. What is *Neptunian* education? This is actually rather slippery, complex territory, as we will discover. Some parts of the answer leap out—Neptune has a natural orientation to *metaphysical questions*, deep *psychological questions*, and *expanded states of consciousness.* The study of *addiction* is in Neptunian territory. Neptune is creative and imaginative, so we might add to our list subjects such as *creative writing, filmmaking, and the whole realm of the arts.*

At the practical, concrete level of astrology, if you have Neptune in the ninth house, you may very well be drawn to any of those educational directions. You may find them meaningful and inspiring. They may even lead you down a road of destiny.

There are deeper waters here. Let me just take you directly to a very Neptune-in-the-ninth-house place by bringing up the idea of *reincarnation.* It is an interesting subject, and of course quite fundamental to the work we do with evolutionary astrology.

My point here is larger though. I am just using the issues reincarnation raises as a launching pad. To begin, I ask your ninth house Neptune a seemingly simple question, "Do you believe in reincarnation?" And your ninth house Neptune, assuming it is healthy and fully functional, might respond, "Well, I definitely remember some past lives. *But reincarnation? I don't know . . .* "

That might seem like a confused answer. How can you possibly feel you remember some past lives but not be sure about reincarnation? What could that mean?

I press you, and here is your explanation: "Maybe what I remember are literal past lives. But maybe they're something I saw on television or in a movie when I was a little kid; I don't remember the television show or the movie, but maybe I have that imagery in my head, and I was so moved by it and so identified with it that now I am *interpreting* it as a memory of a past life. Or here's another thought: maybe there's some kind of ancestral memory. Maybe this 'past life' was lived by one of my ancestors long ago and I'm somehow in resonance with this person through some weird, undiscovered genetic phenomenon or through some more subtle energetic phenomenon. Maybe that's what I am remembering."

Which of these many views is true?

Here we have *three different interpretations* of exactly the same facts. Any one of them could potentially be valid. It all depends on how we connect the dots, so to speak. *And the ninth house is about connecting the dots.* It is where we move beyond facts into *interpretations* of the facts. In the ninth house we seek the Holy Grail of *understanding*. This is why one of its classical meanings was *religion*. That is still a useful, practical ninth house word—especially with mystical Neptune there. But we can stretch the term a bit and call the ninth the house of *belief systems* or *philosophy*.

Let me continue to use the idea of reincarnation as a vehicle for launching into a higher Neptunian orbit. Let's say that we accept the literal notion of past lives, as I do myself. But exactly *what* reincarnates? That's a tough question. If we are "all one" and the individual self is ultimately an illusion, what reincarnates? Buddhists don't like to say "soul," so they often say "the mind-stream" instead. That just sounds to me like different words for the same thing. But the question is subtle. I have a deep faith in the idea of reincarnation, but whoever I was in the past is stone dead—I am a different being, with a different chart and a different path. So, what actually came back into flesh?

I don't doubt that each of you could write a five-hundred-word essay on that subject. Writing such an essay would get you firmly in the ninth house part of your head. If you've got Neptune there, you'd feel right at home wrestling with a juicy metaphysical question like that one, and it would be good for you.

If we were serious about wrestling with that topic, how might we proceed? We would have our own ideas, but maybe we would also seek "expert witnesses." We might turn, for example, to the works of the great psychic, Edgar Cayce, the "sleeping prophet," who brought so much attention to reincarnation here in the Western world. Or maybe we would look to the incredible work of the late Ian Stevenson, a psychiatry professor at the University of Virginia, with over 1,700 case studies of kids who remembered past lives in concrete detail—most of which were corroborated factually in field research. Or Roger Woolger's hypnotic regression work, or that of Brian Weiss. Or what about Gautama the Buddha? He had a few words to say on the subject.

Welcome to the world of Neptune in the ninth house. We are talking about an *intellectual inquiry* into the precise details of the metaphysical mechanisms that govern this universe. We are talking about *sharpening our understanding.*

Implicit in this process is the notion that we can recognize that there are many wise teachers we can learn from. Those words sound familiar, don't they? We used similar language earlier with Neptune in the sixth house. But here we're not talking about the sixth-house idea of *direct contact* with such teachers—rather the ninth-house idea that we can have direct contact with what they have *left behind* for us. In the sixth house, we speak of that mysterious quality of *transmission* that can exist between teacher and student. Comparatively, the ninth house is more cognitive and conceptual. *For it to work, you do not need to know the human being behind the ideas.*

I actually think your dog can receive sixth-house transmission from you—it is that instinctual a process. Dogs are famous for showing guilty expressions, for example. And we might make a case that feelings of guilt are humanity's gift to the dog kingdom! But try asking your dog our famous question, "what reincarnates?" Good luck, right? The point here is that sixth house learning has an instinctual, "monkey see, monkey do" component, while ninth house learning happens much more in the top two inches of your head.

What I'm trying to get at here is a *celebration of learning*—the idea that right views and right concepts get us a lot faster and further down the Neptunian evolutionary road than wrong views. Burdened by wrong views, we can so easily tie ourselves in knots. *With Neptune in the ninth house, there is enormous benefit that comes from establishing in the intellectual mind a correct understanding of our human condition in the universe and of our possibilities in it.*

"Correct understanding" is of course a very slippery concept, fraught with the dangers of dogmatism and various forms of fundamentalism. And those are perilous soul-traps for anyone with a ninth house Neptune. We can be so eager for understanding that we leap into over-simplifications, then defend them like rats with crusts of stale, moldy bread.

Correct understanding often arises from correct questions—especially ones which *subvert our certainty*. Let me illustrate that with an example. Run this idea up the flagpole before a group of astrologers at a convention: *you can see the personality in the birthchart.* Most of them will wonder why you bothered to say it at all, it's so "obvious." But wait a minute—you had the same birthchart when you were five years old as you do today. Do you have the same personality now as when you were five? Obviously, most of us have improved somewhat since we were munchkins. For the majority of us, our present personalities bear only a tangential resemblance to who we were back then. And yet, your birthchart is exactly the same as it was when you were five.

So what is it exactly that we see in the birthchart? Clearly, "the personality" is not an idea that withstands close scrutiny.

That's a didactic point. I am not making it so much for its intrinsic meaning, but rather to illustrate ninth house *critical thinking.* Say all that to a group of expert astrologers, and there are going to be some who get angry and defensive. And, bless them, there are going to be some who listen. They are the ones who make an "A" in their ninth house functioning.

Again, I am just using the idea of astrology here as a vehicle for exploring the larger principles that underlie a ninth house Neptune. We are talking about metaphysical education, driven by the right questions.

Taking it a little further, we might for example learn in an intellectual sense about the laws of karma—that every action, loving or separative, has inescapable consequences. We might grasp that idea in principle—learning it from a book, so to speak. The next day we are driving down the highway and some *macho*-man in a pickup truck is tailgating us. And instead of bedeviling him by slowing down, we pull over and kindly let him zoom by. We even wave at him. In our heart, we were thinking, "what a jerk"—but our pure action will inevitably bear positive fruit in our life, now or in the future.

The point is, we might very well *not have offered that kindness toward someone who offended us unless we had an understanding of the laws of karma.* In our evolutionary journeys, *we* can lead with conceptual understanding, in other words. We do not always have to lead with the heart.

If you have Neptune in the ninth house, keep a pile of metaphysical books by your bedside. Attend lectures, come to classes, sit with teachers.

You are training your mind to lead your soul. You have come to that point in your journey. Probably, in prior lives, your good heart got ahead of your head, so to speak. You need to help your head catch up.

Switching gears here, we all learn in Astrology 101 that the ninth house symbolizes *travel*—but let's stretch that word to include *culture shock,* or *cross-cultural experience.* Without much mental effort, we can include such experiences under the broad banner of "education." Other cultures put the world together in distinctive ways. They have a different view of things than we do. Their views may not necessarily be better, but they are distinct, and absorbing their perspective helps us to ask some productive questions.

I understand, for example, that some Arabic people burp after a meal in order to express appreciation. Why not? In Europe, many women go topless on the beaches. Why not? Some dear Mexican friends once brought something up that they were hesitant to say. I'll never forget it. They said, "*Americans don't like babies.*" At first I didn't understand, then I saw it—in Mexico, unlike America, a baby crying in a restaurant isn't such a big deal. A baby in a stroller gets a lot of positive attention from strangers. It's just a different culture.

Getting at these core beliefs—beliefs so deeply entrenched that we are blind to them—is one of the core evolutionary mechanisms of the ninth house. Travel—and open-hearted contact with foreigners—triggers that process in us. Thus, with Neptune in the ninth house, we keep our "religion" healthy by exposing it to cultural challenges and alternatives.

With Neptune in the ninth house, again we link metaphysics and travel. What do we call travel with a spiritual agenda? We have a name for it: *pilgrimage.* So, faced with Neptune in the ninth house, I might say to a client, "I see pilgrimage in your chart." Here we encounter the archetype of the *sacred journey.*

With this configuration, at various points in your life, the opportunity to undertake such journeys will arise. The laws of synchronicity declare that. Don't miss them; these trips are critical ingredients in your evolution. Go to *holy places* and open your heart and mind to them. Some of these destinations are probably not "official" holy places, like Lourdes or Benares or Jerusalem. Some of them will just be holy for *you.* For one woman I knew, it was an island on the coast of Maine. She described it as her "church." Something spiritual in her was renewed through her annual summer visits there.

Karma, whether we know it or not, plays a role in all of this. Perhaps in a prior lifetime you were a nun in a convent in Tuscany. Maybe while on vacation you will be drawn back to Italy—and the feeling of the place triggers memories of spiritual buried treasure within you. That can work even if you don't remember the past life—although with Neptune in the ninth house, the place will certainly seem supernaturally, goose-bumpy-familiar to you.

The point is that if you have Neptune in the ninth house, various *places* on the planet have energies to which you are psychically attuned for any of a variety of reasons. Exposure to these energies can trigger active evolution in you. Visiting them is a skillful means—a wise thing to do.

Where are these places? You'll either have a feeling of inexplicable attraction to them or you will simply be "blown" there by the winds of karma.

Let me reference what could be a long "footnote" here without actually diving into it. One way to get a possible sense of where you can find these charged places is to have a look at your astro-locality charts. *Astro*Carto*Graphy* and *Local Space* lines often give hints about their locations.

A ninth house Neptune is not always about travel; sometimes we can enter "foreign territory" right at home. Here's an illustration. Let's say someone joins my evolutionary astrology apprentice program with a background in a more conventional style of astrology. Instantly, he or she is having a cross-cultural experience. Without making value judgments, my style of astrological thinking can feel "foreign" relative to other practices. As we look at any system from two different sets of assumptions, two different points of view, we'll often see it more clearly.

As is our eternal custom here, let us not neglect the evolutionary garbage can. Neptune in the ninth house provides one, just as surely as everything else in astrology.

One lower, escapist, energy-leaking quality of Neptune in the ninth house is simply to *hang on the cross of a pre-existent, dead belief system.* This can look like rote participation in a religion that no longer enlivens our souls nor speaks to them. And "religion" here does not narrowly mean the usual menu of Judaism, Hinduism, Christianity, Islam, and so on. As easily, it can imply beating the dead horse of some New Age belief system that is no longer working for us, or even something more secular—the religion of communism, for example, or the religion of endless scientific progress. Essentially, in every case, we are looking at a situation where we get so attached to our opinions—so attached to being right—that it almost becomes like we are "keeping God in his place." Nothing new or fresh is allowed to exist—which, if you think about it, is a pretty excellent definition of death.

A particularly sticky issue with Neptune in the ninth house arises when we reflect on the innate selflessness of Neptune. That wide-open, nonresistant state is its highest expression, but don't forget the dark side of it—that familiar, drifting ghost-state. And the question, "What will it all matter in five hundred years?" Our solar lives *do* matter; we need our egos in order to gather the soul-food of experience in this world. *But what if we make a religion out of being a ghost?* What if we make a religion out of the endless surrender of our right to exist?

This may sound unlikely, but think about it. There are many religions that make a virtue out of silent suffering, as if the highest human aspiration were to hang on a pointless cross. If you have Neptune in the ninth house, be wary of that soul-trap.

The antidote? In classic, high Neptunian fashion, *question the underlying assumptions.*

29

NEPTUNE IN THE TENTH HOUSE

Mission. Service in the world. You are invited to embody some ideal or principle for your community. Doing so entails putting your "little ego-self" aside. Wear the hat humbly and eventually it will fit.

God grant that today I do work that matters.

Leaking Energy: *Becoming a "public utility." Losing one's self in a social role. The trap of fame. The trap of propriety. The trap of social expectations. The trap of the spiritual ego. The trap of self-created "failure."*

One traditional name for the tenth house was *the house of honor*. Fair enough—but it didn't necessarily mean "honor" in the sense of integrity or decency. Back then, it was simply about position and status. Humans have always been concerned about their place on the social totem pole.

Updating that ancient reality to reflect the present state of human monkey-business—putting it in the framework, in other words, of modern astrological practice—the tenth house has become symbolic of one's *career* and *professional life*. That is accurate—but by far the most evocative way I have found to address tenth house issues meaningfully with a client is to speak of it as representing his or her *mission* in life.

"Mission" is perhaps too lofty a term, but I like it; it lifts us out of thinking narrowly in terms of professional categories and money-making. It also takes us beyond the egocentricity of present-day "career" rhetoric—all the *me, me, me* language about how *I* am going to *get mine*, I am going to *make something of myself*, I'm going to *get ahead*, and so forth.

Ambition is not necessarily such a terrible thing, of course. It can correlate with high levels of engagement and creativity, and with making a real contribution to society. The problem is that it just doesn't reflect the actual realities of tenth house motivations—especially when relatively egoless Neptune is there.

Almost everyone has some desire to *leave the world a better place* or to have a positive impact upon their community. Such drives are not utterly and totally *opposed* to our more ego-centered needs for recognition, fame, and money. The point is broader—that these loftier drives are a critical *component* of any understanding of the tenth house. That principle extends to the rest of the planets, by the way, not just to Neptune.

Often, what people are doing in regard to their mission is not directly reflected in what the Internal Revenue Service labels their work. As a practical illustration, when the tenth house is stimulated by transit or progression, we often see more than professional changes. We see changes in a person's *status in the community*. For example, someone gets married; someone becomes single; someone has their first child; the last child leaves the nest; someone retires.

None of those changes necessarily make you any money. So, with the tenth house, we are looking at changes in *the way people in general view us*. We are looking at *what we appear to be* from the perspective of people who do not know us very well. In a nutshell, the tenth house is about *how self relates to community*.

Bottom line, *if you have a planet—any planet—in the tenth house, you have a mission*. That's what any such configuration ultimately means—at least potentially. You've come to a place in the soul's journey where your task is to *develop that planetary function and offer it as some kind of gift to your community*.

Planets in the tenth house typically give us insight into the actual nature of the mission—but there are currently about ten objects astrologers call "planets," while there are approximately 1.7 *gazillion* things you can do "professionally" with your life. So each planet stands at the head of a very long list of possibilities. Logic dictates that they have to be at least somewhat vague in terms of saying exactly what mission we should pursue. Planets aren't useless mission indicators there, but their helpfulness in specifically describing it is limited.

What planets in the tenth house do so much more helpfully and effectively is that *they indicate what part of ourselves must be developed radically before the right mission is magnetized into our lives.* And that's not just a cutesy New Age way of putting it. This is a pure expression of the principle of synchronicity.

As we saw a moment ago, "mission" is a bigger word than "career." Career is driven by ego, and often by hunger, self-importance and insecurity. But "mission" implies that you are plugged into far more powerful dynamos than mere ambition. Mission means that you are preparing yourself to do something that *the community needs you to do.* There is a need out there and you are the answer to it. And so there's a wonderful synergy, potentially, between your own development and events that seem to occur randomly—which is to say synchronistically—in the outer world.

In a nutshell, when you are ready, you get "the call." That's true with any planet in the tenth house.

Now let's add the specifically Neptunian elements to the tenth house mix. So far, we have mostly been talking about the tenth house itself. With Neptune there, for your mission to come and find you, what must develop radically is your own relationship to the part of you that Neptune represents. You have to clean your windows. Essentially, what must flower is your own spirituality—that is one word I could use. Equally, we could refer to your *visionary imagination.* Compassion and selflessness are good Neptunian words too. Developing and expressing them can be part of the process. Psychic or intuitive powers are on the list, as is a general sensitivity to invisible energy-fields. We could speak of your relationship with God—or Jesus or the Dharmakaya or angels or Mohammad or Vishnu.

To say it more succinctly, the task that lies before you is to become an *embodiment of a Neptunian principle that is visible to anyone who looks at the outward shape of your life.* That's an intentionally broad statement because Neptunian principles cover a lot of possibilities, as we just saw.

If, for example, we think of someone who is the embodiment of compassionate or charitable activity in the world—if I invoke, for example, Mother Teresa of Calcutta—we see something of the spirit of Neptune in the tenth house. She embodied the idea of one who is committed to easing the suffering of wretched beings through charitable work. Thank you, Mother Teresa. Her chart is murky both in terms of her time of birth and even her date of birth, so I'm not saying she actually had Neptune in the tenth house. We just don't know. I'm only using her as an example. But thank you, Mother Teresa, for reminding us all of the far limits of the human capacity for compassionate engagement in the world.

That last line is not meant as simple piety towards her. What I am saying is that Mother Teresa has *symbolized* something of the highest expression of Neptune for the human family. And that is the classic action of a tenth house planet—that your life takes on the proportions of a myth *in the minds of people who do not know you.* You thus affect the myths and symbols of your community. In Mother Teresa's case, she of course has had that kind of mythic impact upon literally millions of people—essentially "everyone knows about her."

We do not always need to operate on such a grand scale here—not everyone needs to be Mother Teresa—but we do always need to be mindful of the *public symbolism* of our lives.

Let's continue to merge Neptune with the tenth house. As you are probably beginning to see, it's a somewhat odd marriage of symbols. High Neptune couldn't care less about "fame" or "status." What will any of that *fru-fru* matter in five hundred years? So, you were a very *important and prestigious* monkey in Lower Slobovia for a few years, huh? Try playing that card before the angelic hosts in the Hall of Judgment!

Something in Neptune naturally turns inward, away from the glitz of the world. And yet the tenth house really is *about* the world and our place in it. A lofty, somewhat self-transcendent concept like "mission" is the only possible way to bridge the two symbols—the tenth house and Neptune—in a healthy manner.

Imagine a yogi who spent seventeen years in a cave in the Himalayas, sitting in meditation, fasting, and all of that. And maybe that yogi was found dead in the cave at some point—"late in his career," shall we say. He withdrew utterly from the world and was literally not seen in it for the last seventeen years of his life. But in telling the story, I am invoking Neptune in the tenth. The point is, the reality of that solitary yogi's life has an impact on anyone who hears the story. That yogi might even have had Neptune in the tenth house, and he was succeeding in his mission by embodying another face of Neptune—in this case, not charitable or compassionate action, but rather a *radical devotion to the inner path*. He is a mythic figure; even if we didn't know him, we *know* him.

And so, we have these two very different lifetimes—Mother Teresa and this yogi—one being profoundly relevant to the community in a direct way, and one indirectly relevant to the community, almost accidentally. These are both positive Neptunian tenth house images. Thus, both people become mythic and symbolic beyond their specific personalities. One expressed compassion, the other, inner devotion. Those are both high Neptunian qualities, of course—but there are others, equally precious, and less obviously "spiritual." With Neptune, I always like to add "of *visionary imagination*." In doing so, I roll out one of my favorite illustrations. This man did actually have Neptune in the tenth house, in Cancer, just a few degrees from his late-Gemini Midheaven: *Walt Disney*.

Let me float the idea of Walt Disney as "a great spiritual lighthouse." The language seems a little weird, doesn't it? We are not accustomed to thinking of Walt Disney as a spiritual giant. And in fact, Walt Disney, when you get into the details of his life, was kind of a fascist in a lot of ways, apparently—there were some pretty nasty edges to the guy. But how many generations of humans has Walt Disney touched through his visionary imagination?

Walt Disney, whether he knew it or not, was transforming our relationship to the nature kingdom. Talking dogs, talking chipmunks, a famous and rather human mouse—you know who I am talking about, right? Who doesn't? Walt's Neptunian imagination basically touched *everybody*. Since Disney made *Bambi*, generations of us would feel bad about shooting mama deer.

I'm obviously saying all of this with a smile on my face—but didn't Walt Disney affect the consciousness of generations through manipulating the myths and the symbols by which we came to understand the natural world? That's an easy question. Clearly, he did that. And impacting the collective visionary imagination, affecting our view of all life—is that not spiritual work? It is a pure expression of his Neptune in the tenth house—and even in Cancer, simply for the implicit *caring*.

I love to roll out Walt Disney as an illustration of Neptune's action in the tenth house simply because he is so antithetical to what we would conventionally view as a spiritual teacher. He did not make direct mention of God, souls, pious virtues or any of that kind of "spiritual" stuff, and yet, *he embodied Neptune in the larger sense*. He triggered a transformation of the way we interpret the matrix of reality—and what could be more Neptunian than that?

While we are it, we should add, very concretely, that *film is a Neptunian medium*. Movies are a dream-world. Using film, Walt made his dreams a gift to us all. He developed his dream to a radical degree and found a way to offer it as a gift to the human community. He is an utterly clear expression of the action of Neptune in the tenth house.

And he made a zillion dollars doing it. That's not a problem. It detracts nothing from his accomplishment. It was just the way the world said, "thanks, Walt."

So, increasingly, in this emerging post-religious world that we're creating, we find that healthy expressions of Neptune in the tenth house don't always bear the obvious trappings of "official spirituality." The church, the temple, and so forth, are becoming at least somewhat marginalized in many segments of the human population. They are still here; they may last a long time. But, bottom line, they are no longer the only vessels carrying human spiritual aspiration.

When a younger person with Neptune in the tenth house comes to me looking for career counsel, there are some technical tricks we can employ to narrow career paths down a bit. What planet, for example, rules the sign on the Midheaven, and where is it located? What sign does Neptune occupy? What aspects does it make? But fundamentally, my point is that, in looking at a chart, we are only going to get some general impressions of possible career tracks or missions. There are limits to how specific we can be. As we will see, that is not a problem.

With Neptune in the tenth, trying to support that younger person in the counseling room, I'd be happy to put religious categories on the table as possibilities—such a person might, happily, become a *chaplain*, one who engages in the *ministry* or the *rabbinate*, one who becomes an *imam* ...on and on, in any of these obvious clerical categories. But let us also recognize another possible career track—the *shaman*. Is that a religion? Well, kind of—it is a Neptunian role, for sure, to be a shaman. Or a medicine man or medicine woman. I know that sounds a bit exotic, but let's recognize that the list is long, and those categories would be on it.

Let's stretch a bit further: what about suggesting to that young person that he or she become a *Jungian analyst?* Such an analyst might not be universally recognized as a religious figure, but he or she is certainly doing work with the deep unconscious mind, and that is the realm of Neptune. He or she can be understood as a lighthouse in the community, reminding us of the fact that we are deep psyches on a mysterious journey in this world. That sure sounds like a tenth house Neptune flying high to me. Every Jungian analyst, just by being what he or she is, is an embodiment of that reminder to the community.

Go further: what about somebody who is working as a *hypnotherapist?* Inducing trance in people? Hypnotism—what a mystery that is. Why does that work? What is going on with hypnotism? And what a reference to deep consciousness it is—so, once again, we see that classic Neptunian fingerprint.

Anybody who is working in any of those professional categories is potentially doing higher Neptunian work. Ditto for every *visionary artist.* I made reference to Walt Disney, but really every visionary artist counts here. They all lift us up into the realm of imagination. Ditto for the great storytellers: the *screenwriters*, the *filmmakers*, the *documentarians.* And of course the poets, the painters, the musicians who lift us into another world—sometimes for ten seconds, sometimes for longer, opening that doorway into a transcendent reality. Thank you, Beethoven. Thank you, Led Zeppelin. Thank you, William Butler Yeats, David Whyte, and Dylan Thomas. Thank you John Singer Sargent.

These are all illustrations of the higher expressions of Neptune, whether or not these people actually had that tenth house Neptunian configuration.

Try this: here's somebody with Neptune in the tenth house. I say, "Hey, what do you do for a living?" Answer: "I'm a bartender." That shouldn't surprise us too much either; *a bartender is a Neptunian figure.* A bartender helps you alter your consciousness, right? And isn't that Neptunian?

Let's let that image breathe a little bit. Bartending doesn't sound as lofty as some of the roles I've just been mentioning. Does being a bartender mean that such a person is blowing it spiritually? Mixing margaritas when they should be teaching *kundalini* yoga? I don't think so; I'm not going to be so judgmental.

Maybe you have a glass of wine with your friends after a long week of work. What happens? You feel a deeper sense of connection to each other;

you feel calmer; you feel loving; you feel a certain serenity. You get your own joke, you take yourself less seriously. You feel a lightness of heart and a sense of humor. Think about it: *the alcohol has put you in a more spiritual state of consciousness.* If all the virtues I just listed don't spell "spiritual" to you, I need someone to define the word for me.

So, thank you for being our spiritual master, Mr. Bartender!

Let's invoke a familiar cliché: a bartender who is essentially an underpaid psychotherapist. Not all bartenders are like that, but it isn't a rare phenomenon. How many times has a bartender heard the following from somebody sitting on the barstool—*My therapist would kill me if she ever heard this, but . . .*

Again, my intention is not to make a grand case for a career tending bar just because you have Neptune in the tenth house. But in just hanging out a little while there with Joe the bartender, we expand our sense of what a positive response to Neptune in the tenth house could potentially mean. We expand our compassionate engagement with the diverse expressions of it, going way outside the boundaries of official spirituality—and thus avoiding some of the dangers of self-important piety and judgment.

Remember: what the Divine thinks you are doing and what the Internal Revenue Service thinks you are doing are not always the same thing.

Recall our basic principle, that a planet in the tenth house must be intentionally developed in order for the mission to arise. How do we develop Neptune intentionally? The obvious answer: some kind of *spiritual practice*. Yes—but let's take it down a specifically tenth house road. In the tenth, we experience *status*. We are "somebody." And that is to the ego like sugar is to ants. So a discipline for developing a tenth house Neptune is to let go of all that—to get comfortable with being *nobody special*, nobody important.

How do you feel about a "guru" whom it costs a thousand dollars to see, who has a private jet, and vacations with famous movie stars wearing thousand-dollar sunglasses? Suspicious, right? *To teach something, we must know it*—and Neptune is about a state beyond ego-identification.

Pretentious people cannot teach of a life without pretense.

One practical synchronistic effect of all this is that people with Neptune in this position, on the developmental road to meeting their higher callings, often go through *periods of initiation* in which they feel and appear "unimportant." They go through times in which their spirituality is unrecognized and unappreciated. *And maybe they learn that having their spirituality go unrecognized does not diminish the reality of their spirituality at all.*

When they fully internalize that truth, they are on the verge of a "career breakthrough." They've earned it. They passed the evolutionary test. If I had to write this on a bumper sticker, I'd say that *until we lose all self-importance, we cannot teach the higher mysteries.*

Let's turn our attention to the lower ground. As usual, there is plenty of that available with Neptune in the tenth house. Obviously, we should make reference to *the town drunk*—the person who is publicly identified as an addict or a wastrel of some sort.

On a more subtle level, let's consider the image of a person who lives the life of *a ghost,* or a person who is *hanging on the cross*—someone who has not actively claimed his or her life, but instead seems existentially suspended, like the proverbial deer in the headlights. With Neptune in the tenth, typically such a person is caught in a *public role*, or defined by a *social role*. Every one of us is born into a society, into a social class, ethnicity, economic bracket. Many of us don't land too far in life from where we were launched: in other words, they got us when we were young.

So, to make a short story shorter, maybe a person is eight years old and there she is—one of the kids at the country club. And now, thirty years later, she is one of the drunks at the country club bar. We met her earlier; here she is again, illustrating an empty face of Neptune. How does she feel? There is more than one possible answer to that question, but if she has Neptune in the tenth house, she probably feels as if her life has become a bad movie, that she is *caught in a role.*

Neptune, as we saw right from the beginning, can *drift.* It can slip into a lackadaisical feeling that nothing matters, that none of this will mean anything in five hundred years. And, down that road, the solar ego fails to perform its natural function—so there we sit, at the bar, talking about things that don't matter to us with people with whom we do not feel connected.

That *slow drift*—and a public persona to go with it—is one dark expression of a failed response to Neptune in the tenth house. We didn't claim our own journey through the world but instead allowed ourselves to be *shaped by the expectations of others*, seduced by the path of least resistance in terms of our social identity. And life just kind of got away from us.

Here's another soul-trap. With Neptune in the tenth house, there is a risk of being seduced by *glamour.* That's one of my favorite words—it sounds sort of cheap and modern, but it has an old tradition to it. Glamour was a power that leprechauns had. They could cast glamour on something and make it look more valuable than it was—which is interesting insight into the "glamour magazines." A leprechaun might cast glamour on a bucket of pebbles, then say, "Farmer O'Houlihan, I will gladly trade you this fine bucket of diamonds and rubies for your broken-down horse." And of course the joke was on the farmer, once the glamour wore off.

Glamour attracts us—but it is not real. And, among its many meanings, Neptune is *the planet of glamour.* Illusion, delusion—glamour is a very short step away from those words.

If you were born with Neptune in your tenth house, you may very well find the winds of karma blowing you into situations that have some hint of glamour about them. If you have a middle-class income—and let's start from that common point of view—I would invoke the image of expensively-coiffed high-rollers in glittering casinos in fancy five-star hotels on the French Riviera, dressed in gowns and tuxedos, wearing diamonds, gambling fortunes.

Can you feel the game that I'm playing with you? We look at those "glamourous" people and they're like the gods on Mount Olympus. We envy them. Often we don't want to admit that. I suspect that if we are afraid to admit the attraction, the *glamour* has gotten even more power over us.

How do the people in those casinos actually feel? What does it feel like actually to be there? That's a big, complicated question. Some of them are probably pretty happy, but surely some of them are not. What might it feel like if you're there and you're in the wrong relationship and wrong life, with the wrong people, and you know that but you don't know how to get out of it? And yet, all the while, everybody is looking at you, *projecting glamour onto you.*

Maybe you start to halfway believe it. There's social expectation that you *must* be really happy—being a god or goddess on Mount Olympus, how could you not be happy? Hey, you are even having a good hair day! Maybe, with Neptune in the tenth house, an opportunity such as that arises, you're caught in the web of that rich, glamorous world. You hate it—but you become addicted to it as well.

Now, as always, the antidote to any of these lower expressions of Neptune in the tenth house is the higher expression. I'm aware that my words verge upon sounding silly, but that statement really embodies the most basic active astrological principle. We've seen it over and over again—the energy *will* manifest; it's just a question of *how* it will manifest. Your consciousness—your choices and your decisions—determines the answer.

And so, if you have Neptune in the tenth house, on the road to the higher ground there will arise naturally in you some *interest in consciousness itself.* I don't know what exact form that interest will take. As we have seen, it may be in a religious or spiritual category, it may be in an artistic category, it may be in a psychological category. But there will arise naturally in you an interest in consciousness. We can count on that.

Pursue it! Climb that mountain; radically develop that Neptune in you. Trust those instincts; trust those interests.

And then something strange happens. Follow those instincts and interests where they lead you, and the laws of synchronicity will attract into your life a unique opportunity: *the opportunity to get paid for your spirituality.* I'm being a little crass putting it in those terms—but it often works out exactly that way quite literally. Translating a little more broadly, we might speak of your being *recognized and appreciated socially or collectively for your inner life.* That is actually a more precise way of putting it.

I don't mean to make any kind of jinx out of money, though, because that's often exactly how society says "we appreciate you." And down that road, there may be glamour—and even that is not an inherently bad thing, *unless you fall for it.* You will be equipped to see through it, although it may tempt you at times. But you won't be a ghost. You'll be too real for that.

So we've looked at the low ground and the high ground with Neptune in the tenth house. Here is the synthesis. *You are to be a reminder—or even a direct catalyst—in the inner lives of people whom you do not know personally, or with whom you do not have personal karma.* And that is your mission. I don't want to be too Capricorn-ish about it, but you have signed up for that responsibility. There is the sense of a soul commitment to rise to that level in yourself and to play that role in your community.

Don't blow it, or you will annoy all the angels.

30

NEPTUNE IN THE ELEVENTH HOUSE

Great benefit from the support of a spiritual tribe—visible or invisible. Fellowship; Sangha. Shared practice. Intense development of psychic sensitivity over time. Setting spiritual goals and intentions.

Ready or not, here it comes.

None of us can make it on our own.

Leaking Energy: *Pointless, draining, unproductive social relationships. Social religion. Insidious creep of escapist behavior as psychic sensitivity increases without support of adequate inner practice. Turning away from community.*

There are always two fundamental dimensions to the eleventh house. They're interlocked, although at first they don't seem to be. Traditionally called the *house of friends*, the eleventh house deals with groups of people with whom we have involvement, affiliation, or identification. Secondly, the eleventh house has to do with the *future*—that is to say, with evolutionary processes that gather momentum over time.

Those seem like two very different statements. Let me pull them together for you. It is in their interplay that we come to a full understanding of this piece of astrological symbolism.

Let's say you have a specific ambition, an intention, or a priority in your life—those are all good eleventh house words. It is to become a skilled painter of fine art. Good for you—maybe you have Venus in the eleventh house, and you are right on track. So here's some good advice—*hang out with artists*. Get to know other artists; build relationships with them.

There's other advice that we could give you about becoming an artist, but that admonition should be on the list.

Why?

Because sometimes your enthusiasm for developing as an artist will wane—and if your friends are artists, they're going to be running into you, asking, "What are you painting lately?" They're going to support you, and help you recharge your enthusiasm. They may not even know they're doing it. Their own enthusiasm will be infectious.

At a practical level, they are going to email you to let you know that your favorite brushes are on sale at a particular art supply store. They're going to tell you about a show that's coming up. They're going to invite you to come to Europe with them—at your own expense, of course—to visit the great art galleries.

In this case, you have chosen "your tribe" in coherent support with your personal interests. This simple insight is the bridge that links the two pillars of eleventh house theory: clear *developmental goals and the alliances that support their realization*.

As we mentioned, conventionally the eleventh house is often called the house of "friends." That's actually quite a misleading term. When modern people speak of their friends, they are implying intimacy, deep familiarity, and fondness. Eleventh house "friends" might better be called *associates* or *allies*. Those terms can sound a little cold, but they are closer to the actual experienced reality. Here's the concept, put very starkly: eleventh house friends are people whom you can *use*.

Ouch! That sounds even colder, doesn't it? But there is no exploitation implied here—only *common cause* and *mutual benefit*. These people help you get to where you want to go. You probably do the same for them.

Let's add Neptune. If you are on the right track, even in your early years you will have some Neptunian goals, interests, or priorities. Those can take many forms, but they boil down to prioritizing the exploration and opening of consciousness. That is a healthy response to Neptune in the eleventh house, and you benefit from keeping your eye on that prize as you *think strategically about where and what you want to be when you are old.* To achieve that Neptunian ambition, it is really helpful to have friends who are on a similar path.

I always think of the foundational Buddhist teaching that there are three "Refuges" from the craziness of this world. The first of them is the *Buddha*, who is always there, omnipresent. The second is the *Dharma*—the law of life, the teachings. Follow them, and your life will be easier. And for the third Refuge—the Buddha said, "Look at each other. When you fall down, the others can pick you up." That third Refuge is called the *Sangha*. It basically means *the fellowship*.

There is a wonderfully esoteric—and utterly Neptunian—reading of this last Refuge which I learned from Khenpo Karthar Rinpoche in one of his books. In speaking of the *Sangha*, he pointed out that this fellowship is not completely visible. There are beings in the bodiless, invisible realms who are part of it too. We could call these entities *spirits who take an interest in your practice.* Neptune-fashion, they are compassionately engaged with you, whether or not you can see them.

How do you attract them? Just pray. Just close your eyes and open your mind to deep trans-Neptunian space. Ask for their help. They care. *Where you are now, they once were themselves.*

Bottom line: with Neptune in the eleventh house, your natural and proper goal in life is spiritual development and in order to attain it to your fullest potential, you need the context of a group of like-minded souls.

I can speak personally here since I have this configuration in my own chart—my Neptune lies in mid-Libra in the eleventh house. So let me just say a whole lot with one single word—*thanks!* I thank every one of you. The apprenticeship program is my *Sangha*, or at least part of it. Everyone in the program is part of my fellowship. And because of my membership in these groups—and I want to put "membership" ahead of any reference to my role of "leadership"—you all help keep me on my path. What would I be doing if I weren't doing this? I'd be a bartender, I guess! *(laughter)* Or just sitting in a bar.

So, thank you.

Neptune is about surrendering. Let me illustrate that dimension of Neptune in the eleventh house with another personal story. This one goes right to the heart of it, and it is kind of painful to tell. A long time ago, in the 1990s, I was playing in a band called *Dragonship*, doing a rock opera. And a band is an eleventh house structure—with *ensemble* music, you can only access that absolutely thrilling experience via cooperation with other musicians. So while playing in a band might be personally meaningful, it also requires "allies." There's that classic eleventh house signature.

Here's what happened. It was scary. I woke up one morning with half of my face paralyzed. The condition is called Bell's Palsy. I'd never heard of the disorder before and I felt that I'd probably had a stroke. I literally couldn't move half of my face. I couldn't even close one of my eyes. I went straight to a doctor, of course. I learned that I had "probably about a 75 percent chance of recovering." That statement of course translated in my Saturn-ish mind to the fact that there was a 25 percent chance that I would spend the rest of my life unable to speak clearly. That would be horrifying for anyone—but you can imagine the particular implications for me, given my work.

As I mentioned, I was playing with a band back then. I had this moment with them—this kind of group healing ritual that unfolded very spontaneously. It was nobody's plan or intention. They all made a close circle around me, and I was lying in their laps, as if I were a baby, as they all laid their hands on me, to heal me. I'm not even sure how we got there, into that positioning. But somehow we did.

If you're a Capricorn, with Saturn on the Midheaven like me, welcome to hell! I can give and give. But receiving? That's *hard*. To receive love? Neptunian, eleventh house love? I had to surrender to the love of this circle of friends, in a time when I was patently in terrible need.

Well, obviously, I healed. There are only some faint, residual effects of the Bell's Palsy. And I thank my band. Who knows, logically, how much that healing circle affected the disease or supported the healing? My gut tells me it helped a whole lot.

I want to underscore the essential insight—that I *evolved* in that moment. I had to. I helped myself a lot by being able to receive that love. And that receiving was really tough. That's Neptune in the eleventh at the hard-work level—*learning how to receive from the group.*

To be human is to be vulnerable. It involves interdependency.

Carrying that idea further, in one of the *Star Trek* films—*Search for Spock*, I think—they started out with the self-evident moral idea that "sometimes the needs of the many outweigh the needs of the one." But they quickly began to play with another idea. Poor Mr. Spock—Mr. Capricorn, rather obviously—was in a dire situation. All the other characters had to steal the starship *Enterprise*, breaking all the laws and getting themselves into a world of trouble, in order to go rescue him. And the theme deftly switched to how *sometimes the needs of the one outweigh the needs of the many.*

Sometimes the group—whether it's the crew of a fictional starship or a rock 'n' roll band—has to go to bat for one person who is grossly and grievously in need. If you've got Neptune in the eleventh house, one of the first things you may need to learn is how to receive from the group. That might happen in a way that feels really unbalanced to you, as if you don't deserve what you're getting. But that need—and your heart opening to that love—is part of your eleventh house evolutionary work.

Earlier I mentioned that one dimension of the eleventh house is the setting of *goals* and *priorities*. Any goal or priority that you sincerely feel—and support with appropriate allies—will loom larger and larger in your life as time goes by. You will inevitably *make progress* toward it. Thus, any planet in the eleventh house has a curious property: *it grows stronger as you grow older.*

Careful here, though—that planet growing stronger may not be good news. It depends on your response to it. Jupiter in the eleventh? Will you develop some kind of meaningful success—or just get fat or sybaritic? Mars in the eleventh? Will you develop real courage, enough to defend something precious to you—or just become chronically angry and bitter?

What about having Neptune there? *Will you become a saint or a drunk?* That line oversimplifies a complex topic, but it aims our noses generally in the right direction. Just simply and objectively, with Neptune in the eleventh house, your Neptunian energies will get stronger as you move on past life's middle. The psychic opening will increase, by mechanical astrological law. How you handle that is up to you.

Say somebody asks you to make some predictions for a newborn baby. Maybe you say, "She'll get taller." Everyone laughs. But of course you are right—getting taller happens automatically. That's what I mean by "mechanical astrological law." It operates outside the realm of volition. Anything in the eleventh house gains power as the wheels of life turn.

The question is, can you handle it? Neptune is saying, *ready or not, I'm coming.*

Earlier, when introducing Neptune's core meaning, I mentioned how it correlates with psychic sensitivity. That sounds good until you read the fine print—that psychic sensitivity includes an attunement to all the suffering in the world, all the pain radiating from everybody sitting next to you in the waiting room, the whole energetic ambience around you.

Can you handle that pain? As that psychic opening occurs, there must be corresponding spiritual practice to help you integrate it. Otherwise, you'll become overwhelmed. And that's when we see the darker Neptune manifesting. What is the nature of that darker Neptune? *The ghost, hanging on the cross.* And of course the escapist, the drunkard, the addict. These, as we have seen countless times now, are the dark images. Will they gain power over you as you age, or will you get it right?

I sat with a woman once many years ago. She had Neptune in the eleventh. She was about thirty years old. I encouraged her to recognize that spiritual practice of some sort was going to become more important to her as time passed—and that if she failed to practice, dangerous results could arise and her psyche could become overwhelmed. Almost as an afterthought, I added that she might experience something like dementia. And course I had already emphasized the positive path and the treasures that were available to her on it. Inwardly, I also felt that since she was just thirty years old, thinking about "down the road" in life was probably kind of a safe abstraction for her.

And she burst out crying.

I had hit a very sensitive nerve. Her father had recently been diagnosed with early onset dementia—he was only in his fifties, I guess. She lived in terror that the same thing would happen to her. If I'd known that, I would naturally have been more delicate in how I phrased what I'd said to her. In retrospect, I do feel a sense of the divine hand in this—I was telling her the truth, more than I knew. She had an innate vulnerability in this scary direction. Maybe there are genetic components to dementia—but I was also talking about a way she could lower the risk of developing such a disorder. I was talking about how, with appropriate spiritual practice, these kinds of negative Neptunian manifestations can perhaps be warded off.

There might be people in the medical world who would think that meditation had nothing to do with warding off dementia. I'm not in a good position to argue with them, not knowing much about brain biology. I do know that it is well-established that people who, for example, work crossword puzzles regularly are less likely to come down with Alzheimer's. "Use it or lose it" seems to be a good principle with the brain. And with Neptune, meditation is the antidote to states of dissociation and spaciness—states with a distinct kinship to senility.

Let's not lose sight of the fact that, with Neptune in the eleventh house, something far more glorious is available to you, provided you work toward it with some diligence all your life. The carrot at the end of the stick—or better said, the pot of gold at the end of the rainbow—is the potential of becoming a *luminous elder*, one who is an inspiration to anyone who has the privilege of being near you. The "elder" part enters the equation when we think about Neptune *developing deeply over time*. There are spiritual elders whose presence we relish and cherish. And there are "old people" who just bore the pants off us. With Neptune in the eleventh house, you have the capacity to land heads-up on that one. But you've got to do that deep Neptunian work in *ongoing fashion*, diligently.

And remember: you also need the *right allies*. You need your *Sangha*.

The negative is always the distortion of the positive. I spoke positively about how if you have the goal of evolving spiritually, you need to find friends who are on the same path. Now let's look at the negative side of it. Let's say that you have not clearly established that spiritual goal. Neptune is still there in your eleventh house—so, by mechanical law, you still have some connection with groups of people, some tendency to be drawn into crowds. The winds of karma or synchronicity will blow you into such collective, social situations—*but without the unifying principle of your own spiritual intention underlying your choice of friends, how would these groups be assembled?* What is the common denominator in them? The answer is, your own uncertainty—your own vagueness, your own rudderless, lost *randomness.*

So, what we see in this expression of eleventh house Neptunian dysfunction is a person stretched thin in life by *social entanglements*, distracted by group associations that don't have any particular meaning. The lament becomes, "I guess I have to go to the party on Saturday. Sally would be so sad if I didn't show up. I guess I really should go."

I imagine that on your gravestone: *She went to parties she didn't enjoy. She met a ton of people about whom she didn't give a damn. And afterwards, she always sent a nice thank you note.*

Better to find your natural Sangha and help each other to the top of the spiritual mountain.

31

NEPTUNE IN THE TWELFTH HOUSE

Trance work. Meditation on the transitoriness of all phenomena. Meditation on luminous emptiness as the true nature of mind. Conscious use of loss and reversals of fortune. Acute psychic sensitivity. Regarding the world as a dream. Losing self-importance. The Sacrament of Holy Solitude.

What we are looking for is what is looking.

Leaking Energy: *Psychic shock arising from insufficient spiritual practice. Self-numbing behaviors. Escapism. Spiritual laziness. Withdrawal from life.*

Neptune is the natural ruler of the twelfth house, so when it lies there it takes on tremendous—if somewhat one-dimensional—power. When a planet gets into its own house or its own sign, I always visualize a big dog chasing a little dog down the street. And the little dog gets to its own yard and turns and faces that big dog. It makes its stand. *I'm in my territory. I am Davy Crockett at the Alamo. I am Butch Cassidy and the Sundance Kid, combined.* And usually that big dog is going to hesitate when it notices that "cornered" attitude. A planet gets to its own house and it has that kind of feeling: I'm home, and this is where I am as powerful as I can be.

So with Neptune in the twelfth house, we are looking at not only a powerful but also a very *pure* expression of Neptune. That's why I called it "one-dimensional" a moment ago.

If I had to reduce this energy to one single word, it would be *contemplation.* Or meditation. But because contemplation, meditation, prayer—religious words like that—are so familiar, we numb ourselves a bit by using them. So let me add another, edgier word—*trance.* That one makes people pay a little more attention. We are maybe a little less comfortable with the idea of "entering trance." It seems a little weird, a little suspect. And with Neptune we've got to remember to be weird. This is not safe, church-on-Sunday, spirituality. This is full-on mysticism. And when we three-dimensional, time-bound monkeys begin to have intuitions about the larger framework of actual reality, it gets unnervingly weird. We are not used to the idea of a multidimensional, time-transcendent frame of reference—let alone the direct sensory experience of it. We will see a lot of that with Neptune here in its own house, maxed out.

And yet there is something in our hearts or our essences that can tolerate that spaciousness. We can sense the reality of that bigger framework. When Neptune is in the twelfth house, we see a very clear expression of that particular sensitivity. The questions become: *Can you sit with all that spaciousness and not be undone by it? Can you actually tolerate that level of groundlessness? Can you be that open? Can you stand that much transparency, that absolute vulnerability?* How much of that can you take?

Passively, with Neptune in the twelfth house, we can pretty much guarantee that even if we are looking at the chart of a person who is bitter, materialistic, and drunk in front of the television set most of the time, we will see at least some of these psychic phenomena. He or she might cynically deny them, but they will be there. I envision such a person holding onto the arms of the easy chair, white-knuckled, fearing the abyss they are afraid to name.

Even in the case of someone like that, if you say to them, "sometimes people just *know* things without knowing how they knew them," that person is probably going to agree. He is going to get it. He is going to have had those kinds of experiences. He might have no interest in their larger implications; he may just shrug his shoulders. But he will know that such realities—which transcend logical understanding—are part of life. He was born with an attunement to them, just as some people are born with an innate ability to sing or to play music or to dance.

On the face of it, that might sound like a good thing. But by now you're familiar with both sides of the Neptunian archetype. The response of the human ego to Neptunian input or stimulus can be complicated. With the psychic opening comes a vulnerability to the psychic pollution that surrounds us all. We live in a world full of fear and anger, a world full of anxiety. There are loftier things we can say, but those negatives are out there. We all radiate on those negative wavelengths sometimes.

With any strong Neptune placement, you are tuned into all that. As you open, that hunger to grab the arms of the chair, white-knuckled, arises. We may not know what's happening or label it correctly—but we feel it. Some of that aversive reaction is simply driven by our fear of being vulnerable to things that are indeed pretty scary. We don't want to be swept over Niagara Falls by this wave of rage or despair, or desolation or heaviness.

How can we defend ourselves against all that? There's a pressing question for anyone born with Neptune in the twelfth house. Without certain kinds of spiritual effort, we don't even know where the hurt is coming from. It's like being in a room with a bad smell. You're tired of smelling it, but what can you do? Stop breathing? That works for thirty seconds and then you're going to breathe some more, and the smell will be even worse.

If you have Neptune in the twelfth house, you are breathing the psychic air. How do you deal with that? There is a higher road—but there is also the gaping vertigo of the lower road. And so, consistent with this supercharged position for Neptune, we enter the familiar territory of escapism.

I'm aware that most of what I've said so far about Neptune in the twelfth house has essentially been a repetition of material we've already covered. That should be no surprise, because with Neptune here, we are simply dealing with a very pure and unmodified expression of the Neptunian archetype. The twelfth house does not add much to Neptune; it only intensifies it.

In a full analysis of a specific individual, we would, of course, add elements of individuality by considering the sign Neptune occupies, its aspects, and so on.

One way in which I might begin to address these issues with a client is to say that there is a real danger that you might *not grow spiritually* at all in this lifetime. I would add that this lack of growth could be masked by a belief that you were in fact growing. You would have no idea that there was a problem.

The misleading evidence that you were in fact growing would be that you were having plenty of psychic and spiritual experiences.

These experiences would not in fact be evidence of any current growth—only residual "money in the bank" from prior lifetimes. "Money" is a crude but direct analogy that I like to use. You're born with ten million dollars. Hey, you're rich! And later you die with ten million dollars. You're still rich. *But you didn't make any money.*

Our classic Neptunian phrase—*what will it matter in five hundred years*—has great relevance here. As I roll out that phrase again, what I find useful about it is its ambivalence. On one hand, we know that there is something beautiful and wise about those eight words. They can serve you well and reflect a deep spiritual serenity. Say your flight has been cancelled and you have to check into the airport hotel—a lot of people get really upset, frustrated and angry by that experience. At a time like that, it really helps to have a strong response to Neptune. So you have to spend a night in Chicago and get home tomorrow—what will that matter in five hundred years? There's obvious practical spiritual wisdom in that kind of transcendence.

But, on the other hand, we can also recognize implicit in the phrase the potential for not taking responsibility for our own lives. There can be a kind of passivity in the face of what arises, where we don't lift a finger in our own defense—and where we don't lift a finger in terms of our own evolution. We can simply be lackadaisical. Or lazy. That lack of motivation can generalize across life's big game board—but I'm also linking it specifically to a lazy or lackadaisical quality relative to our own evolution. *Why should I make the effort to explore this gift with which I was born?* I have ten million dollars—that's plenty of money. Why should I make any more?

Well, there is an excellent answer! A moment ago, I referred to "money in the bank" from prior lifetimes. That's just a single phrase, but it embodies the soul of the deepest Neptunian wisdom in the world. Unlike worldly fortunes, this currency is transferable from lifetime to lifetime.

Ask the angels—or ask any reflective old person, for that matter—and they will all tell you the same thing: life is very short. The sheer folly of banging our heads against the wall "to get rich" is vividly illuminated on the deathbed, where we instantly lose every penny. All worldly glory is famously transitory. But if "your treasure is not of this world," the good news is that you get to keep it. Nothing can take it away from you.

And with Neptune in the twelfth, your actions in prior lifetimes have positioned you for a breakthrough in this one. You are potentially burning high-octane spiritual fuel. All you have to do is to make like Captain Jean-Luc Picard of the starship *Enterprise* and say, "Engage."

So how do you actually do that? Start by realizing that there is nothing you need to do first. You have everything in place. In the back of my head, I am hearing Van Morrison singing, "No guru, no method, no teacher."

Have a seat. Turn down the volume on distractions. Pay attention to your mind. That's the sum of it. Your karma sits like a tossed penny quivering on its edge, ready to fall heads or tails. One little quantum moment of effort on your part and you can land heads up. You can walk away with "a hundred million dollars."

What might stop you from claiming that treasure? I have a strange answer: *your own wisdom,* turned on its head. What I mean by that takes us back to our familiar question, what will this matter in five hundred years? On this potentially fruitful evolutionary cusp, there is a real risk of snatching defeat from the jaws of victory simply because *you don't care enough to do anything about it.* That "not caring" can bring us straight back to laziness—or trans-Neptunian consciousness—depending on what form it takes.

The twelfth house is oceanic, containing the whole frothing sea of consciousness. Out of that sea arises the more specific and crystalline structure of the individual ego. So with Neptune in the twelfth house, there is a sense of really "getting the joke" about the ego. We are standing back from it, and in the mirror we see the self-important little monkey demanding life's little bananas. Now, getting the joke about *other people's egos* is usually pretty easy! But getting the joke about our own ego? Losing our self-importance? That's of course really difficult.

Which leads us directly to another opportunity synchronistically connected with having Neptune in the twelfth house: Situations arise in which we get to be "nobody in particular." We have the experience of not being viewed as "special." Nobody thinks we're very important or even very interesting. There are parallels here with some of what we saw with Neptune in the tenth house, although the ultimate aims are quite distinct. Phrases we might use are *feeling anonymous,* or *feeling invisible* or *discounted.*

Think about it for a moment, and you quickly realize that learning to tolerate being anonymous has a lot to do with being egoless—that is, if we accept it and revel in our social transparency. Wouldn't it be fun to be a ghost and move invisibly through all the back rooms of the world where people believe they are having private conversations?

The alternative, of course, is to get completely bent out of shape by "not being taken seriously." That's just an ego feeding-frenzy. And because of the power of synchronicity, that feeding frenzy is about as nourishing as munching magazine photographs of five-star meals. No matter how much we whine, we are still invisible.

This "anonymity" associated with a twelfth house Neptune may not be the story of our lives. If you are, say, a tenth house Leo with Neptune in the twelfth, that solar configuration will shade things. Being a tenth house Leo, you will probably have experiences of being "seen as important." But there will still likely be periods of being sort of ignored—of being invisible—when that Neptune is triggered by transits or progressions.

How do you handle that? Can you be mindful enough to realize that this is a gift? Can you appreciate that you are being offered, via synchronicity, a chance to be *nothing but a great, invisible spaciousness* as you walk through this fashion-show of a world?

Can you "get it" that, at the ego level, that's all any of us actually are anyway?

I am remembering a wise client of mine, a woman of about fifty-five or sixty, with Neptune in the twelfth house. She was talking to me about how she had once been "pretty," but that when she reached a certain age, she felt like she'd become invisible in the world. People just wouldn't see or notice her at all. She joked a lot about how easy it would be for her to shoplift if she felt like it. She could walk out of a fancy boutique watched over by skinny, self-absorbed twenty-somethings, having nicked an expensive Italian leather jacket off the rack—and no one would even notice her. At her age, she just wasn't, as she put it, "in the game" anymore.

There was a mix of humor and playfulness, along with a dash of bitterness, in her words. She wasn't painfully upset about it—but that invisibility was also a little frustrating to her. Basically, God bless her, she was using it as an evolutionary opportunity. She was working with it. She was getting the joke. And it was stoking the fires of her evolution in twelfth house Neptunian fashion. Her ego was going "poof."

Do we exist if nobody is paying us any attention? There's a classic

Neptunian question.

I was standing in line in a grocery store some years ago. It was a long line. And just to pass the time, I picked up *TV Guide* and opened it at random to an interview with Julia Roberts. And my respect for her went off the charts as I read it. She was asked, "What is the greatest misunderstanding that the public has about you?" And Julia Roberts had the most delightful answer. She replied, "That I am fascinating." All of a sudden I was thinking, I'd like to have dinner with that woman! She doesn't have Neptune in the twelfth, but it's strongly placed in her chart—in Scorpio in the fifth house in a very tight square to her Leo Moon. I think she's gotten that one right!

This kind of experience of anonymity could be viewed as misfortune, but of course there are worse misfortunes in this world. For millennia, astrologers have viewed the twelfth house as troublesome and ominous of terrible losses. While I don't want to overdo that perspective, it is simply grounded, practical astrology to recognize that there is observable truth in it: the twelfth house does indeed correlate with things not going as we had hoped.

What we must remember is that the loss of *anything that supports an identity to which we are attached* can be a springboard into higher states of consciousness. As the structures which support ego collapse and erode around us, we can simply feel sorry for ourselves, thinking of ourselves as victims—and, for one example, find solace in the whiskey bottle or the pharmacopeia.

But we can do better than that. There are "right uses" of apparent loss or misfortune, and they are in classic Neptunian territory—territory that is amplified by Neptune's presence in its own natural house. How many people have awakened spiritually as a result of life-threatening disease, divorce, or bankruptcy?

Now, it is profoundly important to affirm that we don't always have to lose things or suffer in order to grow spiritually. It's just a method that sometimes works—and one that has a natural correlation with the twelfth house. I want to be really careful not to slip into the dangerously oversimplified perspective of framing the twelfth house as "unlucky." We read that idea in a lot of astrology books, but let's really trust the symbols and invite them to speak. How many houses are there? Twelve, of course. Astrology is a cyclical system, and this is the last of them, so the twelfth house must correspond to *the end of a cycle.*

Everything that is born must die. Everything that comes together in this world must fall apart. There are no exceptions to that. That is a universal truth—one that is the very essence of a deep understanding of the twelfth house. Thus, in the twelfth house, things *naturally die.*

Add a fundamental truth about human psychology—sometimes things come together in a way that we like *and we try to hold them together that way forever.* That natural reflex of *clinging* is antithetical to a twelfth house Neptune. This configuration is about *learning to learn from endings.* In doing that, you are simultaneously learning to accept the way things actually are. Nothing is permanent; everything changes. You can accept that notion "in your heart"—or you can learn it the hard way, which is in your life.

Remember when you were little and you went on vacation? Maybe your family went to the beach for two weeks. And as the second week began, you started to feel this terror and despair that the week would soon be over and you'd have to go home again. And you wished the vacation would never end.

This anxiety about something over which you have no power at all—the passage of time and the changes it brings—ruined half of your vacation.

Maybe you figure that out. Welcome to the higher ground of Neptune in the twelfth house. Or maybe you just suffer futilely, feeling a sense of doom hanging over every good thing that arises in life—there's the lower ground.

You get older, maybe a little wiser. Maybe you go on another vacation. You are enjoying the beach, but—in your greater maturity and wisdom—you are also aware that part of the joy of this vacation is that it *will* come to an end. You understand that if you were to just stay on vacation for the rest of your life, that beach would begin to feel depressing and empty. The vacation *has* to end; that's actually part of why and how it works. This attitude reflects you maturing—and coming to understand that the twelfth house is simply part of a natural cycle. "It's all good," as they say.

When we see a strong twelfth house focus of any sort, the laws of synchronicity suggest that such people are "studying endings" in this lifetime. One way to say it is that they are transforming that child's attitude about the end of a vacation to the wiser adult's attitude. That's an effective working metaphor for the evolutionary process we are exploring. It is about *learning how to let things go gracefully.* With Neptune in the twelfth house, you simply signed up for that lesson in this lifetime. Objectively, you will experience losses, endings, and finalities. Each one of them has the potential effect of opening up a psychic door into higher states of consciousness. If you can digest these endings, they become precious to you. You realize that you have learned something from the apparent loss, that you have evolved because of it.

That lesson can take fierce forms sometimes, but it is true and real.

I used a keyword phrase at the start of this chapter that I heard attributed to St. Francis of Assisi: *What we are looking for is what is looking.* I've always loved that line. What we are seeking spiritually is the thing inside us that is watching us. What is it exactly that is looking out through your eyes? You're not really this monkey-body. You're not even those eyes.

Whatever it is, that thing *we are looking for* is not fully or totally of this three-dimensional world. Whatever it is, it existed before your body did—and it will continue to exist after your heart stops beating. Where? How? These are maybe the most mysterious questions in all of life. Reflecting on them is part of having Neptune in the twelfth house.

But *becoming* that thing that is looking out through your eyes, switching the locus of your identity out of the monkey-business and into trans-Neptunian spaciousness, is the essence of your goal and your path in this lifetime. Lucky you, you are positioned to get there.

Part Four

Neptune in the Twelve Signs

32

SIGNS: THE GREAT ANIMATORS

Neptune crawls along slowly, spending an average of about fourteen years in each of the twelve signs of the Zodiac. For that reason, some astrologers treat its sign position as relatively insignificant, dismissing it as "merely generational." By contrast, these same astrologers often call the faster-moving bodies "the personal planets." I believe this to be misleading language. For starters, *all* the planets are "personal"—you feel each one of them in your bones. If, for example, you have Neptune in Scorpio, one of its layers of meaning is that your spirituality is tied up with your sexuality. We might discuss your feelings about maintaining eye contact with your partner through the point of orgasm. If that doesn't sound "personal" enough for you, I'd like to hear something that is!

There is nothing abstract or "merely generational" about Neptune's sign position. The energy of the sign permeates the planet, making Neptune in Scorpio a very different beast than Neptune in Capricorn or Sagittarius. Still, as we will see, the fact that so many people in one's age group all have Neptune in the same sign is significant. In that sense, it is indeed generational. Equally significant is the fact that there are always "lost Neptune tribes" whose ghosts walk among us—Neptune signs missing from the current population. Try to find someone with Neptune in Taurus, for example. Neptune kissed Taurus goodbye on March 20, 1889, and won't be there again until May 21, 2038.

So Neptune's sign positions do indeed set the tone for periods of history. That's an idea we will explore deeply a little later. Right now though, my main point is that you have a deeply personal relationship with Neptune, and its sign position is a huge piece of that puzzle.

WHAT EXACTLY ARE SIGNS?

Signs represent the psychological energies that animate us. They are what give people "vibrations." They correlate with the *values* that underlie our choices in life. Should you quit your job and move to Costa Rica? If you are a Cancer or a Capricorn, think twice before doing that—your natural values are more naturally oriented to home, work, and stability. Those values work well for you. But if you are a Sagittarian or an Aquarian, pack your bags for Costa Rica—the value of "coloring outside the lines" is a wise one for you.

Maybe I describe a woman as being "constantly caught up in relationship dramas." Based on that simple portrait, I ask you a question about her: is she an introvert or an extrovert? You can't answer. Being caught up in relationship dramas is a *behavior*. That puts it in the astrological category of the houses, not the signs. Equally, we find both extroverts and introverts in those kinds of situations—but when we see those relationship dramas, both will rather reliably have planets in the fifth, seventh, or eighth houses.

Introverts, however, can usually be recognized by lots of planets in the Water signs—Pisces sometimes, but especially Scorpio and Cancer. You'll often find introverted Capricorns too. Extroversion, on the other hand, tends to happen more in the Air and Fire categories.

My favorite "tweet" on this subject is that *we are our signs and we do our houses*. Now of course, "being" and "doing" are interactive concepts, and the reality is not so black and white. But keeping a clear sense of the distinction between signs and houses adds precision to our practice.

A QUICK TOUR OF NEPTUNE IN EACH SIGN

We already understand the basic drives represented by Neptune, for good or for ill. We have seen how our understanding is further focused by a knowledge of Neptune's major aspects and its house position. Now we take it a step further by grasping how the sign in which we find Neptune adds another distinct tonality to the mix.

I will be briefer here than I was with Neptune through the twelve houses and its aspects to the rest of the planets. That's not because the sign is less important, nor because it is "merely generational." Part of the reason I am briefer is that some of these sign positions have only abstract relevance in the present time—again, think of Neptune in Taurus. Mostly, it is because we have already explored Neptune's houses and aspects in detail. All we have to do here is to reframe and retool some basic concepts, turning "doing" into "being."

I want to present this material in tabular, telegraphic form as it relates to the individual, then in the following chapters to look at some broader implications of Neptune's sign changes that do indeed impact us all generationally and historically.

NEPTUNE IN ARIES

Underlying Archetype: The spiritual warrior

Developmental Aim in Consciousness: Clarity and focus in the presence of fear and shock; spiritual courage.

Essential Strategy: Facing fear. Defending one's spiritual path. Bold action in seeking mystical stimuli.

Appropriate Spiritual Hero: One who has some value for which he or she would be willing to die

Synchronistic Correlates: Adventures; crises; dramas; do-or-die moments.

Sidetracked, Distracted, and Addicted: Pointless battles against illusory foes; crippled by fear; passionate about trivialities; forever unforgiving; holding grudges; desire for martyrdom.

Shadow: Drunk on anger

See Also: Neptune in the First House, Neptune in Aspect to Mars

NEPTUNE IN TAURUS

Underlying Archetype: The spiritual animal speaking no human language

Developmental Aim in Consciousness: Return to instinctual, natural spirituality; union of Mind with the physical body; peace, calm, and serenity.

Essential Strategy: Staying close to nature; paying mindful attention to the body; exposure to silence; music; cultivation of simplicity.

Appropriate Spiritual Hero: The "wise old Navajo;" the "Taoist master planting beans"

Synchronistic Correlates: Links with animal and plant kingdoms; messages from the physical body.

Sidetracked, Distracted, and Addicted: Mere materialism; boredom; endless repetition.

Shadow: Life defined purely by the satisfaction of the animal appetites

See Also: Neptune in the Second House, Neptune in aspect to Venus

NEPTUNE IN GEMINI

Underlying Archetype: The spiritual teacher; the spiritual student

Developmental Aim in Consciousness: Alertness to moment-to-moment consciousness; attention to the senses; mental clarity and right thinking.

Essential Strategy: Commitment to endless learning in a spirit of openness and genuine curiosity; to be continuously humbled by the enormity of the larger truths.

Appropriate Spiritual Hero: The genuine sage who is endlessly surprised

Synchronistic Correlates: Exposure to teachers and teachings; attraction of cognitive dissonance into one's life; sensory contact with other dimensions.

Sidetracked, Distracted, and Addicted: Living in one's head; theory and thinking blocking direct experience; spiritual dilettantism.

Shadow: Being right all the time

See Also: Neptune in the Third House, Neptune in aspect to Mercury

NEPTUNE IN CANCER

Underlying Archetype: The Great Mother

Developmental Aim in Consciousness: Opening the heart to compassion; deep devotion.

Essential Strategy: Committed love in all its forms; courageous openness to the inner life; willingness to feel deeply.

Appropriate Spiritual Hero: The Healer; The Nurturer

Synchronistic Correlates: Opportunities to learn from familial situations; wounds that open the heart.

Sidetracked, Distracted, and Addicted: Self-absorption; fearful defensiveness; mind-dulling resistance to change.

Shadow: Absolute defensiveness

See Also: Neptune in the Fourth House, Neptune in aspect to the Moon

NEPTUNE IN LEO

Underlying Archetype: The Performer

Developmental Aim in Consciousness: Faith in one's own spirituality; spontaneous spiritual generosity; naked humanity.

Essential Strategy: Betting on yourself in spiritual matters; acting as if you were one step ahead of where you actually are; expressing your soul's nature loudly and clearly—and doing those three things with a sense of humor about yourself.

Appropriate Spiritual Hero: The artist unafraid of embarrassment

Synchronistic Correlates: Opportunities to express one's self; creative engagement; leadership.

Sidetracked, Distracted, and Addicted: Spiritual self-importance; crippling, arrogant pride.

Shadow: The Hypocrite

See Also: Neptune in the Fifth House, Neptune in aspect to the Sun

NEPTUNE IN VIRGO

Underlying Archetype: The Devoted Disciple; the Servant of Humanity

Developmental Aim in Consciousness: Spiritual skills and techniques; humility.

Essential Strategy: Long-term commitment to spiritual practice; seeking teachers.

Appropriate Spiritual Hero: The true and authentic guru

Synchronistic Correlates: Encounters with teachers; opportunities to lose one's self-importance via service.

Sidetracked, Distracted, and Addicted: Neurotic repetition of ineffective spiritual techniques; empty ritual; loss of self in the face of meaningless duty.

Shadow: Volunteered slavery

See Also: Neptune in the Sixth House, Neptune in aspect to Mercury

NEPTUNE IN LIBRA

Underlying Archetype: The Fair Witness; the True Soul Mate; the Devotee of Beauty and Rapture

Developmental Aim in Consciousness: Tolerance for paradox; aesthetic rapture; the highest refinement of human love and companionship.

Essential Strategy: Exposure to beauty; learning to see both sides of everything; finding companions on the spiritual path.

Appropriate Spiritual Hero: The artist in full flow; the spiritual lover

Synchronistic Correlates: Encounters with art and beauty; exposure to periods of creative renaissance; meetings with soul mates.

Sidetracked, Distracted, and Addicted: Confusion of the sexual and the spiritual; laziness; fear of commitment to anything.

Shadow: Eating candy in a comfortable chair, forever

See Also: Neptune in the Seventh House, Neptune in aspect to Venus

NEPTUNE IN SCORPIO

Underlying Archetype: The Shaman

Developmental Aim in Consciousness: Honesty with one's self; contact with occult sources of spiritual energy; making death our counselor.

Essential Strategy: Recognition that unresolved psychological issues thwart spiritual development; seeking inner power necessary for evolutionary breakthrough; energizing one's self via sacred sexuality.

Appropriate Spiritual Hero: Medicine man or woman; mystical psychoanalyst

Synchronistic Correlates: Encounters with intense life-and-death drama; transformative sexual experience; being faced nakedly with one's own issues.

Sidetracked, Distracted, and Addicted: Bitterness; sexual confusion; subjectivity clouding objectivity; endless self-pity and grief.

Shadow: A resolution to be dead

See Also: Neptune in the Eighth House, Neptune in aspect to Pluto and Mars

NEPTUNE IN SAGITTARIUS

Underlying Archetype: The Seeker; the Pilgrim

Developmental Aim in Consciousness: Aligning one's psyche with cosmic principles, and living for them.

Essential Strategy: Immersion in spiritual learning; commitment to right thinking; cross-cultural spiritual experience to shatter parochialism.

Appropriate Spiritual Hero: The Wise Fool

Synchronistic Correlates: Contact with shocking, mind-stretching, "foreign" spiritual experience; contact with powerful teachings.

Sidetracked, Distracted, and Addicted: Needing to be seen as "right about everything;" settling for oversimplification; intellectual laziness masquerading as "faith."

Shadow: The Fundamentalist

See Also: Neptune in the Ninth House, Neptune in aspect to Jupiter

NEPTUNE IN CAPRICORN

Underlying Archetype: The Wise Elder; the Wizard

Developmental Aim in Consciousness: Radical self-discipline and deep objectivity in spiritual matters; spiritual responsibilities toward one's community or tribe.

Essential Strategy: Spiritual practice; time spent alone; questioning "common sense;" making the spiritual path real via doubting and testing it.

Appropriate Spiritual Hero: Gandalf; Merlin; Dumbledore

Synchronistic Correlates: Mountains to climb; hard tests; forces that compel early maturation; responsibilities toward those who are less evolved.

Sidetracked, Distracted, and Addicted: Crippling logic; the need to "control reality" by not allowing it to go beyond the boundaries of conventional reason; materialism, pure and simple.

Shadow: The paranoid, controlling tyrant

See Also: Neptune in the Tenth House, Neptune in aspect to Saturn

NEPTUNE IN AQUARIUS

Underlying Archetype: The spiritual revolutionary

Developmental Aim in Consciousness: Freshness and originality; seeing spiritual experience directly, free from the weight of traditional metaphors and explanations; the banishment of false guilt and shame.

Essential Strategy: Thinking outside the box; learning to maintain focus without the helpful support of traditional social-spiritual structures; renewal and re-visioning.

Appropriate Spiritual Hero: The Awakener; The one who turns the page of history

Synchronistic Correlates: Encounters with doubt; encounters with errors and lies in traditional teaching; having "the rug pulled out from under" one's beliefs; living in times of radical and fundamental social and religious change.

Sidetracked, Distracted, and Addicted: Hooked on negativity and rebelliousness for its own sake; spiritual quirkiness.

Shadow: Cold dissociation from the deeper psyche or soul

See Also: Neptune in the Eleventh House, Neptune in aspect to Uranus and Saturn

NEPTUNE IN PISCES

Underlying Archetype: The Mystic

Developmental Aim in Consciousness: Absolute transparency; perfect compassion; decoupling of awareness from "personality."

Essential Strategy: Meditation; trance; contemplation; prayer.

Appropriate Spiritual Hero: The wise hermit meditating in the cave; the "invisible saint" living anonymously in the ghetto—or at the Country Club

Synchronistic Correlates: Psychic experiences; pressing evidence of the existence of other realms; living in times of profound spiritual renewal.

Sidetracked, Distracted, and Addicted: Overwhelmed by one's own sensitivity; escaping into oblivion or the blurred anonymity of underachievement.

Shadow: The drunk; the addict

See Also: Neptune in the Twelfth House, Neptune in aspect to Jupiter

33

HOW NEPTUNE'S SIGN CHANGES THE MUSIC

Let's take a look at the "generational" impact of Neptune's sign changes in a very clear and specific way: the way it leaves its unmistakable fingerprints on our ears and our souls via the soundtracks of our lives.

Neptune's reputation among astrologers generally triangulates among mysticism, inebriation, and general flakiness. None of that is wrong, as we have seen. But we can also make a case that Neptune *defines reality* as we actually experience it—and that definition is partly about what's actually "out there" and partly nothing but a matrix of our own attitudes, interpretations, and assumptions. How does a tree look to a Navajo shaman? How, by comparison, does it appear to a university botany professor? How does a woman's body look to a monk from the eleventh century—or to a modern feminist?

Whether we recognize it or not, half of what we think we see "out there" is in fact the mythic belief-system that we carry between our ears. This Neptunian function clears our eyes—or blinds them— very unmistakably at the level of individual perception. That's what we have mostly been exploring so far. But as we consider Neptune's slow passage through the twelve signs of the zodiac, we can also see how it leaves its signature on the underlying mood of the times, collectively.

As Neptune changes signs, the underlying tone of our communal reality-dream changes. With its 165-year orbit, the planet spends an average of about fourteen years in each sign, although that varies a bit. Almost like clockwork, with each new sign Neptune enters, the collective mood shifts.

There is nothing subtle about it. The implications are vast and cover a wide spectrum of cultural tastes, attitudes, and fascinations. But there is no barometer more sensitive to these Neptunian sea-changes than *popular music.* The songs we hear on the radio, in clubs, or just as we walk down the street reflect nothing less than the soul of the times. Perhaps more directly than any other indicator, they mirror our collective heart. They are the dream we are dreaming. And Neptune's sign changes, in harmony with the music, illuminate the story.

We could just as readily follow Neptune's footprints through other cultural areas that express *style* and *fashion*: tastes in clothing, in film, graphic art, architecture, food. Really, we could talk about any area of life that is amenable to being shaped by an injection of Neptunian human fantasy, attitude and desire. Following up on all of them would be an interesting project, but it would be book-length. My aim here is to just take that single barometer of the Neptunian mood—popular music—and watch it register Neptune's sign changes. We will learn about music—but we will also learn to feel very directly the emotional tonality of Neptune's presence in various signs.

I choose music because it, along with film and clothing fashion, is so widely dispersed through society that essentially "everyone knows about it."

One quick technical note: in common with the rest of the planets, Neptune's path forward through the zodiac advances, then loops back in retrograde motion. Usually that means that its entry into a new sign is a bit complicated—it crosses the boundary, retreats back into the previous sign, and re-enters the new one. Sometimes it straddles the cusp as often as five times. Ditto for its exit from a sign. To avoid getting bogged down with a tedious list of dates, I will simply state the year in which Neptune *first* touched a new sign and the year in which it was *last* found there. You will see some overlap and apparent contradictions in the dates. For example, Neptune first touched the Scorpio cusp in 1955, but then twice threaded back into Libra, at last exiting Libra and entering Scorpio solidly in early August 1957.

Astrology always works, but sometimes it just hits you between the eyes. Examples might be America's infamous "September 11th" occurring with Pluto sitting on the Sagittarian Ascendant of the most commonly used chart for the USA—or the Fukushima nuclear catastrophe happening the very day that Uranus transited into Aries. I find the correlation between Neptune's entrance into a new sign and changes in popular music to be in the same spectacular and obvious category.

Let me prove it to you. Here, I want to concentrate on living memory—and thus the charts of people you have actually met—so I'm only going to go back as far as 1928, when Neptune crossed out of glitzy "Roaring Twenties" Leo into Virgo.

NEPTUNE IN VIRGO: 1928-1943

Virgo is the sign of the *Servant*, and in astrology's usual shadows-and-light style, we see "the Virgin" straddling the thin line between positive humility and the horrors of humiliation. Positively, Virgo values precision and excellence; negatively, it can become picky and overly critical—of itself as well as of others. If it is too hard on itself, it descends into labyrinths of shame, self-doubt, and self-sabotage.

As Neptune crossed in and out of Virgo, the world was on the brink of experiencing the massive collapse in confidence called the Great Depression. Our very Neptune-in-Leo experience of the Roaring Twenties was about to hit the wall of Virgoan reality. It is tempting here to talk about Neptune entering Leo in 1915 and ushering in the Jazz Age with all its gloriously Leonine color, extravagance and fru-fru, but as I indicated earlier, I'd prefer to focus on those currently living—and my apologies to a few elders who are still around with their natal Neptunes in the sign of the Lion.

Neptune first touched the Virgo cusp in September 1928, retrograded back into Leo the following February, and entered Virgo finally and solidly in late July 1929—just three months before the bottom fell out of the world economy. Collectively, via the Great Depression, humanity attracted a chance to study that strange land that hovers between our two Virgo poles: humility and humiliation.

Think of the popular music of the 1930s and the mind immediately goes to the so-called "Big Bands" of the era. We see them in groups of fifteen or twenty players, in formal Virgoan tuxedos and gowns, under the leadership of names we still recognize: Benny Goodman, Duke Ellington, Woody Herman, Harry James, Glenn Miller, the Dorsey brothers, Count

Basie, Artie Shaw.

Call the images up in your memory or, more likely, from films you've watched—and consider what you see through the lens of Neptune in Virgo: everyone is dressed in natty, almost aristocratic fashion. Can you imagine showing up for one of those shows in a T-shirt? The music is played mostly from scores—right notes are clearly defined, and wrong ones would stand out like sore thumbs. Hitting one would probably get the player fired. The musician's task is, in a sense, to *obey* and to *play it correctly*—and to do so as "the servant" of the band leader. The very social structure of the bands reflects Virgoan hierarchy and values.

Note that the Big Bands bore the names of their leaders, many of whom were famously despotic. There's the Virgoan servant-and-master signature again. Meanwhile, the dancers on the floor, dressed in their finery, were dancing according to *established structure and method*—again, with a "right way" and a "wrong way" to do the steps always clearly defined: the *jitterbug*, the *Lindy hop*, the *Balboa*, the *Carolina Shag*.

You didn't just wiggle in those days. You did it right—or people would notice. Feel the Virgo?

There is in all of this "Virgo-osity" a clear, anxious response to the Depression, as people struggled to reclaim and reaffirm their dignity and sense of social position. Beneath the smooth facade, one can almost sense the underlying anxiety of both the musicians and the dancers—what if I get this wrong? What if I screw up the music or the steps? How far will I fall? *What will people think?*

I would like to add a couple more points about the music in this Neptune-in-Virgo period. First, it was a time when the federal government became a great sponsor of the arts in various Depression-related social programs. Conservatives and liberals will have different ideas about all that, but there is the clear Virgo signature in the servant-and-master structure. The government became a *patron.*

Perhaps more importantly, I'd like to point to two great voices in the realm of folk music, both of whom articulated a more honest, direct, "working man's perspective" on those hard times. First, there is Woody Guthrie. He was probably America's best-known folk balladeer of the period. Listen carefully to *Goin' Down the Road Feeling Bad,* or even better, take in the explosive lyrics of *This Land Is Your Land,* and you will get chills realizing what was actually happening back then, behind the gauzy, insecure fantasies.

The second folk voice I want to mention here is Huddie Ledbetter, known as Lead Belly. His songs about the often dreadful experience of being black in America during the Great Depression still feel raw, present, and agonizingly honest. Many of us know *Cotton Fields* and *Goodnight, Irene,* which he composed. Or try this couplet from a song that he didn't write, but which he made famous: *The Midnight Special*:

> *Knife and fork are on the table, ain't nothing in my pan.*
> *And if you say a thing about it, you have a trouble with the man.*

That's just a couple of phrases, but they say so much about the pain of Neptune in Virgo: lack, humiliation, and oppressive servant/master social hierarchies.

But then go back and watch—compassionately—a clip of Benny Goodman leading his elegant band, as human beings struggled to affirm their dignity in the face of loss and adversity. Neptune in Virgo clearly gave the Great Depression a soundtrack—and maybe a little glimpse of the higher realms in a dark time.

NEPTUNE IN LIBRA: 1942-1957

Courtesy, civilized behavior, and simple manners are the domain of Libra. The sign is ruled by Venus, the goddess of grace. We are talking about Serious Romance—from the waist up. We are talking about character, *savoir faire*, and the basis of simple social harmony between people.

The Libran symbol of the Balance-Scale suggests opposites in perfect equilibrium: an ounce of lead and an ounce of gold dust. Or male and female. Or Jack and Jill. With Neptune there, we see a *spiritualizing (Neptune) of the idea of relationship (Libra)*—and, like everything else in astrology, that every front has a back. Lifting human love into a realm of refinement and idealism is the higher meaning of Neptune in Libra—but of course it comes packaged along with a great potential for unrealism and ungrounded expectations just begging for disillusionment.

Romantic projection, which is very much in the domain of Neptune in Libra, thrives on separation. Lonely hunger—and its comforting, compensatory delusions—carried poignant meaning during that nightmare time. Against the backdrop of the sheer Plutonian horror of World War II, the unabashed romanticism of Cole Porter's 1943 *You'd Be So Nice to Come Home To* struck a resonant note—especially as we realize that many couples were physically separated by the war and haunted by the knowledge that they might very well never see each other again. "Coming home" to the loving arms of an idealized partner surely animated many a moment of transcendent, comforting imagination in foxholes across Europe, Asia, and the Pacific.

Then the soldiers came marching home from war, hungry for the imagined comforts of marriage, home, and family—and for songs that harmonized with the romantic Libran mood. Accordingly, Neptune's passage through Libra was the age of the great lovestruck crooner. Frank Sinatra. Tony Bennett. Patti Page. Perry Como. Bing Crosby. Rosemary Clooney. Dean Martin. Eddie Fisher. Dinah Shore. Peggy Lee. Doris Day. Nat King Cole.

The tune that topped Billboard's Top 100 in 1952 epitomizes it all: Jo Stafford's *You Belong To Me.* At the time, I am sure the sentiment it expressed was innocent beyond reproach. Times have changed. Notice how nowadays simply telling someone that he or she "belongs to you" feels anachronistic and vaguely suspect. Not with Neptune in Libra! Then, the Neptunian dream of the world was utterly, unquestioningly romantic. *We all wanted to dissolve into each other.*

NEPTUNE IN SCORPIO: 1955-1970

With Neptune in the sign of the Scorpion, we would expect a much more intrusive, psychologically honest, less romantic, and frankly sexier musical style to emerge. Accordingly, out went the crooners and in came rock 'n' roll. Paraphrasing a line from the previous paragraph, we are now talking about Romance—*from the waist down.* Elvis shook his pelvis and nothing was ever the same again.

Debates rage about the exact date of the birth of rock 'n' roll. Clearly it owes a vast debt to African-American blues artists and to working-class white Europeans displaced into Appalachia. But our subject here is not the question of where or how rock 'n' roll originated. Our subject is the Neptunian mood of culture as reflected in changing popular tastes. We are not paying attention to scholarship here; we are listening to the radio.

Neptune hit the passionate, uninhibited, erotic sign of the Scorpion in 1955—the year that saw the chart debuts of Elvis Presley, Little Richard, and Chuck Berry. What was the first rock 'n' roll record? You can start fistfights among musicologists with that question. A strong contender is Bill Haley and the Comets' *Rock Around the Clock*. The linchpin of the argument is simply that it was the first rock 'n' roll single to rise to the number one position on the Billboard charts. It did that in the summer of 1955, keyed to Neptune's Scorpionic signal.

I watched a video once that showed the very white, very Neptune-in-Libra, crooner Pat Boone singing Little Richard's *Tutti Frutti* in a very white nightclub. I almost felt sorry for the man. *"A whop bopa-a-lu, a whop bam bam, tutti frutti, oh rooty, tutti frutti, oh rooty ... Got a gal named Sue, she knows just what to do ..."*

Then the videographer brilliantly cut to Little Richard himself singing the song. The raw, strange, and distinctly *single entendre* sexuality of the tune blasted right through Boone's bowdlerized reading of it. *She knows just what to do* didn't refer to housework. Collectively, the repressed Libran libido had given way to the Scorpionic roar of sheer, enthusiastic hunger—from the waist down.

With Neptune in Scorpio, we now had the soundtrack for that epochal cultural change we call *the sexual revolution*.

Let me digress for a moment. In saying all this, we are presented with a classic Neptunian evolutionary opportunity: I imagine that you are feeling strong opinions forming. Was it "good" that graphic sexuality made itself felt in the music? Or did it represent a degradation of human culture compared to the more "romantic" music of Neptune in Libra?

The point is not that we need to answer the question—it is actually the polar opposite: that we *don't* need to answer it. We only need to observe it, and perhaps to trust that in all of this there are forces manifesting from the trans-Neptunian realms—forces we can witness but never fully understand.

NEPTUNE IN SAGITTARIUS: 1970-1984

Rock 'n' roll loudly metamorphosed into "Rock." Sagittarius is of course ruled by Jupiter, the exuberantly nymph-impregnating King of the Gods. As Neptune entered that sign, in the music *bigger became better* and *nothing succeeded like excess.* The volume got louder. The hair got bigger. The tickets got more expensive. People wanted to dance, so after a while disco arose and took over. Sequins replaced blue jeans. Performance moved from concert halls to stadiums. Woodstock happened in '69 with Neptune still in Scorpio and couples merrily bonking in the mud—but soon the outdoor music festival, attracting attendees in populations the size of small cities, became the dominant cultural form.

Bands that had made their mark in the 1960s became huge businesses—apart from our evaluations of the music as an art form, just think of the *marketing* of the Rolling Stones, the Who, Led Zeppelin, the Bee Gees, Stevie Wonder, Crosby, Stills & Nash, Earth, Wind & Fire. New supergroups arose—Boston, Foreigner, Styx, Electric Light Orchestra.

Sagittarius is the great Traveler, and its cross-cultural fascinations made themselves felt in the music too. *Reggae* came out of Jamaica and left fingerprints on popular sensibilities that one still hears today. The huge success of the Police was based partly on the savvy marketing of their reggae-tinged music to the non-English-speaking world. Led Zeppelin began using the drum rhythms of northern Africa. The general Sagittarian stretching was pan-cultural, as well as embodying the general obsession with more, more, more, and the cult of "The Next Big Thing."

Sagittarius carries the archetype of the Philosopher, and music became "big" in concept as well as volume. Think of the metaphysical ambitions, both musically and lyrically, of the "prog rock" bands of that era—Genesis, Yes, the Moody Blues. You had to be *deep*, although of course being sexy still helped. That's true no matter what sign Neptune is traversing.

Bigger and bigger and bigger and bigger, like blowing up a balloon but not knowing when to stop—we all know where that leads: limits are reached, brick walls loom. Sagittarius must inevitably collide with Capricorn.

It's not just a good idea, it's the law.

NEPTUNE IN CAPRICORN: 1984-1998

Neptune's passage through Capricorn, a sign ruled by restrictive, controlling Saturn, manifested musically in two very different ways. One was the explosion of the popularity of *country and western* music, which began to erode the long reign of rock 'n' roll. The other was the dominant cultural position achieved by *hip-hop* or *rap*, which, in a very different way, did exactly the same thing.

Capricorn carries a great respect for tradition, and "country" is a very traditional musical form in at least a couple of ways. Musicologically, it is typically structured in conventional verse-chorus-bridge format. Often the chords are simple. There is a more-or-less standard array of instrumentation: guitar, bass, drums, fiddle, and pedal steel guitar.

Someone with a good ear who didn't speak a word of English could figure all that out just by listening to the *sound* of Country and Western music. With relatively few exceptions, no musician or song went very far in that world if they departed from those Capricorn-ish structures, customs, and musical mores.

Perhaps even more significantly, in its *lyrical content* country music also tends to reflect traditional "Capricorn" values: *true love, marriage, family, church, and patriotism.* As Neptune entered Capricorn, there was a great hunger for a return to these kinds of values—values diametrically opposed to the perceived excesses correlated with Neptune's passages through Scorpio and Sagittarius.

Epitomizing this trend, country megastar Garth Brooks released his first album in 1989, not quite midway through Neptune's passage. He is the second best-selling solo artist in musical history, after Elvis Presley. By January 2012, his sales had surpassed those of the Beatles.

I mentioned that Neptune's time in Capricorn manifested in a second way. This parallel expression of the archetype made an entirely different *sound* than country and western music, but once we understand astrology, we can easily see the same symbolic DNA behind it. Here I am talking about the complex phenomenon of *hip-hop* music—also called *rap*.

Let's start with something very practical lurking behind hip-hop's cultural message. At a core level, Capricorn correlates with a fascination with *tools* and all things *mechanical.* It's fitting that reliance on a new breed of *drum machine*, such as the Oberheim DMX and Roland 808, was typical of many hit songs from this period—really in all the popular musical genres. But rap music simply could not have existed without these machines.

Neptune-in-Capricorn's *machine connection* goes further. Musically, the essence of the hip-hop form is to chant rhyming verses over a beat extracted from an existing song recording—and that extraction was accomplished via another mechanical tool—a device called a *sampler.*

A third tool, the *MIDI-based sequencer*, came to be a dominant recording device too—and, again as with the drum machine, its impact was felt across all genres, not just rap, even though it was critically essential to that form. Sequencers first appeared in 1983, just one year before Neptune entered Capricorn, and they literally changed the sound of popular music. Who needs a musician when a computer can play the whole string section for free? Who needs a band when you can have an entire orchestra in your bedroom?

Again, my own opinion looms: to my ears, sequencers and drum machines spawned some music so utterly boring and repetitive that no human hand could have possibly created it. But they also freed creativity from some practical shackles, giving artists without resources options that would have been unimaginable even a decade earlier.

Back to hip-hop in particular. The timing of the genre's entry into popular awareness is irrefutably connected with Neptune's entry into the sign of the Sea Goat. 1983-84 saw the early rise of seminal rap artists Run-D.M.C. and LL Cool J. In 1986, the Beastie Boys' album *Licensed to Ill* was the first rap album to reach number one on the Billboard charts. Generally, the "golden age" of hip-hop is seen to run from the mid-1980s through the early 1990s—right in synch with Neptune's passage through Capricorn. Billboard editor Paul Grein called 1990 "the year that rap exploded," based significantly on the huge success of Public Enemy's album *Fear of a Black Planet.*

In terms of lyrical content, rap is controversial. In fairness, it is essential to add that the form contains a diversity of voices advocating a wide range of viewpoints. In the popular mind, much of hip-hop is violent, male-dominated gang-oriented, and utterly phallocratic—fraught with degrading images of females as "bitches and hoes."

To call male dominance over women a "traditional value" is of course—at the literal level—sadly correct and accurate, if ironic. Opinion again: *I hate that.* If you are reading this book, you probably hate it too. But there it is—to me, a sad delusion, but consistent with the patriarchal shadow of Neptune in Capricorn.

Meanwhile, Garth Brooks was singing about true love, marriage, family, church, and patriotism. Nobody would confuse rap and country.

But conservative values and the creation of and skilled use of tools—any astrologer can see the signature of the Sea Goat behind all that.

NEPTUNE IN AQUARIUS: 1998-2012

Key words for Aquarius: Innovation. Diversity. Independence. Technology. Rebellion. Revolution. When Neptune entered Aquarius, the impact upon music was immediate and profound, and reflected that vocabulary.

Aquarian technology drove it all. MP3 encoding, which reduced the size of digital music files to manageable proportions, had been standardized as early as 1991, but by the late 1990s its use was widespread. In 1998, right on Neptune's Aquarian schedule, MP3.com was launched. The Digital Millennium Copyright Act was enacted. And, most critically, *the first MP3 players hit the market.*

On January 9, 2001, Apple released Version 1.0 of iTunes—and the world of music was changed forever. By what? Again, our answer: Aquarian technology.

Napster, starting with perfect Neptunian timing in 1999, made music free—and naturally, this was an appalling calamity for that very Capricornian institution: the music *business.* Napster was shut down a couple years later for *pirating,* in Aquarian "outlaw" fashion, the intellectual property of recording artists—an Aquarian battle still being fought in myriad forms all over the world. And of course that issue goes far beyond the realm of music.

Closer to our purposes here, we observe that these distinctly Aquarian technological developments created enormous changes in the mood, place, and nature of music in society. They virtually destroyed the "music industry" in its previous monolithic form. The big labels shrunk, laying off vast hordes of employees. In Aquarian fashion, however, small-time artists were able to thrive. They often found digital niches, fans, and outlets for their music. MySpace and Facebook, launched in 2003 and 2004 respectively—with Neptune in Aquarius—created Aquarian mechanisms for musical outreach and contact.

Meanwhile, in another technological development, streaming Internet radio took off, creating an unprecedented *diversity* of radio stations—and, critically, in individualistic Aquarian fashion, a digital sea of *ever more isolated* styles.

It is tempting to devote ten thousand words to the correlation between Neptune's passage through Aquarius and the epochal cultural revolution symbolized by Facebook and "social media" in general. I am going to resist that temptation and stick with looking into that flawless mirror of the cultural mood that we call popular music.

Successful artists abounded during this Aquarian period—Eminem, Usher, Beyoncé, Alicia Keys, Nickelback, Destiny's Child—but the real musical news with Neptune in Aquarius was simply *Future Shock*. To me, the main impact of Neptune's passage through Aquarius almost undercuts my whole argument: in truth, there was *no longer a single, recognizable form of popular music*, as there had been for at least many decades. As a culture, we no longer had that unity. Instead, each one of us had a thousand channels—and earbuds—standing between us and the world.

NEPTUNE IN PISCES: 2011-2026

With the previous six signs, we have the great advantage of hindsight. Neptune only first touched Pisces in 2011. I am exploring all this just a few years into the process, with many years left to go and the flower not fully open. Much of whatever music Neptune's return to its own sign will bring us is still mostly unrecorded—and perhaps not even imagined.

Meanwhile, looming over all of this is a huge wild card of uncertainty. As we just saw, Neptune's passage through Aquarius brought music into the Digital Age—and that change came packaged with the classic Aquarian concern with individuality and personal uniqueness. If you like bisexual Samoan reggae music played strictly on traditional instruments, there is a channel out there for you. Don those earbuds, and welcome to paradise. The looming uncertainty is, *will there ever again be a single, recognizable form of popular music?* Or has Neptune's time in Aquarius been a game-changer? I don't know, and it's too early to tell.

But there is one thing we as astrologers do know for sure: Neptune is very strong in Pisces. And there is another point I believe we can reliably assume: Neptune seems to have a natural connection with music.

Putting two and two together, my guess is that somewhere, there is a five-year-old genius sitting down at a keyboard for the first time. One might envision him or her laying down the first steps toward a music of *entrancement*, its notes *hypnotizing* us into an attunement to the next dimension. That would be utterly Neptunian—and, in Pisces, Neptune's energy is pure and unalloyed.

Jimi Hendrix, shortly before he died, was asked about his next project. He spoke of "sweet opium music." Well, maybe Jimi is back, and he is now that five-year-old I just mentioned.

Keith Richards of the Rolling Stones once said something to the effect that "90 percent of all popular music is dreck." And of course he is right. Works of true genius are precious for their rarity. That has always been true, and it will surely be true of Neptune in Pisces as well.

Think of Neptune in Virgo and all the silly, scared, formulaic "dance music" it spawned.

Think of Neptune in Libra and all the sappy, forgettable, unrealistic love songs it oozed.

Think of Neptune in Scorpio and the plague of recordings it generated that reduced human intimacy to a transaction of the genitals.

Consider Neptune in Sagittarius and the pretentious, tendentious, self-glorifying dimensions of the puerile "rock anthems" it sired.

Think of Neptune in Capricorn and how it cranked out music so boring and predictable that only a machine could have accomplished it—and a machine did!

Think of Neptune in Aquarius and how it shattered the power of music to be a unifying cultural force by isolating us into self-interested boutique genres and exclusionary categories.

Neptune in Pisces will surely not be immune to that kind of trivializing poison. We will get—perhaps we already are getting—saccharine, juvenile "spectacles" and "entertainment" which will not be remembered beyond the lifespan of a guppy.

But maybe somewhere Jimi Hendrix is sitting down at that keyboard to take us further into the Piscean ethers. Maybe Claude Debussy has been attracted back into the flesh by inaudible angels in the material air. Perhaps a fresh audience has been reborn, an audience that is worthy of Beethoven's tenth symphony—the one he died before he could finish. Perhaps we will attract him too. Perhaps we have earned that right. Perhaps we are spiritually hungry enough.

Hidden in the sugar, behind the perfumed clouds of improbable light, I believe that the power of Neptune's return to its own sign heralds a musical renaissance.

34

NEPTUNE'S TRANSIT THROUGH PISCES

We just skimmed over Neptune's passage through several signs, observing its impact upon one specific category of human expression: popular music. Let's take a deeper and more multi-dimensional look at the planet's current passage through Pisces.

Neptune touched the Piscean cusp for the first time in a century and a half back in 2011. It will not be finished with that sign until the beginning of 2026. So we who are alive now find ourselves in a rather magical position in human history. The last time Neptune was in its own sign was 1847 through 1862, shortly after it was officially discovered. No one, in other words, who remembers it is still around.

Astrological experience teaches us that when a slow-moving planet passes through its own sign, the event leaves its mark on the historical period in an unmistakable way. Let's calibrate our perceptual instruments here by first tuning into a couple of illustrations of this rulership principle. We are lucky: in relatively recent years, we have all experienced two examples of this kind of sign-planet reinforcement involving outer planets. We'll consider them before we delve into Neptune's current situation.

Pluto's passage through Scorpio started back in late 1983 and ran into 1995 when Pluto crossed over into Sagittarius. For some of you current thirty-somethings this will seem like ancient history—maybe a bit lost in the misty memories of childhood. The rest of us, a little older, will remember those times vividly.

This is potentially a huge subject and I want to be careful not get totally lost in it. My tactic here is to demonstrate how powerful the passage of planet through its own sign can be, and how it changes the course of history.

PLUTO IN SCORPIO

When Pluto crossed into Scorpio—its own natural sign—the event was a powerful jolt to the collective human unconscious. It was time for us, Scorpio-fashion, to look at a lot of things we had been afraid to consider or admit. So what happened? The terrible AIDS epidemic really took hold. Suddenly, talking a lot more honestly about that classic Plutonian and Scorpionic subject—human sexuality—became a question of survival.

Scorpio and humor are joined at the hip, of course—as are sex and humor. Most jokes, when you really stop and reflect on them, are actually about taboo material. There was a joke going around back in those days; maybe you remember it. One five-year-old says to another, "I found a condom on the patio." And the response: "What's a patio?"

It's funny, for sure—but that joke is also a time capsule of a very Plutonian period in human history. Condoms had previously been a somewhat "impolite" subject, but evolutionary necessity reared its irrefutable, synchronistic head. In a sense, we *had* to talk about condoms or we would die. Ditto of course for gay sex. Even among progressive heterosexuals, there had been a general attitude of, "Fine, I respect your lifestyle—but just please don't get too graphic about it." That had to end too.

I think that the ensuing dialogue has blossomed now, a generation or two later, into our present far greater acceptance of gayness as a natural condition. It's one of the great goods that came out of the AIDS epidemic, as Plutonian honesty and reflection were synchronistically pressed upon us all.

Again, Pluto is of course "always somewhere." But when it is in Scorpio, it is particularly powerful. Between 1983 and 1995, it was as if the entire world went through a major Pluto transit all at once.

Still on the subject of sex, during the Pluto in Scorpio period, *pornography* became much more mainstream. A lot of that was due to technology. People now had VCRs—videocassette recorders—at home, so they no longer had to face the stigma of going to the sleazy "dirty movie theater." If they wanted to, they could watch porn at home, with a vastly reduced chance of public embarrassment. That made it a lot more accessible to women, for one thing—which, in turn, somewhat humanized the story-lines.

Make of pornography what you will, but clearly, it exploded during the years when Pluto occupied its own sign. A positive development? A negative one? Remember, our main aim here is to explore Neptune, and attachment to opinion only blinds us there. Pornography is what it is—and no astrologer could miss the connection between Pluto's time in Scorpio and the relative mainstreaming of the genre.

Pluto in Scorpio wasn't just about humanizing and acknowledging sexuality. *It was about very many things that had previously been kept hidden, denied, shamed, and rationalized.* It seemed for a while as if everyone was suddenly in a Twelve-Step program. It almost became a badge of honor—and I think that is actually a fair assessment: it takes courage to be in those kinds of programs. Some of the most transparently honest clients I have ever seen are dried-out alcoholics who owe a great and ongoing debt to Alcoholics Anonymous. And under Pluto in Scorpio, the twelve-step programs expanded to include Narcotics Anonymous, Overeaters Anonymous, and, of course, Sex Addicts Anonymous.

In every case, a "dark, shameful secret" was invited out of the closet and into the bright light of day—at least within the context of individual meetings.

Meanwhile, due to the literary success of Anne Rice, the *vampire* practically became the national bird. Were those vampire books the epitome of Pluto in Scorpio? That sounds like an easy question to me. All the "vampires" were released from the collective unconscious.

URANUS IN AQUARIUS

Here's the take-away for our limited purposes here: *When a planet is in its own sign, the volume goes up on it.* We can see that so clearly in retrospect with Pluto's passage through Scorpio. And we can expect the same with the present passage of Neptune through its own natural territory, Pisces.

But let's not go there quite yet. Here's another example of a planet's passage through its own sign, even closer to the present time. Remember the passage of Uranus through Aquarius? That ran between 1995 and 2003, so all of us, even you younger folks, had front row seats.

With the revolutionary energies of Uranus hyped to the max, we would expect an absolutely fundamental paradigm shift at the social and collective level. Unlike Pluto in Scorpio, this would not have to do with taboo material surfacing—that is Pluto's domain, not that of Uranus. Instead, we would envision Aquarian triggers: *changes in the social order, acts of individual genius or independence that changed the world, and technological innovations that altered the rules of the game.*

So what happened? Famously—and right on schedule—September 11, 2001, came along. Once you clear away the obvious outward drama of those attacks, the underlying bones of what happened go beyond explosions, extremism, and conspiracy. *What really happened was that the nation-based world order that we had understood since we were children came crashing down.* The so-called "War on Terror" is unprecedented in a number of ways, first among which is that it pits a nation against—what? Not another nation, but rather something more like an *idea* that joins people across national boundaries. Even to say, as some pundits do, that it is the war of Western civilization against the Muslim world—a kind of repeat of the Crusades—is completely wrong. Most Muslims are peaceful people, just as appalled by the extremists as anyone else. And of course many of the extremists were not born in Muslim nations.

Fear not, I am going resist the temptation to evaluate the War on Terror. Exploring it is not our point here. Our point is that, with Uranus in Aquarius, whether you like it or not, *a few people got a new idea and utterly changed the way we experience our world.* How can a nation fight a war against an unboundaried, ill-defined group of people united only by a common view of things and a global technological web? You can't bomb an idea. Maybe we can answer that question someday—but it is a new game, with new rules and a new game-board. That is the point.

A little while ago, talking about music in relation to *Neptune's* passage through Aquarius, we saw how it correlated with the digital revolution that transformed the face of the recording industry. Those years were a very Aquarian time for humanity since Uranus was there for a lot of it too, mostly toward the end of Neptune's passage. As we saw, the way technology "changed the music" is consistent with Neptune's passage through Aquarius—but it is even more fundamentally linked to Uranus being there. That's because we are talking about *game-changing acts of genius and innovation.*

Going further with the technological side of this Aquarian-Uranian fusion, we can add the launch and incredible success of the Toyota *Prius*. Hybrid cars are everywhere now; they clearly have something to do with the future of driving. The *Prius*, which first went on sale in Japan in 1997, marked the beginning of that change.

Likely, even vaster in its implications was the mapping of the human genome, completed during that same period.

Once again, my aim here is not the full exploration of the astrology of those years. It is simply to "calibrate our dials" as we contemplate the meaning of Neptune's passage through Pisces. Clearly, when an outer planet is on its own turf, we can expect to see its tattoo on the times.

NEPTUNE IN PISCES

As in all things astrological, Neptune's passage through Pisces will bring good, bad, and everything in between. Individuals respond well or poorly to astrological stimulus—but at the collective, social level, we usually see *every possibility expressed.* There are just so many of us on the planet that the canvas is broad enough for there to be space for everything from the trashiest responses to the loftiest ones.

Consistent with the Neptunian archetypal field, we will undoubtedly see *escapism* raised to an art form—designer psychedelic chemistry, virtual reality, a pulse of drug use and abuse, a rise in alcohol consumption. I suspect that before it is over in early 2026, you will be able to go down to your local Big Box store and buy some kind of computerized helmet and bodysuit that lets you experience being Superman having sex with the cyber-porn star of your choice, complete with a virtual orgasm. This will raise the word "nerd" to the level of a true psychiatric category—and I am sure that the pharmaceutical companies will come up with a psychoactive antidote for it!

New Age people of the truly terminally "uber-positive" variety will, as usual, foresee a massive leap in consciousness, flying saucers to the rescue, a change in our very DNA, and the onset of a golden age of peace, love, and understanding.

That's all hype, naturally. I doubt it will happen like that. After all, Neptune has passed through Pisces many times in human history, and we still haven't seen that kind of mythical golden age. And yet, in those childish fantasy-images, we glimpse something of the true Neptunian archetype. It correlates with the human capacity for spirituality.

So, staying grounded, I expect an incremental boost in *the human fascination with consciousness itself.* I believe that it's happening already, right now. One way to express it is that *"everyone on the planet will spend '3 to 5 percent' more time in some kind of mystical state."* You too! I suspect that you've already meditated a few more hours this year than you did in 2010.

Angels looking down from their heavenly ramparts will note a few signature phenomena here on Earth. For example, I conjure up the image of *a vicious drug dealer on the Mexican border gazing transfixed for a moment at the Milky Way ... a hard-hearted, woman-beating pimp on the South Side of Chicago hypnotized for thirty seconds by a perfect rose ... a flatlined, ear-pierced, tattooed, neo-Nazi skinhead punching the wrong button on his car radio—and, for thirty seconds, being spellbound by the sound of Beethoven's ninth symphony coming over the airwaves ...*

Obviously, these are metaphorical images, but I suspect they are accurate, even literally. I suspect they are unfolding widely right now, individually, one at a time, virtually unnoticed—and yet powerful in their cumulative effect. Each individual contributes something to the collective ambience. With Neptune in Pisces, one at a time and generally unnoticed, people are lifting themselves a little higher. Gradually the whole world is lifted a little higher too. We are not talking about some lightning bolt of global transformation, but rather about an incremental push in a Neptunian direction.

In a nutshell, as I speak now in 2013, *humanity is ready for a spiritual reawakening.*

I say this, hopefully, with some lead in my shoes.

THE MIRROR OF HISTORY

As history has demonstrated, the Neptune-in-Pisces change is not subtle—but it is not black-and-white either. When it is over, Earth will still be Earth, and people will still be people. But, along with all the Neptunian escapism and waste and delusion, I believe we will also see *a new spiritual beginning for all humanity.* I could speculate about its nature, and we will get to that in a little while. But first, I want to look into the mirror of history and see what it can teach us. I have a second agenda in doing so. I am aware that my phrase—a new spiritual beginning for all humanity—sounds very grand. I believe it is true, but looking into the mirror of history will show, not only its outlines, but also its limits. Humanity has experienced Neptune's passage through its own sign many times. Each apparition has been different, of course—that's always the way it is. But in studying the common threads, we can perhaps "clean our windows" a bit in terms of understanding what is trying to happen before our eyes right now.

I will focus quite a lot on *religion* here. It has always been humanity's most primal barometer regarding the higher Neptunian possibilities—and often of the lower ones too. I choose the subject of religion here, much as we chose to look at music a while ago, simply because it is such an excellent flag in the wind. Almost as easily, we could look at art, social customs, and the fictional stories we tell ourselves. Those are Neptunian as well.

Let's start our historical investigation of Neptune's journey through its own sign with the roots of Christianity.

As usual in matters of religion, there is an initial *visitation of divine energy and magic*—followed by it all being codified, institutionalized, and rationalized by later bureaucracies and "Departments of Theology." Generally they strangle most of what was actually vibrant and alive in the beginning. Christianity illustrates this process rather unerringly.

Jesus came along sometime early in the first century, maybe a little earlier. Neptune was not in Pisces yet. Four rather different versions of that story are told in the gospels of Matthew, Mark, Luke and John. Much of the rest of the Bible's New Testament is actually not the story of Jesus, but rather the story of St. Paul bringing the Christian message to the Roman Empire. That's where we will concentrate.

Paul began his journey to "Asia"—modern Turkey, really—in about 45 AD. Neptune was still in Aquarius then. And he was very nearly tarred and feathered for his troubles. But in 47 AD, Neptune entered Pisces, and his message exploded across the pages of history. *Christianity essentially owes its early roots to Neptune's passage through Pisces.* From a historical or academic perspective, the chances of Christianity having taken hold as a world religion without its eventual association with the Roman Empire was very slight—and that marriage took off under the Piscean rays.

Let me go a little more deeply into this particular example to help us understand the broader cyclical dimensions of this whole process of awakening. We will learn some principles here that generalize across the pages of history and carry us far outside the Christian realm.

Let's start by thinking some dark thoughts about Aquarius—which of course comes before Pisces. Focusing on the negative side of that sign, we remember that technically, Aquarius is a Fixed sign of the Air family.

Fixity, expressed negatively, is simply rigid—think of *rigor mortis.* And Air is mental energy; it is about *ideas.*

Put them together and you get—on the unfortunate side of the equation—the notion of *stubbornly rigid ideas.*

Add Neptune to the mix, and you see *spiritual ideas* that have lost their elasticity and their ability to excite and enliven anyone. The scholars and the bureaucrats have eclipsed the mystics.

This morbid condition is eternally the natural prelude to Neptune's entry into Pisces and the spiritual awakening it implies. Before the spiritual renaissance can happen, there is a period of spiritual deadness, in which *dull, unchanging ideas and interpretations of the divine* have replaced genuine magic.

For the Roman Empire, during the time of Jesus, that morbidity took the form of the worship of gods in which few people still had any faith. In fact, Julius Caesar himself had been declared a god, postmortem. Roman citizens were required to go to the temple and offer sacrifices to him—or they would pay what amounted to a traffic fine.

History always feels distant. The trick is to re-enter it through imagination. Can you imagine a sophisticated Roman patrician thinking, "Damn it, I need to go offer money to the ghost of a dead politician, or they'll fine me fifty bucks." It must have been laughable. It must have been a cynic's paradise.

But remember that no matter what the period of history, people always have Neptunes. Therefore they always have a need for some contact with the divine, with magic, with higher realms. *Under Neptune in Aquarius, religions often simply have run out of fuel.* They are dead or dying, at least in terms of their ability to enliven anyone. This arid soul-desolation sets the stage for Neptune's entry into Pisces. It worked for St. Paul and it will likely work for us today too.

In fact, we will soon see evidence for exactly that.

I am going to jam into fast-forward here. I want to cover a lot of history without getting bogged down in it. Unless I note otherwise, every event and date I am about to mention correlated with Neptune being in Pisces. Like all anecdotal evidence, the story of St Paul's preaching to the "seven churches of Asia" could be a lucky coincidence. But when you follow the next two thousand years, I believe the clues add up—and cast an encouraging light on our present times.

Sticking for a while with the Christian framework, Theodosius the Great—the Roman emperor from 379 to 395—made Nicene Christianity the official state religion of the Roman Empire. *St. Paul had won*. Ironically, the only ones left to worship the old Roman gods were you and me—the astrologers, who still speak of Jupiter and Mercury and Venus.

There is—no surprise—a strong connection between Neptune in Pisces and the *advance of Buddhism* as well. There are various tellings, but the standard version is that in about 58 AD, Emperor Ming-Ti introduced Buddhism to China. Much later, in the sixth century—either 538 or 552 CE, depending on which historian one consults—a delegation sent by a Korean prince arrived at the court of the Emperor of Japan. The Koreans brought with them Buddhist *sutras*, an image of the Buddha, and a letter from the Korean prince praising the dharma. This was the official introduction of Buddhism to Japan.

St. David brought Christianity to Wales in 550. That might not be a big deal to you, but, hey, I'm Welsh through my dad's side, so I thought I would toss it into the pot in honor of my paternal ancestors. The old "pagan" religion had burned out; people were ready for something new and fresh. In that case, it was Christianity.

Here's a big one, maybe the most impressive event of all.

Neptune was in Pisces from May 701 until February 716, inclusively. Our attention now switches to the Muslim world. The year 711 brought the Islamic invasion of Spain and the establishment of the Moorish culture there, which endured for centuries and left a huge mark on Spanish society. A year later, in 712 AD, a Muslim state was established in what we now call Pakistan. The truly amazing thing is that by 715 AD, a Muslim empire stretched all the way from the Pyrenees to China, with Damascus as its capital. Astonishing how fast that happened! And this was before Facebook, folks.

There were many religions in those lands—and yet none had the resiliency nor vitality to resist the conversion to Islam. There are bloody tales to be told there, as there are with Christianity's various forced conversions. But the deeper story is simply that after Neptune's passage through Aquarius, *the people were ready for something new.* They were ripe for contact with fresh "trans-Neptunian" energy. The first blush of Islam brought that *juju* to them—just as St. Paul had brought the fire of the early Christian faith to the jaded, spiritually hungry Romans.

May 1192 AD saw Neptune again crossing into Pisces, where it remained until early 1207. Illustrating the potentially lunatic dimension of this energy, the Fourth Crusade was originally intended to conquer Muslim-controlled Jerusalem. Instead, the Crusaders invaded and conquered the Christian city of Constantinople, which was the capital of the Byzantine Empire. This cemented the "Great Schism" between the Eastern Orthodox and Roman Catholic churches.

None of that is very inspiring—but consider how "inspired" you would have to be to leave home and hearth and go out into *terra incognita* with only your broadsword and your faith, however misguided it might have been. Something was in the air . . .

Neptune was back in Pisces between March 1520 and the end of 1534. The Catholic church had a bad case of "Aquariosis." It had become rigid, formulaic and mechanical, as well as profoundly corrupt. Famously, "indulgences" were being sold—you could pay a small fee and be forgiven for almost any sin. It was almost like a politician "fixing" a traffic ticket in exchange for a bribe. *How dead has a religion become when a custom such as the sale of indulgences is tolerated and expected?*

A Catholic priest named Martin Luther had had enough. In 1517, still with Neptune in Aquarius, he posted his "95 Theses" on the church door at Wittenberg—and in 1521, with Neptune in Pisces, the die was cast: he was condemned as a heretic and excommunicated, setting into motion the Protestant Reformation. By 1529, Henry VIII of England had summoned the "Reformation Parliament" and begun to cut England's ties with the church of Rome.

Again, the history quickly becomes complex, and I don't want to get lost in recounting it. But once more, observe the Neptune-in-Pisces fingerprints that underlie the Protestant Reformation: *an old religion has become formulaic. People were ready for a change. They were ready for a fresh visitation of energy.*

And since we are talking religion here, *chocolate* was brought from Mexico to Spain in 1520! That's fun to say, but let's also remember that an addiction to chocolate is hardly rare.

Illustrating the mad side of Neptune in Pisces, we come to the infamous *Salem witch trials*, which occurred during Neptune's 1684-1698 passage through Pisces. Showing similar fanaticism, in 1685, Louis XIV banned all religions in France except Roman Catholicism, which triggered much bloodshed and led to more than fifty thousand Huguenot families leaving France. Consistent with the higher dimensions of Neptune, in 1687, King James II of Great Britain issued the Declaration of Liberty of Conscience, which guaranteed tolerance of all religions.

In all of this, the specifics are of historical interest, but what I encourage you to underscore in your own mind is simply that *people were thinking in religious terms during these times;* Neptunian questions, for good or for ill, had become major motivators of human behavior. That is really the point.

The last historical time Neptune entered Pisces was April 1847, only crossing finally into Aries in October 1861. The correlations here are dramatic too. *Spiritualism*—which involved communion with the dead and with beings in other dimensions—swept through the English-speaking world. It was not an orthodox religion with an official canon, but more like a spiritual movement—something akin to the New Age culture of the 1980s and '90s. The nearest thing the American Spiritualists had to a "Bible" was the 1847 book, *The Principles of Nature, Her Divine Revelations, and a Voice to Mankind,* by New York state clairvoyant Andrew Jackson Davis. In Europe, we might similarly point to *Le Livre des Esprits* by the Frenchman Allan Kardec, published in April 1857.

Spiritualists themselves often cite March 31, 1848 as the birthdate of their faith. It is in controversial but culturally significant territory that on that date, the Fox sisters, Kate and Margaret, of Hydesville, New York, claimed contact with a spirit—something they were allegedly able to demonstrate to observers via various rapping noises. Arthur Conan Doyle, of *Sherlock Holmes* fame, became a major figure in the movement that arose around them and the worldview they embodied—a movement that attracted Abraham Lincoln, as well as Queen Victoria and Prince Albert. Clearly, Spiritualism was not a movement only among uneducated or otherwise marginalized people.

Make of it what you will, Spiritualism was an utterly Neptunian creature—happening right on schedule with Neptune in Pisces. Society was ready. Numbers vary, but one report I read informed me that in 1850, out of an American population of about twenty-three million people, *eleven million* of them claimed membership in a spiritualist church. Naturally, none of this appears in our high school history books.

Personally, I've got to say that I am a believer. I know there have been scandals and frauds and hoaxes galore, and that you can't believe everything you hear. But I've been blessed with the chance to speak several times for Fellowships of the Spirit at Lily Dale, New York. Lily Dale is a surviving representative of the spiritualist tradition, which had its roots right up there in that chilly part of the world. Anyone can visit Lily Dale, and if you have any interest in these matters, I would recommend it. The short version of my story is that they have made a believer out of me, both through objective demonstration and through their obvious qualities of honesty, intelligence, and integrity.

On a different note, I don't think it's too much of a stretch to call *communism* a religion. That is obviously a bit ironic in that communism is nominally opposed to any religion at all. And yet it is—or was—a passionate belief system that gave meaning and direction to many people's lives for well over a century. And Karl Marx published the *Communist Manifesto* right on Neptune-in-Pisces schedule, on February 21, 1848. Again we see the familiar situation: people were ready for something new, something in which they could believe.

BACK TO THE PRESENT

Religion is a complex subject. John Lennon, just before he was taken from us all, famously invited us to *"imagine no religion."* And of course we can sympathize with his point; there is perhaps no other force in human history that has led to so much pointless bloodshed, stupidity, and inhumanity. But Lennon wisely added a question: *"I wonder if you can?"*

I am not sure it is possible. We all have Neptunes—which means that, whether we like it or not, it is our fate as humans to have a point of contact with realms beyond all logic and imagining. And we all have both ninth house and Sagittarian functions, which are desperate to connect the dots and make some sense of those transcendent perceptions.

As much as I love John Lennon, I have to answer his question negatively. I really cannot imagine a world without religion. I think it is hardwired into us. All I can imagine is that we might "clean our windows" more thoroughly, and let a purer light come pouring through.

Once while reading one of Jonathan Kellerman's wonderful murder mysteries, I came across a quote that stuck in my mind. Kellerman wrote, "Religion makes good people better and bad people worse." That pretty much says it all, doesn't it?

With Neptune back in Pisces until 2026, we can expect an awakening—and a big dose of religious craziness, unrealism, delusion, and probably "God-inspired" bloodshed, rape, and mayhem. History suggests that this is the shape of the package. In the "crazy department," back in 879 AD, with Neptune in Pisces, the Pope and the Patriarch of what became the Eastern Orthodox Church excommunicated each other. I could imagine the old Monty Python crew covering that one! And remember the Salem witch trials.

Religion definitely can make bad people much, much worse.

Our point is certainly not that having Neptune in Pisces is simply a positive thing. That would be naïve—not to mention that it would reflect an ignorance of history, or at least a very selective reading of it. The sole point is that when Neptune is in Pisces, *people's attention is on spiritual matters*, as it needs to be in order to set the stage for spiritual renewal.

What can that mean in today's world?

The first thing I want to say is that I actually have no idea. Life is unpredictable. We astrologers see archetypes in action, and we have a leg up on other professions when it comes to understanding the marrow in the bones of synchronicity. But consciousness interacts unpredictably and creatively with these "predestined" archetypal fields of possibility—for what it's worth, that is my entire philosophy of astrology in a single sentence. What humanity will actually *do* with Neptune in Pisces is not a question that can be answered through technical astrological analysis. Ultimately, it is a question that will be answered by seven billion human hearts.

In this present cycle, Neptune first touched the Piscean cusp on April 4, 2011. Amazingly, the April 25, 2011 issue of *Time* magazine bore a bold cover story: *What If There Is No Hell?* Under those words was the phrase: "A popular pastor's best-selling book has stirred a fierce debate about sin, salvation and judgment." Reverend Rob Bell had wondered—in print—if perhaps God's love was so vast and so perfect that He would allow no one to burn in hell for eternity. Naturally, there was no shortage of representatives of the First Church of Bitterness and Idiocy who were up in arms. They seemed to have a deep psychological need for people unlike themselves to be tortured for eternity. Again, religion makes bad people worse.

What I would like to underscore here with this *Time* story is simply that, right on schedule, a major *news* magazine in the United States happened to run a cover story on a *spiritual* matter. This was astrology-in-action in a very real way. For me, it set the tone for the following fifteen years—much of which still lies ahead.

At a far more concrete and lasting level, we see the effects of Pope Francis I upon the Roman Catholic Church. He was elected as the new Pope on March 13, 2013, and of course he has been upsetting the applecart ever since. Many of us—including myself—are praying he is not assassinated. Certainly that energy is out there around him. Such is the level of resistance the old guard puts up as they begin to feel the ground eroding out from underneath their feet.

Pope Francis has dismayed some of his critics by reaching out across religious "party lines"—and I actually think that simple observation might be the key to understanding humanity's present state of Neptunian evolution and renewal. Have we not come to a time in which a simple realization I am about to describe is dawning in the minds everywhere—at least in the minds of everyone currently enrolled in Earth's program for the "spiritually gifted and talented?" And by that silly phrase, I don't mean saints and gurus. I mean the kinds of people who are evolved enough to see that hatred and violence solve very little, that love is the higher path—people such as yourselves.

And here is the realization to which I refer: that words like God, Allah, the Dharmakaya, Christ, Jehovah, Vishnu, Brahma, the Higher Power, and so forth *all mean about the same thing*.

Cultures vary—but not as much as they used to vary. We are famously in "the global village" now, and that is not just a catchy phrase. It is a reality. On the nightly news, we see Christians and Muslims slaughtering each other. That gets a lot of coverage. Humanity loves explosions. What we don't see are the "gifted and talented" Christians and Muslims watching that bloodbath with the same horror and incomprehension, knowing that they are perfectly capable of sitting down with each other, making eye contact, and comfortably seeing divinity in each other despite their cultural differences.

You are like that. I am like that. And the best news is simply that *we are not rare.* John Lennon said, "*You may think that I'm a dreamer, but I'm not the only one . . .* "

Isn't this *underlying unity of world religions* an idea whose time has finally come? More to the point, doesn't what I am saying appear *so utterly* obvious to you that it seems weird that I am sounding as if I am sharing a great revelation with you?

But this fundamental human spiritual unity was not always so obvious, as history proves. It is clearly not obvious to everyone even today—and similarly none of the great Neptunian historical shifts we have already detailed here involved entire societies turning left in lock-step. Still, I believe that we are witnessing a major evolutionary shift—and one that comes with some serious birth pains. *We are witnessing a shift from a diversity of culturally-based, ethnic religions into a unified global spirituality.*

I don't want to hype this—as I said earlier, I am not prophesying some golden age. Neptune in Pisces is simply about a paradigm shift in the fundamental metaphors that underlie the human relationship with the trans-Neptunian realm. In a sense, John Lennon was right when he asked us to "imagine no religion." He wasn't asking us to imagine no spirituality.

In a government census, people are often asked about their religion. One of the boxes they can check is "none." A lot more people, especially younger ones, are checking that box lately—but when the question is followed up, one often hears that they are "spiritual but not religious."

I think that's the direction in which the wind is blowing.

Earlier in the book, speaking of the ongoing sextile of Neptune and Pluto, we explored the emerging union of spirituality and psychology—the idea that *we can no longer envision an authentic spiritual life without a commitment to doing personal work on our own wounds.* That, I believe, is part of this monumental Neptune-in-Pisces shift too. It is another dimension of the emerging new spiritual paradigm.

As we have seen, this emerging union of spirituality and psychology is ultimately inseparable from the discovery of the trans-Neptunian realm, with its own synchronistic correlates: the emergence of transpersonal psychology, energy healing, body-mind-spirit syntheses, the shamanic renaissance and so forth. And let's put evolutionary astrology on the list too.

I would add yet another piece to the puzzle: *the convergence of physics and mysticism.* Religion and science have often had an uneasy relationship.

They still do, in many ways. And of course science itself *is* a religion to many people. Mention astrology to one of its "high priests," and you will see as much foaming at the mouth as you would if you suggested pork rinds to a Muslim or an uplifting experience of homosexual love to a Mississippi Baptist.

And yet, I believe that the division between science and spirituality is healing—that science, at its best, is simply human reason struggling toward the truth of things, and that in this emerging epoch, religion can no longer viably resist objective truth. As the Dalai Lama—a figure at least as exemplary of all this change as Pope Francis—put it, "If scientific analysis were conclusively to demonstrate certain claims in Buddhism to be false, then we must accept the findings of science and abandon those claims."

Can we imagine a spirituality so robust that it can pass any critical test of reason or analysis, while still speaking meaningfully to anyone in any culture—and simultaneously keeping us psychologically honest about our own evolutionary processes?

I believe the roots of that kind of collective spirituality are what is trying to emerge between now and 2026. And I believe that, in your bones, you all know that. That is who you are and that is why you are here on Earth in this extraordinary time.

Part Five

Neptunian Transits, Progressions, & Solar Arcs

35

NAVIGATING NEPTUNIAN TIMES

Let's look at the possibilities that arise during periods of particular Neptunian emphasis in a person's life. By "Neptunian emphasis," I mean the whole range of moving or developing kinds of events that involve the planet Neptune. These happen in two fundamental categories:

The first one involves ways that the planet Neptune itself can move through your chart, triggering various configurations by forming critical aspects. This first set of techniques embraces Neptune's actual transits and also its motion by solar arc. (Via progression, Neptune's motion is essentially too slow to warrant practical attention—it might only move two or three degrees in your whole life.)

The second fundamental category of Neptunian stimulus occurs when *any* transit, progression or solar arc triggers the position of the natal Neptune itself. In other words, we might see your progressed Sun forming a conjunction with the place Neptune occupies in your natal chart, while transiting Saturn trines it.

We will parse all this out in individual detail, but there is one principle that runs through everything we will explore next: *you are free to make a total mess out of a Neptune time and you are free to get it right.* The astrologer's job is to aim your nose in the right direction, not to predict which way you will aim it. In other words, as in all applications of evolutionary astrological "prediction," we release ourselves from the bondage of trying to announce in advance what is going to happen to anybody. Where we make our stand is on the more accurate and philosophically justifiable ground of *predicting questions* and—within the limits of our own wisdom—suggesting the best answers.

GRAPHING THE HOLY GRAIL

I want to start off with an image that will crystallize some slippery ideas that play a pivotal role in our understanding of all these Neptunian events. The horizontal axis of this graph represents *time*—vast swaths of it. The vertical dimension represents levels of *consciousness*—and the higher, the better.

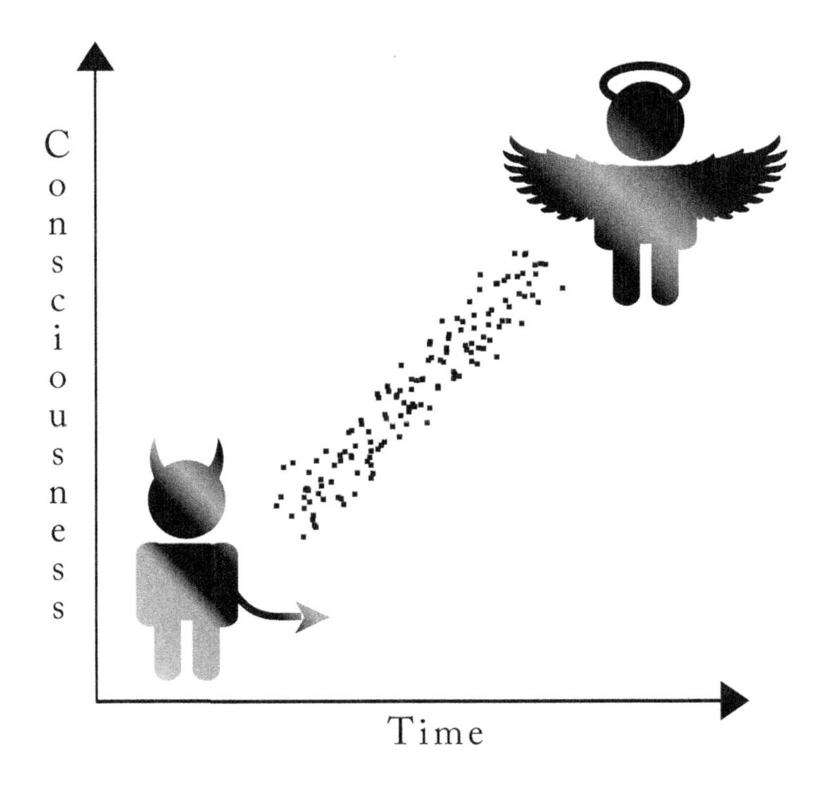

As we study this line very carefully, we see that it is composed of a vast number of individual dots or points. Each one represents a person, and the dot tells us where he or she is on the evolutionary journey.

Somewhere, let's say up near the top end of that line, we look at one of those dots through a magnifying glass. "Oh, look at that—it's His Holiness, the Dalai Lama." There he is, way up there, no surprise. Not far away, we maybe see Bishop Desmond Tutu or Carl Jung. Now we look down considerably lower: "Oooh, there's the dork in the Ford F350 pickup truck who cut you off in traffic last week." Now, that dork might not actually be "the worst person who ever lived." Way down lower on the graph, we see goons from death squads—and CEOs pouring carcinogens into the water supply for fun and profit.

But I chose the dork and the Dalai Lama as examples for a purpose. What exactly is the difference between them? Fundamentally, the answer is that the Dalai Lama simply has a more "spacious" consciousness than does our dork. The dork's driving behavior has shown that he believes his problems can be solved through aggression. The Dalai Lama had his nation attacked, stolen from him under incredibly cruel circumstances, and he said: "Don't strike back. Violence solves nothing."

That must have been difficult. When you've been kicked in the belly like that, it takes a whole lot of "evolution" to have fully internalized the principle that violence begets violence.

The difference between the dork and the Dalai Lama, then, is not fundamentally one of intelligence. But we might fairly say that the "spaciousness of the consciousness" of the Dalai Lama compares favorably with the spaciousness of the consciousness of the discourteous fellow in the pickup truck. Who's to judge, but I feel subjectively that I am on pretty solid ground saying this. In saying it though, I skirt the edge of a very non-Neptunian place of judging—defining our graph in terms of who I don't like and all the people of whom I disapprove. I want to avoid that black hole; I want to stay as close as I can to truth. Our hold on that higher Neptunian ground gets shaky when we judge other people.

And yet, we're not being *entirely* judgmental about this. Anyone can look into the eyes of an evolved person and sense that quality of depth. It's not an exotic perception. It is kind of like sensing intelligence or kindness in someone—not 100 percent reliable, but a commonplace part of daily life. The word "discrimination" should be introduced here. It is not the same as being judgmental, although of course they are cousins and we need to be careful about our own subjectivity.

Now, let's tie all of this more directly into Neptunian developmental events. Remember the vertical axis of our graph, running from the lowest states of evolution to the highest states of evolution. And I speak of the line being composed of dots, and each dot represents a human being. But what about the horizontal axis, representing time—and thus, possibilities of development?

So far, we have looked at the graph in static form. But now we add life to it—we put the microscope on any one of those dots, and we see that most of them are gradually moving upward and to the right. Some of them are moving fast; some are moving slowly. Their speed does not depend upon their position on the graph either—you might look up at the high end of the graph and see dots that are not moving very quickly. *Just because you're very evolved doesn't mean you're currently evolving in a rapid way.* There are people who get stalled at fairly lofty states in the journey.

When we look down towards the bottom, left-side of the graph, where we're looking at people who "live for shopping," or spend most of their time hating or competing or raging, some of them are actually moving pretty fast. It's like comparing smart kids in the first grade to duller ones in college.

Go further. Take any one of these dots and watch it from cradle to grave. Basically they all make some progress over a lifetime—maybe a little, maybe a lot, but there is usually some progress. But look more carefully—really look at the moment-to-moment *microstructure* of the process. *The dots speed up and slow down.* Hypertext any of those dots—remembering that they represent human beings—and we can see their birthcharts and their transits and progressions.

When a dot is moving fast, it represents a person going through a period of Neptunian stimulus.

There's our bottom line. *Periods of Neptunian stimulus correspond to periods in which one's consciousness might be becoming more spacious.* In a moment, we will get to why I put the "might" in there. So far, all this is parallel to more conventional astrological ideas, such as the notion that Mercury periods correspond to educational opportunities and Venus periods to intimate developments. Here the developmental focus is Neptunian.

One more step. What about that "might?" Here is someone going through just such a Neptunian time—her progressed Sun is making an aspect to her natal Neptune, for example. We put the magnifying glass on her dot, expecting rapid motion. *And it's frozen in place.* It appears that no evolution is happening at all.

How can that be? Simple—she may be in a Neptunian time, but she is *making a weak response* to it. Hypertext her biography—here she is, sitting in front of the television with her third Budweiser, dreaming of shoes.

Neptune does not "evolve you." You evolve yourself. Neptune correlates synchronistically with a time of *evolutionary opportunity*, that's all. You are ripe and ready, and synchronicity declares everything—and everyone—you need is in place. On the other hand, what will it matter in five hundred years? There's TV and there's beer . . .

This point is absolutely pivotal. *Consciousness is not generated through an unconscious or automatic process*. The evolution of your consciousness is not analogous to the growth of your body. You're born a kid and you get bigger. That happens automatically; that's the karma of the physical body. But consciousness is generated through voluntary, intentional processes. There are a variety of voluntary, intentional processes that can generate it, and that's what we've been talking about throughout this book.

As we've seen, each person's optimal methods are different, each person is faced with different challenges. For each person at a given time, there are effective methods for triggering this evolution. But the bottom line is that evolution never happens automatically—it happens through choice and intention. And it happens—if it happens—during times of Neptunian stimulus.

Once again, my favorite line here is that "consciousness is not generated through an unconscious process." I like that line a lot. I got it from a gentleman by the name of Rodney Collin, who wrote *The Theory of Celestial Influence*. I believe Collin stole it from George Gurdjieff. I don't know who Gurdjieff stole it from. There's a long, wonderful line of thievery here. Feel free to steal it from me.

So, in a Neptunian time, we have an opportunity to create more spaciousness in our consciousness—to clean our windows. All the laws of synchronicity support us during these periods, which is to say that along with the inner pressures, concrete opportunities are there as well—the teachers we need are there, the circumstances are there, the resources are there. All the tools are in place. All you have to do is to simply rouse yourself up and take advantage of them.

Will you do that or not? The answer is not in your chart. The astrologer doesn't know; it's not the astrologer's job to know. We're not predicting anyone's fate—we're way beyond that. Under Neptunian stimulus, you can choose to move your little dot up that graph, heading for that high corner. Or you can sit there, doing nothing— escaping, really, hiding from the opening that is trying to unfold inside you.

Sometimes I introduce our dork-and-the-Dalai-Lama metaphor with a client, and then I come to the punchline: "During this period, you have a chance to become less like a dork and more like the Dalai Lama." That never fails to get a good laugh. Or maybe I say "less like Britney Spears and more like Mother Teresa." Or "less like Kim Kardashian and more like Pope Francis"—pick your bad examples and your good examples. I mix and match a little bit so I don't always repeat myself. And of course, times change. If anyone comes into contact with this material in twenty years, I have no doubt that they will have an abundance of good and bad examples to peruse.

Saints and fools are never in short supply.

SOME VERY HUMAN CONSIDERATIONS

Maybe we find ourselves sitting with a client who has just come through a period of transiting Neptune crossing through an opposition to his Sun. The event is over and he did well with it. You can see it in his eyes. There is a depth there that was not there last time you saw him.

Further evidence for his success is the fact that there is *no evidence of failure*—he did not become addicted to anything, there were no escapist behaviors, he didn't get into a delusional state and go haring off after a self-destructive relationship, a phony guru, or a get-rich-quick scheme.

The Neptunian energy had to do *something*. In the absence of the negative, we can generally assume the positive.

Given that happy situation, here's a way to both advance the conversation with the client and deepen rapport. Simply say, "*I want to acknowledge and honor what you have accomplished, invisibly, over the last two or three years.*"

Rather reliably, you will immediately see a big smile on the client's face. *He is so happy just that somebody sees it.* That's because one reality of this world is that huge Neptunian victories plus five dollars get you a *latte* at *Starbucks.* I don't mean that statement cynically. It is a reference to the fact that society simply does not value these kinds of psychic and spiritual developments, nor does it even have much language to recognize them. It is important—and encouraging—to remember that a person can just *nail* a Neptunian period and have nothing to show for it outwardly, materially.

SPIRITS IN THE MATERIAL WORLD

There was a gentleman once who went by the name of Gautama. After a considerable period of questing for the meaning of life, he found a tree and he just sat under it. Now, visualize Gautama—just a guy sitting under the Bodhi Tree. And now, here he is a little bit later, having attained enlightenment, *and he is still just a guy sitting under a tree.* Did anything happen? No, not materially.

We constantly hear that we live in a "materialistic society." It's become a cliché, and so we nod our heads and tend not to think too deeply about the words. We imagine it means that we live in a world in which people are obsessed with money and material comforts. True enough, but *the ultimate expression of materialism is our belief that we are in fact material objects.* It includes the notion that all that really matters—all that is truly real—is what we can see in the material world.

Astrologers themselves tend to be materialistic in this way. I don't mean they are money-hungry or anything like that. I just mean that so often their main concern seems to be what the atoms and the molecules are going to do in response to some astrological stimulus.

That's not a taboo question, not at all. But it is a narrowly material one, literally. So, sometimes a Neptunian event occurs in the life of a client, and "nothing happens." It would be more accurate to say that *the "something" that happened was simply not visible.* It didn't happen where the astrologer was looking—which was among the atoms and molecules of this world.

This is one reason why simply acknowledging the reality of your client's inner victory is such a fine way to build rapport.

Let's bring this closer to everyday reality, make it more human, more like what you actually see in the counseling room. Erase Gautama and instead picture a woman in her early thirties. She's sitting on a park bench. She's going through a Neptunian time. She's got a two-year-old son who is off somewhere visiting Grandma and Grandpa. She has been married for five years. She reads *Elle* magazine and *Cosmopolitan* and sometimes envies her girlfriends who are still single. She's a little frustrated with her husband. He's a good guy. He loves her and she loves him. But the relationship isn't as passionate as it was when they first met.

So there she is, in a Neptunian time, sitting on a park bench, alone, chewing on all this. As she first sits down, she's kind of depressed and frustrated. And synchronicity has struck: she's tempted by somebody else—her old boyfriend from college just "friended" her on Facebook. He'd love to get together "for a cup of coffee." You know the story. She is sexually tempted and she's anxious and she's all bent out of shape.

Astrologically, she's in the midst of progressed Venus squaring Saturn, while *transiting Neptune makes a trine to her seventh house Mars*. Can she clean her windows?

In the process of this Neptunian flow, she sits down on that park bench and *comes to the realization that she will surrender to her marriage.*

I choose my words carefully there. It is not that she "settles for her marriage." I intentionally didn't say it that way. There may be some element of that "settling;" I want to be Plutonian enough to acknowledge that there's some taste of that—but the deeper point by far is that she has *surrendered to being married*. She has accepted it. "This is my life. I love my child. I want to do a good job of being a mother. I want to do a good job of being a wife. I will adjust to the realities of my marriage as it is, and I will work on them."

And then she gets up from the park bench and walks away.

From a material point of view, *nothing happened*. She sat on a bench and she got up. From a deeper point of view, something absolutely pivotal just unfolded in that woman's life. It will have material effects; it will affect the course of her journey. But not yet. Neptune happens inside us—at least at first.

There's something very beautiful about this little tale. If you can grasp it, you've understood something central to any Neptunian period: *most of what is truly important in such a time happens invisibly*. It is more centered in the category of "realization" and less focused on actual existential events, even though there are always those synchronistic correlates we've been discussing.

Let's go a little further with the woman on the park bench.

Maybe, in her uncertainty, unease and temptation, she goes to a fortune-telling astrologer who sees Neptune interacting with that seventh house Mars. The astrologer predicts, "You will meet someone. You will have a love affair." When Neptune interacts with relational or sexual symbolism in the chart that is a classic prediction—a tragic love affair, or one based on illusion or simple lust. Such predictions often prove objectively accurate.

But let's go back to the storyline as I'm telling it. This woman "surrenders to her marriage." That turns out to be a very beautiful thing, once she has lived with it for a while. It represents *spiritual maturation* for her. And yet, materially, "nothing happened."

You can almost imagine the fortune-telling astrologer being disappointed when the woman keeps her knickers up, so to speak—that she didn't have a love affair, as predicted.

Isn't that perverse? But there are even deeper levels of toxicity in this kind of astrological prediction.

This young woman—whom we are considering respectfully and compassionately—finds herself in a classic human dilemma. She is tempted by her old boyfriend. And let's honor the fact that there was even a certain authenticity to that relationship, and maybe some things were left unresolved in it. She's quite tempted—but not only for the sorts of reasons a pornographer would understand.

In the light of those very human understandings, what happens when she goes to that astrologer who predicts that she "will soon have an affair?" Is that prediction helpful? Quite the opposite. Here she is, *one inch away from having an affair* and fouling up her marriage and probably screwing up her child. One inch away from it—and an astrologer, "speaking for God, channeling the universe," announces that she is "destined" to have an affair. It's "written in the stars."

There's her green light. There's her encouragement to "surrender to the inevitable." *She was also one inch away from getting it right*—and that old-school astrologer pulled her in the wrong direction.

"Self-fulfilling prophecy" is the term often rolled out here, but we are talking about something even more delicate. Souls are hanging in the balance sometimes as they come to sit with us for astrological counsel. That's why I have a *moral* problem with fortune-telling. I've just illustrated it; that's what I mean. That kind of astrology could have been actively destructive to the spiritual growth of this woman.

Now, a grounded modern astrologer understands objectively that one of the things Neptune hitting that Mars could possibly mean is an affair. And we might even open our hearts enough to recognize that maybe an affair isn't the end of the world, and maybe somebody needs to go through something like that as part of an evolutionary process. Let's put that on the table too; let's not be prim or shy about it.

But may God protect us from the dark karma of leaving out the core idea, which is that Neptune is about accepting, surrendering, opening up, figuring out how to be most loving towards ourselves and towards the people around us.

SYNCHRONISTIC CORRELATES DURING A NEPTUNIAN PERIOD

I've been banging the drum for the realization that we can do well with a Neptunian period and "have nothing outwardly to show for it." That's really the most critical concept here. But we can't ever separate astrology and synchronicity. Through synchronicity, we almost always find some kind of manifestation cast like a shadow into the three-dimensional, molecular world. As we have seen, synchronicity links the inner world with the outer world of sensory experience, so there's almost always some connection between inner Neptunian realization and things that appear to the eye.

The underlying, unifying theme of synchronistic manifestation under Neptunian stimulus is that the universe is supporting you in any effort you make in the direction of exploring consciousness. That phrase—exploring consciousness—refers to a very diverse range of phenomena; not everybody needs to do Kundalini yoga. For one person, going to Mass might be the ticket. For another it could be hiking to the tops of mountains with a backpack—and, once on the peak, remembering to sit there and gaze for a while.

The synchronistic point is that such outward events are simply more likely to "pop up" for you during Neptunian times. They arise by what we are taught to call "chance."

A classic expression of all this is that is we tend to *encounter spiritual teachers* during such periods. Illustration: your telephone rings and you pick it up. It's a friend of yours who "happened" to think of you. She tells you about a Lakota medicine woman who is giving a talk at a bookstore downtown. Your friend feels like going, but she doesn't want to go alone. "Do you want to come?"

There it is—synchronicity in action. This opportunity has been offered to you—that phone call is a direct manifestation of cosmic law under Neptunian stimulus. *Your response, however, is in the category of freedom.* Maybe you say, "I'd love to!" You go, and you sit in the presence of this medicine woman, and she just blows you away. Even though you are only one person in an audience of a hundred, something is triggered in you. Maybe she is saying words you have heard before, but you seem to be hearing them for the first time. Is it her voice? Is it that you are now ready to truly hear? Synchronicity suggests that both statements are true and that *your consciousness is mirrored in the outer world, just as the outer world—in the form of that wise woman—is mirrored between your ears.*

On the other hand, maybe your friend calls with the invitation and you say, "I'd love to, but I'm too busy." You hang up the phone. The laws of synchronicity declare that doors will open. Freedom declares that you have a choice about whether you pass through them.

The take-away for the counseling astrologer? A client comes to sit with you during such a Neptunian time. Knowing the meaning of the symbolism, you say: "Be alert. Your telephone might ring, for example, and a friend might be inviting you to attend an event with a spiritual teacher. Think seriously about going, because at times like this, magic is afoot!"

Two days after your session, the client's telephone rings—and, because of your good astrological counsel, he or she is *more likely to recognize the synchronistic signature* and agree to attend the lecture.

That's simple imagery, but it represents how astrological counsel actually works. It's why astrology can be helpful—it alerts people to the synchronistic terrain of their evolution in a given time. That counsel can ally with their own intuition and free will and help lead them to the higher ground. That is the true purpose of our work—not to dazzle people with our amazing predictions, but just to help them.

Of course you might speak of a "phone call from a friend," while what actually happens is that your client sees an ad for the Medicine Woman's lecture in the newspaper. Maybe it's not about a Lakota medicine woman at all, but rather about a lecture on hypnotherapy or Jungian dreamwork. Still, you've alerted the client to the evolutionary possibility.

Let me stick with encounters with spiritual teachers for a moment more. Any Neptunian event can bring them into your life, but let's imagine that we have a Neptunian event that involves the third house or the ninth house. Those symbols are particularly connected with *education* and *information*—with correcting your conceptual relationships with the universe and with consciousness. Such stimuli could easily coincide with an encounter with teachings. Ditto for any association of Neptune with the planet Mercury.

Maybe you happen to have Taurus on the cusp of your ninth house, so Venus is its ruler. Venus does not intrinsically have an association with teaching and conceptual kinds of things—but for you personally, it does. With Taurus on the cusp of your ninth house, when we see Neptune interacting with your Venus, it should alert us to the presence of teachers or teachings.

Here we are moving in the direction of a more technical kind of astrology—and later we will explore all this in more "cookbook" fashion. But notice how the principles are exactly the same. Teachers or teachings? As we look specifically at the chart, we can evaluate the probability that such events will reflect the synchronistic manifestation—that if there are third house, ninth house, or Mercury associations, then, yes, the probability of encountering teachers is higher.

If such associations are absent, we are probably going to look for other kinds of Neptunian manifestations. We will list some of them in a moment.

Let's tweak the story of the medicine woman and her lecture. You are sitting in the audience with a hundred other people. Your chair is halfway back from the podium. Right in the middle of her talk, the speaker seems to look right into your eyes for a few seconds. Something transpires in the resonant space between you and her. If you babble about it, you will sound deluded and self-aggrandizing. But it was real.

Here, in this example, we have probably moved away from third house or ninth house symbolism. This is more personal, more primal—something passed between you and that particular woman. We are now likely talking about some *sixth-house* correlate—something to bring in the ideas of *lineage, transmission*, and *spiritual mentoring*. Maybe your natal Neptune, under some current stimulation, lies in your sixth house. Or maybe the stimulant—the transit or progression—is in the sixth house.

Most of what I've been saying here about Neptune events has been focused on one category of synchronistic manifestation: teachers and teachings. That's just been an example. There is so much more that might happen, signaled by the details of the chart. During Neptunian times, weird things happen. Psychic or intuitive events abound. You have amazing dreams. Contacts with archetypes—and the stories that reveal them—pop up. You are drawn into the making of a film, you discover *The Lord of the Rings*, you start writing fiction. (Remember, imaginative creativity is part of Neptune.) Metaphysical books fall off bookshelves. You see a ghost. Amazing, numinous "coincidences" abound. You remember a past life. Someone you love dies in a magical, mystical way you'll remember forever.

The list is effectively endless—and each category of Neptunian event has its technical astrological correlates, which will usually be present in each case. What are they? We covered a lot of it earlier in talking about Neptune in the houses, signs, and planetary aspects. We will look at in more granular detail before we are done.

Let me spin out one more example. Say you have transiting or solar-arc Neptune stimulating your fourth house. I'll just make up a story here; there are a billion of them I could tell. Let's imagine you are in a period of your life when you're house-sitting a lot, moving around and feeling kind of rootless and "between lives." During such a time, somebody might ask you where you live and you laugh out loud.

That's purely material astrology—while Neptune is in the fourth house, there might well be some uncertainty in terms of where you actually call home.

But let's dig deeper. The people whose house you're going to occupy will be in Europe for a month. It happens that they have a beautiful haven of a place on a hill, with a big view of the sea. Recall that earlier, in talking about the connection between Neptune and geographical places, I pointed out how mystics are drawn to the ocean, the desert and mountain tops. The underlying principle is that mystics seem to like spacious views—which in turn supports a "spacious view" of the interior life.

So, here you are with Neptune passing through your fourth house, and the opportunity arises to house-sit a home on a hill with a view of the sea. There's the synchronistic fingerprint. But think about it: doesn't that sound like the universe helping you out with your Neptune transit? Through synchronicity, it has provided you with the support of that magical house in that magical place.

A really deep psychological astrologer might say all sorts of helpful, spiritual things to you during such a time—but without an awareness of these material synchronicities in relation to location, maybe he or she wouldn't notice the connection to that home on the hill. There would be a loss there—not so grievous a loss as might arise with a purely materialistic astrologer—but a loss nonetheless.

The key point here is that in working with Neptunian events, while we need to honor the interior richness of them, we are better astrologers for not forgetting *entirely* about the material world!

We could speculate further. Maybe on the bookshelves of this ocean-view house there is a fine collection of philosophical or spiritual literature. Maybe it is full of Buddhist icons or Christian icons. Maybe there is a mask that belonged to an Inuit shaman from the eighteenth century. It is still vibrating. Again, the house itself seems to be supporting you.

On a more subtle plane, maybe the people vacationing in Europe who live in the house are genuinely conscious beings who relate gratefully and mindfully to being on a mountain top overlooking the sea. They use it as a spiritual opportunity and appreciate the energy of whatever iconography is in the house. They have created a vibration there themselves, and—lucky you—you get to enjoy that good *juju* and soak it up for a month. All of that enhances your response to the Neptune transit in a uniquely fourth house way—which, through our knowledge of astrological technicalities, we can now specify and concretize, thus *supporting your mindfulness.*

And, with Neptune, mindfulness is what it's all about.

FOULING IT UP

Along with the "good" synchronicity, there will always be a red carpet rolled out that leads straight to the garbage can. That's part of the Neptunian synchronistic field too.

Feel like getting drunk? Bourbon is on sale this week. Want to escape into sex? Here's an attractive person, hot to trot, with no strings attached. Want to numb out? Here's a pusher, whether he represents the Zeta gang in Mexico or a pharmaceutical company. Those opportunities will all be present too.

It's just your own mind, calling you, wherever you look.

36

LOSS: NEPTUNE'S FIERCE GIFT

Fearmongering and astrology share a long history. I don't want to contribute to it. Naturally I want to keep the work honest, and I know that life can be very difficult sometimes. But I also want my clients to leave my office feeling encouraged—not that I mind if they are a bit "sobered" too. Sometimes a bracing challenge or two is mirrored in the stars. It is my job to help the client look into that mirror.

There is one principle in which I have come to believe with absolute confidence: always, without fail, no matter how grim the vision in the mirror, there is higher ground. There is purpose in what happens to us in life. And there is always a way to get through it.

With all that said loudly and clearly, we enter some potentially shaky territory. *We cannot study the transits of Neptune for very long without realizing that they often correlate with loss*—sometimes with truly grievous loss. Emphatically, they do not *always* indicate loss. But as astrologers on the front lines of existential reality, we need to be prepared—and to help prepare our clients—for these kinds of eventualities.

LOSING A JOB

Say, for a concrete example, there is some contact between transiting Neptune and your Midheaven—or perhaps you have natal Neptune conjunct your Midheaven and it gets triggered somehow via transits or progressions or solar arcs. *And you lose your job.*

Now, such a passing configuration does not *mean* that you're going to lose your job—it can have other meanings too, which we will weigh later on. But a classic synchronistic correlate of a period of Neptunian stimulus is *the loss of some existential structure that is critical to the support of your identity as you have grown accustomed to thinking of it.* Losing a job is a good example of that, especially with the Midheaven or the tenth house in the Neptunian crosshairs.

Say you've had this same job for twenty-seven years—so long that it is just "there" in your life, without question, like gravity. You no longer even consider whether or not it is fulfilling to you. It has simply become one of the "givens" of your life. Naturally, over the years, your entire identity has become deeply enmeshed with your position in this company. Suddenly, they downsize. Goodbye, here's your golden parachute—which turns out to be made of lead. *So who are you now?* Your social identity can no longer defined by this job. And the challenges go way beyond the practical questions of paying bills. How do you respond now when a friendly stranger says, "Tell me about yourself? What do you *do*?"

Hopefully, your identity was never *entirely* defined by your professional position. But even if you have other foundations for it—relationships, faith, hobbies, community projects—it was inevitably at least partly defined by your work. For most of us, what we do for a living plays a big role in how we think of ourselves.

And now you don't have it anymore.

Once this transit is over, if you land on your feet, you will understand this job loss as a fierce blessing. Or, if you cannot digest it spiritually, it might send you reeling into oblivion.

Recycling an old joke from earlier, picture me, sitting in front of a class of students doing absolutely fantastic Steven Forrest impressions. But what if one day I wake up to discover that people no longer enjoy my "fantastic Steven Forrest impressions?" What if suddenly nobody is interested in astrology, nobody's buying my books, nobody wants to come to my Apprenticeship Program?

Well, to put it mildly, that would be a real personal crisis for me. What's my alternative? "Do you want fries with that?" Astrology is all I know how to do. I've been at it for fifty years. I have no other skills.

I can't help but laugh thinking about it, *and that is because it is so terrifying.* My laughter is purely nervous. Who would I be if I didn't wear this hat? Who would *you* be if you weren't wearing your hat? Could that loss destroy you or me? Of course it could; we're human.

But is it possible we could digest such an experience of loss of public identity and turn it into spiritual wisdom? Well, if you have Neptune engaged with a tenth house feature in your chart, maybe that's what's going on. Maybe that's the evolutionary opportunity. Maybe that's why, in our example, I described someone unexpectedly losing the job he or she had held for twenty-seven years. Neptune works that way sometimes. Loss can be part of its synchronistic field.

If somebody comes to me while he is going through some professional reversal of that nature, I want to respect the difficulty of it. But I also want to underscore that there is higher ground, that there is a way through this dilemma. There is meaning in this. This is not a random event. The universe has offered this opportunity to lose an outworn identity.

Are you actually your job? And, deep down, does it still feed your soul?

If you find yourself having this experience, remember, Neptune-fashion, that you are going to lose that job sometime anyway. Everything changes. Why not now? You're going to have to retire or you're going to have to die. Sooner or later, you're not going to have this support. It's transitory, like everything else in this world. Do you really want to build your mental foundation on those shifting sands? The universe is offering you this opportunity now. Get through the nightmare with grace and faith and there is higher ground on the other side of it. We can promise you that much—*that higher ground is part of the same Neptunian archetypal field that brought the loss.*

During times of such Neptunian loss, the last thing you or I or anyone else wants to hear is that "this is God's plan; trust it." We are terrified. We feel like a victim in a random universe. The existential rug is pulled out from underneath us. And there's seemingly nothing we can do about it.

So, you've lost your job. "Quite a spiritual lesson for you"—I would never say those words to a client. They are too glib; they dismiss the human difficulty of it all. But they are actually the bottom line: to put it simply, *loss is arguably the greatest spiritual lesson we face in life,* and it is very commonly part of the Neptunian experience.

IT'S NOT JUST ABOUT LOSING A JOB

In the foregoing illustration, we've been looking at Neptunian events in connection with the tenth house—thus, we are in the category of loss of identity in connection with our profession—or more broadly, with our place in the big, public world. Loss can naturally occur in other areas of life. With Neptune triggering your seventh house or your Venus, for another example, maybe a major relationship or a marriage ends. If you've been part of a couple for a long time, your identity is very tied up with the relationship. And suddenly you find yourself single. That piece of your identity is not there anymore. Can you live without it? Who are you without that person as your partner?

Again, I want to underscore that such loss is not reliably a rigid prediction. You can't categorically state that when Neptune hits an area of your chart you will experience tragic losses there. There are other possibilities too. But it is helpful to be mindful of the possibility of such an experience, to put the idea of loss on the table.

One point is certain—with Neptune, there's always going to be *a loss of some identification with the little self.* That's basic to "cleaning the window." It may be subtle and internal rather than outwardly obvious—a loss of a belief that is no longer serving you, for example. It might be *some dimension* of your identity rather than feeling like the whole enchilada—within a long marriage, for example, maybe it's not about divorce, but rather about dropping some aspect of how you relate together. Illustration: two people might realize that their baby names for each other have gotten stale, and that using those names is holding them back in a less mature stage of their development as a couple. So goodbye to the Hot Chick and the Cool Dude, goodbye Rocky and Bullwinkle, goodbye Romeo and Babycakes.

I opened this "predictive" section of the book with an image of a woman in her early thirties sitting on the park bench. To commit to being a wife and good mom, she has to let go of what had been a fundamental part of her sexual self-image—let's call it the *passionate femme fatale.*

Oh, how heartbreaking! I mean, God bless all of you women who have hung on to your passionate femme fatale! Let me speak for heterosexual men everywhere and say thank you, thank you, thank you! You put the sparkle in our eyes.

And it's fun to say that, it makes us laugh, but my intent here is serious. This poor woman sitting on the park bench—let's look at her with human compassion, always our clearest Neptunian lens. To remain in her marriage with a clear heart, to be a good mother to her child, she has to let go of something truly precious: what I am calling her "passionate femme fatale."

In neon letters ten feet tall, *this is not about giving up her sexuality*—I'd never tell anybody to do that—but rather about her surrendering a more youthful, *mate-seeking version* of her sexuality. She needs to get past that developmental stage. She must release her identification with the part of herself that is *preoccupied* with sexual attractiveness. And that hurts! That's the loss of something she values, and not for crazy or unworthy reasons. But everything changes, which means everything born must die. There is no more Neptunian perspective than that. *Part of her identity has to die in order to make room for evolution into possibilities she cannot yet imagine.*

I think it's fair to say that those of us who are on the far side of, say, their forty-fifth birthday know what I am talking about. It's emphatically not about giving up our sexuality, but it is about letting it breathe in a way that younger people don't *need* to understand—letting it evolve into something very different than what animates a person who is still habituated to hunting for a partner or partners. As always with a Neptunian event when it is navigated consciously, something is lost and something *we could not previously have comprehended* is gained.

THE CRUX OF THE MATTER

Here's solid advice for anyone going through major Neptunian stimulus: "Sit back, take your time, reflect—because *you don't know what you're doing now*. You are confused. Just accept that condition, know that it is purposeful and transitory, and that way you will avoid some major blunders." In the previous chapter, we used the sample of "the dork and the Dalai Lama." And the Dalai Lama can understand the dork, but not vice versa because *a gallon can understand a quart, but a quart cannot understand a gallon*. I love that volume metaphor. It is very precise. In a Neptunian time, your consciousness is, rather literally, "gaining volume." Loss comes in when some old identity-structure is standing in the way of that expansion, whether or not we know it.

Often, when you're dealing with a client who has a genuine spiritual foundation, someone who is not too defensive, they'll respond to these words with gratitude. Just knowing that there is a *reason* they're confused is a comfort. And of course, with some confidence, we can also let them know when "they won't be confused anymore"—when the Neptunian period will be over, in other words.

But here's the better statement, the deeper statement, where we enter the truly profound territory: in a Neptunian time, it's not just that you *don't* know what you're doing, it's that you *can't* know what you're doing.

And that is an entirely different statement. The sleazy used car salesman cannot understand the saint. Our dork is baffled by the Dalai Lama. No "explanation" will suffice to resolve that dilemma—explanations just rearrange the furniture in the person's head. What our dork needs here is an *expanded* head. He needs more volume. The quart needs to become a gallon. Then, and only then, can he understand.

This is the heart and soul of the Neptunian process. *Consciousness expands first, and then, into that expanded space there flows visionary inspiration for what we might do next in the outer world.* And that practical piece—what we might do next—is almost secondary, a mere footnote compared to the evolutionary step.

If this sounds vague or unclear to you, here's a way to ground it in realities you have already experienced in your life. If we had asked you, back when you were eleven years old, what you wanted to be when you grew up, you probably would have had an answer. *How valid would that answer be for you today?* When you were twelve, you had a crush on somebody. *Are you sad that relationship didn't work out and turn into a marriage?* Similarly, in a Neptunian time, your level of awareness must expand—otherwise there will be no sufficient basis to sustain the new vision. The only way the sleazy used car salesman can understand the saint is to become a saint himself.

Loss, in the outward sense, creates the space into which this new, expanded awareness can express itself biographically—later on. So, naturally, you are confused in a Neptunian time. You just haven't caught up with yourself yet. Don't let that worry you!

The most useless and futile thing you can do in a Neptunian time is to try to solve your problems.

Don't just do something, sit there. That's an easy pronouncement to make—but it's hard to follow, especially when you're feeling anxious.

Needless to say, if you've got pressing problems, it's very tempting to try to solve them. The woman sitting on the park bench feels sexually and romantically frustrated. That's pressing! She's tempted to have a fling with her old boyfriend, the one who contacted her on Facebook.

Let's say she does that. Apart from our reflections on the potentially destructive impact of that fling on her marriage and her family—just putting all of that aside for a moment—what do you think will actually happen? If she has an affair with her old boyfriend, what's your best guess about the outcome of it? We all know the general patterns of life. So—she has the big affair with the old boyfriend, and maybe her marriage falls apart because of it, and there's that whole familiar "country and western" melody. And most of the verses are about loss created by our own errors and foolishness.

What's the next scene? She's two or three years down the road in a relationship with the old boyfriend—and she's sitting on a park bench, feeling a little romantically and sexually frustrated. Back to the proverbial square one.

Right? How many times have you "learned" that one?

Her belief that the solution to her problem is to explore things with the old boyfriend is really just an example of her rearranging the existing furniture in her head. That's all she's doing. She is operating within the framework of her old state of consciousness. That's all any of us can ever do until we've done the inner Neptunian work of actual evolution. Loss is really just a side-effect.

This woman is in a Neptunian time, so her real solution lies in becoming "less like the used car salesman and more like the saint." She needs an expansion of her consciousness. Specifically, as we have seen, she needs to develop an understanding of human sexuality that isn't so much based on the sexual logic of youth. She is poised on the threshold of beginning to understand that physical love can blossom in a deeper, more lasting way as we move forward through the years together. With Neptune trining her seventh house Mars, she is on the cusp of a *breakthrough in awareness* that will actually allow her to go forward that way, not just replay old patternings. She can learn, in her body, that in physical love between two people committed to each other over the long haul, sex doesn't necessarily go downhill, but it does get different. And as her consciousness opens up to the difference . . . well, she's less like the dork and more like the Dalai Lama.

She moves up on our famous graph.

That expansion is the work she must do *first* in order to actually solve her problem. It requires more than rearranging the outward biographical furniture. It requires cleaner windows.

THE VISION QUEST

In a Neptune time, you need a vision. And, through employing the personalized, chart-specific, processes and mechanisms that we've been pursuing, a vision will come. You can count on that. This is one of the laws of the universe. It will not fail.

To get at this idea of a vision quest with clients, I often adopt a mock-censorious voice and accuse them of "having no vision for their lives." In using a preachy voice like that, what I'm trying to do is to make fun of the similar voice inside their own heads—a voice that is giving them grief for feeling a bit lost. Remember: in a Neptune time the problem is not that you don't know what you are doing, it's that you *cannot* know what you are doing. For that reason, we must release the idea that "not having a vision" is inherently a personal failure—and replace it with a sense that such clueless periods are part of a natural developmental cycle and really nothing to worry about. In giving ourselves grief for lacking a vision, we're not honoring the fact that Neptune means that your old visions have played out and you're in the process of getting a new one—one far richer than anything you've known before. That process just takes a while. There is no problem at all.

You have no vision! The ego hears that and immediately arms its photon torpedoes. Confronted that way, almost anybody is going to get defensive. I mean, who wouldn't? The natural response to "such an insult" is: "Who do you think are you to say that to me? *Of course I have a vision for my life!* I have values! I stand for things. I know who to vote for. I know my favorite color. I like Mexican food, and Led Zeppelin, and Maui, and Zinfandel wine in a real wine glass, and I hate Fox news, and I love my cat," and on and on.

Ego shrouds itself in its favorite armor: *opinion.*

Because people are sensitized and reactive in a major Neptunian period, we have to be gentle with them. As we have seen, they may experience frightening outward losses in the concrete sense, or at least a kind of disenchantment with the way thing are in their lives. Even without material loss, the "lost" feeling alone is scary—and also potentially the most powerful evolutionary rocket fuel there is. We need to nurture it. We assure the client that he or she is simply shedding an old skin and that it is perfectly natural that some of the old "position papers" don't seem to work anymore. *There is nothing they have to do*, other than cultivating mindfulness. And the fruit will fall from the invisible tree into the visible, biographical world in due time—when the Neptunian stimulus moves on.

A simple image appears in my mind's eye, one that I believe puts a smile on the faces of the angels. Here's a person in a Neptunian time. She is listening to her old favorite record, one she's loved since she was in college. *And she gets up and turns it off.* Her angels are smiling, not because they dislike the music, but because she was *mindful.* The part of her that holds the "official position" that she likes this particular music is nothing but a mechanical, memorized habit. The present reality of what she has become is no longer moved by that melody. *And she noticed that.* The momentum of past opinion did not define her present reality. It's a small image, but it encapsulates the heart of the matter.

So, if you're not what you were, what are you? *You don't know.*

Can you step out of the dubious comfort of an outworn identity into that fertile spaciousness, into that vast *groundlessness*—and thus receive the new vision? Can you get out of your own way? Your soul is struggling in that direction. That's an inner process. It has a strong kinship with meditation. And, as we have seen, through synchronicity, you might get some outward help in the form of losses; structures that have supported the old identity fall away. You lose the job. Your partner meets someone new. Your knee goes out and you can't dance anymore. Synchronicity also brings gifts we are more inclined to appreciate—we meet teachers, precious books fall off shelves at the right moment, magic is afoot.

THE DARK SHADOW

We have already looked carefully at the dark side of Neptune in the natal chart—one dimension of it being that it tempts us with various forms of numbness and escapism. During periods of Neptunian stimulus, these same kinds of threats loom pressingly.

In naming the devils here, it is critical that we stretch our imagination beyond merely worrying about overdoing drink and drugs. I learned this years ago with a client. She was a little older than me, and sort of "New Age" before that term was part of the culture—a long time ago, in other words. We were both part of spiritual group. She came to me for a reading with Neptune heading for a conjunction with her natal Sun. In my inexperience, I offered an offhand comment about escapism—but immediately assured her that for a lofty soul such as herself there would be no worry from that quarter.

And then she disappeared from the radar screen—stopped coming to our meetings, went poof. About two years later, toward the end of the Neptune transit, she returned—*about forty pounds heavier.*

Nobody asked what she had been up to. It was pretty clear: she'd been eating potato chips and ice cream. Why? Here's a clue: *a belly full of food and a load of sugar in your bloodstream can numb you out as surely as four shots of tequila.*

So, one behavioral manifestation of Neptune's shadow during such a period is a heightened tendency toward escapism in its myriad forms. The key insight is that this phenomenon is not driven fundamentally by "weakness" in a person's character. Its origin lies in a failure to adapt, via some spiritual effort, to an opening of the psychic sensitivities. This is not only a more accurate understanding, it also has a great practical advantage. Unlike blaming someone for "weakness," it actually points directly toward the remedy: *make that spiritual effort.* You've earned a breakthrough. Don't squander it on weight gain.

Reminding us again of Neptune in the natal chart, such Neptunian periods can bring out the "ghost" in people. We can "hang on crosses." We can drift into dark, lost dimensions characterized by a total lack of inspiration, wondering what all of this will matter in five hundred years. Those are all soul-cages just as sure as emptying vodka bottles.

Another Neptunian temptation arises during such times, and this one doesn't get mentioned nearly as often as the others: *a nostalgic retreat into the past.* Here's the logic behind it. The future is uncertain; we don't know how it will turn out. And uncertainty fills us with anxiety. There is a corollary to this. One thing we all know for sure about the past: *we survived it.* No matter how bad things looked in the past, you are here now. It all turned out OK. You made it through. You are still among the living. *You want to go back there.* That's why a kind of conservative reaction can rise during a Neptunian period—a person tries to hold together his or her old life: the job that is no longer meaningful, the religion that is no longer working, the marriage or relationship that no longer has any relevance to us or which has descended into complete ritual.

It's tempting to say that the universe does not allow us to hold the past together—that loss arises and the old structures disappear and we simply must move forward. Sometimes it works that way. A partner leaves us, for example. What can you do? You get fired from the job. As we have seen, these losses are Neptunian events. But it's too simplistic to say that Neptune always works that way. Sometimes people do successfully hold the old reality together—long past the time that it is feeding them in any meaningful way. This is ultimately just another form of Neptunian escapism. I guess we could call it *an escape from the future.*

What has such a person gained? Here's a parallel question: what would it feel like to start over again as a freshman in high school? Wasn't it bad enough the first time around? Not to be cruel, but people who fall into that soul-cage essentially become the *zombies* of the world—the walking, breathing, living dead.

Talking about the Shadow side of anything astrological can be depressing. I guess it should be! And none of us are immune. We can recognize ourselves in these dark mirrors. To be human is to be sitting on the evolutionary razor's edge, right at the frontiers of your own potentials. That inevitably means that we all fail sometimes. That is such a universal reality that feeling bad about it—or worse, feeling guilty about it—is futile. It's like feeling bad about breathing.

The only standards by which we might actually benefit from judging ourselves are the classic Neptunian ones. First and foremost, can you have compassion for yourself, no matter what? It all starts there. Second, can you recognize that others are in similar predicaments, and that's why they behave badly sometimes too? There's compassion again, this time aimed outwardly.

And finally, can you sit back down and embrace that wide-open emptiness and openness? Can you get back to the endless, joyful task of cleaning your windows?

37

NEPTUNIAN TRANSITS, PROGRESSIONS, & SOLAR ARCS: HINTS AND SPECIFICS

Neptune is an archetype. When it looms episodically in your life via transits, solar arcs or progressions, there is a certain pattern of "astrological DNA" in the mix no matter what form the technical specifics take. But naturally, transiting Neptune sextiling the Moon is a different beast than solar arc Saturn squaring natal Neptune. Part of our craft lies in learning to open the full specificity of the astrological language. We quickly collide with questions of which house that Moon occupies or from what sign of the zodiac that Saturn square is emanating. The details ramify at warp speed, moving us merrily toward increasing precision—if we can surf the waves of information.

One result of all this potential complexity is that a true astrological "cookbook" covering the full range of technical possibilities would weigh more than a sumo wrestler after a food tour of New Orleans.

All that we have been pondering so far in this "predictive" part of the program is an attempt to decode the basic logic of a Neptunian period in the life of an individual. It has taken me a while to cover it all, even in general terms. It's rich territory—even when we leave out references to the astrological specifics.

My hope is that you can apply the general theory creatively to whatever is going on in your own chart or the charts of people who come to sit with you.

What I want to do now is to try to help you do that by offering a few hints about how to handle various passing Neptunian configurations. This is about as close to a "cookbook" as I want to get.

What follows are "tweets" and "bumper stickers" rather than long essays. Please take them in the context of everything we have explored already—and not only in the last couple of chapters, but really in everything we've seen, right from the beginning of this book.

Earlier, for example, we explored the meaning of a *natal* aspect between Neptune and Venus. When Neptune *transits* through an aspect to your natal Venus, some of those same archetypal potentials are likely to manifest—but in a "transitory" way. If you are experiencing such a Neptune-Venus transit, please reconsider that previous natal material in the light of what is now emerging in your life—just frame it as a passing opportunity or condition.

I would say the same if Neptune transits into a new house in your chart; spend some time with earlier material about the meaning of having natal Neptune in that house "permanently," in your birthchart. It requires a little translation, but the translation is not difficult.

Again, the possible range of combinations is vast, but as we saw earlier, all aspects are about integration. That's a principle that works by transit or progression just as reliably as it does in the context of birthchart analysis. *So think first about how the two energies might look if they were on the same team.* Don't take too seriously the conventional astrological idea of "good and bad" aspects. Just remember that if the two planets are connected by a hard aspect, the integration requires more work. That is balanced by the increased danger of laziness with the easier ones.

Going further, the progressed Sun contacting natal Neptune is not quite the same as transiting Neptune contacting the natal Sun—but the two archetypes are the same. You would use a lot of the same language in either case. In what follows, we'll deal with them as if they were interchangeable. That's not quite right—but again, the alternative is a book that would weigh more than you do.

In carrying these ideas toward precision, you will soon enough be on your own—at least beyond these basic guidelines. Even an unabashed astrological "cookbook" quickly runs out of steam. It might suggest the meaning of Neptune transiting through an aspect to Venus—but what if that Venus lies in the twelfth house in Aquarius in a conjunction with the

Moon? Or maybe Venus lies in Cancer in the tenth house. Those are far from interchangeable situations.

Even the cookbooks fail.

There is no real alternative except to learn to *think astrologically*. Start by asking yourself, what exactly is the nature of that natal structure? The birthchart is the "root prediction," as I called it in *The Changing Sky* years ago. With that understood, ask yourself what house and sign the stimulating body occupies. Then integrate, integrate, integrate! What do these two forces look like when they're working together toward an evolutionary goal? What might a wasteful war between them look like? How might they agree to not grow—and thus have no war at all, but no progress either?

Astrology is very articulated language with a large vocabulary. How would you respond if someone asked you, "What does French say?" There is no substitute for actually learning the language. Below you will find some brief verbal formulas that suggest a framework for thinking specifically—and astrologically—about Neptune's interaction with each of the planets and each of the houses. We look at each possibility both positively and negatively. In other words, we talk about the specific escapist correlates of each one, as well as the higher integrative, evolutionary intentions. We look outwardly, through the lens of synchronicity, at what "might be happening" in the physical, biographical sense. And we make some distinctions between the easy and the hard aspects.

And remember, all of this is nothing but the shorthand version of a few basic hints. Listen to your intuition, trust it, and jam away!

NEPTUNE AND THE SUN

In the Alchemical Cauldron: Ego and spirituality are making space for each other. We may need to take a strong stand for our right to follow our own path. We need a vision. The personality must become spiritually sane enough to cope with radically expanded sensitivity.

Synchronistic Correlates: Opportunities to connect with teachers and teachings. Loss of that which supports identity and ego. Psychic experiences. Retreat.

Escaping into Addiction: Egocentric spiritual delusion. The "sleepy refuge" of commitment to failure.

In Hard Aspects: Shocks to the self-image. Enforced humility. Loss and failure. Experiences of anonymity or invisibility.

In Easy Aspects: Gifts of the spirit. Abundant support and opportunity, which you must find the motivation to seize. Feelings of drifting.

The Price of Failure: Escapism. Agreement to "hang on the cross." Giving up. Defeat.

NEPTUNE AND THE MOON

In the Alchemical Cauldron: The human heart is merging with mystical perceptions. Love is expanding. The path of devotion and adoration. Daring to feel deeply. Great Dreams. Vulnerability as a spiritual path. Magic normalized.

Synchronistic Correlates: Psychological sensitivity. Domestic concerns; love and its price in the context of family. Encounter with one's soul tribe. Search for one's natural home. Intensified dream-life.

Escaping into Addiction: Appointing one's self as a "public utility" to be used by others. Hypochondria. Whining. Accepting victimhood.

In Hard Aspects: Feeling emotionally overwhelmed. Reaching limits and the edges of sanity. Feeling rootless or homeless. The "motherless child."

In Easy Aspects: Tenderness in others opening our hearts. Surrendering. Sweet tears. Sleepiness.

The Price of Failure: Self-indulgence. Weakness as a choice. Dependency on others. Selfish entitlement.

NEPTUNE AND MERCURY

In the Alchemical Cauldron: Three-dimensional intellect encounters evidence for a multi-dimensional reality. The widening bandwidth of perception. Finding the words. Spiritual education. Correction of wrong ideas.

Synchronistic Correlates: Weird perceptions. "Seeing things." Encounters with spiritual teachers and teaching. Omens and signs. Inexplicable sensory experience.

Escaping into Addiction: Compulsive worry. Mistaking information for spirituality. Compulsive talking. Endless, pointless busyness.

In Hard Aspects: Mental confusion. Confused speech. Fruitful, but difficult, intellectual effort in spiritual matters. Really stretching the mind.

In Easy Aspects: Flowing into understanding. Blossoming of wisdom. Eloquence. Danger of mental laziness. Feeling that "I already know everything I need to know."

The Price of Failure: Decisions based on erroneous beliefs. Misperception. Retreat from evolution into mere dogmatism. Talking as a way of suppressing the truth.

NEPTUNE AND VENUS

In the Alchemical Cauldron: Merging personal and transcendent love. Aesthetic rapture as a spiritual path. Serenity and adoration triggering evolution. Body and soul in intimate accord.

Synchronistic Correlates: Sacred sexuality. Contact with beauty, whether it is natural or human-made. Encounters with soul mates. Peacemaking and forgiveness.

Escaping into Addiction: Only seeing one's spirituality in others. Compulsive, ungrounded romantic dramas and expectations. Sheer laziness. Sugar-trance.

In Hard Aspects: Love banging on the door. The cost of love. How badly do you want him/her? Disillusionment in love. Abandonment. Encounters with ugliness. Feeling shaken.

In Easy Aspects: Being charmed into evolution. Being seduced. Love as pure Grace. The slippery slope. Lazy self-indulgence. Vanity. Love doesn't have to be hard all the time. Opening the heart.

The Price of Failure: Time wasted on unworthy partners. Mistaking genuine soul-connection for actual, practical compatibility. Eating chocolate instead of meditating while the opportunity passes.

NEPTUNE AND MARS

In the Alchemical Cauldron: Courage and mystical sensibilities merge. The spiritual warrior. Facing fears. The spiritual adventure. Spiritual passion. Sexual passion as a path. "Fear is the mind-killer."

Synchronistic Correlates: The moment of truth. Now or never. Sudden breakthroughs. Life-changing adventures or misadventures. Stress. The warrior's sacrifice for those s/he loves.

Escaping into Addiction: Sexual compulsivity. Addiction to rage. Addiction to watching sports.

In Hard Aspects: Scary perceptions. "Seeing a ghost." The life-changing event for which you did not ask. The spiritual ordeal.

In Easy Aspects: Naturally coming to "the mountaintop." Integration of the erotic and the mystical. Mistaking hormones for a spiritual connection.

The Price of Failure: Misplaced anger. Soul eclipsed by anger or fear. Rage rotting the soul. Division and duality confirmed. Loss of passion or libido.

NEPTUNE AND JUPITER

In the Alchemical Cauldron: Self-confidence and spirituality merging. Pride, in both the positive and negative sense. Evolutionary opportunity seized. Contact with inspiration. Contact with spiritual heroes.

Synchronistic Correlates: Every dog has his day, even spiritually. The door opens. Your main chance. The teacher appears.

Escaping into Addiction: Inability to resist any temptation. Megalomaniacal spiritual delusion.

In Hard Aspects: Overreaching and overestimating the self—with an equal chance of the opposite. Finding that balance.

In Easy Aspects: Your good karma bears fruit. Mystical opportunity "falls from the sky." Recognize and claim the gift—and don't sleep through it.

The Price of Failure: Missed opportunities. Spiritual puffery. Slipping into glamour, ego inflation and spiritual pride. Accepting the "guru award" and believing it.

NEPTUNE AND SATURN

In the Alchemical Cauldron: Discipline and long-term commitment complementing spiritual aspiration. Method. Skillful means. The reality check. Effort. Practice, practice, practice. Spiritual maturation.

Synchronistic Correlates: Austerity and lack. Time spent alone. Useful disillusionment. Encounters with step-by-step methods. Breakthrough resulting from relentless effort.

Escaping into Addiction: Compulsive explaining and "debunking" of the miraculous. Emotional isolation as a self-protective tool.

In Hard Aspects: Cherished illusions crash. Spiritual hunger that is hard to satisfy. Difficult lessons that help us grow up.

In Easy Aspects: Hard work finally paying off. One more step as the final catalyst for breakthrough. Growing up without noticing it. Procrastination robbing us of an evolutionary opportunity.

The Price of Failure: Spiritual stagnation. Feeling cut off from the Divine. Feeling uninspired. Mere ritual.

NEPTUNE AND URANUS

In the Alchemical Cauldron: Fearless questioning of received wisdom. Rebel Buddha. Individuality on the path. Rejection of external authority. Doubt. Trusting the authority of your own experience.

Synchronistic Correlates: Rebellion against socially expected "religion." Endings with former teachers. The bold spiritual decision leading to breakthrough—and perhaps to exile.

Escaping into Addiction: Making everyone else wrong. Hooked on spiritual fads. Dissociative disorder as a means of self defense.

In Hard Aspects: Doors slammed. Shunning and excommunication. Buying "the pearl of great price." Painful price of truth, integrity, and authenticity.

In Easy Aspects: Flowing into spiritual individuality. Finding one's own natural path or method. Descending into quirkish spirituality, tempted by easy answers.

The Price of Failure: Continued conformity that becomes stultifying. Hypocrisy deriving from "not wanting to hurt anyone's feelings." Adopting flaky beliefs in lieu of genuine searching.

NEPTUNE AND NEPTUNE

(Note that transiting Neptune forms aspects with its natal position, as does solar arc Neptune)

In the Alchemical Cauldron: A purely Neptunian period. Meditation, compassion, and cleaning the windows.

Synchronistic Correlates: Circumstances support evolutionary breakthrough.

Escaping into Addiction: Drunkenness in all its forms.

In Hard Aspects: How much do you want it?

In Easy Aspects: Don't sleep through it!

The Price of Failure: A missed opportunity that will not return again for a long time.

NEPTUNE AND PLUTO

In the Alchemical Cauldron: Psychology and spirituality complementing each other. The interdependency of both kinds of "inner work."

Synchronistic Correlates: Psychological wounds that inhibit one's evolutionary potential surface. Spiritual support appears "at the critical moment."

Escaping into Addiction: Getting hooked on "powers." Psychological insight without compassion or humor. Fascination with "the dark side of the Force."

In Hard Aspects: The inner work pushes you very hard. You may need to cry, but find it difficult. You may need to forgive, but find it nearly impossible.

In Easy Aspects: Your inner work has earned you a breakthrough. All it takes is a little more effort. Don't let laziness or passivity snatch defeat from the jaws of victory.

The Price of Failure: Either staying caught in the fugue of endless self-absorbed psychology or avoiding personal growth via a "flight into light," which is to say hiding from pain in some religious or philosophical rationalization.

NEPTUNE AND THE LUNAR NODES

In the Alchemical Cauldron: Prior-life memories are entering consciousness, directly or indirectly.

Synchronistic Correlates: Meetings with people who seem strangely familiar. Past-life regressions, dreams, and memories. Visits to places with which one is inexplicably familiar. Psychic readings.

Escaping into Addiction: Repeating the past and justifying it defensively.

In Hard Aspects: One's evolutionary journey is hanging in the balance. Will you relive the south node past—or will your spirituality serve your higher north node intentions?

In Easy Aspects: The spiritual insight and support that can come from an accurate grasp on one's exact karmic issues and patterns. Gaining such insights and doing nothing about them.

The Price of Failure: Just a missed opportunity, with the sadness of that feeling leading toward mild, unlabeled despair and increased vulnerability to "turning it all off."

THE HOUSES UNDER NEPTUNIAN DEVELOPMENTAL PRESSURE

Do remember to look at the much more in-depth material about *natal* Neptune's placement in each of the twelve houses. With minor translation, those perspectives cast light on Neptune's house transits—which last an average of fourteen years—or the solar arcs, which last for something more like three decades. With events that endure over so much time, it is often difficult subjectively to sort out one's birthchart from their glacial pace, so there is a natural blurring between the natal and the transitory configurations.

In every case, the meaning of the Neptunian house-event is considerably more vivid when it hits a sensitive point within the context of the house. Perhaps there is a planet resident in that house—Neptune's passing conjunction with it will be flavored not only by the nature of that planet, but equally by the material we explore here. Extending this reasoning, we realize that each planet in the birthchart lays out a network of sensitive invisible *trigger points*—points that are in aspect to the natal planet, in other words. Some such trigger points naturally fall in the house through which Neptune is currently passing. They're like trip wires—when Neptune hits them, an avalanche of symbolism is precipitated comprising the whole array of houses, signs, and planets involved.

Illustration: Maybe you are writing a fantasy novel while Neptune transits your third house. You get stuck as Neptune forms a transiting square to your natal sixth house (think *mentors*) Saturn (think *elders*). You respond consciously. Rather than staying stuck, you hire an older editor who is very hard on you—but improves the book.

With Neptune in the first house by transit or solar arc . . .

If you get it right: You behave boldly, even selfishly, if necessary, in order to claim your right to experiences that actually contribute to your evolution. You can't simultaneously do this correctly and keep everyone happy and approving toward you.

If you get it wrong: You miss the boat and become an actor on the stage of life, a ghost who lost his or her way.

With Neptune in the second house by transit or solar arc . . .

If you get it right: You do not underestimate yourself spiritually. You instead behave in a way that befits your level of evolution. You support yourself with the proper spiritual tools.

If you get it wrong: You beat the dead horse of spiritual methods you have actually outgrown. You fail to employ simple, practical solutions to the problems that are holding you back.

With Neptune in the third house by transit or solar arc . . .

If you get it right: You trust the strange messages your senses offer. You listen to the inner voice. You find your voice as a spiritual teacher. You seek teachings and teachers.

If you get it wrong: Tension arises between the reality of your perceptions and your socialized voice. This mental confusion undercuts the clarity and authority of your voice.

With Neptune in the fourth house by transit or solar arc . . .

If you get it right: You find or create a safe space for your sensitive inner work. You find your spiritual family and your natural spiritual home.

If you get it wrong: Your family turns you into a ghost who serves them. You settle for living in alienation, with your spiritual life a well-kept secret.

With Neptune in the fifth house by transit or solar arc . . .

If you get it right: You embrace your creativity as a spiritual path. You find spiritual ecstasy. You resolve old karmic attractions, releasing yourself and others from repeating unproductive patterns.

If you get it wrong: Your hunger for spiritual ecstasy misdirects into mere appetite. You get into trouble with some pleasure overdone.

With Neptune in the sixth house by transit or solar arc . . .

If you get it right: You seek your spiritual mentors. You practice, practice, practice, thereby creating healthy spiritual habits. You use service toward others as a chance to get over yourself.

If you get it wrong: You become so defined by your duties and routines that you become invisible as a person. Robed in what appears to be virtue, you have given up your own path.

With Neptune in the seventh house by transit or solar arc . . .

If you get it right: You seek your natural soul partners in friendship and intimate love. You find people who can corroborate your mystical perceptions. You establish a spiritual basis for intimacy and trust.

If you get it wrong: You fall in love with people who fail you. You trust the wrong people. You hang on the cross of empty, meaningless relationship.

With Neptune in the eighth house by transit or solar arc . . .

If you get it right: You unify spirituality and sexuality. You prepare consciously for death, no matter your age or longevity. You encounter invisible powers. You may help—or at least be present—when others are dying.

If you get it wrong: You dissipate energy in sexual drama. You become morbidly absorbed in thoughts of death. You withdraw into darkness.

With Neptune in the ninth house by transit or solar arc . . .

If you get it right: You seek teachings that deepen and correct your metaphysical understanding. You surrender to inherited wisdom traditions. You undertake pilgrimage.

If you get it wrong: You descend into dogmatism and rigidity, perhaps into fanaticism. You become parochial and narrow. You make a religion out of personally hanging on a cross.

With Neptune in the tenth house by transit or solar arc . . .

If you get it right: You seek a spiritual mission in the world. You get "the call" and heed it. You become a lighthouse in your community. You may accept an initiatory period of "being nobody special."

If you get it wrong: You become a public utility. You are an actor on the stage of life, not liking your own part. You drift, never satisfied, seeking "destiny" but too lazy to find it.

With Neptune in the eleventh house by transit or solar arc . . .

If you get it right: You prioritize your long-term spiritual goals and act accordingly. You find your natural spiritual fellowship or tribe. It supports and serves you, and vice versa.

If you get it wrong: You drift into pointless socializing with people with whom you share very little of substance. Your goals are vague and dreamy, too uncertain to guide you.

With Neptune in the twelfth house by transit or solar arc . . .

If you get it right: You make a big effort to open your psychic centers of perception. You do spiritual practice in some sense of the term. You accept loss as a teacher. You are willing to be unrecognized.

If you get it wrong: You are overwhelmed by your own sensitivity, taking refuge in some form of escape or numbness.

I do emphasize that all the foregoing material is intended mostly as an aid to your memory. We explored these archetypal transactions—both in terms of planetary aspects and houses—much more deeply earlier in the book. And the moment you really go beyond memorizing key words and look *integratively* at an actual birthchart—that's when you've entered the realm of true astrological artistry. That third house Neptune in Scorpio, which is conjunct Venus and square Mars from Aquarius in the sixth, is currently experiencing a trine from transiting Neptune in Pisces and the seventh house, and ... you get the picture. You need to assemble a lot of pieces.

Part Six

Chart Examples

In his Astrological Apprenticeship Program, Steven generally presents some theoretical material, then works with the charts of class members using their shared personal stories as a way of demonstrating the practical application of the ideas he has just taught. What surfaces is often emotional, personal, and thus not for public consumption. Confidentiality is the quintessential ethical principle in counseling, and that stricture applies in the "AP." Only Steven's students have access to the recordings and transcripts of those private parts of his classes. The illustrations of Neptune's action that follow are of well-known people, both because of the universal usefulness of their recognizable names and biographies and to respect the privacy of Steven's students.

38

THE PROOF OF THE PUDDING

Synthesis and integration—those are the north stars of astrological analysis. No single configuration has reliable personal meaning outside the context of the whole chart. Moon in Pisces? We might start with the notion of "sensitivity." But what if there are nine planets in Aries? Or nine planets in Cancer? If, in other words, if someone asks about the meaning of the Moon in Pisces, the right response is not "sensitivity"—but rather "show me the chart."

In what follows, I am going to break that rule. I want to take a brief look at the action of Neptune in the lives and charts of a great many people. Ignoring most of the astrological context inevitably creates distortions and a loss of perspective. That is lamentable—but the alternative is even less appealing: a full analysis of even one birthchart would require many pages, and most of the material would only be indirectly relevant to our main topic of Neptune.

Synthesis and integration, again, are the great arts in the craft of astrology. In many of my other books, audio and visual recordings and webinars, I've tried to illustrate those larger principles as best I can. Here, it will be more of a quick zoom through a varied astrological landscape as we try to see the principles we've explored in the previous pages come alive in the actual human biographies of familiar public characters.

The people mentioned in what follows are the good, the bad and the ugly. To pick subjects, I just roamed through the Astro-Databank database choosing anyone who grabbed my interest. Hopefully, they'll grab your interest too.

As a loose organizational principle, I have arranged these illustrations according to Neptune's house position. Earlier chapters in which I explored the significance of each house provide the theoretical foundation. I won't repeat any of that groundwork in detail here. If something doesn't make sense to you, just go back and read the relevant house chapter again. In many cases, I also make reference to astrological aspects. Again, earlier chapters flesh out the underlying thinking.

NEPTUNE IN THE FIRST HOUSE

Born with Neptune in Leo in her first house, *Marilyn Monroe* epitomizes so much of what we have been exploring. The first house is what we present to the world. Having Neptune there lends a fluid quality to the social persona. With a client, I will often describe it as "wearing the mask of the master actor." And with Marilyn, we can take that very literally. Obviously, she was a fine, professional actor. But the point is deeper. There is a tale about her walking down Fifth Avenue in New York with a friend. She wore a headscarf and a raincoat, and no one noticed her. This was at the height of her fame. Suddenly she said to her friend, "Do you want me to be *Her*? Watch." And she transformed herself instantly into "Marilyn"—and within thirty seconds she was surrounded by fans and autograph seekers. That's perhaps the best Neptune-in-the-first-house story I know. It says it all.

Marilyn Monroe was a very talented actor. She was also, as we all know, a classic tragic figure, her life fraught with loss. The circumstances around her untimely death are murky, but certainly, her increasing addiction to prescription psychiatric drugs was a huge factor—and that's a classic Neptunian issue too. Relationships were a painful area of her life, and Neptune played a role in all that as well, being in opposition to her seventh house Moon-Jupiter conjunction, as well as trine her Venus. In reference to her two marriages, her biographer, Donald Spoto, quipped that her marriage to Joe DiMaggio collapsed "when he discovered that she was Marilyn Monroe," while her marriage to playwright Arthur Miller collapsed "when he discovered she wasn't." It's a funny line—but not if you are living it.

If you're interested in a more integrative look at Marilyn Monroe's chart, you might enjoy a webinar I recorded about her and Mexican painter

Frida Kahlo. You can find it online at: http://www.forrestastrology.com/store/webinars/chart-reading-frida-marilyn-detail

Another master actor, although of a very different nature, is *Woody Allen*, also born with Neptune in the first house—in Virgo this time, giving him that unparalleled capacity to play the Virgoan "nerd," just as a Marilyn's Leo placement made her name synonymous with glamorous "stardom."

For the sheer chameleon-like charm of Neptune in the first house, there is no example so clear as former American president *Bill Clinton*, born with Neptune in Libra in the first, conjunct both Venus and Mars. One can see the signature of his sexual downfall in that configuration too.

For the purely visionary dimensions of Neptune in the first house, poet and writer *Maya Angelou* stands out, as does the visionary Englishman *William Blake*. More currently, for visionary creativity, we might consider singer-songwriter *Taylor Swift*, born with Neptune in the first house in the midst of an earth-shaking comic traffic jam right on her Capricorn Ascendant. Neptune is conjunct her Ascendant along with Uranus, Saturn, and Mercury—an impressive chart befitting a leader and a spokesperson for a generation. It will be interesting to watch the Capricorn "Elder" symbolism open like a flower in her life. I suspect her best work still lies ahead.

NEPTUNE IN THE SECOND HOUSE

Money, as we saw earlier, is not the only consideration in the second house—but it is part of the symbolism and often a pressing dimension of daily life, so let's start right there, with dollars and cents. There has always been a complex relationship between money and the spiritual path. Born with Neptune in the second, the synchronistic principles animating people's lives often manifest as a kind of up-and-down *surreality* around finances, as if the universe were trying to get them to think about how much power they are going to assign to money. I'd like to use three examples here. The first is Apple Computer founder *Steve Jobs*, who had Neptune in the second in Libra. The second is the "naughty" American author of a few generations ago, *Henry Miller*, with Neptune there in Gemini (and conjunct Pluto). The third is *Pope Francis I*, born with Neptune in Virgo in the second house.

Steve Jobs was born into relative poverty, along with the initial emotional insecurity that often goes with being adopted. And of course he became one of the wealthiest human beings on the planet—and he accomplished that rags-to-riches feat in classic second house fashion by designing a set of *fundamental tools*—and remember, tools are resources that support life, and are thus second house material—that many of us nowadays find essential to life as we have come to live it.

Meanwhile, in a very different way, *Henry Miller* became an expatriate, moving to Paris in 1930 with virtually no money at all in order to work on his masterpiece, *Tropic of Cancer*. (Recall that his Neptune lies in Gemini, the sign of the wordsmith.) For most of the 1930s, he was dependent financially on French writer *Anais Nin*, who was born with Neptune in nurturing Cancer directly opposite her Moon—luckily for Henry!

Pope Francis I, modeling himself after Saint Francis of Assisi, has railed against the financial extravagance of the Roman Catholic church, famously refusing to live in the papal mansion at the Vatican, preferring simpler quarters. I can do no better than to quote his own words here: "We have created new idols ... and the golden calf of old has found a new and heartless image in the cult of money and the dictatorship of an economy which is faceless and lacking any truly humane goal." He went on to say that the heart of our collective suffering "is in our relationship with money and our acceptance of its power over ourselves and our society." There's the high Neptunian perspective on the second house.

NEPTUNE IN THE THIRD HOUSE

Perception, thought, and speech—this is the classic triad of functions underlying the third house. As we saw earlier, the delightful word *heresy* is helpful here too. That's because there is nothing more heretical than questions, and questions are the lifeblood of the third house. Let's start with one of my favorite heretics, psychologist *James Hillman*, author of *We've Had A Hundred Years of Psychotherapy—And The World's Getting Worse*. The title says it all. You can imagine the enemies he blithely made with those twelve heretical words.

Following is a broader quote from him, redolent of third house Neptunian values, motives, and symbolism:

> *Not just any talk is conversation; not any talk raises consciousness. Good conversation has an edge: it opens your eyes to something, quickens your ears. And good conversation reverberates: it keeps on talking in your mind later in the day; the next day, you find yourself still conversing with what was said. That reverberation afterward is the very raising of consciousness; your mind's been moved. You are at another level with your reflections.*

Given the mystical and occult qualities of Neptune, its placement in the third house can bend one's perceptions in those spooky directions. Try horror novelist *Stephen King* as an example. He has Neptune in Libra in the third. The scary dimensions of his work come from his first house Pluto—which is, of course, sextile his Neptune—along with his Scorpio lunar south node. His third house Libran Neptune simply adds the artistry and mystery to the way he conveys his edgy tales.

Neptune is the chameleon, taking on many different forms. Think of the mind-boggling character changes achieved by comedian *Lily Tomlin.* Hearing *her voice change* as she performs can give you goose bumps. For sheer adaptability and curiosity—another pair of third house qualities—we might look to British entrepreneur *Richard Branson*, who started out with a record company and parlayed it into an airline and is leading the way into "space tourism" as founder of the Virgin Group. Note that his record company illustrates the notion of *media*, while the airline and the space flights are forms of *transportation*: both third house domains. Branson's Neptune lies in the third house in Libra, in a tight conjunction with Mars.

Spiritual teacher *Ram Dass* has Neptune in Virgo in the third house square his Sagittarian Moon. The double-dose of Mercury energy here tells the tale: its communicative vibration permeates both the third house and Virgo. Few human beings in recent generations have been so skillful at articulating Neptunian truths in a way that brings ancient wisdom into the framework of modern culture, values, and language.

Finally, consider the tragic case of *Alan Turing*, born with Neptune in Cancer in the third house. A brilliant mathematician, he essentially broke the Nazi *Enigma* code, which played a pivotal role in the Allied victory in World War II. This is a real classic: Neptune's action can be to *fog* and *obscure* something, and here it is in the house of communication—one could hardly come up with better symbolism for "secret codes." Turing is arguably the "father of the computer," and prophetically spoke of a time when "ladies will take their computers for walks in the park." After essentially saving Western civilization and inventing the human future, Turing was arrested, tried, and convicted of "gross indecency" in 1952 because of his gay orientation. Destroyed, he ate a cyanide-laced apple in 1954 and put the lights out. It is tempting to honor the man with a longer analysis here. Suffice it to say that his Neptune squared the conjunction of his Libra Moon and his south lunar node in the sixth house, and thereby hangs the tale.

NEPTUNE IN THE FOURTH HOUSE

Seeing into the heart and soul of another human being—and heart and soul are the essence of the fourth house—is of course impossible. Seeing a person's outward *home* and *family* are easier tasks. And home and family are concrete expressions of fourth house energy. With Neptune in the fourth house, one danger lies in becoming a *ghost within a family system.* Is this the case with *Prince Charles* of England, the Prince of Wales? I don't know how he feels—again, who can see into another's heart and soul? But I do know that Prince Charles has Neptune in Libra in the fourth house, conjunct Venus. And I know that he has spent his whole life right up to the socially-conventional age of retirement, in a state of perpetual waiting to become King Charles—a family role. Has he felt lost? Has he felt overwhelmed by a family role he never truly chose? I can't answer that. His intimate complexities with Princess Diana and Camilla Parker Bowles are of course reflected in the strong Venusian overlay on his Neptune as well.

The fourth house is deeply psychological, and one cannot speak long about psychology without thinking of the father of the field, *Sigmund Freud*—born with Neptune here, strongly placed in Pisces. Using the word "psychology" could mislead us about the fourth house, however. Psychology, as an academic discipline, misses the more visceral and direct qualities of true fourth house experience, especially with transrational, sensitive Neptune there. Such a configuration bypasses mere theory and links the conscious mind directly to the well of imagery that we call the collective unconscious.

Fittingly, the award-winning, uber-successful film director *Steven Spielberg* has Neptune in this position in Libra. His personal imagination has left its stamp on the imaginations of at least a billion people. There's a poignant dimension to Spielberg's relationship with the specifically fourth house dimensions of Neptune too. He was raised Jewish in Cincinnati. As the only Jewish child in his school, he bore the brunt of a lot of anti-Semitism. That prejudice took on added punch; he grew up hearing horror stories from Holocaust survivors who were being tutored by his grandmother. Thus, the *family myth* (fourth house) was charged with the ghostly Neptunian imagery of *victimhood*. Out of the well of that pain came one of his masterpieces, the film *Schindler's List*, for which he won the Academy Award for Best Picture of the year—with transiting Neptune sextile his Pisces Midheaven.

NEPTUNE IN THE FIFTH HOUSE

Here we see the active link between spirituality and creativity, as well as the connection between mystical states and ecstatic release. My mind immediately turns to *Bruce Springsteen*, born with Neptune in the fifth house in Libra in conjunction with peripatetic Mercury and the soulful Moon. Bruce and I are the same age. I did my senior year of high school in New Jersey, and I used to go watch him perform when he was just another kid playing the local clubs. He looked like he was having fun then—and now, almost half a century later, I still get the impression that he's having fun. Losing one's self-conscious ego in that sheer exuberant rock'n'roll joy is the marrow in the bones of a fifth house Neptune, and Springsteen illustrates it.

That's what we see. What interests me most here is what we cannot see—the mystical trance into which Springsteen must enter to conjure up his muse. That state of creative receptivity is the inner, meditative dimension of this configuration.

While thinking of performers who apparently enter an energized, ecstatic state while they are onstage, I also think of *Mick Jagger* of the *Rolling Stones*, born with Neptune in Virgo in the fifth house.

When we think of fifth house pleasure, the mind often naturally turns to sexuality. *Erica Jong*, author of the then-controversial book *Fear of Flying*, had the same Virgoan Neptune in the fifth as Mick—and "wantonly" stuck out her tongue for the world to see in much the same symbolic way.

A darker illustration is *Bill Cosby*, who was also born with Neptune in Virgo and the fifth house. (Or so it seems—there is some controversy about his time of birth.) Up until recently, Cosby would've been a benign representative of this energy, but lately, allegations about him drugging women in order to force himself on them sexually have put him in the category of a cautionary tale. He allegedly escaped into sexual ecstasy at the price of his moral compass—his healthy ego function of ethical self-control swamped by desire, just like a drunk unable to resist that fourth or fifth glass of whiskey. By the way, I would say that the 12:30 a.m. time suggested as probable for Cosby in Astro-Databank has been strongly supported by the transit of Pluto over his calculated Midheaven—an astrological event which coincided with his public downfall and humiliation.

NEPTUNE IN THE SIXTH HOUSE

At its best, Neptune in the sixth house embodies spiritual discipline, humility, and the receiving and giving of initiation, as our human wisdom traditions are passed down the generations. The first person I name here is relatively obscure, but he played a huge role in my own early life. He is astrologer *Ronald C. Davison*, born with Neptune in Cancer in the sixth, opposing his twelfth house Sun. I never met him, but his simple book *Astrology* did more to set me on the path I've followed all my life than anything else I encountered in print back then. I practically memorized that book; I went through at least two copies of it.

On a vastly broader scale, consider *Mohandas Gandhi*, born with Neptune in the sixth house in Aries, opposing his twelfth house Sun. How many souls have been inspired by his humble example of spiritual discipline and nonviolence? His spiritual discipline was so complete that when the assassin's bullet entered his body, he said the name of God—*Ram*—as he fell.

Music is a trance-inducing spiritual practice, with a long tradition of teachers and students passing magic down the line. There are many examples here, but consider seminal jazz bassist *Ron Carter*. In addition to his recordings and performances *in support of more famous soloists*, he embodied his sixth house Virgoan Neptune by teaching in the music department of the City College of New York, guiding younger musicians. Similarly, to many country singer *Johnny Cash* was more than a musician. As both a musical and cultural role model—and a humble Christian—he embodied his Virgo Neptune in the sixth house. It opposed his twelfth house Piscean Sun. Accordingly, Cash fell into Neptunian addiction—and lifted himself back out of it, showing the way to sobriety and integrity for many others.

The luminous, brief, and tragic career of classical cellist *Jacqueline du Pré* illustrates her aesthetic Libran Neptune in the sixth house perfectly. The heady cocktail of freedom and discipline that underlie her recording of Sir Edward Elgar's *Cello Concerto in E minor* is a legend in the world of classical music. Thinking of the "lineage" aspects of the sixth house, let's add that when du Pré was just sixteen years old, a patron gave her the first of her two Stradivarius cellos. I don't want to overemphasize illness as a sixth house reality, although there is a pattern of it often seen there. Jacqueline du Pré was diagnosed with MS in her late twenties. Thus, she *lost the gift the gods gave her.* Tellingly, she continued to teach master classes as long as she was able to do so.

Finally I mention *Chay Blyth*—not a household name, but he lived his sixth house Neptune in a way that illustrates the extremes of human self-discipline. His first feat, accomplished with a friend, was to row an open boat across the Atlantic Ocean. After that, he sailed solo around the world. That has been done many times, but Blyth did it the hard way—he sailed the infamous Southern Ocean the "wrong way," beating against the often gale-force prevailing westerly winds. Alone out there in the freezing, windy cold for ten months, skirting the edge of icy death countless times, I suspect a man has a chance to think some profoundly Neptunian thoughts. I might add that he had the Sun in Taurus in his first house conjunct quirkish Uranus, and they both tightly trine his Neptune. His vessel was named *British Steel*, and that might have been his own "middle name" too. He certainly earned the right to it.

NEPTUNE IN THE SEVENTH HOUSE

In the seventh house, we enter the realm of intimacy with all its possibilities and perils. I think first of a man who is quoted perhaps more than any other person in modern history—English poet and playwright *Oscar Wilde*. His Neptune lay in Pisces just a couple of degrees below the western horizon. My rule of thumb is that when a planet is within 2.5° of the seventh house cusp I see it as "conjunct the cusp." Seeing sixth house dimensions to Wilde's relationship to Neptune would not be an error, but ignoring its seventh house components would be a grievous one. The simple facts of his life support that seventh house argument perfectly: Wilde was not only an inspired artist, but also a gay man who was jailed for two years and ultimately destroyed physically and financially, all because of whom he loved. There's that Neptunian signature of *loss*. The details are messy and too complex to explore fully here. Essentially, Wilde filed libel charges against the father of his lover Lord Alfred Douglas. He was egged on by Douglas because of their father-son issues. And that backfired. Douglas himself had an eleventh house Arian Neptune in a telling opposition to his fifth house Libran Venus.

One might think of the seminal modern astrologer *Dane Rudhyar*, born with a Neptune-Mars conjunction in Gemini on his seventh house cusp. Gemini underscores the need for wide experience—and Rudhyar indeed married five times! Seventh house relationships are not always sexual, though. Perhaps more importantly, we might consider the intimate Neptunian contact Rudhyar made with his many astrological clients.

Extending the seventh house, as we should, beyond marriage in order to include everyone who has a major, life-shifting impact upon us, we might think of *Carlos Castaneda*, who was born with Neptune in Leo in his seventh house. And of course meeting the very Neptunian figure of the shaman don Juan altered the course of Carlos' life.

Back to the classic seventh house domain of marriage, think of actor *Paul Newman*. His long marriage to Joanne Woodward expressed his seventh house Neptune in Leo perfectly. She was not only a consummate actor who won an Academy Award for "Best Actress," she was also actively interested in the Neptunian fields of astrology, palmistry, and psychic phenomena. When asked about sexual temptations outside his marriage, Newman said, "Why go out for hamburger when you can have steak at home?" Their marriage lasted for fifty years, until Newman's death.

NEPTUNE IN THE EIGHTH HOUSE

Some of the relationship language we would naturally use for the seventh house applies to the eighth house as well. The two houses are not interchangeable, as we explored earlier in the book, but they do overlap in the area of *bonded intimacy*. We just spoke of Paul Newman, with his Neptune in the seventh. Now I mention *Joanne Woodward*, his wife, with her Neptune in Virgo in the eighth house, opposing her Pisces Sun, which is in turn conjunct her Venus. The seventh house puts a lot of emphasis on the diplomatic skills of "getting along" with another person. Illustrating the stormier, more passionate qualities of the eighth house, Woodward, when asked about the apparent "contentment" of her marriage to Paul Newman, responded: "Who's contented? We may divorce next year. But we like each other a lot and have great respect for each other. We feel very comfortable together. We don't believe in being together all the time. We spend about half the year together, and have nothing in common." Truth on the table, eighth house fashion. That Paul Newman could "take it" was probably one of the keys to their long partnership.

The eighth house "occult" path, as we saw earlier, involves establishing relationships with energies or entities beyond this visible world. A fine illustration of that principle lies in *Jane Roberts*, one of the first "channels" in recent times. She brought "the Seth material" into the world through the doorway of her eighth house Neptune in Leo—and her empowering relationship with an invisible spirit.

Jim Morrison, poet and singer in the 1960s band *The Doors*, was born with Neptune in Libra in the eighth house. In his leather pants, he oozed seductive sexual energy, illustrating the sexy Libran-Venusian addition to the inherent *juju* of the eighth house. Accordingly, Morrison was named in a number of paternity suits. Yet he remained bonded to his "cosmic mate" (his own words) *Pamela Courson*—who was, appropriately, born with Neptune in her seventh house.

As we just saw with Jane Roberts, Neptune is mystical and the eighth house carries the signature of occult experience. Jim Morrison, in performance, was often likened to a shaman. The roots of that part of his *persona* ran, deep and authentic, right from his earliest years. As a child of four or five, he witnessed the accidental highway deaths of some Native Americans in New Mexico. This memory became a big part of his life and was brilliantly captured in the film *The Doors* by director Oliver Stone. The occult dimensions of the eighth house are slippery to discuss. Here are Morrison's own words:

> *Me and my mother and father and my grandmother and grandfather were driving through the desert at dawn. A truckload of Indian workers had hit another car or something—there were Indians scat-*

> *tered all over the highway, bleeding to death. So we pulled the car up... And all of a sudden I realize that they didn't know what was happening anymore than I did... and I do think, at that moment, the souls or the ghosts of those dead Indians —maybe one or two of 'em, were just running around, freaking out, and just leaped into my soul, and I was like a sponge, ready to just sit there and absorb it... And they're still in there. It's not a ghost story, it's something that really means something to me.*

Sadly, Morrison destroyed himself, Neptune-fashion, with alcohol and drugs. His sensitivity overwhelmed him, and we lost a great voice—but not before he had haunted the minds of a generation with his weirdly powerful imagery and reckless *persona*. "I am the Lizard King. I can do anything." It takes a certain kind of personality to deliver a line like that and not be laughed off the stage for it. I saw the Doors play a couple of times in their heyday. When Morrison delivered that line, the hairs on the back of my neck stood up. He *was* the Lizard King.

One more illustration—and here we see the darkest possible face of the charismatic shamanism of Neptune in the eighth house. Jim Morrison only destroyed himself. *Jim Jones* took hundreds with him in the tragic mass suicide in Guyana of the members of The People's Temple, which he led. He had Neptune in Virgo in the eighth house.

And then, finally, there is *Adolph Hitler* himself, born under that Neptune-Pluto conjunction in Gemini, with the planetary pair lying four degrees apart in his eighth house.

NEPTUNE IN THE NINTH HOUSE

Connecting the ninth house with "religion" is accurate enough, but the word can be misleadingly narrow. The ninth house refers broadly to all systems of "mythic" belief—the values by which we impute meaning to life. Fittingly, master mythologist *Joseph Campbell* was born with Neptune there, in Cancer, in square aspect to his Arian triple conjunction of Sun, Jupiter, and Mercury. His book *Hero With a Thousand Faces* and his PBS series *The Power of Myth* probably did more to bring an interest in mythology back to life in the modern world than anyone else, with the possible exception of Carl Jung.

In a more narrowly religious vein, fallen evangelist *Jimmy Swaggart* has Neptune in Virgo in the ninth house. Interestingly, the planet is almost unaspected, which gives it an unfettered quality, as if it had a mind of its own and could operate independently of the rest of the chart. Virgo can set impossibly high standards, which of course are a breeding ground for guilt and shame—which, paradoxically, can then often "act out" in the world as bad behavior. The Reverend Swaggart's voracious and hypocritical appetite for prostitutes and pornography came to light in 1988. In 1991, after his public tearful repentance, he was arrested for driving on the wrong side of the road—and again found in the company of a prostitute. He stepped up to the pulpit after that episode and announced to the crowd at the Family Worship Center, "The Lord told me it's flat none of your business."

Swaggart is still preaching as I write these words, but his star fell after that one.

To balance that dreadful tale, I'd like to spotlight one of my favorite Christians—U2's singer *Bono*. With his efforts to ease the burdens of African poverty and other good works he has undertaken, he actually walks the talk that Jesus talked. Fittingly, Bono has Neptune in Scorpio in his ninth house conjunct his eighth house Scorpio Moon and opposing his Venus and his Mercury. Let's also mention *Edgar Cayce*, "the Sleeping Prophet," with his ninth house Taurean Neptune conjunct his Moon. Raised as a conventional Christian, he was startled to wake up from one of his psychic trances and learn that he had been speaking of prior lifetimes.

We are on shaky ground with *J.R.R. Tolkien*'s time of birth. The rectified chart shown in Astro-Databank gives him Neptune in the ninth house—and the planet is surely conjunct Pluto, in Gemini. I am inclined to accept this chart for a lot of reasons—the creative, child-oriented, fifth house Capricorn Sun, the south lunar node in the linguistic third house—but mostly for that ninth house Neptune. *The Lord of the Rings* is arguably the most broadly influential treatment of the *Quest motif* in English-language literature, and there is no motif more quintessential to the ninth house than that one. Frodo Baggins' outer search may be fanciful, but his inner one speaks universally to almost everyone.

NEPTUNE IN THE TENTH HOUSE

Having Neptune in the tenth house links two very disparate realities—on one hand, the spiritual life of our soul and, on the other, our public persona, which lies so much in the realm of the ego. The perils inherent in the synthesis are enormous, as we explored earlier. One who in my view got the integration beautifully right is the late, great *Paramahansa Yogananda*—born, like J.R.R. Tolkien, Henry Miller, and Hitler, under that world-changing conjunction of Neptune and Pluto in the 1890s. In good Gemini-fashion, Yogananda found words for that which is beyond all language. And he still inspires millions of us.

In thinking about Neptunian spirituality, we often have to go beyond the obvious category of religion. Many people play public roles that bring us back to the Neptunian heart of imagination, magic, and enchantment, and not all of them wear robes and funny hats. Who could top *Walt Disney* for that honor? He was born with Neptune on his Midheaven, in Cancer, square his Moon and his Ascendant. His vision has shaped the myths and symbols of our world. I like author *Frank Herbert* a lot in this category too. With his Neptune in Leo in the tenth, he wrote the transcendent masterpiece of science fiction: *Dune*, which linked religion and psychedelia with a story of the birth of a new religion.

Comedy helps us get over ourselves, so it's no surprise that many comedians are very Neptunian people. The jokes get funnier after the kids have gone to bed, of course—and so it is fitting that the man who essentially defined late-night humor on television, *Johnny Carson*, had Neptune in the tenth house, appropriately placed in in Leo. Moving Neptune forward into Sagittarius and more modern times, *Russell Brand* and his tenth house Neptune have kept us laughing—and, once the chortles stop, thinking too. Are the clowns of the world spiritual teachers? Once you see how they take the starch out of the human ego, it is difficult to say no.

The "town drunk" is an expression of the sadder side of a tenth house Neptune. In that familiar term, we see the Neptunian signature of escapism matched with the tenth house elements of public image and reputation. I think of singer *Tom Waits*. In his tune *Emotional Weather Report*, he laments, "High tonight, low tomorrow." Just four words, but they eloquently capture the mundane pitfalls of Neptunian escapism. I would also reference the world's most beloved rascal, *Rolling Stones'* guitarist *Keith Richards*, whose reputation as "a junkie and drunk" is outlived only by his ... longevity. Both men have Neptune in Libra in the tenth house. I suspect both of them have more moments of sobriety than their reputations might suggest. How else could they have given us such gifts of artistry and emotional catharsis?

NEPTUNE IN THE ELEVENTH HOUSE

This is the one I claim for my very own. I was born with Neptune in the middle of Libra in the eleventh house, pretty much dead square my Sun. With that configuration, my spiritual life benefits from the support of a "congregation." Accordingly, I feel so much gratitude for my Neptunian *sangha* or fellowship in the Apprenticeship Program. I feel like I get paid to do my spiritual work, and kept on track by all of you who have sustained it over the years as students, clients and readers.

Thank you!

Some enterprises that are spiritually significant to individuals at a personal, private level can only be accessed cooperatively and collectively. Playing in a band is one fine example of that principle. Nobody can do that alone. Singer, songwriter and band leader *Neil Young* has lived that life for half a century, touching millions of people. He has Neptune in Libra in the eleventh, conjunct Jupiter. Ditto for singer *Adele*—she was born, apparently, with Neptune in Capricorn there, although there is some uncertainty as to her time of birth.

Making a memorable film must be profoundly satisfying, but no one can do that alone either. Epitomizing the *auteur* aspect of film direction, we might think of one of the bright stars of the golden age of European cinema, *Federico Fellini*, born with Neptune in Leo in the eleventh house. Like Neil Young, Fellini had Neptune conjunct Jupiter, suggesting success developing over time and a lasting legacy that results from it.

Miraculously, we have a reasonably accurate time of birth for the man who embodies the Italian Renaissance perhaps more than any other, *Michelangelo Buonarroti,* born with Neptune in Scorpio in the eleventh house. Vatican politics—an eleventh house matter—were ever-present for him, but even more tellingly, we can see how his reputation as one who could "channel the divine" through his art has grown over time to its present fabled proportions. It is almost hard to remember that he was an actual human being—although an evening with his chart goes a long way toward correcting that blind spot. Michelangelo's Neptune was conjunct genius-Uranus and in a tight trine to his Pisces Sun—which of course in turn was deeply receptive to Neptunian inspiration.

Albert Einstein—like Michelangelo, another Piscean with his Neptune in the eleventh house—provides a parallel study in inspiration. For our purposes here, the most fascinating piece of the puzzle with Einstein is how, over time, he has been transformed from a scientific figure into a mystical one, to the point that he became the model for everyone's favorite "Jedi master," *Yoda,* in the *Star Wars* sagas. At the mythic level, Einstein still embodies the emerging Neptunian synthesis of physics and mysticism.

Politics—again, a quintessential collective eleventh house activity—can be deceptive and full of illusion, intentional and otherwise. Disgraced American president *Richard Nixon* was born with Neptune in Cancer in his eleventh house, opposing his Capricorn Sun. How did he feel in the closing years of his life, as the dark face of Neptune came to full flower inside him?

My final example here is *Playboy* magazine founder *Hugh Hefner*, with his Leo Neptune in the eleventh house. I immediately think of the tacky, tawdry "glamour" of the eleventh house "fellowship" that surrounded him. To be fair, he has been an active philanthropist and thus has also been associated with a lot of people who were motivated by Neptunian compassion. But who could doubt that *glamorous* (Leo) *airheads* (Neptune) have been in short supply in his life either?

NEPTUNE IN THE TWELFTH HOUSE

With Neptune in its natural house, its energies are pure and powerful. Such a person will have mystical and psychic experiences—we can count on that. What we cannot count on is the person's response to them. Do they get so scared that they slip into staunch denial—or into some form of self-numbing escapism? Or do they rise to their own perceptions and follow them where they lead?

It is helpful to remember that even when successful in their responses, such individuals do not always appear "religious." A very fine example of that principle is *General George S. Patton* of World War II fame. He was born with Neptune strongly placed in Taurus in the twelfth house, opposing his Scorpio Sun. Patton famously believed in reincarnation and felt that he had actually been the Carthaginian military genius Hannibal in a prior life, among other military figures. Stories about Patton's metaphysical openness are abundant, but here is one of my favorites. As they prepared to invade the Italian peninsula in 1943, a British general said to Patton, "You know, George, you would have made a great marshal for Napoleon if you had lived in the nineteenth century."

Patton's answer: "But I did."

Inventor *Nikola Tesla* was born with an ultra-strong Neptune, lying in both Pisces and the twelfth house, trine his Sun and square his Mercury. Tesla's genius was nearly matched by the constant Neptunian pattern of loss and betrayal in his life. He essentially invented the modern age. That sounds like an extreme statement, but where would we be, for one thing, without the alternating electrical current that allows electricity to be delivered long distances over power lines? Tesla's invention. Where would we be without the basis for radio, telephone, and television? Again, essentially Tesla's inventions.

As a student, Nikola Tesla went through what, in the language of this disenchanted world, would be described as a "nervous breakdown." Judge for yourself. The following is taken directly from Tesla's brief Astro-Databank biography:

> *During the malady he observed many phenomena, strange and unbelievable. His vision and hearing intensified beyond any normal human capacity. He could sense objects in the dark in the same way as a bat. It was a period in which his sensitivities were so heightened that the flashes of light that he had seen from the time he was a kid now filled the air around him with tongues of living flame. Their intensity, instead of diminishing, increased with time and seemingly attained a maximum when he was about twenty-five years old. His responses were so keenly tuned that a word would become an image that he could feel and taste. It was during this time that he had one of his most famous ideas, that of the rotating magnetic field and alternating current induction motor.*

Let others call that a "nervous breakdown," if it pleases them. To me, it sounds like a *direct experience of the trans-Neptunian realm*—and something that would have been honored and valued in a more enchanted time. Nikola Tesla's twelfth house Piscean Neptune was a gift to us all, but the story of his treatment by this world will put tears in your eyes. He spent his last years in New York City feeding pigeons whom he called "my sincere friends."

For pure creative inspiration, it's hard to rival singer and poet *Leonard Cohen*. He was born with Neptune in Virgo in the twelfth house, fittingly in a conjunction with artistic Venus. That both art and sexual love have been his "gurus" is easily discerned in his biography. His five years in a Buddhist monastery illustrate the highest mystical aspirations of this configuration. The deep inner opening symbolized by Neptune in the twelfth house allows inspiration to flow—but it is not only inspiration that can pass through that wide-open doorway. In his song *Anthem*, Cohen gives us the often-quoted line, "There is a crack in everything. That's how the light gets in." There's a man who understands Neptune!

Light flowed abundantly into the mind of the brilliant Welsh poet *Dylan Thomas* too—but so did the whiskey which ultimately killed him. Thomas was born with Neptune in Leo in his twelfth house, squaring his Scorpio Sun. We might say similar things about the "cracks" in *Grateful Dead* guitarist and band leader *Jerry Garcia*. He was born with Neptune in Virgo in his twelfth house, very nearly unaspected. In 1986, he experienced a diabetic coma. And in 1995, he died of a heart attack in a drug rehabilitation facility where he was struggling with his addiction to cocaine and heroin. Yet again, we see the fingerprint of the dark Neptune, as another great light in the world went out.

That completes our whirlwind tour of the various faces of Neptune in the lives of some of the actual human beings who have shaped our world. Again, each of these human stories deserves its own chapter. None of these brief comments reflect anything like the full power of an integrated astrological analysis. In sacrificing that depth and breadth, what I hope I've accomplished with this warp-drive roller coaster ride through dozens of people's lives is to establish an overview of Neptune's action in a variety of contexts.

The principles we have been exploring are robust and reliable. My hope is that by seeing them in action like this, your faith in them will deepen. I hope that all this will give you the confidence to use them in your own journey—and perhaps to help you help others in the endless process of cleaning their own windows.

CONCLUSION

EUCALYPTUS TREES

While on a teaching trip to Nelson Bay, Australia, late last July, I had a rare moment alone. I was sitting in a car in a grocery store parking lot, waiting in the shotgun seat—but it was Australia, so I was subliminally flummoxed, as usual there: sitting on the left side of the car, not the right. As an American, I felt like I was in the driver's seat, but there was no steering wheel and no pedals.

And July meant it was midwinter.

Australia is a good place to wonder about things. Mad parrots squawk. The moon, at least to these northern-hemisphere eyes of mine, is even backwards, filling in from left to right. Orion stands upside-down in the night sky. And I myself was upside-down, hanging miraculously from my feet on the bottom of the earth, with a mind to match.

Through the "windscreen," looking out over the car's "bonnet"—their language keeps us North Americans guessing too—I saw a line of eucalyptus trees. I was in the midst of teaching an edition of the seminar upon which this book has been based, so my mind was primed in dizzy Neptunian fashion. I started thinking, *"eucalyptus trees . . . "*

Am I simply looking at a line of eucalypti? Or am I looking at an *image* of trees in my brain, believing them to be "out there?" And if anything is in fact actually "out there" at all, what is it exactly and how does it compare to what I think I am seeing? Those trees are mostly empty space, atoms being mostly vacuums. In seeing them, I am only connecting the perceptual dots in a way that says at least as much about my five human senses as it does about the natures of the trees themselves.

Further befuddling me, whatever those trees are, I am looking at them through the *lens of time*—which is also, quite possibly, a human construction. That tree was once a seed. Someday it will be dust. Beyond time, the tree is all those things at once—so does "a tree" have any true, separate existence at all?

Even trickier, trees are living things. Am I looking at some kind of alien consciousness going very, very slowly? Is the tree *noticing me noticing it?*

Is the tree in my head noticing the rest of my head noticing it?

OK, I freely admit it: you really had to have been there.

As I read these words, they seem sophomoric and obvious—like bad poetry from an overly serious fourteen-year-old. My experience of the eucalypti was real—one of those true moments of lucid, vertiginous, luminous understanding—of *getting it.* But trying to put the perception into words, however clear or eloquent they might be, results in linguistic blither that falls somewhere between comedy and catastrophe.

The underlying point is that my experience of those eucalyptus trees was not cognitive or verbal, even though I am trying—and failing—to translate it into that framework. There is nothing I could say about it that I couldn't have said, still wet behind the ears, back in college. I could parrot Buddhism and quantum mechanics pretty well even then.

How do we *talk* about consciousness? That's what I have been trying to do throughout all these pages you've been reading. I hope I haven't sounded like a blabbering fool—or worse, some academic "talking head" rattling off out of his depth, while drinking coffee from a Styrofoam cup.

Thirty years ago, I closed my second book, *The Changing Sky*, with Ezra Pound's *Canto 120*. It has been in my mind ever since.

> *I have tried to write paradise*
>
> *Do not move*
> *Let the wind speak*
> *That is paradise*
>
> *Let the gods forgive what I*
> *have made*
> *Let those I love try to forgive*
> *what I have made.*

Take away all the pretty, compelling words in your head, and what is left? Is that remaining silence the essence of Neptune? No, not exactly—

that's close, but "silence" doesn't go far enough. Take away all the cluttering concepts too—all the opinions, ideas and interpretations—and we are getting closer. *Let the wind speak*. Let naked alertness remain—and never confuse this non-thinking state with torpor. As Henry Miller put it, we must "stand still like the hummingbird." That is the essence of pure Neptune, god of the sea, standing "still" on the shoreline—a shoreline that marks the boundary between the solid ground of everyday life and the vast waters that surround us, and from which we once arose—what, in this book, we have been calling the trans-Neptunian realm.

Was there actually a line of eucalyptus trees out there? Niels Bohr, one of the founders of quantum mechanics, once said, "*Everything we call real is made of things that cannot be regarded as real.*" This is science, not metaphysics. He is of course talking about atoms and their constituents—which are still described as "things" in high school science class. But in quantum mechanics, those quarks and muons and bosons and neutrinos, et al, are more like ghosts of possibility, winking in and out of this world, their existence literally depending on whether or not we are looking.

And these little whimsies are the building blocks of life. You are made of them. Me too. And all the eucalyptus trees as well.

So are we here at all? *What are we, really?* Niels Bohr quipped, "*A physicist is just an atom's way of looking at itself*"—only he wasn't simply joking.

It sounds crazy. But apparently it isn't crazy. And that leaves us—we humans—as the crazy ones, believing in a delusional reality of solid bodies and cold separation. *Materialism* is not just an attitude of money-addled, existentialist selfishness—it is emerging as a nearly universal psychotic condition: a hallucination, and a truly terrifying one.

Am I talking madness here? If I am, then all the physicists of the past century are insane too. They are basically all on board with quantum theory. Gary Zukav, in his terrific book *The Dancing Wu Li Masters*, famously sounded the battle cry: "*The statistical predictions of quantum mechanics are always correct. Quantum mechanics is the theory. It has explained everything from subatomic particles to transistors to stellar energy. It has never failed. It has no competition.*"

And the universe that quantum mechanics describes is truly weird, and utterly Neptunian—Niels Bohr again: "*If quantum mechanics hasn't profoundly shocked you, you haven't understood it yet.*"

Science and mysticism are converging—that has become one of the truisms of our present age. Like most gems of wisdom, every time we hear the words repeated, they get a little more shopworn. That doesn't make them any less true. Supported by an astrological perspective on humanity's emergent knowledge of the trans-Neptunian realm, we can plainly see that a new paradigm of planetary consciousness is coming into focus. As I described way back in the second chapter of this book, I believe that one dimension of the shift into post-religious, universal, psychological spirituality is the healing of the long schism between science and mysticism.

That schism has been with us for so long that many of us have come to take it for granted. As astrologers, we are accustomed to attacks from scientists who label us "pseudo-scientific"—as if we *wanted* to be scientists, as if we wanted to be members of their church. But taking sides in that debate is sheer folly at this point. The train is leaving the station. Max Planck, usually seen as the father of quantum mechanics, said it best: *"A scientific truth does not triumph by convincing its opponents and making them see the light, but rather because its opponents eventually die and a new generation grows up that is familiar with it."*

I think Max Planck's point holds beyond the boundaries of science—astrology's star is rising on that same, paradigm-shifting tide, while its passionate, witch-burning "debunkers" simply pass away, presumably with their opinions intact. Planck was born with Neptune in Pisces—strongly placed, in other words. Prophetically, he also said, *"Science cannot solve the ultimate mystery of nature. And that is because, in the last analysis, we ourselves are a part of the mystery that we are trying to solve."*

And that line brings me right back to those eucalyptus trees in Nelson Bay, Australia. Even though trying to write about my experience there makes me sound like a babbling old fool, I know that what I experienced subjectively in that parking lot was real—maybe more real than what I am experiencing now, thinking that I am sitting at a desk, writing these words. I believe that in that brief moment my "windows were pretty clean," to use the metaphor we have employed throughout this book. I think my consciousness and those trees entered into a kind of unity in that moment—or maybe I should say that a preexistent, primal unity that had been there all along broke through my normal delusional condition.

Quantum mechanics is only a bit over a century old, but humans have been thinking about this kind of thing since the beginning of time. When I was a young man getting my degree in Religion at the University of North Carolina, I took a course in Gnosticism—a Near-Eastern faith that rose up around the time Christianity was getting established. Gnosticism was very astrological. In its cosmology, we "fell from a realm of Light" down through the seven planetary spheres, merrily taking on the bad qualities of each planet as we spiraled downward into our present miserable condition. These dark planetary deities—the authors of all our various delusions—were known as *Archons*. Our only hope was to reach back up past them, via *gnosis*—knowledge, wisdom, consciousness—to return to the realm of Light: a celestial region beyond the power of the Archons.

The highest—thus the worst—of these Archons was called *Yaldabaoth*. We know it today in its Roman guise as the planet Saturn. And of course back then Saturn was the outermost of the known planets. The Gnostics did not know of Uranus, Neptune, or Pluto, nor of the trans-Neptunians. They lacked that critical part of the map homeward. To them, Saturn was the final boundary before deep space.

In the Gnostic cosmology, Yaldabaoth created the other six planetary demons. He stood like a stone wall between us and the higher realms of Light, *tricking us into believing that he was the ultimate reality.*

Gnosticism sounds quaint and archaic until you stop and think about it for a moment. Then it might give you goose bumps. Has Saturn—the planet of cold reason and "common sense"—fooled us all into believing that it is God? Has "rationality," separation, and materialism—all Saturnian qualities—successfully sealed humanity off from its higher potentials and possibilities? Has it not, in Gnostic terms, tricked us into believing that it is the ultimate reality?

Compare the nature of Saturn to the nature of the Biblical Jehovah and it gets really scary. That judging male God of Judaism, Islam, and Christianity's Old Testament definitely bore Saturn's fingerprints. He was pretty good at dispensing justice, but not so good at mercy. His most famous quote is probably, "Thou shalt not." Doesn't that old western religion of punishment, shame, and patriarchal tyranny bear the stamp of the dark Saturn—the Archon that rules this world by tricking us into believing that it is the ultimate and final divinity?

What toxicity have we been enduring for the past three thousand years?

And what happened when we discovered Uranus—the first "god" beyond Yaldabaoth? What happened when we began to break Saturn's spell? Late in the eighteenth century, that discovery marked the revolutionary "beginning of the end" of that dark Saturnian dominion. The absolute authority of the Church began to fail. Kings failed at the same time. The Uranian human right—and human ability—to *question everything* emerged in ascendancy.

Then along came Neptune, showing us the "window" through which we can peer into the higher realms: through Pluto, and beyond it, into the endless mystery of inner and outer space.

The Gnostics were right, in other words—and they foresaw all this two thousand years ago. So what does it all mean? Is humanity itself ready now to "return to the Light?" I am too much of a Capricorn to go all breathlessly "New Age" on you—don't worry! But I can say objectively and confidently that we now have the map that shows the way home. That map is what this book has been about.

To me, the most cogent language about cleaning our Neptunian windows has arisen in Vajrayana Buddhism, especially in its *mahamudra* tradition. Those teachings describe the ultimate nature of our minds—and of reality itself—as *luminous emptiness*. I've never encountered a better metaphor—nor, by the way, one more consistent with the view of reality revealed by quantum mechanics. Most Buddhists affirm that "emptiness" is the nature of all worldly phenomena—that ultimately, there is nothing "really" out there, that it is all mind.

And remember: "mind" is not something happening inside your skull. Your skull is an illusion too!

None of this makes a lick of Saturn-sense, of course. But it sounds exactly like Max Planck and Niels Bohr, doesn't it?

A thousand years ago, by the banks of the river Ganges, the master Tilopa offered some fine teaching to his student Naropa—these are both major figures in the northern Buddhist tradition, but telling their story is not my point here. The teachings themselves are the point.

Tilopa's words have come down to us as a precious text—to me, the single most compelling document in Buddhism. Formally, it is called the *Mahamudra Upadesha*, but it is often more simply called the *Ganges Mahamudra*. In it, speaking of the nature of the mind, Tilopa said to Naropa . . .

For example, it is like looking in the middle of the sky and not seeing anything.

> *For example, just as the nature of space transcends color and shape, and just as space is therefore unaffected or unchanged and unobscured by the various colors and shapes that occur within it, in the same way the essence of your mind transcends color and shape . . .*

That "empty sky" metaphor has always been powerful for me. Beneath the thoughts in my head, there is a kind of empty spaciousness—something formless and wide-open, like the empty sky. When I am aware of it, I feel my window is pretty clean. When I beheld those eucalyptus trees, that was the window through which I was looking—whatever "I" means.

Buddhist literature often makes reference to this kind of "emptiness." The word is a hard sell in the English-speaking world. If a friend says "I am feeling so empty," you give her a hug. But this "emptiness" is more like what Niels Bohr and Max Planck were discussing—and proving. It is the startling realization that there may in fact be no physical world out there at all. That perhaps it is all mind. As the great British physicist Sir James Jeans famously put it, "*The universe begins to look more like a great thought than like a great machine.*"

The magnificent Vajrayana teacher Thrangu Rinpoche, in his commentary on the *Ganges Mahamudra*, encouragingly pointed out that, "*This is something that anyone can experience directly by looking at their own mind.*" The trans-Neptunian realm is always there, in other words. We can all "experience it directly" if we want to try—but Thrangu added that: "*it is something that no one can conceive of. You can experience the mind but you cannot accurately think about it, because it transcends the realm of thought . . . It is like . . . the midst of the sky or the midst of space. The nature of your mind is beyond thought, but nevertheless it is your mind, so it is not beyond experience.*"

I think that Thrangu Rinpoche would have understood what I was trying to say about those eucalyptus trees.

Personally, I delight in all this! I delight in realizing that people meditating upon their own experience of the mind two millennia ago could come so close to what physicists have more recently discovered—and proven—in their particle colliders and in the hearts of exploding stars. And isn't it strange that Neptune—for so long reviled by astrologers as spacey and unrealistic—is actually emerging as the planet that most directly engages us with the true nature of raw reality? It turns out that it is Neptune, not that tricky "Archon" Saturn, that has its feet on the ground—except that there is no ground, just luminous quantum emptiness.

So how do we get on with this great work? How do we clean our windows?

There are broad answers that have relevance to everyone—we will look at the main one in a moment—but the point of this book has been that each person's Neptunian path is distinct and individual. The time of Saturn's "one-size-fits-all" religious rules ended 235 years ago, with the discovery of Uranus. My purpose in writing these pages has been to illuminate as best I can a wide range of effective spiritual practices—practices reflected in each person's natal chart via Neptune's house, sign, and astrological context.

Life is short and precious, and it is sad to think of anyone's good heart going to waste under Saturn's repressive thumb. Your path is your own. *You don't need no stinking rules.* Have a look at the mirror in the sky and you will see your road reflected there. Follow it, if you choose.

The poet said, *"I have tried to write paradise. Do not move. Let the wind speak. That is paradise."* Yet, here I am, nearing the end of this long line of words, not letting the poor wind get a word in edgewise. It's a writer's fate, a teacher's fate—an astrologer's fate—to weave a web of phrases, all the while hoping they point to something beyond themselves, perhaps to a beckoning line of eucalyptus trees somewhere.

How does it actually feel to be transparent to the universe? Or let's start on more familiar ground: what does it feel like to be transparent to another human being? Wide-open? Not defended or judging at all? No intervening opinions, resistance, or suggestions? We all know the answer. The word is *love*. To love the universe—and each other, and yourself—in that fashion is the quintessential, nonresistant heart of Neptune. Love is what arises when your window is squeaky clean.

Buddhists speak of *bodhicitta*—loving-kindness—as the root of all practice. The Dalai Lama went so far as to say, "My religion is kindness." In Judaism, the Torah exhorts you to "Love your neighbor like yourself" (Leviticus 19:18) and to love God "with all your heart, with all your soul and with all your might" (Deuteronomy 6:5). Hinduism has its core *Bhakti* practice of ecstatic, loving devotion to the Divine. Meanwhile, Islam commands believers to treat all people with *birr*, which essentially means deep kindness. I know less about Islam, so I asked my friend and publisher in Turkey, Bariş Īlhan, about it. Here is what she said: "In Islam God said *I was a hidden treasure and I loved to be known*, so He actually created the world through love." In the Christian tradition, Saint Paul said it so eloquently in this familiar passage from the thirteenth chapter of First Corinthians: "Though I speak with the tongues of men and of angels, but have not love, I have become sounding brass or a clanging cymbal." And even the Beatles sang, "All you need is love." They were right too.

Let me go a little further down the road with Saint Paul. He added, "And though I have the gift of prophecy, and *understand all mysteries and all knowledge*, and though I have all faith, so that I could remove mountains, but have not love, I am nothing."

To *understand all mysteries and all knowledge*. I doubt anyone could ever get that far. But we keep trying. That's part of what makes us human. And we keep making progress, and that progress is accelerating rapidly. That's been the point of this concluding chapter, and really of this whole book. Our knowledge and understanding of those two mirrored mysteries—mind and sky—has exploded. We are poised on the edge of an extraordinary evolutionary leap. We actually *can* remove mountains. But can we, both as humans and as astrologers, keep love in the equations?

Because without it, we are nothing.

Do not move. Let the wind speak.

Thank you.

ABOUT THE AUTHOR

Steven Forrest is the author of several astrological bestsellers, including *The Inner Sky*, *The Book of the Moon*, *The Book of Pluto*, and the new classic *Yesterday's Sky*.

Steven's work has been translated into a dozen languages, most recently Chinese and Italian. He travels worldwide to speak and teach his brand of choice-centered evolutionary astrology – an astrology which integrates free will, grounded humanistic psychology and ancient metaphysics.

Along with his busy private practice, he maintains active astrological apprenticeship programs in California, Australia, North Carolina, and Europe. He is a founding member of the Ethics Committee of the International Society for Astrological Research (ISAR). About Steven's readings, Jungian analyst Robert Johnson says, "I have had several charts done in my lifetime and none of them—but yours—have escaped the astrologer mistaking so much of the chart as a sounding board for his own ego. You have recovered the divine art to its noble status."

See his website www.forrestastrology.com for more details.

LEARN ASTROLOGY WITH STEVEN FORREST

Interested in learning more about Steven's unique approach to astrology? For a listing of lectures and workshops that are available in a variety of audio and video formats, go to: http://www.forrestastrology.com/store.

Better yet, join the many successful students who have completed **Steven's Astrological Apprenticeship Program**, where he teaches both the specific techniques of interpretation and the style of presentation that have made him one of the most successful and influential astrologers in the world. Steven takes great joy in passing on the teachings and strategies that have worked for him over the years through his Apprenticeship Program.

The Apprenticeship Program presents students with a rare opportunity to learn astrology in a supportive environment of like-minded individuals, who together create a feeling of community and connection, leading to bonds that last throughout life. Some come to the program to train professionally, while others come for personal or spiritual enrichment.

Steven's apprenticeship groups are currently meeting in North Carolina, Southern California (near San Diego), Northern California (north of San Francisco), Australia, and Europe.

After attending their first in-person official Apprentice workshop, students gain access to a private student-only shop with over 10 years of Steven's private teachings, recorded in audio format, and also available as pdf transcripts of select programs.

Learn more at www.forrestastrology.com

Printed in Great Britain
by Amazon